Jimmy Curran

Scotland's Greatest
Athletics Coach

Craig Statham

When you run the quarter-mile, come out of the blocks full tilt. And when you hit the back stretch, kick a little harder. Then you'll come 'round the turn into the home stretch … and you'll be all done in and a black curtain will be clouding your sight. This is where champions are made! This is where you get up on your toes and sprint to the wire!

First published in 2020
Newbattle Books
52 Newbattle Abbey Crescent
Dalkeith, Midlothian
EH22 3LN

ISBN: 978-1-5272-6317-8

Cover design: Heather Macpherson, Raspberry Creative Type
Book design: Craig Statham

Printed and bound by Martins the Printers, Berwick-upon-Tweed

This book is dedicated to Jimmy's family members and former athletes who generously gave their time to ensure its accuracy, but did not live to see its publication.

Tom Danaher
Larry Lattomus

It is the nature of man to rise to greatness,
if greatness is expected of him.

John Steinbeck

Contents

Acknowledgements

When I first delved into the life of Jimmy Curran, there was virtually nothing written about him that was immediately available in the public domain. What history I could find told of a life that deserved a book, but even in-depth research would likely not be able to draw out enough information about his life to write 90,000 words of text. But after some days of scouting the internet, mostly in digital newspaper archives, it became clear that a book was indeed a possibility. So, as is my way, I dove right in and contacted family members, and from there my seed of an idea turned into the first page, and then the second, until I finally had the semblance of a book. But getting there required more than old newspapers. Central to this book were an array of individuals, some who were related to Jimmy, some who were trained by him, and others who were acquaintances. All were bound together by a love and respect of their patriarch, their coach, their friend, the small, funny Scots American with the rolling Rs. Without them there would be no book about Jimmy Curran.

It is common when writing a book to find one person that emerges as a hinge around which the book revolves. That was most definitely the case with this book. Before I started writing in earnest I contacted one of Jimmy's granddaughters, Laurie Danaher, and asked for her blessing to write about Jimmy. From her first reply it was clear that she was going to give me her full support. And so it proved. She has, from that first contact, answered every question, offered information, encouragement, support, advice and opinion. And as the book neared its conclusion, she proofed the text. And she also scanned all the family photographs, many of which you can see in this book. This biography would have been a much poorer effort without Laurie's help.

In 2017 Laurie and her sister, Alanna Berger, made a visit to Scotland, and we met at a hotel in Peebles, where Alanna brought out those photographs. Alanna was also a great help, and offered anecdotes

ACKNOWLEDGEMENTS

about Jimmy whenever asked.

Laurie and Alanna's brother, Tom, came on board early in the project. With the added benefit of actually having run in one of Jimmy's teams, he provided much information, and no doubt had lots still to offer. Sadly, however, Tom died suddenly in 2015. This book is dedicated to him.

Stephen Curran is the last of Jimmy and Janet's grandchildren to bear the Curran name. He provided a number of wonderful stories that added colour to the book, and also offered up an early photograph of a moustachioed Jimmy wearing his Hussars cap.

I met up with Mike Lewis while he was on a golfing trip to Scotland. Over coffee and cake at the Elephant House in Edinburgh (birthplace of Harry Potter) he kindly recalled memories of his grandfather's exploits.

A number of other family members remember Jimmy, and were kind enough to pass on stories, and offer encouragement. Thank you to Jeannie Cornelius and Nan Harr.

Younger family members didn't have stories about the family patriarch, but did offer encouragement via a private Facebook group, and for that I am grateful.

Jimmy's immediate family no longer exist in Galashiels, but an extended family does still thrive in the town. Whilst giving a talk to the Old Gala Club, I met a number of members who offered information, encouragement, and made me aware of a trophy presented by Jimmy to the local school. Thanks to Jason Curran and Janette Adams, amongst others.

Jimmy's last team ran in 1961, which meant that a small, dwindling band of former students would still be alive. I set out to find as many as I could. I initially made contact with the man who Jimmy considered to be one of the best two athletes he ever trained – Henry Thresher. Henry's view of his former coach, that he was a wonderful human being who had a positive impact on his life, would be repeated by virtually all former students I spoke to. As well as a phone call, Henry kindly sent me a letter about his former coach. To him I give my thanks.

The next former athlete I spoke to was Larry Lattomus. His enthusiasm for the book, and the information he sent me via email, convinced me the project was a viable one. Sadly Larry died in 2017. This book is dedicated to him. His children Jeff Lattomus and Jennifer Lattomus Donley continued their father's enthusiasm for the book, and put me in touch with their mother, Diane Carey, who corrected some facts in his biographs and provided additional information.

From the same team as Thresher and Lattomus came Gus Ormrod, and like his compatriots he gave his time and information freely, glad that someone was finally paying respect to his former coach. His wife Jackie and son Augustine were equally supportive.

In 2016 I made contact with Paul White, who entered into our correspondence with gusto, and kindly provided me with a detailed document he titled *How Sir James Michael Curran Influenced My Life*. I cannot underestimate the importance of this document in giving me an in-depth insight into the man that was Jimmy Curran.

Equally helpful was Jef Evans. He had an insight that none of my other interviewees had, as he was both a student athlete and a coach. He sent email after email with insightful information that, along with Paul White's document, gave me a far greater understanding of who Jimmy was. Even 57 years after Jimmy's death, Jef's love for the man shone through brightly. Jef was also integral to my speaking to Andy Anderson.

Andy sent me much information by email, and we had an extended chat on the telephone in which he gave me a wealth of information, his tongue perhaps loosened somewhat by our shared Scottish heritage.

An article in Mercersburg Academy's magazine saw a number of emails pinged my way, and from these came helpful snippets of information that further built the story of Jimmy's life. Christopher Montgomery, Harry Pickle III, Hank Spire and Harper Girvin all gave freely of their information.

ACKNOWLEDGEMENTS

Bob Batdorf kindly gave his opinion on Jimmy's coaching methods.

I was also contacted by Joe Silverman, who offered his encouragement.

In virtually every case Jimmy's former athletes offered up information that was retained only in their memories. I am honoured that they trusted me to put these personal stories into print.

My one real regret when tracking down former students, was failing to get in touch with Rolando Cruz, despite calling in the help of Villanova University, Mercersburg Academy and various libraries in Puerto Rico.

Most of Jimmy's athletes have passed away. As such, I made a concerted effort to contact their families (often children, but sometimes grandchildren). The internet has opened up a wealth of ways to track people down, and I used them to my advantage.

One of the stories that eluded me for some time, was that of Albert Robinson. His common surname made it difficult to find family members, but I eventually tracked down his grandson, Art Whiting. Art kindly cleared up his grandfather's sudden retirement from athletics whilst still in his prime.

Another teammate of Robinson, Harry Goelitz, proved less elusive, thanks in great part to his less common surname. Gary Goelitz, Frank Blossom and Amy Blossom, kindly provided me with a wealth of information.

One of the more interesting athletes was Chuck Taylor, as he was the only one I am aware of that travelled to Europe with Jimmy. His son, David Taylor, kindly supplied much information about his father, as well as previously unknown information about the trip to Europe.

Carol Rick Gibbons kindly provided information about her grandfather, Marvin Rick. She also allowed me to view a photograph of Rick, in his team uniform on the SS *America* as he travelled to the 1924 Olympics.

Barney Berlinger Jr kindly provided information and scanned a number of documents from his father's scrapbook.

Jerry A. Madden kindly provided information about his father-in-law, Steve Szumachowski.

Reid Kellam kindly provided background information about Austin and Byron Kellam. Jack Milne Jr kindly attempted to recall information about his father's time at Mercersburg, and Benjamin G. Gifford kindly sent me information about his father, Pax Gifford, that allowed me to complete his biography.

Seth Cagle kindly recalled much about his father's life, as well as his father's memories of his roommate, Charles Moore Jr. He also usefully scanned a rare postcard detailing the upgrade of the Jimmy Curran Track.

A number of families that may have held interesting information did elude me, most especially those of Allen Woodring, Allen Swede, Harold Barron, Larry Shields, Bill Cox, John Payne, Dick Foran, Paul Cowie and Jeff Kirk.

One could not write about Jimmy Curran and not visit the source of many of his achievements and much of his fame – Mercersburg Academy. So, I took time out of a family holiday to drive to the school. My great thanks go to Doug Smith for taking time out of his schedule to take me on a tour of the school grounds, delve into the school archive, and for providing access to digitised files and rare books. A tour through the school track and grounds, as well as lunch in the canteen, gave me an insight into Jimmy's experiences that I could never have garnered from documentary sources.

An important source of information would have been David Emory, who served as one of Jimmy's coaching assistants towards the end of his career. Sadly David passed away not long before I started writing. However, I was lucky enough to track down his son, David Emory Jr, who provided some wonderful stories, for which I wholeheartedly thank him.

Thanks must go also to Lee Owen, editor and publications director at the Academy, who printed a short article, written by me, in

ACKNOWLEDGEMENTS

the Mercersburg Magazine. This led to me accessing a number of former students.

Jason Bershatsky, Director of Alumni Relations, kindly attempted to track down Rolando Cruz. Although his attempts came up blank, he pointed me towards Cruz's university, Villanova, where Matthew V. Gwin, Senior Director of Engagement Activities also attempted to find Jimmy's elusive pole vaulter. Again, despite attempts to track him down, I finally had to call it a day and admit defeat.

Personally digging into archival material is often the most fruitful way to do research, and to that end I visited a number of libraries, archives and schools. The first of these was the Royal Highland Fusiliers Regimental Museum in Glasgow, which holds an incredible archive of documents, photographs and an unpublished book by Jimmy's senior officer, Lieutenant-Colonel Henry Kelham, detailing a day-by-day account of the Boer War. This was the foundation upon which the chapter titled *Kelham's Warriors* was built.

With Jimmy hailing from the Scottish Borders, it was incumbent on me to visit the Hawick Hub, which holds much of the area's archival material. It was here that I sourced the criminal record book for Galashiels, highlighting the chequered pasts of Jimmy's siblings.

In an attempt to access more detailed information about the various amateur athletic societies in Scotland, a fruitful visit was paid to the National Records of Scotland.

The National Library of Scotland offered access to the *Galashiels/Border Telegraph*, a newspaper that holds a wealth of information, but which has not yet been digitised. The Library's incredible maps website (maps.nls.uk) helped in tracking down various landmarks related to Jimmy's youth, not least where he lived and the cemetery he used as a makeshift track.

Thanks also go to Galashiels Burgh Primary School, for allowing me access to photograph the only known gift from Jimmy to the town which I could track down.

On my previously-mentioned trip to the United States I used

some time to visit the New York Public Library. As well as providing access to a couple of hard-to-find books, my membership gave me digital access to the *International Herald Tribune*, which allowed me to (finally) track down information about Jimmy's teaching trip to the MacJannet School in France in 1935.

A number of libraries, archives, schools and universities attempted to track down information about alumni. My thanks go to them for taking time to undertake research for me that was, in most cases, incredibly enlightening, and ultimately led to further information.

The University of Pennsylvania took many athletes from Mercersburg Academy, and therefore I contacted them for information on a number of occasions. My thanks go to the various staff members who helped me. They are Joseph-James J. Ahern, Senior Archivist at the school, Tim Horning in the archives, and Charles Cobine, Digital Outreach Librarian at the Van Pelt Library, and Charles Dorman, Associate Director of Athletic Communications. Also incredibly helpful was Dave Johnson, Director of the Penn Relays, whose knowledge on the various individuals I was researching was impressive. Discussions with Dave saw several changes to the text.

Bob Lee, Director of Communications and Marketing at Columbus Academy, provided excellent information about former teacher Jack White.

Barry Cantwell was the athlete thrown out of Mercersburg with Harry Goelitz. Information about him was kindly provided by Sigrid Perry at Northwestern University.

Emil von Elling was the only coach about whom I attempted to track down further information. Verna Gilson at the Beardsley Library kindly looked into his archive.

Julie Bartlett Nelson, Archivist at the Forbes Library in Northampton, Ma., kindly attempted to track down information about Calvin Jr and John Coolidge's time at Mercersburg.

I was intrigued by Jimmy's visit to watch Sydney Wooderson take part in the Mile of the Century. Vicky Clubb of the University of

ACKNOWLEDGEMENTS

Birmingham in England, kindly attempted to track down information from Joe Binks' papers in the National Athletics Archive.

Thanks also to Paul Dudman at the University of East London who very kindly pored through the archive of the British Olympic Association in an effort to find information regarding the offer, to Jimmy, of a post training the 1916 British Olympic team.

Clayton Ruminski at the Hagley Museum and Library attempted to track down Jimmy in the archive of the Reading Iron Works. Unfortunately none existed.

Thanks to Roger Hull, researcher at the Liverpool Record Office, for providing information on the Cunard Hotel.

Thanks to Steve Smith and Kaitlyn Pettengill at the Historical Society of Philadelphia for locating photographs of Jack Roden and Jimmy. The Society also answered my questions regarding the Meadowbrook Club Year Book.

The Free Library of Philadelphia kindly copied an obscure newspaper article for me.

Laura Schieb at the Rauner Special Collections Library attempted to track down information about the Professional Coaches' Association of America. It proved as elusive in the library collection as it was in digitised newspapers.

Justin J. McHenry, Director of the Franklin County Archives, was extremely kind in sending me scans of Jimmy's naturalisation papers.

Helen Stec, at Tufts University, kindly attempted, albeit unsuccessfully, to track down information about Jimmy's stint at Donald MacJannet's summer school in Angon, France.

Kara Nadine Alexander and Michelle Denise Dalmau at Indiana University went beyond my expectations by scanning two images from an extremely obscure and difficult-to-find book, and by allowing me to use them in this book.

Thanks go to Holly Roper at the University of North Carolina at Chapel Hill who provided information that allowed me to complete Bob Black's biography.

JIMMY CURRAN

Christine Ameduri, archivist at the McDonough School, kindly provided information about Harvey Reed.

Tom Wharton, assistant archivist at Phillips Exeter Academy, attempted to find information about Jimmy's job interview at the school. Despite being unsuccessful in his search, thanks are given.

Thanks to Ann Mosher who attempted to track down some articles and photographs in Temple University's Special Collections.

Jim Bishop of the St Andrew's Society of Philadelphia spent much time delving into archives checking if Jimmy had ever become a member of the Society, and if he could find a link with the sculptor R. Tait McKenzie.

Whilst Jimmy's family, former athletes, their families and the staff of Mercersburg Academy and various other school and archives provided the foundation upon which this book was built, a wealth of others filled gaps and provided additional information that allowed me to satisfy my need for accuracy. I thank each and every one of them.

Thanks go to Meilyr Emrys for providing valuable information on the (sadly largely forgotten) Welsh athlete, Percy Smallwood.

Thanks also to Ellen Boer and Andrew Boer, relatives of Michael Strauss, the journalist who wrote numerous in-depth articles about Jimmy in the 1950s. They pointed me in the direction of their father and grandfather's archive at the Historical Society of Palm Beach County, to whom thanks are also extended for sending me articles.

Drew Keeling, a historian with an interest in mass migration, kindly provided one of his publications regarding the cost of shipping fares. He was also amenable to emailing back and forth regarding various shipping issues, and these conversations helped greatly inform my understanding of transatlantic travel in the early 20th century.

Thanks also go to my friend of 46 years, David Hume, who now lives in Galashiels, and walked me around the Eastlands Cemetery to work out where Jimmy had trained.

Evelyn Anderson and Jayne Jackson confirmed my suspicion that the two race judges standing with Jimmy in one of the photographs

in

ACKNOWLEDGEMENTS

this book, were indeed William and John Torrie.

There were a small number of books that directly related to Jimmy, he having competed against, trained or had an acquaintance with, each of the book subjects. Each provides an insight into an aspect of Jimmy's life, and also the wider athletics world. These are *Hot Foot: Walter Knox's Remarkable Life as a Professional in an Amateur World* by David F. Town, *The Little Wonder: The Untold Story of Alfie Shrubb World Champion Runner* by Rob Hadgraft, *The Runner McGough* by Tommy McGuire, *Mr Struth: The Boss* by David Mason and Ian Stewart, *Struth: The Story of an Ibrox Legend* by David Leggat, and *Immortal of the Cinder Path: The Saga of James 'Ted' Meredith* by John Jack Lemon. Additional thanks must go to John Jack Lemon for sending me a copy of his book (free of charge), in the midst of the coronavirus pandemic. I look forward to reciprocating by sending him a copy of this book.

Thanks also go to Kelly Stewart, daughter of Jimmy Stewart, who kindly answered my question regarding her father.

Jim Gerencser of the Carlisle School Indian Resource Center kindly allowed me to use an image of Joe McHugh.

Sandra Strang was extremely kind in attempting to uncover information about the Port Elizabeth Scottish Association.

I contacted Gala Harriers with a view to accessing any archives they might hold. Unfortunately these no longer exist, but club member Neil Renton did kindly provide information, most notably regarding his dual role as a council officer researching Jimmy for inclusion in the Scottish Borders Sporting Hall of Fame.

This book, like my previous one, relied heavily on numerous US and British digital newspaper archives to mine obscure information. One of these, Old Fulton NY Postcards, warrants a mention, and can be accessed at www.fultonhistory.com/Fulton.html. The website is run by a Fulton resident called Tom Tryniski. It contains a wealth of information, and long may it continue to be a free resource.

Should I have missed anyone who provided help, I apologise profusely. No slight was intended.

Cover photographs and vignettes

COVER PHOTOGRAPHS AND VIGNETTES

Notes

Language

This story takes place mainly in two countries, both of whose primary language is English. There are, however, small differences in the spelling of certain words, and I had to decide whether to use US English or British English. For no reason, other than it is the version I use personally on a day-to-day basis, I chose British English. Where US English occurs within a quote taken from a written source, or is used in common terminology, such as Pearl Harbor, the original spelling is used.

Timings

The means of recording the time run, and distance or height jumped, have changed several times over the years. In the early years detailed in this book, runners were measured to one fifth of a second. Greater accuracy was introduced at the 1912 Olympics, with runners measured to one tenth of a second. However, timing to one fifth of a second remained common. Neither are absolutely accurate as they were recorded by hand-held stopwatches. Fully electronic timing was not introduced to the Olympics until 1964. This book denotes the time in the manner it was printed in newspaper reports of the time i.e. either as a fraction or in decimal format.

Soccer and football

I thought long and hard about how to differentiate between the two sports known by the term 'football' – soccer and gridiron. I determined not to use the term soccer, as this is not how Jimmy would have referred to it. I could see no simple way to do this, so ask the reader to be aware that the two sports are represented, and to use context to discern between them.

Foreword

While I am neither a track and field specialist, nor a writer, I am uniquely situated to submit this foreword. Jimmy Curran was my grandfather, who we knew as papa, and someone who formed the background story of my childhood and those of my siblings and cousins. His energy, discipline and persistence were legendary in our family and set the bar for subsequent generations.

How did it begin? Craig had already started writing about my grandfather and found a photo of Jimmy Curran on my Facebook page. In March 2015 I received a message: 'Looking at the story of your grandfather, I would like to write a book about his life'. Really? So I forwarded it to members of the family and we were impressed by Craig's track record. I thought if he could write a book about Bruce Springsteen, why not write about my grandfather as well!

Craig is an expert researcher, and as such, archive material is not lost in the depths of dusty libraries and forgotten news clippings. Craig digs deep. He finds obscure information and records, and brings back a life one would have thought totally forgotten. Craig tells the tale of my grandfather's life in the army, then as a civilian supplementing his earnings running as a professional, and finally as an immigrant to the USA. The book is not just about my grandfather, but also about the young men he coached. Craig has captured the flavour of the sporting environment in those days. The working man who ran for prize money being barred from amateur sport, and hence the Olympics, went on to coach at America's elite schools. Jimmy Curran helped plant the seeds for what we now see as the norm today: excellence in training methods, diet, self-belief and total commitment. For the athletes reading this book, you might be fascinated by the standards of the professional runners back in the early 1900s, particularly in Scotland.

I started out reading about my grandfather. By the end of the book I was reading about somebody else – Jimmy Curran, the man. Thank

JIMMY CURRAN

you, Craig, for taking the baton and running with it.

Laurie Danaher
London, 2020

Prologue • 290

The sun was only just breaking the horizon, casting long shadows over the resplendent grounds of Mercersburg Academy, an elite prep school in southern Pennsylvania, as Jimmy Curran, the school's 58-year old Scottish athletics coach, walked towards its five-hole golf course. On any given day he could be seen around campus wearing a tartan sports jacket, topped off with a green and white tammy, and if he was feeling particularly patriotic, a kilt. But on this particular morning in August 1938 he sported slacks and a shirt, with a sun hat for protection. He carried with him two sandwiches, a gallon jug of water and ice, a three iron and three balls. His goal was to finish as many holes as possible before tired legs or the setting sun forced his retiral. He steadied himself on the tee, lined up his shot, swung, and peered into the morning sky as the ball, made in Scotland, sped away from him.

*****

He was a diminutive man, stretching 5'4" on a good day, 'only slightly taller than the average jockey.' As the years passed, and he added some pounds and his skin loosened, reporters began likening him to the Irish actor Barry Fitzgerald. But in his youth, with his dark hair swept back, he had been a dashingly handsome man – his prominent ears, jutting lower jaw, and ski slope of a nose, greater than the sum of their parts. He had arrived in America, or Ameriky as he liked to cheekily call it, virtually penniless, but with a job awaiting him in Reading, Pennsylvania, and the desire to prove himself as one of the finest middle-distance runners in the world. Within weeks the job was gone, victim of the financial panic of 1907. But he used his athletic prowess to procure coaching posts at, first, the University of Pennsylvania, and then Mercersburg Academy. The boys who ran for his teams were the sons of presidents and industrialists, but despite this immense social gulf

1

between teacher and students, they were immediately drawn to the little Scotsman who could outrun them all, and whose wit had them doubled over with laughter.

Jimmy's time at the University of Pennsylvania had been more than fortuitous. He had served under America's dean of coaches, Mike Murphy, and his team. For three years their vast knowledge had seeped through, and he had utilised what he had learned on the University's cross country and freshman track teams. When he took the step up to head coach at Mercersburg, Murphy's teachings flooded from him.

The soft tone early photographs of Jimmy belie a toughness that saw him drive him and his boys to mine hidden reserves. He taught his athletes techniques that allowed them to run faster, jump higher and throw farther, and when their bodies told them they could do no more he used psychology to eke out further milliseconds or millimetres. But, unlike many of his contemporaries, he was no tyrant. There was no screaming at athletes, or pushing them beyond breaking point. He treated them fairly and respected them, knowing they would reciprocate when the gun was fired.

By the time the ball left his club on that morning in 1938, he had become a Mr Chips-like character, and tales of his achievements, and his legendary wit, all told in a mock Scots brogue by students and fellow coaches, flew around the cinder tracks of the eastern United States like gossip at a racetrack.

*****

The round had begun the previous evening at Jack's Drugstore in Mercersburg. The tale has taken on many twists over the years. In one telling Jimmy was drinking a soda, and the conversation came around to Scotland's place as the home of golf. Someone (it could have been 'an Irishman or, worse, an Englishman') questioned whether golfers were indeed real athletes. Scotland's national game had been slighted, the gauntlet had been thrown down, and it was Jimmy's duty to defend its honour. Another has the druggist telling Jimmy the story of two farmers who played around 150 holes of golf as a bet. With a shrug of his shoulders and a scrunching of his nose, Jimmy looked at the druggist and, in his Scots brogue, still strong after 30 years away from his homeland, dismissed the farmers' feat: 'I kin do better.' He would later tell one of his grandsons that he simply wanted to show what a man of his age could do. Whatever the truth, and it may well be that the actual story is an amalgam of all three, Jimmy's mind was made up – he would take on the Academy's golf course. In the process he would further cement his legendary status. As Jimmy would prove time and again, he never refused a challenge. Indeed, he thrived on proving he was capable of meeting any that arose. And if it included walking long distances and golf, then all the better.

Seventeen years later, in 1955, he played a round of golf with his grandsons, Mike and Jim Lewis. Their mother, Jimmy's second daughter, Mary, warned them to limit him to 18 holes. After they had finished their round he wanted to play again but they refused and made their way to the clubhouse where they ordered sandwiches. They watched their grandfather head for the restroom as they waited on their food, and as they were being served they looked out the clubhouse window to see him on the first tee with another group. He was unstoppable, driven by an inner spirit. His granddaughter, Alanna Berger, conveyed a similar story, noting that she would often caddie for him on local golf courses. After he had completed a round, he would immediately be ready to go again, while she would be exhausted.

*****

By noon an American-made ball had replaced the Scottish one which, according to Jimmy, was lying too close to the turf. By dinner time the crowd reached into the hundreds; the story goes that, fearing that the 58-year-old would not last much longer, two doctors and an undertaker were amongst the throng. But the worst he suffered was a swollen ankle, sustained after a bee sting.

As he passed 285 holes, one onlooker urged him to reach 300. Jimmy looked at the man and, with a mix of disdain and tiredness, told him 'You're only doing the talking, it's me that's doing the walking.' Jimmy was looking for an opportune moment to end his day's work, having fulfilled his goal many hours earlier. The moment came at 8.12pm, on the 290th hole, with a 25-foot chip in. He'd had enough. He picked his ball from the hole, and headed for the clubhouse. Not only could he now say he had completed 290 holes of golf in one day, covering almost 35 miles, but he also now had a couple of stories to add to those that played upon the stereotypical parsimonious Scot he loved to portray himself as – there were, he dryly told listeners, no green fees, and the three golf balls with which he had begun his round had grown into five.

Jimmy's feat was considered interesting enough that, three months later, the story was published nationally in Robert Ripley's *Believe It Or Not*.

Chapter 1 • The Queen's Shilling

Fifty-eight years before Jimmy chipped into the 290th hole on the short Mercersburg Academy course, he was born into a large family in the Scottish border town of Galashiels, or simply Gala as it is often known. It sits halfway between the Scottish capital, Edinburgh, and the English border, nestling comfortably in the lee of a range of low-lying hills, and in the 19th century, as the buildings expanded outwards, so it seemed that the hills were spilling into the town.

Galashiels had experienced a gradual growth for hundreds of years. Scotland's Industrial Revolution, coming on the back of the Enlightenment and the Agricultural Revolution, allowed Glasgow, Dundee, and Scotland's other urban centres to prosper. And rural towns eagerly followed. The town's geographic situation may not have initially appeared particularly noteworthy, but in every rough there may be found a diamond. Galashiels had two.

When the town's first settlers agreed on their situation, on the banks of the Gala Water, they chose well, their decision proving to be the town's making, allowing it to flourish. For the defining need of the Industrial Revolution, advancing apace through the hills, glens, towns and cities of Scotland, was fast flowing water. Where there was water there emerged mills. And where there were mills there was growth.

And then there were the rolling grassy hills surrounding the town. These proved a perfect food source for the Black-faced and Cheviot sheep which were so integral to the ever-growing wool industry. Indeed, so integral were they that by 1798, when the industry was just beginning to thrive it was estimated that in the county of Selkirkshire there were 118,000 sheep occupying 148,000 acres of grazing. With such natural resources Galashiels had the means to cement its place at the rural heart of this industrialisation. It did so with gusto.

The weight of wool being worked on in the town went from 722 stones in 1774 to 2,916 stones in 1791, and 21,500 stones in 1833, whilst the number of spinners quadrupled from 1780 to 1791. To cope with this continual unfettered growth, eight mills were erected between 1792 and 1826, along with a new lade and a cloth hall. The technological advances continued unabated and by 1840 the hand-loom weavers had been almost wholly replaced by power looms sited in great manufactories.

In 1833 a reporter noted:

> Having lately had occasion to visit the thriving town … I was delighted to witness the prevailing stir and bustle. On conversing with some of the most extensive manufacturers, I was informed that orders were coming in far faster than they could be completed, and that while Galashiels cloth still maintained its predominance, the manufacture of woollen checked shawls of various colours, lately introduced, are now brought to great perfection.

The arrival of the railway, in 1849, and the subsequent branch line to Selkirk seven years after that, saw the woollen industry truly explode. The number of mills rose from 13 to 22 in the 40 years from 1851 – often vast brick affairs with endless rows of windows, and chimney stacks that dominated the skyline. That year Galashiels showed its strength at the Great Exhibition in London, when the town provided the largest single contribution, one of 'very superior character', to the woollen industry exhibit, which was in itself the largest of all the exhibits, with 2,016 feet of hanging space.

An industrial powerhouse nation requires a far greater workforce than that of a rural economy, and to cope, Scotland's population in the 19th century rose from 1.6m to 4m. The knock-on effect of this enormous jump was that people required to be fed and clothed, and Galashiels was well-placed to fulfil the latter. But the town's population at the turn of the century was entirely inadequate if full advantage was to be taken. Thus the 19th century saw the population of Galashiels growing continually – 844 in 1801, 5,919 in 1851, until 1891 when it stood at an impressive 17,367, an incredible 2,057% increase from 90 years earlier. But natural growth alone could not meet such a demand and almost two-thirds of those living in the town in 1881 were outsiders, finding their way from elsewhere in the Scottish Borders, and further afield.

And as the population grew it required to be housed. Dorothy Wordsworth, on a tour through Scotland with her poet brother William, in 1803, wrote of Galashiels that a 'townish bustle and ugly stone houses are fast taking place of the brown-roofed thatched cottages.' The house-building continued apace, expanding outwards into the town's hinterland, as the old greywacke stone buildings were joined by brick-built ones made possible by access to rail transport. But the quality of the new housing stock was poor, breeding poverty on a grand scale. Families, often numbering 10 or more, lived in cramped, unsanitary conditions, where, without the medical means to prevent or cure, disease and illness spread like wildfire. Toilets were usually a communal stone or wood affair housed in the building's backland, whilst bathing was done at one of the town's six bath-houses, and laundry at one of eight wash-houses. Death hung over the town like a coastal haar.

And a growing population requires an infrastructure capable of supporting it. Around 1800 the town was served by 22 tailors and clothiers, 17 wrights, 10 tanners, five shoemakers, three bakers, and two candlemakers, amongst others. A century later the tailors and clothiers had grown to 65, the bakers to 18. The town was overflowing with businesses offering every imaginable ware needed by the townsfolk; 85 confectioners and fruiterers, 69 grocers, 38 booksellers and stationers, 34 private gardeners, 19 dressmakers, and even 14 music teachers.

In the 19th century the infant mortality rate in Scotland, and beyond, was incredibly high. By mid-century around 120 of every 1,000 live births in Scotland died. Forty years later it had actually risen slightly to 129 – around one in eight births. The real heart of this epidemic of infant death was in urban areas, with families in Glasgow faring especially badly. But Galashiels was by no means immune.

From 1849 to 1853 the town suffered three cholera epidemics, due in great part to the 'impassable streets, greasy footpaths, and reeking middens … a rank luxuriance of filth.' The Police Commissioners refused to spend money on labour to obviate the squalor, and so the task of cleansing the town fell to 'old men and mere youths on the footpaths and roadways, progressing at a snail's gallop, an inch an hour.' But the passing years and a growing understanding of disease did not bring with it action, and in 1867, a further threat of the same disease saw an investigation into the state of the town's wells which were 'totally unfit for domestic use.' Four years later smallpox and scarlet fever ravaged the town.

*****

It is unlikely that many families escaped heartache amongst such deprivation and disease, and the Currans, led by John and Ellen, were no exception. In October 1875, John, the youngest of the five children, aged just four years old, contracted scarlet fever, which was thought to emanate from tainted milk. Without the benefit of penicillin, not discovered and used as a treatment for another 67 years, John suffered a sore throat, fever and rash for around eight days, before dying in the family home at Overhaugh Street. As was common at the time, when the next child to arrive was a boy, a mere 10 weeks later, he too was named John. But the family's grief would not end there. Three years later, 10-month old Jane-Ann became infected with whooping cough. The cough can be so violent as to cause sufferers to vomit or even break ribs, but often the effect on infants is much less aggressive and they are afflicted with only a mild cough, but stop breathing for short periods. On New Year's Day, 1879, she succumbed, and the Curran family was once again thrown into mourning.

Within three months Ellen was pregnant once again. The death of her youngest child was still vivid, but the new life inside her helped to focus her thoughts elsewhere. And just over a year after Jane-Ann's death, and only weeks after William Ewart Gladstone had graced the town with his immense oratorical skills during the Midlothian Campaign which would see him elected Prime Minister, the family welcomed a new son, and as was the Scottish way he was named James, after his grandfather. As a Roman Catholic he would, nine years later, be given his confirmation name, Michael.

At the time of Jimmy's birth the family was living at 1 Bank Court, in the centre of Galashiels. Over the following years they would move around to the nearby Overhaugh Street and Bank Close, eventually returning to Bank Court by 1906. And it was here that the six surviving Curran children, four boys and two girls, grew up, surrounded by their extended family of grandparents, uncles, aunts and cousins.

James soon became Jimmy and he was enrolled, aged around five, at St Andrew's Roman Catholic School, built just a year before he was born. He arrived at a highly opportune time; in 1872 the Education (Scotland) Act had been passed, ensuring that every child up to the age of 13 years old acquired a certain educational standard, and that Scotland would emerge with the finest education system in the world.

*****

As the century progressed, the number of social outlets grew in tandem. Although Galashiels lacked the daily bustle and vibrancy of major population centres, such as Glasgow and Edinburgh, it heartily took part in major celebrations – a welcome counterpoint to the sweat and blood poured into the wool industry's carding machines.

In June 1887 the town only undertook small celebrations for Queen Victoria's Golden Jubilee and, as such, locals travelled by train to cities as far afield as Newcastle to partake of greater festivities. On the evening of the 21st, as darkness descended, Jimmy would likely have looked on as his brothers played on the streets of Galashiels with squibs and crackers, and set a vast bonfire alight on Market Place. The townsfolk made their way to the top of the town's surrounding hills and there they set alight further fires and at one point in the evening 62 fires, burning across the Borders, could be seen from the top of Meigle Hill.

A year before the Diamond Jubilee celebrations, in 1897, it is likely that Jimmy was one of thousands of Galaleans who watched a vast public demonstration to commemorate the centenary of the death of the poet Robert Burns. Led by the town's brass band a vast array of marchers – friendly societies, millworkers, sports clubs – made their way to the public park where they were entertained by a choir and orchestra performing songs by Burns, culminating in a rendition of *Auld Lang Syne*. Jimmy's love of Burns' work would never leave him – 14 years later he would stand up at a social meeting of the Scottish Border Club of Philadelphia and sing Burns' *Braw Lads O' Gala Water*.

The following year it is likely that he partook of a celebration to mark the Diamond Jubilee of Queen Victoria who, less than a year previously, had become the country's longest-reigning monarch. Perhaps in response to the muted events of a decade previously, the town went all out with mass gatherings. Three days of celebrations ended with over 10,000 people gathering at a fête in the Public Park where a 35 feet high bonfire was lit, whilst the summits of some of the surrounding hills burned bright, as they had a decade earlier, with smaller fires.

In 1904, the town even hosted Buffalo Bill Cody's Wild West Show, as part of one of eight European tours dating from 1887 to 1906.

But as was often the way in areas of rampant poverty, many chose a more Bacchanalian release from the tough and mundane daily life. On payday it was commonplace for men to walk straight from their place of work to the public house where they would proceed to spend much of their earnings. This social problem prompted the rise of the temperance movement. It spread throughout the country and had made its way into Galashiels by the early 19th century. A century later groups such as the Good Templars, the Band of Hope and the Total

Abstinence Society abounded, whilst temperance hotels pervaded the town. But despite the prevalence of such groups and businesses the impact they had was limited, competing, as they were, against public houses numbering into double figures.

The resultant drunken working class men (and quite often women too) and their feral children did not sit well alongside what was, in the Victorian era, a Draconian approach to policing that would, today, be referred to as 'zero tolerance.' The Curran family did not avoid the long arm of the law, and Jimmy's brothers faced the wrath of the court several times. In 1883 Michael was brought before the magistrate for fighting, and the following year Edward was charged with a breach of the peace for 'uttering oaths and making a noise to the annoyance of the lieges.' Three years later he was in trouble once more, this time for throwing stones, and at the end of the century Jimmy's youngest brother, John, was convicted of a breach of the peace. But it was Michael who came up with the most ingenious method of being hauled before the local magistrate. In an attempt to impress two local boys he loaded a firearm (a one inch long replica cannon) with gunpowder, injuring the face and eyes of one of the boys. The charge was dropped.

Jimmy appears to have avoided the town bobbies, either through good behaviour, youthful cunning, a slice of luck, or a mix of all three.

*****

The scale of the Galashiels woollen industry by the mid-19th century was such that the town was almost wholly reliant on its success. Any major downturn promised to have far-reaching, if not industry-ending, consequences. And so it proved. By century's end Galashiels was largely reliant on the North American market. But the introduction of successive US tariffs devastated the Galashiels industry, with one firm's transatlantic sales dropping from around £25,000 a year to £2,000. And as if to kick a man when down the industry was pushed further into decline by the introduction of cheap imports, mainly brought in from continental Europe and Yorkshire.

With less work available, men and women left the town for employment elsewhere, and between 1891 and 1901 the population of the town fell sharply, and for many of the younger males, especially in the mid-1890s when the prospect of war was looming in South Africa, a stint in the army was often the only viable option.

From the early 1880s to 1901 the number of men in the British Army rose from 124,000 to 430,000, while the population of the country took only a modest jump from 34.9m to 41.4m. As Jimmy was growing up he watched two of his brothers enlist – Michael to the Royal Scots Fusiliers and then the King's Own Scottish Borderers (KOSB) in 1886. In 1894, his brother John joined him.

By the time of Jimmy's 18th birthday, in 1898, he was working for the family of recently-deceased local brickmaker and hotel proprietor Samuel Gillan, taking on roles as varied as labourer, groom, and barman at the Royal Hotel. But he was dissatisfied with the mundane life. Less than a month after his birthday he travelled to Dumfries where, on 28th January, he stood before Lance Sergeant Samuel Castle and enlisted in the 3rd Battalion of the KOSB, a militia battalion that often farmed out recruits to the regular army. His life was about to change dramatically.

The militia was a reserve army force, the forerunner to Britain's Territorial Army. It had long-existed in Britain, dating back to the days before the union of the four countries. In the early 19th century, with the threat of a Napoleonic invasion growing in likelihood, a bolstered militia appeared to be a necessity if the regular army was fighting on the continent. And so, men from all over the country were conscripted to serve, although those with money could pay another to take their place. The threat of invasion ended at the Battle of Waterloo but the militia continued on as an arm of the British Army, albeit with conscription replaced by a voluntary sign-up.

By the time Jimmy accepted the Queen's Shilling, men would attend for training, all the while retaining their civilian job. Aside from the financial benefits (they would receive pay and a retainer), they would meet up with like-minded individuals, whilst dipping one's toe in the water of army life to garner whether it was comfortable.

Jimmy's first months were spent travelling back and forth to the regiment's base at Hannahfield Camp, half a mile south of Dumfries, just east of the River Nith. His days were spent in the grinding monotony of army life – instilling an unquestioning obedience, weapons training, daily drills and marches, as well as frequent manoeuvres on the Kingholm Merse – a routine that had served the British Army so well for so long.

The daily drudgery of army life was occasionally broken. On 19th July, as the men were in the midst of a drill, a fire in an annexe of the Crichton Royal Institution, a mental asylum situated the length of a running track from the camp, elicited a response. Jimmy, along with his fellow volunteers, marched quick-time to the scene and 'rendered very valuable assistance.'

*****

As a youth Jimmy had been aware of his natural running talents, and had trained as best he could with limited facilities. In an era when running tracks were only available in larger towns and cities he found the next best thing. On the south-eastern edge of Galashiels, lying in the shadow of the Gala, Abbots and Netherdale mills, with trains rumbling by beyond, was Eastlands Cemetery. It was split into two rectangular sections. The most westerly of these was almost rectangular and the outer path totalled 452 yards, just 12 yards longer than the standard quarter-mile distance. Jimmy was friendly with the son of the church sexton and the two pounded their way around the gravel paths:

> They had cinder paths in the graveyard and it was
> better than any track in the district except that it was
> square instead of round. So we could run on it in the
> winter, wearing tennis shoes instead of spikes. Could

14

you imagine when they saw the footprints in the snow in the morning?

By the time he joined the army he was fit and fast. He still had much to learn about the art of competitive running, but he had the ingredients necessary for success – speed, endurance, and an unquenchable spirit and desire to win.

Jimmy's first known opportunity to test himself came soon after enlistment. In August the regiment marked its centenary with five days of celebratory events, which included a number of sporting events. On the 20th the regiment made its way to Castledykes Park, home of the Dumfries Hibernians football club, where two regimental football teams faced off against each other. The game was followed by dinner, before the men made their way to the Merse for four hours of sport. The substantial monetary prizes attracted 300-400 entries, Jimmy and his elder brother John among them.

A competition area was roped off and events got underway with a novelty race, where potatoes were placed a yard and a half apart and competitors had to pick them up in their mouths and place them in a bucket. After much merriment the more serious events began – Jimmy was involved in at least three. He ended up with two first places, in the 100 yards handicap, and the half-mile, and also finished second in the long jump. His brother, as well as finishing second behind Jimmy in the half-mile and third in the obstacle race, was awarded first prize for having the neatest uniform. In the evening the men were entertained by bands and soldiers playing and singing songs such as *The Scamp Of The Regiment*, *Battle Morn*, and *Scotland Yet*.

After recovery from the day's hectic activities the soldiers started early the next morning, marching from camp to Greyfriars Kirk in Dumfries. Led by pipe and brass bands, which took it in turn to play, they were joined en route by volunteer detachments. Jimmy and his fellow Roman Catholics were given special dispensation to attend the Protestant service by the town's bishop. What followed was a service of hymns and prayers and a long address by Rev. Roger S. Kirkpatrick. The service ended with the singing of *Onward Christian Soldiers*, and a rendition of *God Save The Queen*. They departed to the strains of the militia band playing *I Canna Leave The Auld Folks Yet*. Afterwards Jimmy and his fellow Catholic soldiers headed to St Andrew's Pro-Cathedral to celebrate Mass.

On Monday 22nd, with a hot sun blazing down, the men were inspected by Colonel Vernon Chater before being put through a drill on Kingholm Merse. A large crowd of spectators looked on as one half of the regiment launched an 'assault' on a farmhouse, defended by the other half. As the attackers pulled closer to the defensive positions the defenders retreated, pulling back to a golf house at the head of the Merse. As they moved forward past the farmhouse they began to charge the retreating defenders with the pipes playing in the background. A 'ceasefire' was called, likely to much disappointment, and the men made their way back to the barracks, to the strains of *Blue Bonnets Over The Border*, for a parade and inspection. The following day, the last of the centenary celebrations, another parade was held after which the men attended a concert at the Regimental Theatre.

The men barely had time to rest their heads before they were set to depart for major military manoeuvres on Salisbury Plains. After a night of disturbances in Dumfries, during which soldiers fought with the local police force, the men loaded onto trains at 6am and headed south.

The trains carrying Jimmy and the rest of the Borderers south from Dumfries were but a small part of a massive operation, the largest ever, to enable over 53,000 troops, their horses, and their ordnance to converge on a rural patch of southern England. Sam Fay, the General Manager of the Midland and South Western Junction Railway, highlighted the enormity of the task he had faced in getting 26,000 of the men to and from the area – a 1,000-yard long temporary platform, called Ludgershall Station, was erected and over 60 trains, which laid end-to-end would have measured 10 miles, transported men in and out on a single line.

The men were split into two armies, the Northern and Southern. The Southern, led by General Redvers Buller, was to act as an invading army, pushing northwards from the south coast. South of Salisbury they would be met by the defending Northern Army, led by the Duke of Connaught. The KOSB was under the command of Connaught.

After alighting from the train at Ludgershall Station before daybreak, Jimmy and the men of the KOSB were marched to Homington Camp. For the following five days, in the late-August heat, they undertook preparations, until 1st September when 'hostilities' between the two armies began, and the 3rd KOSB marched from Homington Camp to Fovant. The march would be the first of many, an attempt to replicate wartime conditions, and instil in the men an understanding of the levels of endurance and discipline they would need in a conflict situation. After breaking camp for the night, reveille was sounded at 2.30am on the morning of the 2nd and after a moonlit breakfast the men were on the march again, to Charlton Down, and by the 3rd they were back at Fovant. The relentless marching of the first two days being broken up only by marches through small villages where the men attempted to glean information about the outcome of the battle taking place in the Sudan between 25,000 British and Egyptian troops and 52,000 Mahdist warriors.

The first 'clashes' between the Northern and Southern armies came on 3rd September, and by the end of the day Buller's army had made substantial advances into Connaught's territory. The men spent Sunday in camp, attending church services and a concert, and news began to filter through about the British Army's victory at the Battle of Omdurman in the Sudan. Jimmy and his fellow soldiers turned out and cheered as the artillery fired a salute by cannon.

After more marching on the 5th, Jimmy and his fellow soldiers in the 3rd KOSB were ordered to assault the Southern Army at Stockton Wood, but just as the Brigade was forming, and the monotony of the previous week was about to be broken, the ceasefire was sounded. For two more days the men marched until they crossed the River Avon at Little Amesbury in pursuit of the 'enemy' but, after exchanging fire on Normanton Down, once again the men were frustrated by a ceasefire.

On 8th September the combined armies made their way to Boscombe Down, where they were to be reviewed. With them flooded in thousands of spectators, attracted by the biggest military spectacle Britain had ever seen, and fortified by the events in Sudan being relayed to them in the country's newspapers. So great in number were the soldiers and onlookers that they would have appeared, to anyone observing from the distant hills, like a blanket laid atop the flat green lands. At 11.20am the men began their march past, as Field Marshal Lord Wolseley, and a vast array of Knights, Lords, Dukes, Earls and MPs took their salute. It took two and a half hours for the 49,000 soldiers, their 10,000 horses, and 219 guns to pass the great and good assembled before them. The British Army, Wolseley told his staffs, was indeed 'a grand army.' With the review complete the spectators flooded onto the plain, and 49,000 became 130,000. On the Battalion's final day at Salisbury, they marched out of camp, heading for the railway station, to the strains of the bands of the 1st and 4th Staffordshire Regiment. Train after train headed out, 63 in total. The KOSB departed at 4pm and arrived in Dumfries the following morning. After breakfast in the barracks square the men were dismissed.

In early October Jimmy travelled north to Hamilton, just south of Glasgow. It appears that army life was to his liking; he signed up to the Highland Light Infantry, the regular army. The HLI was a relatively new regiment in the British Army, formed only one year after Jimmy's birth. But, perhaps cognisant of its want of longevity, it had quickly built its own traditions – whereas the Scottish regiments tended to wear kilts, the HLI wore trews and, unlike most other regiments, remained clean-shaven.

In late-December 1898 Jimmy's new regiment, based in Crete, made their way home. After touching back on home soil they took advantage of some much-deserved leave, before travelling to

THE QUEEN'S SHILLING

Devonport on the south coast of England. It is likely Jimmy travelled south with them. They were based in Raglan Barracks and Tregantle Fort for much of the coming year and, as had been the case whilst serving in the militia, Jimmy spent much of his time coping with the mundane routine of army life. The success of the previous year's manoeuvres at Salisbury saw the exercise repeated, albeit on a smaller scale. Then it was back to Devonport again.

*****

But whilst the majority of Jimmy's army life was made up of marching and manoeuvres, opportunities to pass time in a more leisurely fashion did arise. Sport in the military had begun to gain support from officers in the mid-19th century. It was seen as a way of boosting morale, instilling comradeship, improving relations between the ranks, encouraging healthy inter-regimental competition, and increasing fitness. At military academies such as Woolwich, Addiscombe and Sandhurst it began to play a central role in training regimes. By the 1850s Woolwich held an annual athletic meeting, and also hired a professional bowler to teach recruits cricket, whilst at Addiscombe a bi-annual athletics meeting was in place. Lower rank officers enthusiastically organised events to test soldier against soldier, battalion against battalion, and regiment against regiment in the sporting arena. But a lack of absolute support from the upper ranks saw to it that the events were not woven into the fabric of army life.

Gradually support did come, albeit when senior staff came to the conclusion that sport could help improve many of the army's current failings. And these failings became patently clear when, in 1862, cadets at Sandhurst Military Academy mutinied against harsh treatment, poor food, and pettiness by some of their officers. What followed was a three-day siege which ended only when the well-respected Duke of Cambridge arrived and berated the cadets.

The military response was to commission a report by General

JIMMY CURRAN

John Fox Burgoyne. Burgoyne's findings, published in 1864, were the catalyst for greater organisation of sport in the military, arguing that 'outdoor manly exercise' such as football, cricket, gymnastics and racquets would all help to avoid a repeat of the incident at Sandhurst. By the 1870s many regiments were holding annual athletic events, but it was the publication, in 1876, of two articles in *Field* magazine, which saw athletics in the military achieving national significance. One railed against the modern soldier's lack of fitness, a problem for which the proposed solution was 'voluntary permanent training.' The military response was speedy – a week later the Army Gymnastic Staff announced a 'grand military athletic meeting.' That June saw the first annual athletics meeting and by the time of the First World War had grown into a meeting of national importance. In the 1890s Tim Harington, an officer from the King's Regiment, admitted to doing 'very little soldiering' due to the time he spent playing 'cricket, rugby, association [football], tennis, racquets, hockey, etc.' By the time Jimmy joined the army in 1898 sport was an integral part of military life. And he took every opportunity that arose to test himself. Whilst he had likely run in races as a teenager it was whilst serving his country that the lethal mix of athleticism, speed and endurance began to mature. And his superiors encouraged him.

In August 1899 Jimmy competed in the Hamilton Garrison Sports, but could only manage to place in throwing the cricket ball.

A month later he was back in Devonport, competing in the Garrison Games, and it was here that his true potential started to become clear. On a day attended by most soldiers based in the Plymouth and Devonport area, Jimmy defeated all before him, taking first places in the 120 yards, the 440 yards, the mile and the hop, skip and jump. He had proved himself one of the best athletes in the British Army. Events elsewhere were to quickly dash hopes of his military career being an endless stream of sporting events.

Chapter 2 • Kelham's Warriors

For many centuries there existed a profitable exchange of goods between the east and west, known as the spice trade. In later years, Spain, Portugal and Holland all scrambled for supremacy. They utilised overland trade routes such as the Silk Road, but in response to the blocking of these routes by the Ottoman Empire in the 15th century traders looked for alternate routes. This led to an oceanic route being established around the southern tip of Africa.

In 1652 the Dutch East India Company established a base at Table Bay, a natural harbour near the Cape of Good Hope, a peninsula on the south-western edge of the African continent. Although never meant to be any more than a point at which to replenish food and water, many Dutchmen were soon forced to journey into the interior to farm land, when the local Khoikhoi tribe refused to supply them with meat. They became known as Boers, or literally, farmers. A colony was formed.

Realising its importance of this stopping off point, the British seized the Cape in 1795, briefly relinquished it in 1803, and gained it back in 1806. This led to strained relations with the Boers, and these deteriorated further as slavery was abolished, and the English language was enforced in the colony's courts. In response the Boers migrated north and east, in what was known as the Great Trek.

This led, in the 1850s, to the creation of two Boer-controlled provinces – the Orange Free State and the South African Republic, also known as the Transvaal. The British controlled lands to the north, and two provinces – Cape Colony and Natal – to the south. But any thoughts that the two factions would live peaceably alongside one another was shattered with the discovery of diamonds at Kimberley, in the British-controlled Cape Colony, in 1867.

In 1877 Britain annexed the Transvaal in an attempt to create a federal British-controlled state and this led, for a few months in 1880-81, to a conflict, which ended in defeat for Britain, and the return of the

KELHAM'S WARRIORS

Transvaal to the Boers. Five years later, in 1886, gold was discovered at Witwatersrand in the Orange Free State, and so productive were the seams that by 1898 a quarter of the world's gold was extracted from Witwatersrand rock. To service the gold fields, the town of Johannesburg was founded. What followed was a huge influx of British migrant workers, or *uitlanders*, into the region. Relations between the two became increasingly fractious, with the Boer government restricting the voting rights of the *uitlanders*, whilst taxing them heavily. In the mid-1890s they built a railway from Pretoria to Delagoa Bay in Portuguese East Africa, effectively bypassing British tariffs at the ports of Natal and Cape Town.

The response to this continued provocation, was the Jameson Raid. This was an attempt, in 1895, to stoke an uprising amongst *uitlanders* in Johannesburg. Its failure was miserable

By 1899 the region was at boiling point. Joseph Chamberlain, the British Secretary of State for the Colonies, demanded the *uitlanders* be given full voting rights, and in an attempt to threaten the Boers into acceding to these demands, posted troops on the Transvaal border. Almost simultaneously Paul Kruger, President of the Transvaal, sent an ultimatum demanding the removal of troops within 48 hours or war would be declared. The *Daily Telegraph* bristled at this 'grotesque challenge', its response being one of anger and defiance: 'Mr Kruger has asked for war, and war he must have.'

On 11th October the Boers entered Natal and the Cape Colony, eliciting a declaration of war from Britain.

*****

During October the men of the HLI took a physical exam, to deem whether they were healthy enough to be sent to South Africa. The doctors 'were much struck by the eagerness manifested by the men to pass as fit for service.' The regiment was then split into two groups. The larger would make their way to South Africa as part of the Highland

Brigade, an historic grouping of regiments consisting, during the Second Boer War, of a phalanx of Scottish army regiments – the Black Watch, the Seaforth Highlanders, the Argyll and Sutherland Highlanders, and the HLI. A rump, made up of those who failed to pass the medical test, had not attained sufficient service, or were too young to serve, remained behind at Raglan Barracks in Devonport. Being only 19 years old, Jimmy fell into the latter group.

The main body headed by train to Southampton where they boarded HM Troopship *Aurania*, bound for Port Elizabeth on the south-eastern coast of South Africa. Buoyed by a sanguine expectation of victory, the biggest fear amongst the men being that they would arrive too late for the action, but this was quickly dispelled by senior officers who made it clear that the war was going badly. If this anxiety was prevalent amongst the men on their way to South Africa then it was even more pronounced for those left behind at Raglan, and Jimmy noted the soldiers' worry that 'the war would be over before we could get into it.'

Almost three weeks later the soldiers reached South Africa, being forced to disembark at Cape Town due to an overwhelming need for them at the front. They spent the next week defending the railway between Beaufort West and Deelfontein, gradually moving north east until late November by which time they had reached the Modder River. Only one month after landing in South Africa the British soldiers, known to the Boers as rooineks, literally translated as red neck, on account of the fact that their necks, unused to the beating sun, turned red soon after arrival, were about to face their Boer opponents in earnest for the first time.

In the early hours of 11th December the Highland Brigade advanced in columns towards the Magersfontein Ridge. British artillery had pounded the Boer positions throughout the night in an effort to impair their effectiveness, but, as would more markedly be the case 15 years later during the First World War, it did little more than alert the defenders to the impending attack. Furthermore the attackers were unaware of a forward trench. And it was into this trench that the men of the Highland Brigade walked. An alarm was tripped and the Boer rifles flashed with a volley of bullets so thick that Arthur Conan Doyle, already a famed writer, who had volunteered to serve in South Africa as a medic, argued that 700 men died in the first five minutes. The Brigade commander, Major-General Andrew Wauchope was killed within seconds, followed almost immediately by two of his senior officers, John Coode and Gerald Goff. The 1st Battalion of the HLI had been held in reserve, so its losses were relatively small compared to other regiments; it lost 14 men, with 80 wounded. One man was awarded the Victoria Cross.

News filtered back to the remainder of the regiment at Devonport. Those who had remained behind took the loss of their friends and comrades badly. One soldier, in the early hours of 12th December, drowning his sorrows after the news, partook of too much spirit, fell out of a third floor window, broke his neck and died. His fellow soldiers at the barracks wouldn't have to wait long before the opportunity for revenge presented itself.

On 3rd January 1900, four days before Jimmy's 20th birthday, he exited the camp at Devonport with 58 others, all wearing a knitted tammy presented by the Plymouth and District Caledonian Society, and boarded a train to Southampton. On the dock of one of the largest ports in England a large crowd cheered as they, and over 2,500 soldiers from other regiments, boarded the HM Troopship *Kildonan Castle*. As the ship was on only its second voyage, it was, according to its captain, 'a picture of comfort and convenience in every particular, and as clean as a lady's drawing room' despite a fire having broken out on its maiden voyage. As it pulled out of the harbour at 5pm, the flag was dipped and soldiers and civilians hurrahed each other. Jimmy looked down on the dockside where the Southampton Borough Police Band playing a range of tunes including *God Save The Queen*, *Rule Britannia* and *Auld Lang Syne*. He was leaving Britain for the first time in his life. He wouldn't return for over three years.

JIMMY CURRAN

Almost immediately upon setting sail the suffering of the men began. For many, unused to sea journeys, seasickness kicked in. Men were ill throughout the ship (especially in the mess hall) and those not stricken needed a 'strong stomach' to cope with the sight of the seemingly endless flow of vomit. And for those whose constitution could cope with the rolling of the ship there was the voluntary rigour of inoculation against typhoid, more commonly known at the time as enteric. This measure was considered desirable, for 'when men are huddled together in camps or trenches or in beleaguered towns under war conditions, typhoid tends inevitably to break out amongst them and speedily becomes a regular pestilence.' And so, army chiefs resolved to address this threat by inoculating the men heading to war.

Anti-typhoid fever inoculation had been developed by Almroth Wright, a British pathologist, but there was disagreement amongst those evaluating the programme as to its safety and efficacy. As such the inoculation of troops headed to South Africa was made voluntary. This in itself might not have had a detrimental effect on the programme, but the inoculation had intensely negative, albeit temporary, side effects; Lieutenant-Colonel Henry Kelham, the commanding officer of the 1st Battalion of the HLI, who had travelled on the *Aurania*, complained that it made him feel 'as if someone had beaten my head heavily with a broomstick', whilst Winston Churchill, travelling to the war as a correspondent on the *Dunottar Castle*, noted that 'inoculation against enteric fever proceeds daily … the next day sees haggard forms crawling about the deck in extreme discomfort and high fever.' As a result, take up was low, with around 95% of men declining immunisation. If indeed Jimmy did accept his dose, it would have been administered not far from port, but it is likely that he refused. In all, over 57,000 British soldiers contracted typhoid during the Boer War, with over 8,000 succumbing, more than were killed in battle.

Illness aside, the trip promised to be a monotonous one, dominated by on-board marches. But any thoughts of a mundane journey were briefly laid to rest when a young private called Patterson appeared on deck. Due to his age he had been disallowed from travelling to South Africa. On hearing this judgement, he had immediately left the camp at Devonport and made his way to Southampton, where he stowed away on the *Kildonan Castle*. The army authorities, believing he had deserted, issued a warrant for his arrest. On 5th January, believing the ship was too far from port to turn back, Patterson turned himself in to officers. Although he was warned he would be punished for this breach it was not expected to be severe, and his wish was granted when he was told he would be allowed to fight alongside his fellow soldiers in South Africa. Two days later, as Jimmy woke to celebrate his 20th birthday, the ship docked at São Vicente in Madeira. But a dampener was put on this small break in the endless carpet of ocean when a soldier called Leslie Cowan died from pneumonia. He was buried at reveille. A second soldier, Edward Lafford, would die four days later. A man had also fallen overboard and drowned during the *Aurania's* trip.

Seemingly endless miles of brilliantly clear blue ocean were finally broken as the African continent appeared to port. Following the coastline, the ship passed Robben Island, and reached Cape Town on 21st January. Before them lay Table Mountain, flanked by the smaller Devil's Peak and Lion's Head, but any thoughts of the natural wonders before them soon disappeared as Lord Roberts, commander of the British forces, boarded and gave a rousing speech. Disembarking they headed immediately to the front to join those who had preceded them, arriving alongside General Hector MacDonald, known as Fighting Mac, who assumed command of the Highland Brigade.

MacDonald was the son of a Black Isle crofter and had begun his military career as a private in the Gordon Highlanders. During the Second Afghan War his bravery in the face of the enemy saw him offered either a Victoria Cross or a commission. He chose the latter, making him one of the very few soldiers who moved from enlisted man to officer. In an odd coincidence he received his commission on 7th January 1880 – the day Jimmy was born. By the time he took charge of the Brigade it was traversing the veldt on a seemingly endless trek through South Africa.

The word veldt is derived from the English 'field', but the two should not be confused. It is open, undulating land made up of grass, mimosa, acacia and other vegetation, and covers vast swathes of southern Africa. Its appearance changes with the seasons – the rain yielding a verdant grassland, the beating sun turning the lushness into a landscape of brown, cracked earth. Littered across the vast expanse of virgin land, like ships bobbing on an infinite ocean, and breaking the beautiful, hypnotic monotony, are small boulder-strewn hills known as kopjes that would, in the coming years, provide much needed cover in the heat of battle. But as graced as South Africa was with great physical beauty, it was also cursed: the blazing sun burned the pale skin of foreigners, dust storms and tornadoes uprooted tents, slashing icy rain caused flash floods, and, worst of all, wondrous but deadly electrical storms threw military camps into disarray, killing mules and horses, and, on occasion, a soldier. It was a heavenly setting, and it was hell on earth, all neatly rolled up into one vast juxtaposition.

But as deadly as the landscape could be, it paled next to the Mausers of the Boer troops. For Jimmy, and those who had not witnessed the Battle of Magersfontein, the danger they posed was soon brought starkly into focus. On 5th February, as the men marched through the Koodoosberg area, the Boers poured volleys of bullets down upon them. This distant attack ended at dark, to be replaced by a howling dust storm. Similar attacks continued throughout the month, and the cost was high; on 7th February the Highland Brigade lost 10 men, with a further 65 wounded. The men then marched through a series of nondescript towns and farms, until 15th February when, at Wegdrai Drift, Jimmy looked on as the 7th Infantry Division attacked the small Dutch village of Jacobsdaal.

Two days later the HLI was split from the Highland Brigade and sent to Klip Kraal Drift, a decision that the regiment's officers believed to be a concerted attempted to split the 'kilts' and 'trews.' When the men arrived at their destination they were met by three dead British soldiers, 20 wounded, and a landscape filled with dead and rotting horses and oxen. The smell was overwhelming, and the fever and diarrhoea, known by the men as Modders, reached endemic proportions. Lice were so plentiful that killing them became a pastime amongst the men, who kept tallies of the numbers killed. At the end of the month Jimmy had his first sight of the Boers up close when General Piet Cronjé, his wife, and over 3,000 soldiers, were captured and brought to the Drift. They appeared a disparate lot – none had uniforms, most wore squash hats and mufti, and some carried umbrellas and bundles. That evening, sitting on the freezing veldt, the British officers allowed them to break up two wagons and set them alight. With the strains of Boer hymns pouring out into the night, Jimmy watched as the sparks trailed up into the still African sky, reaching out for the Southern Cross overhead.

On 5th March the regiment marched to Jacobsdaal, the site of action two weeks earlier, through driving rain, then scorching sun, and weighed down by a greatcoat, rifle and 150 rounds of ammunition, and 'accoutrements.' After a nine-day stay the men entrained for a through-the-night journey to Naauwpoort, where, perhaps due to a number of irate telegrams from Scotland sent to Lord Roberts and Fighting Mac, complaining about the perceived slight of detachment, they were re-incorporated into the Highland Brigade.

Jimmy's first months in South Africa had seen a number of serious actions against the Boers, interspersed with tedious, lengthy marches, zigzagging the country to the north-west of Basutoland. Over a 15-day spell, as April turned into May, the men walked over 100 miles, passing through towns such as Bloemfontein, Bushman's Kop, Rietfontein, and ending up in Winburg. After a short stay the marching began again, first to the Zand River then on to Ventersburg where the locals presented each of the men with grey Terai hats decorated with a tartan patch and dark green cock feathers.

On 22nd May the men started a march to the town of Lindley, but before they reached their destination they were engaged by a Boer force which was dug in to the crest of a hill. Realising the route to Lindley was barred, a land-based naval gun was brought forward and soon cleared any opposition. More fighting took place over the next few days, with men often advancing at walking pace, even as they were faced by 10,000 Boers, a lesson that would go largely unlearned until the ravages of the First World War forced a rethink of military strategy. They had marched 130 miles in eight days; with typical British middle-class understatement a weary Kelham lamented, 'March, march, there seemed no end to our peregrinations, nearly every town in Orange River Colony [has] heard the pipes of the HLI.' So tough had been the march that their boots and clothes were in tatters (they were replaced by khaki serge), and they were moving from town to town on 'all the worn-out animals and broken-down carts in the country.' And the cost was high; more than one man killed for every two miles marched. Around 60 years later, in front of the Main Hall at Mercersburg Academy, Jef Evans, later to become a track coach at the school, and his wife Marty, stood watching an octet singing a song, which had been made popular by the folk boom of the late 1950s, called *I Marched to Pretoria*. From behind them came a soft voice. It said, '*I* marched to Pretoria. It was a long way and no fun!' It was Jimmy, an old man now, recalling those long marches he had made when he was a mere boy, singing that very same song.

War is a fine balancing act. A soldier learns to smoothly transition between the aggression and fear of conflict and the joy of victory. And so just a day after staring down the hot barrels of the Boer rifles, Jimmy and his fellows marched through Heilbron, accompanied by pipers and buglers, and wearing the Terai hats presented them in Ventersburg. Here their sacrifices were acknowledged, as the head of the Brigade, Fighting Mac, addressed the men. 'Humph' he grumbled in his own inimitably cantankerous way, 'I cannot help saying you have done very well. You mind your feet. I will take care of your bellies.'

But Mac had limited control over his promise. The Boers had begun to attack supply convoys, carrying away their spoils. As well as the food (and 60 bottles of champagne bound for Kelham), they swept away the HLI's mail – the men weren't just becoming hungrier, they were becoming demoralised. And they were surrounded. Battered by freezing rain and a cutting wind, all Jimmy and his comrades could do was dig into strong defensive posts around the town of Heilbron. When the soldiers of the 5th Fusiliers finally broke through to them, the men were down to the last of their reduced rations. One officer tried to make light of the situation – 'Why, you don't look thin' he joked, 'we heard you were all starving.'

And still the marching continued. On to Frankfort, then south to Reitz. On 5th July they woke to a hard frost on the ground, with a mist lingering just above it. The men were beginning to feel the full effect of the South African winter. As the regiment marched they were aware of the constant threat of snipers, but this means of warfare did little more than temporarily slow the advance, like a wasp bothering an elephant. But the Boers were aware that there was more than one way of skinning a cat – as the infantry moved forward they did so through blackened grass, set alight to hinder the grazing of the regiment's oxen. On one occasion Jimmy watched as a mile-long fire, four feet high drove towards the men's camp. He and his fellow soldiers lined up along a 30 feet wide track and used sacks to beat out any sparks that crossed it.

Henry Kelham had his own way of unwinding. While much of the regiment languished in what were often little more than shanty towns or camps surrounded by endless veldt, he spent much of his free time shooting birds, informed by Edgar Layard's book *The Birds of South Africa*, and game. Another book noted that 'hunting in the South African veldt is as pleasurable as it is beneficial. The morning rides through the bush have an indescribable charm.' Each of Kelham's expeditions to find new prey to bring to the dinner table was documented in minute detail in notes that would be used in the regiment's publication, the *Chronicle*, and his own account of the war. Indeed, he shot so many creatures during his time in South Africa that it seems miraculous any living things still survive on the veldt. No bird or animal was safe – guinea fowl, partridge, korhaan, quail, duck, teal, snipe, hare, springbok, blesbok, rhebok, steinbok and a range of others, were all fair game. Anyone reading Kelham's account of the war could be forgiven for thinking that the conflict was of secondary interest to his hunting achievements.

And his extended forays into the veldt with his Lee-Metford rifle did not go unnoticed. After one solo expedition he was faced with a rampaging Fighting Mac. As Kelham sat astride his horse, the heads of two blesbok at his feet, his superior boomed 'Humph! You've been shooting. I call it a grave breach of discipline. Rejoin your Battalion at once!' That evening an order was circulated, no doubt coming from MacDonald, and aimed squarely at Kelham – ' Shooting is strictly forbidden on the line of march'. Some 23 years later, the two blesbok heads looked down on Kelham from his study wall, as he wrote his memoirs.

But if Kelham, and likely other senior officers, attempted to fill their days with lighter moments, the lower ranks were also not averse to a little horseplay (and occasionally some outright theft). For part of the war Jimmy worked in the officers' mess, and took advantage of his proximity to the personal effects of his moneyed superiors to purloin two brass candlesticks belonging to General Douglas Haig.

The possibility of a substantial battle with the Boers was rising. On the morning of 23rd July, with a bright sun burning through the cold morning mist, the men marched towards Retief's Nek – a narrow pass bounded on both sides by white cliffs, and defended by Boer soldiers. To soften up the defences, two 5" guns bombarded the defenders for three hours before the men moved forward over open country in 'a rather desperate frontal attack.' They went in two groups, Jimmy's G Company traversing to the right behind Kelham. As both parties joined up and moved forward, Boer snipers began to pick off those who raised their heads. Eventually HLI troops neared the Boers, but could go no further and the two foes became locked in a stalemate. Under cover of darkness, illuminated somewhat by burning grass, they retreated.

Casualties were high – six killed and 20 wounded – albeit less than Kelham had expected.

The main battle was followed by a number of smaller skirmishes, and Jimmy was part of an advance under darkness to take a 'Gibraltar-like' hill. In the morning light it became clear to the Boers that their position was much weakened, and they began to retreat. Jimmy and his fellow soldiers advanced from the hill, and met with only sporadic resistance. The HLI excelled in the fight, even drawing praise from the normally curmudgeonly Fighting Mac, who compared them to 'goats among the rocks and hills' – G Company was singled out for special praise. The operation proved an overwhelming success with the surrender of 4,000 Boers under General Hendrik Prinsloo, 1,800 horses, three artillery guns and a convoy of wagons, albeit tempered by the escape of Commandant Olivier and 2,000 Boers to the north.

In early August the men were on the move again, north-west to Harrismith, one of the most loyal British towns. After setting up camp at Swallow Bridge, Kelham rode the six miles to town, looking on as Fighting Mac, 600 mounted troops, and pipers proceeded to the town square. As the Free State flag was replaced with the Union flag, most of the townspeople sang *God Save the Queen* and *Auld Lang Syne*. Festivities aplenty followed with champagne flowing freely, and a brawl between an English doctor and the Dutch Landrost only added to the fun of the occasion.

And still the marching continued; 12 miles on 5th August, 14 miles the following day, then a further three days of marching that saw them pass through Bethlehem, and then on to the shell that once was Lindley. By the 13th, the men were on their way to Heilbron to remove Boers from the ridge at Spitz Kop. Heavy fighting saw five killed and 32 wounded. But the objective was achieved. As the wounded were moved to Cape Town, the remaining men undertook another series of marches in the country north of Basutoland, beginning in Heilbron on 25th August, and ending in Bloemfontein over a month later. Each company was then sent to garrison a nearby town, with Jimmy's G Company assigned to Smithfield, which they reached after a three-day march.

Jimmy spent his first weeks in the town rebuilding defences and renewing paths. Picquets were placed on the surrounding hills for a week at a time, and when his week was up Jimmy would return to the town and spend a week on guard. The time in town was luxurious in comparison to the previous months living in bivouacs, the men being billeted in brick huts. Aside from the Boers cutting some telegraph wires, Jimmy's first month was a quiet one. Time was spent building a fort and playing cricket against the local club. The locals even organised sports on New Year's Day, but unfortunately for Jimmy he was on duty and didn't compete. But despite the relaxed atmosphere, the threat of an attack was ever-present: on 23rd November A Company, garrisoned in Dewetsdorp, surrendered after an attack, with 50 killed and wounded. Thereafter the main garrison, now at Wepener, fought off sustained heavy attacks over a period of days, whilst a Boer force of 2,000 men was halted at Commissie Drift, only five miles from Smithfield.

By early 1901 Jimmy's company had been split from the main body of the regiment for three months. But Boer attacks necessitated a move north, under Colonel Hughes-Hallett, by the companies at both Smithfield and Rouxville. On Jimmy's birthday, 7th January, he spent much of the day readying for his company's march. The following day the men, accompanied by a large troop of local men, women, children and assorted animals, began their trek, passing through various towns and farms in an arduous trek that would last for the next month.

And while Hughes-Hallett and his ragged band of detached warriors headed in Kelham's direction, his superior was ordered to undertake a march to Aliwal North. This would ordinarily have seen the two groups meet on the Smithfield-Wepener road, but the threat of a Boer attack was high, so Kelham opted to take a convoluted route through Basutoland.

How G Company finally met up with Kelham is unknown. They may have followed in Kelham's footsteps, or may have about turned and moved directly south towards Aliwal North when Kelham's route through Basutoland became clear. Regardless, they were, by late March, stationed in Jackalsfontein, and it was here that they welcomed a visit of a football team from A Company who had emerged victorious at a recent tournament. G Company team took on the regimental champions and won by 3 goals to 2.

A Boer threat still existed and the HLI was awake to it. But for all intents and purposes the war had wound down. With the threat decreased the head of the Brigade, Fighting Mac, was called to India, and thereafter Ceylon, where he served as Commander-in-Chief of British troops. A telegram bearing his departing address to the men noted, 'I am so intensely proud [of the Highland Brigade] whose deeds shall ever live in my memory. With soldiers so well disciplined, enduring, and humane, the burden of command has been easy and success certain and it is with the deepest regret and feelings of profound admiration for your many sterling qualities that I now bid you farewell.'

Then, in late May, an order came to move 100 miles south to defend Queenstown for three weeks. But this time the regimental move would be in the comfort of steam trains – or so the men thought. Jimmy entrained at Knapdaar, whilst Kelham's Regimental Headquarters did so at the 'tin shanty' that was Myburgh Station in Aliwal North. Men, animals and equipment were loaded onto open trucks, and for the next three hours they huddled together against the freezing winds thrown at them by worst of the South African winter. Jimmy's journey was not so bad; those travelling from Aliwal North had to contend with the fear of being killed by a drunken train driver, who tore down the Stormberg mountains at breakneck speed, all the while blasting the train whistle. But then, just as the men, wet, cold and miserable, believed they were about to be reunited with the companies they had not seen for so many months, they were told they were to remain split up, stationed in various towns, both in and around Queenstown.

Three weeks of 'civilisation, peace and plenty' were ended by an order to converge on Dordrecht, where the winds and knee-deep snow moved Kelham to describe the weather as 'about the coldest place in

South Africa … absolutely Arctic.' Jimmy was dispatched, along with the rest of G Company, to Barkly East, a 'dull and isolated little town' and one that would be his home for the next year. And while Jimmy withered in the Barkly East outpost, the rest of the regiment headed north again, back to the slightly warmer climes of Aliwal North, to defend the string of blockhouses that stretched 80 miles along the Orange River from Bethulie to Herschel.

Eventually G Company's second detachment from the main body of the regiment came to an end. In early May 1902 the men marched for four days from their long-time base in Barkly East to Dordrecht, where they boarded a train to Bethulie to defend the stretch of land from Rhenoster to Venter's Drift. Here Jimmy finally partook of the 'joys' of living in a blockhouse.

A blockhouse was usually a circular construct erected as close as possible to the water's edge and built of two skins of corrugated iron, the gap between them filled with rubble. The roof, also built with iron, was painted to blend in with the adjacent landscape. It was surrounded by a system of trenches and a coil of barbed wire. Each was manned by seven men, who would have 15 days' supply of food and water. The structures stood about a mile apart. Over the following months the Boers mounted attack after attack, most small, but some much larger – Fouche's troops from the south, Kritzinger's from the north. They raided by night, and sometimes day, and the HLI doggedly defended their corrugated havens. The relentless threat caused a morbid despondency to descend upon many of the men. Eighteen months into Jimmy's war, a new saying began to grow in popularity – 'I wonder if this is our last moon.'

And if the threat of death from a Boer bullet did not induce the breakdowns, for which sleep was the only available treatment, a variety of other dangers lurked: an in-spate Orange River claimed the lives of three soldiers in a six-week period in late 1901, cobras searching for the beef buried by soldiers would attack any unsuspecting target, and in Jimmy's case, when he finally found his way into a blockhouse, he nearly lay down on top of a scorpion. There was, however, an upside: enteric fever, endemic when the men were based in towns, all but disappeared in the clean air and fresh water. And odd happenings no doubt amused the men greatly. A local farmer's ostriches were dying in great numbers and, suspecting foul play, he complained to Kelham. After one was opened up it became apparent that they were eating the cartridge shells left by the soldiers practicing their accuracy.

Despite rumours of peace circulating amongst the men, casualties continued to mount on both sides as fights between the two opposing armies continued. And then, on 31st May, it ended. Over 25,000 men, Britons and Boers, had paid the ultimate sacrifice. Jimmy had come through the conflict completely unscathed. At the close of the Second World War he would tell members of the Greencastle Rotary Club that his conflict was a 'picnic' compared to the First and Second World Wars.

G Company was quickly moved back to Aliwal North, and a heavy snowfall welcomed its return. Within days the 1st Battalion was given orders that it would be leaving the base for Port Elizabeth. On 22nd June, despite hopes that they would remain to celebrate the coronation of King Edward VII, an event that was eventually postponed, the men boarded trains at 10am and 2pm for the 300-mile journey south. Once again they did not travel in carriages, but in cattle trucks. Jimmy, as part of G Company, was on the second of the trains and, as it pulled out of the station, was treated to a rendition of *Auld Lang Syne* by the band of the Connaught Rangers. Unlike the earlier departure, he didn't have the pleasure of being waved off by a large crowd. The journey took two days with numerous hold-ups, as trains travelling south had to give way, often causing delays of up to two hours. Even the beauty of the landscape had lost its appeal after three years of criss-crossing it, although when the spectacular sight that was the flat-topped Karoo koppie mountains called Koffiebus and Teebus came into view, many a soldier's head was no doubt raised from its slumber. But the boredom and frustration reached epic levels after the refusal of an engine-driver and fireman to start work before 4am caused a delay of almost seven hours.

Port Elizabeth was unlike most of the towns the regiment had frequented in the past two and a half years. It was, according to Kelham, a 'treat', one of the best stations in South Africa, although the weather was unpredictable and tended towards the cold, wet and windy.

On arrival the men marched to Fort Nottingham, a mile outside the town, and pitched their camp. With the threat of flying bullets now a thing of the past, they began organising football, cricket and golf matches to fill the days. Jimmy watched from the sidelines as the 1st Battalion soldiers played games amongst themselves, and against local teams and other regiments. His first chance to show his footballing skills came in July in the inter-company tournament. Two wins saw G Company enter the final as favourites, but they failed to live up to their previous form and I Company strolled to a 2-0 victory.

Whilst football was the sport most frequently played by the soldiers, Jimmy was soon to have the chance to once again show off his athletic prowess. The annual long-distance race was held on 16th November, and Jimmy was ready, having trained in the weeks leading up to the race.

The track was 1¼ miles long, and fairly flat with a short downhill section towards the finishing line. Bookmakers were there in abundance and they installed Private Johnston of B Company as favourite. On race day a 'furious gale' pummelled down onto the first half-mile. But the elements did not appear to phase Johnston, and the bookmakers' faith seemed well-placed as he entered the final 100 yards in the lead. But Jimmy had timed his race well. Putting in a sprint he passed the leader to take the honours (and 10 shillings) by 20 yards. Jimmy's three years on the veldt, where staying alive had been foremost in his mind, had not blunted his desire, or speed.

Jimmy had cemented his place as the finest runner in the regiment. But he was aware of a young Lieutenant, only 20 years old, called Wyndham Halswelle. Tall, with dark hair swept back, and a moustache, he looked the quintessential English gentleman, albeit one who considered himself Scottish, as if he had stepped from the pages of a Jane Austen novel. His unerring desire for fair competition, the consummate amateur athlete, did little to obviate this view. He refused to run in spikes and would always start from scratch, whatever the handicap conferred upon him. Clearly Jimmy had to take this youngster on and beat him. The match was set up at a regimental sports in late 1901. In the 100 yards race both men started off scratch. But Jimmy had an advantage; he wore spikes and loose clothing, while Halswelle lined up in his uniform. He proceeded to run 10⅖, showing Jimmy a clean pair of heels to win by six yards. Jimmy, showing the potential for spotting raw talent that was to serve him so well for the next 60 years, and aware of Halswelle's potential and weaknesses, took the youngster under his wing. He was, Jimmy later recalled, 'a natural runner, as awkward as natural runners go, with unlimited speed and no end of courage. He never seemed to weaken and ran his best under fire.' But for all his talent he didn't have the killer instinct. Jimmy began to teach him how to win.

The sport continued unabated. In the last days of the year an inter-company cricket championship was organised. Always willing to turn his hand to any sport Jimmy took part in the last two of the three matches. His place as last man (generally the least talented batsman) appears to have been justified; he scored no runs and his team lost both games.

But the joy of sport was tempered by the drudgery of marches, which the men undertook with a grudging acceptance. On the morning of 11th December the battalion paraded and set off on the eight-mile long road from Fort Nottingham to Zwaart Kops. Jimmy travelled as a Lance Corporal, having been promoted three days earlier. The marchers were accompanied by the usual camp-following stray dogs – 'a motley crowd of happy mongrels.' On arrival the men were issued with Maconochie beef, bread and cheese, and a pint of beer, before a shooting competition. Caked with the unenviable mix of dust and sweat, the men bathed in the Zwaart Kops River before about facing and returning to camp.

But sport was soon on the menu again – with the biggest event being the New Year's Day athletic meeting at Port Elizabeth. On the first day of 1903, civilians from across South Africa joined local residents and soldiers to take part in the Port Elizabeth Scottish Society's Annual Games at the Westbourne Oval. On a 'delightful' day, with music from the HLI band and Prince Alfred's Guard band ringing in the ears, the HLI athletes gave a good account of themselves. Jimmy took part in these events but perhaps deliberately, and definitely wisely, he avoided the races where Halswelle was running. For the star of the show was, beyond any doubt, Jimmy's protégé. The competition looked decidedly average against a man who was clearly a top class runner – in the 100 yards he made up 10 yards on his opponents to win in a time of 9 ⅘. In the 220 yards he won easily in 22½ seconds. And in the 880 yards, with all runners starting from scratch, again he was victorious, in 2.10. He was also expected to run the 440 yards, but was sleeping when the race was run. Jimmy didn't wake Halswelle up, evidence that as early as 1903 he was using a training technique – a variation on later techniques such as transcendental meditation and the relaxation response – that would serve him well for the next 60 years. In his final year as a coach, 58 years later, he would still be using this technique with his athletes.

41

Chapter 3 • The Long Journey Home

On 12th January 1903, just five days after Jimmy's 23rd birthday, he and his fellow soldiers were about to leave the country that had been their home for three years. At 9am they marched from Fort Nottingham to Port Elizabeth harbour, where they boarded HM Troopship *Plassy* for the journey north up the east coast. After a hearty send off by the locals, the ship was on its way up the east African coast. It stopped briefly at Durban and then passed through the channel that separated Mozambique and Madagascar before a further brief stop at the mist-covered Comoros Islands. But despite these all-too-brief sojourns the days were an endless monotony of sea, sea and more sea. As the boredom grew the gambling increased, boxing competitions were organised, smoking concerts held and bingo and card games became the order of the day.

Ten days after departure, as the journey was nearing its conclusion, and as they passed Somaliland and entered the Gulf of Aden, the men of the HLI and the 4th Mountain Battery of the Royal Garrison Artillery began a three-day on-board sports. But this was not a run-of-the-mill sports day – the layout of the ship's deck inhibited any possibility of holding many traditional athletic events. As such, this was less a sports event than three morale-boosting days of fun. The first two days were set aside for preliminary events, with the finals being held on the third and final day. Three-legged and pillow races were augmented by less traditional events such as tilting the bucket and placing the pig's eye. Jimmy was second in both these events, and also in the obstacle race in which he had to manoeuvre his way through sails formed into funnels, and a network of ropes.

Thirteen days after its departure the ship docked at Aden, a parcel of land at the tip of the Arabian peninsula that was ceded, in 1838, to the British, who used it to stop pirate attacks against shipping en route to and from India, and viewed it as a potentially major port, around

42

which the trade of Europe, Asia, and the southern hemisphere would hinge. The stay in the port lasted less than half a day before the ship continued on, passing through the Straits of Bab-el-Mandeb into the Red Sea, onwards towards Suez where, due to the ship having stopped at the plague-infected port of Durban, the men were sent to be disinfected at a quarantine station at the Well of Moses where stood a number of wells filled with warm sulphurous-tasting, virtually undrinkable water. Dropped off at a jetty, the men boarded native scows for the short journey to the shore. When they entered the disinfecting house, Jimmy and his comrades were ordered to make no noise and strip naked, and then they and their clothes were both suitably cleansed.

Free of any lingering disease and lice the men returned to Suez where the *Plassy* docked the following day. With some hours to kill, the men made their way into the town, where they admired the mosques, took in the bazaars, but left with a sense that it was something of a disappointment. On their return they boarded two trains to take them north to Cairo, leaving early evening and pulling into the square at Qasr el-Nil barracks at 2am.

The men, despite having arrived from the excellent accommodation at Port Elizabeth, were hugely impressed. Taken over by the British in 1882, the barracks was situated in the heart of Cairo and, covering 10 acres, it contained two squares, each of which was surrounded on three sides by living quarters and offices. The fourth sides were bounded by the River Nile upon which diabeah sailing boats made their way in and out of the city.

With no war to fight, the sporting events and military competitions started almost immediately upon the regiment's arrival. These included five-a-side football, cricket, athletics, and the Annual Cairo Rifle Meeting, in which the HLI struggled due to having been based in the windy Port Elizabeth. Jimmy is believed to have won the quarter and half-mile championships.

On 10th March the battalion marched to the Well of Moses, the site of their earlier disinfection, on the first of several days of military manoeuvres. The following morning Jimmy and his battalion, along with the 4th Mountain Battery, two Royal Fusilier companies, a squadron of the 11th Hussars, a Mounted Infantry company, and a detachment of the Royal Army Medical Corps, made up Red Force whose task it was to defend the 'retreat' of a defeated army from Cairo, against a Blue Force, made up of battalions including the 2nd Berkshires. Over the following days the Reds acquitted themselves well, winning many of the skirmishes. The 11th Hussars, in particular, distinguished themselves. The manoeuvres took Jimmy to much of the area around Cairo and he passed through, amongst other places, the Mokattam Hills, wondering at the ruins of Memphis, and the Pyramid of Saqqara.

His time in the army was nearing an end, having signed up for an initial period of four years. He did, however, have a problem. His regiment was about to head east to India, giving him a tortuous journey home when his enlistment ended. A simple solution presented itself in the form of the 11th Hussars. They were about to leave for the Curragh Camp, a military barracks in County Kildare, Ireland. So, on 25th March, with Galashiels very firmly in his sights, Jimmy, despite being below the height requirement, was transferred to his new regiment, reverting to the rank of private in the process.

Given this transfer, it is unclear whether Jimmy was able to join his former comrades after their weekly church parade on 29th March, as they formed up and marched to the northern square where, after an address by Major-General Reginald Talbot, they marched past him in single file and were each presented with the Queen's South Africa Medal. Jimmy's, whenever he received it, bore a clasp for both Cape Colony and Wittebergen. He also won the King's South Africa Medal, with clasps for 1901 and 1902, but again it is unknown when he received it. His former comrades in the HLI received theirs in a ceremony in Egypt on 24th December 1903.

The final phase of Jimmy's army life began on April 17th when the 11th Hussars left Cairo by train, bound for Alexandria. Three days later he boarded the SS *Dunera* and, after a journey westward across the

Mediterranean and through the Strait of Gibraltar, the ship turned north and headed for the port of Queenstown on the southern coast of Ireland. Eleven days after Jimmy had left Egypt he arrived back in the United Kingdom, over three years after he had left. The regiment proceeded by train to the Stewart Barracks at the Curragh.

Jimmy's army career had been impeccable. He had served well and never incurred the wrath of his military superiors for behavioural issues (as many of his colleagues regularly did). But in June his conduct began to deteriorate, and as a result he forfeited his good conduct pay. It is likely that this sudden out-of-character behaviour was related to the health of his brother Edward, languishing close to death with phthisis, tuberculosis of the lungs, in Galashiels's Eastlands Hospital. Tuberculosis, in its various forms, was rife in Scotland at the turn of the century. In 1901 there were 130 deaths from the disease in the counties of Roxburghshire and Selkirkshire. Nine days after Jimmy was pulled up for his misdemeanour his brother finally succumbed.

And so it was back to the drills that had blighted his early career. The testing of the men's competency with a rifle was undertaken, and the crossed rifles stitched onto the sleeve of Jimmy's uniform, evident in contemporary photographs, attest to his having achieved a high level of competency.

In July the Royal Visit of King Edward VII and Queen Alexandra to Ireland brought some welcome relief from the incessant boredom. Jimmy and the Hussars headed to a Dublin strung with flags and decorations, but still reeling from the death of Pope Leo XIII. Jimmy and his fellow Hussars lined the route between the Bank of Ireland on College Green and Dublin Castle as the Royal procession entered the city. Two days later the regiment was in Phoenix Park, a vast green space sitting on the River Liffey just west of Dublin, to be reviewed by the King.

In early August Jimmy was granted a furlough and made his way back to Galashiels, where he was reconciled with his family for the first time in almost four years. On the 8th he headed to Gala Park for the

JIMMY CURRAN

Primrose Sports. Each year in Galashiels the Primrose League, a conservative political organisation, ran an amateur sports day. In 1903 the crowd reached around 2,000 as a range of distinguished local guests looked on. Jimmy took part in at least three events. But news of his sporting exploits had clearly filtered back home, and the handicapper accordingly awarded Jimmy a low starting mark in both the flat races he was due to take part in. Jimmy's main event was the half-mile, and in a field of 25, he won his heat, but then, running off four yards, he trailed in third, well behind his fellow backmarker, W.A.M. Watson from Edinburgh. He couldn't better this placing in the 440 yards; entering the home straight in the lead, his efforts to remain at the front were frustrated by two athletes running off a better handicap. In the obstacle race he finished second. Jimmy had laid out his stall, even if he hadn't set the heather on fire.

But Jimmy had his final months of army life to complete. So it was back to the Curragh. Once again the mundane daily army life was broken up by sports events. On 24th August he lined up for his new regiment in the Army's annual athletic meeting at Curragh's Cricket Ground. He took part in at least two races – the mile and half-mile. Before the Duke of Connaught, the 11th Hussars' band, and a large crowd, Jimmy put on a stunning show, winning easily in the mile and crossing the line in equal first in the half-mile. His success in these races would, upon his death 60 years later, be noted in several obituaries.

As October arrived Jimmy had only three days before his term in the army was over. But first he took part in an inspection by the legendary Major-General Robert Baden-Powell, saviour of Mafeking and soon-to-be founder of the scouting movement. And then his life as a soldier was over. A civilian once again, he headed back to Galashiels.

Chapter 4 • Gala Hailes Villa and the Mighty Glasgow Rangers

After his military travels, Jimmy returned to a family who had seen him only fleetingly for the past four years, moving back into the family home. He was 23 years old. But an extra mouth to feed meant that Jimmy's return to civilian life would require him to find a job. It is not clear what work Jimmy initially took, but he was eventually to be found behind the bar in one of the many public houses in Galashiels.

Sporting outlets were plentiful, and Jimmy immediately threw himself into the local scene. Like many of his contemporaries, he was caught up in the football craze that had grown in Scotland in the latter part of the 19th century. Football had a strong hold across the Borders, with teams representing all the larger towns, and many of the smaller ones. By late 1903 he was playing for a team called Gala Hailes Villa, also known as The Blues, in the Border Senior League. It was a tough sport, governed by few of the rules that exist today. One derby game between the two Galashiels teams, Renton and Villa, was ended before half time after rough play culminated in a fight breaking out between the players. In Jimmy's first season the team struggled in the league and finished in a lowly position. But lack of league form wasn't replicated in the Dudley Cup, and the team went on a run. By April they had reached the semi-final, where in a replay they defeated Walkerburn 4-2. A month later Jimmy and his fellow players headed back to Earlston to take on Cumledge Mill in the final. Gala was 2-0 up at half time, and despite losing a goal in the second half they emerged victorious. After they were presented with the trophy, they placed it on the front brake of their bus and drove back to town where they were met with a 'hearty reception.'

Over the next two years Jimmy played for the Villa with little success. But despite the team's mediocre performances Jimmy was a stand-out. That he had caught the eye of others was made clear in 1906. In order to raise funds for a new football pavilion in Galashiels a series of friendly games was organised against Scotland's top three teams – Heart of Midlothian, Glasgow Rangers, and Glasgow Celtic. A month before the first game the cream of amateur players in the Borders were invited to play a trial game, at Mossilee in Galashiels, to choose the representative team. Jimmy was deemed good enough and turned up on 4th April to pull on a red strip against the White team.

But things didn't go quite to plan. From the off the Reds were hemmed into their own half and Jimmy, playing inside right, was well marshalled by the Whites' Walker and Ormiston. Gradually the Reds came back into the game and, perhaps a little undeservedly, took the lead. Struck by this sudden and unexpected deficit the Whites rose to the challenge and scored, first, the equaliser just before half time, and then the winner in the second half. Jimmy didn't do himself justice. He was competing for the inside right position with the Duns player John Blaikie, and was soundly beaten. After the match the players retired to the Royal Hotel for tea.

Jimmy's hopes of playing against Heart of Midlothian were dashed, but the unsuccessful eleven would play in at least one of the following games against either Rangers or Celtic. And so it was that Jimmy was called up to play the second of the three games, against Rangers. Although Rangers were, on the season's form, the weakest of the three teams, they soon highlighted the difference in level against their Borders opponents. Rangers took the field with an under-strength team, any hope this may have inspired for a Borderers' victory was soon extinguished and as the teams left the field at half-time the score was 4-1 in favour of the Glasgow team. The second half provided little succour for the home side, and Rangers added a further two goals in a one-sided game. Jimmy was largely anonymous, failing to even warrant a mention in the subsequent newspaper report which called the Border XI 'a somewhat moderate lot' with the forwards taking the brunt of the reporter's ire, being described as 'very disjointed, combination being at a discount.'

It was quite clear from these games against the very best

opponents that Jimmy had reached his level in football. It was a good level to reach, higher than most achieve, but Jimmy knew as well as the next man that he didn't have the ability to take the step up to play for and against the top level teams.

But before Jimmy had any chance to dwell on his future in the game he had the most important game of his career to play. The mediocre form of 1904 and 1905 was gone, replaced by performances that saw the team come within a whisker of winning the league, with the decider against Selkirk on the last day of the season. A Hailes Villa win would secure them the league, whilst a defeat would see them lose it. Jimmy was a different player than the one who had faced the Whites and Rangers in the past month. From the off he set about Selkirk, firing in two early shots and generally causing problems for the Selkirk defence. Although he failed to score, Villa went in at half time 3-0 in front. In the second half Jimmy once again took the game by the scruff of the neck, at one point running the length of the field with the ball, before shooting wide. Once the fourth goal went in, Villa enjoyed almost total domination. Taking advantage of their unassailable lead, and therefore the league title, the players began to have fun for the last few minutes. Jimmy, along with fellow forward, and future cousin, James Mabon, moved into defence, allowing the defenders to play up front. Jimmy was, according to the local newspaper, the pick of the forwards. After the game the teams retired to the Waverley Inn where the presentation of the Paul Shield took place. That evening the players and their supporters marched through Galashiels, holding the trophy aloft and 'cheering to their hearts' content.'

This was Jimmy's last game for Gala Hailes Villa. At the same time he was playing football, he was competing as an athlete throughout the borders and beyond. Football was a diversion. In order to take the step up to the next level he could not afford to allow his focus to be drawn by a sport that was, essentially, a pastime. From now on athletics would be first and foremost in Jimmy's thinking.

Chapter 5 • The Best Half Miler in Scotland

In the early 19th century footraces tended to be traditional, in that each of the competitors ran the same distance. On the face of it, it was the obvious way to pit man against his fellow man, with the fastest taking the honours. But there was a huge drawback in that it was the same individuals invariably winning almost every race, as well as the fact that it encouraged 'pot hunting' – runners touring the high value events purely to fleece locals of the prizes on offer. As such the number of entries fell, until at some meets only a handful of crack runners were turning up. The fun runners had figured out there was little point in taking part in a procession. The crowds concurred and the entry money used to pay the winners decreased in tandem. To maintain the popularity of athletics, event officials addressed this inequity by introducing a handicap system, whereby the fastest runners were placed at the rear of the field, with the other competitors placed at intervals ahead of them, with the very slowest runners at the front. The aim was, in theory, for all runners to cross the line around the same moment. The crowd would leave entertained, and the athletes, regardless of where they had finished in the race, felt they were competitive.

Handicappers were employed to give each runner a mark, in a systematic way. They would glean information about as many runners as possible – mainly from newspaper reports, club and meet officials, and fellow handicappers – and from this information extrapolate out a mark they believed each runner should be running off.

But determining just how capable a runner actually is, is not an exact science. Handicappers often got it wrong. This was partly due to the fact that rating an athlete's performance is inherently subjective, his form could change from week to week, or he could tour the country, beyond the gaze of those paid to study his progress. Or, in need of a better mark, he might put in a series of slower times than he was capable of. The handicappers were not only fighting to remain up-to-date with the latest form of all athletes, but also with a coterie who were determined to increase their chances of winning races by manipulating the handicapping system in their favour.

As morally questionable as the posting of slower times than one was capable of was, it could be argued that it was not actually cheating. A runner, might, for example, eat a large meal before a meet and the effect of this would be to slow him down naturally. But out-and-out cheating to relieve the authorities of their money did exist. A Scottish runner called Bill Struth, who went on to become arguably the greatest-ever manager of Glasgow Rangers Football Club, and ran at many of the same meets as Jimmy, recounted how he fleeced a meet at Porthcawl in Wales:

> The mark they gave me … was grossly unfair, and made it impossible for me to win. I decided to do something about it. Professional running wasn't for the weakling. [They were] tough days, but challenging and exciting. I've always thrilled in a challenge. As we lined up, I slipped my number from back to front, eased my way along the avenue of spectators as though chatting to them and I wasn't really a competitor. I stole 20 yards and as the pistol barked, I was away. The finishing post was out of sight of the starter. So when I breasted the tape, and was handed a voucher, which, I was informed, could be cashed at the local bank, I dashed to the tent, gathered up my clothes and ran for my life, still in my running strip, for that bank. I knew the protest would be raging behind me. I simply had to get out of Porthcawl without a moment's delay. I was lucky. The bank was open, and though the clerk looked at me in astonishment, he didn't waste any time in handing over the cash when I explained I had a train

> to catch. Then came another race against the clock, to the station. My luck still held. I jumped on the train as it was steaming out of the station. I had no idea where it was going but I was at last clear of the irate officials.

Struth was only doing what he had to do – he had slept the previous night in the competitors' changing tent and had no intention of reliving that particular ignominy. The story has an equally amusing postscript. Years later, perhaps lightly touched by guilt, and much to the amusement of the Porthcawl officials, Struth, albeit now a rich man, paid back his ill-gotten £5 gains, ten times over.

Such tales of deception in the pursuit of monetary gain were commonplace. In 1915 Jimmy recounted a similar story. In the 1880s, a runner called Chip Herbert took part in a race at Nottingham Forest's football ground under an assumed name and was given a mark of 80 yards. It soon became apparent that he was faster than the scratch runner. As he crossed the finishing line in first place he continued his run, through the changing tent to pick up his clothes, and straight into a waiting cab which took him to the local train station, where he caught a train for Liverpool and boarded a ship to America. Those betting on him, his backers, cleaned out the bookmakers.

Another highlights the absolute lengths some would go to in order to increase their winnings, is that of a runner called Moons Hill, competing in the 130 yards handicap at the 1883 Powderhall New Year races. Hill 'turned out to be Cameron of Liverpool, and when his wig slipped off he was glad to follow suit.'

*****

At the beginning of the 20th century there was a fissure running directly down the middle of sport in Britain and America. It was as wide as the ocean that lay between the two countries. On the one side were the amateur authorities – those who saw sport as a pastime competed in by men purely for the love of the sport. On the other were the professional athletes – those who took part for financial gain. For years they faced off against each other, figuratively, the former driven by a healthy wedge of self-righteousness, the latter by the mighty pound and dollar.

The Amateur Athletic Club (AAC) was founded in England in 1866, and its constitution, in line with those in many other sports, laid out that no manual worker could join. This rule caused great dissent, even amongst many who promoted the case for amateurism, who argued that it was an attempt to socially engineer athletics, by contriving to restrict participation to the most privileged in society, thereby creating an equivalent of the class system. Appalled, they fought back vigorously. The ensuing furore saw the AAC collapse, replaced, in 1880, by the Amateur Athletic Association (AAA), an organisation whose aims were broadly similar to the AAC but promoted athletics as a sport for all classes.

For 15 years after the creation of the AAA there was little consensus on the definition of amateurism. To remedy this, a conference was held in Anderton's Hotel in London in 1895. Representatives from the AAA, the Amateur Swimming Association and the National Cyclists' Union met and agreed that an amateur was:

> One who has never competed for a money prize, or monetary consideration, or for any declared wager or staked bet; who has never engaged in, assisted in, or taught any athletic exercise as a means of pecuniary gain, and who has never taken part in any competition or public exhibition with any one who is not an amateur.

The following year the Scottish Amateur Athletic Association (SAAA), founded in 1883, took this definition word for word. Four years previously they had come to an agreement with the Scottish Cycling Union (SCU) to jointly govern athletics and cycling in Scotland. It was a marriage of convenience, aimed at maximising audiences at sporting events by offering both athletic and cycling races at a single venue.

When Jimmy left home to join the army in 1898, athletics in the Scottish Borders was on the cusp of a massive change. Before 1896 virtually all athletics in the region was professional, but a growing number of runners were beginning to compete in amateur events. Seeing the Scottish Borders as ripe territory to build amateur athletics, and all the while expanding their empire, the SAAA worked with some local men to found the Scottish Border Amateur Athletic Association (SBAAA), a regional satellite to promote the amateur code in an area roughly covering Edinburgh, Carlisle and Berwick-upon-Tweed. The following years saw athletic clubs throughout the Borders become affiliated to this body. They enthusiastically organised events, and athletes were equally enthusiastic in their participation. Despite early failed attempts by the SBAAA to secede from its parent body, the hegemony of the professional events in the Borders had been effectively challenged, and an alternative put in place. By the time Jimmy returned from his military service, the amateur code, in its formative years when he departed Galashiels, was now well and truly established in the region.

This organisation of amateurism, despite its internecine struggles, brought with it a desire to protect itself against those it perceived to be profiting from their talents – the professional. On the face of it, amateurism was the very antithesis of professionalism – athletes competing against each other for the love of the sport, unencumbered by the lure of corruption and financial gain, the desire to compete trumping the desire to win at all costs. Indeed, some took this idea of purity to a level that even in the 19th century was considered excessive. Baron Desborough, a sportsman who attained the very highest level in fencing, rowing and punting, saw training as a corruption of athletic purity, believing that pitting one man's natural ability against another's was the true measure of one's athletic prowess. Wyndham Halswelle's views initially mirrored Desborough's – when Jimmy first met him he ran in his army boots, refused to train, take racing seriously, or run off a handicap – although he would later accede to Jimmy's demands that he at least gave himself the best possible chance of victory. Generally, however, amateur athletes did train, and competed for non-monetary prizes which were quite often of substantial value. Alfie Shrubb, the great English runner, was able to 'fill a small room … [with] the silver cups, canteens of cutlery and medals he collected.' This was also the case with Eric Liddell, Olympic gold medallist in 1924, and Jimmy's nephew through his marriage to Janet, whose prizes were so numerous that he took to giving them away to friends. In reality the line between amateur and professional was a thin one. Many amateurs took training, diet, and an athlete's shoes and dress seriously. Failure to do so would mean defeat, and athletes, amateur or professional, do not compete to be defeated.

Those who ran amateur athletics believed they held the moral high ground and that professionalism was an inherent evil destroying not only the sport of athletics, but the moral fibre of both athletes and spectators. And so they launched vitriolic attack after vitriolic attack on the professionals. They believed it was their duty to highlight the moral turpitude of professionalism, arguing that 'no sooner is a business element imported than corruption is introduced, the contestants are inspired with other motives than that of success in the race – honour, distinction and emulation – it needs all the relentless opposition of our strictest disciplinarians successfully to defend the purity of amateur sport.' And the administrators of amateurism were only too happy to oblige. In 1933, J.K. Ballantyne, who had been present at the setting up of the SBAAA 37 years earlier, denounced professionalism in the Borders, painting it as a den of iniquity, dominated by bookmakers, frequented by spectators who were drawn by anything other than the sport, and competed in by athletes who 'resented' their 'sordid' reliance on the cash offerings and would, if the opportunity presented itself, rather run under the amateur code.

And so, professional athletes were eyed with unending suspicion, and treated with utter disdain by those in the amateur authorities who basked in their own moral righteousness. The AAA, fearing for the future of amateur athletics, considered the threat a two-pronged one – amateurs competing as professionals, and professionals entering amateur events. So, in an effort to minimise these perceived threats, they launched sustained attacks on both.

Individuals and teams fell foul of the rule banning amateurs from competing at professional events. Over the years many amateurs lost their status and were banned from competing on the amateur circuit due to having benefited financially in one form or another. The most famous British case was that of Alfie Shrubb.

Alfie Shrubb had started running as an amateur in 1899 and made the move to professional six years later. By 1908 he had built a small fortune taking on all-comers at distances from one mile to the Marathon. He was the dominant force at one to 15 miles, and widely considered the greatest middle- to long-distance runner in the world. Even today he could make a reasonable claim to being the greatest of all time. The move from amateur to professional was an obvious progression for a man of Shrubb's stature – he had the ability to make sums of money that he could only have dreamt of off the track. His early forays into professionalism were disguised as he attempted to retain his amateur status. But the amateur authorities eventually caught up with their most famous asset and, after much deliberation, Shrubb was banned from the amateur circuit.

Considered equally as heinous as those amateurs competing at professional events were the professionals using pseudonyms and other underhand means to compete at amateur meets in an effort to procure the non-monetary prizes, or to institute a betting scam. This was, in the eyes of the amateur authorities, theft. So, in 1882, the AAA set up a fund to prosecute those professionals who passed themselves off as amateurs. And the Association was not backwards in taking impostors to court, generally on the basis they had defrauded local amateur associations of the non-monetary prizes that were being competed for. These prosecutions quite often ended in a jail sentence. Two years after the fund was established, William 'Curly' Bamford competed under the name of Walter Adnett, a known amateur, at Crewe Athletic Festival and won a prize of gold studs and cuff links valued at £3. Caught, he was sent to Knutsford Jail for one month's hard labour.

Professionals would fire off the odd pejorative barb. In the late 1920s R.W. Harrison, captain of Cockfield F.C., noted what he perceived as the hypocrisy that served as the foundation stone of amateur athletics:

> The amateur who sports plus-fours and knows the best people, travels in comfort, lunches before the match, dines after it and stays at the best hotels keeps his status. The stocky built, bow legged Durham pit lad goes without lunch, crowds into a United bus, receives five shillings for tea, contents himself with a pie or a snack in a side street and consequently is a professional.

And Alfred Downer, detailing the committee that revoked his amateur status, pulled no punches:

> There was such a sanctimonious look on every face in the room, that one would have thought we were being tried for manslaughter.'

The amateur authorities would never completely rein in those who wanted to bend the rules. It was an age of abject poverty and one's conscience counts for little when there is a need to feed one's family.

*****

JIMMY CURRAN

Where there were sporting events, there inevitably followed a desire to gamble on every imaginable outcome. And so bookmakers flooded into Scottish athletics meetings – amateur and professional – fleecing the crowds of their hard-earned money. The amateur authorities looked on aghast as what they considered a subversive element tore at the very heart of their Corinthian dream. And they were vocal in their opposition. In 1903 a letter signed by W.G.M. Oliver of the SCU and D.S. Duncan of the SAAA noted that:

> Of recent years the presence of bookmakers at Amateur Athletic and Cycling Sports in Scotland has become such a clamant evil [that the SAAA and SCU] have been at their wits' end for a remedy. Not only has the presence of these betting men affected the attendance of the better class of citizens at Sports' Meetings, but it has in many instances a demoralising tendency on the competitors. Charges of non-trying, foul running and riding, and other malpractices have from time to time been dealt with summarily where proved, but it is an open secret that other offenders in a similar fashion have gone Scot free.

Whilst the amateur bodies can often be accused of scaremongering to further their own ends, in this particular case they were at least partly correct – cheating was rife. In 1906 a correspondent for the *Edinburgh Evening News* detailed a discussion, overheard on a train, where one professional athlete described to another how he had been involved in race fixing at a recent athletic event in the Borders. The reporter lamented the fact that the competitions of the past, between the 'lithe shepherd' and the 'virile worker,' had been replaced by the corrupt professional pocketing the rich prizes on offer.

But whilst bookmakers were certainly viewed as a problem, the real issue was the fact that the potential winnings they offered spawned men who were willing to fix races in their favour to hugely increase those winnings, men known as backers.

A backer could operate in various ways. He could, for example, simply support an athlete financially, then gamble on their winning races. Others would pay a quality athlete, or even multiple athletes, to throw a race, allowing money to be placed on the longer odds of a lesser athlete, secure in the knowledge that the race was fixed and their winnings virtually guaranteed. But occasionally the backer would be the bookmaker himself. Faced with making a loss on a hot favourite, he might pay that man to lose the race, thus turning his loss into a profit.

Backers of the best runners were commonplace at the turn of the century. The Canadian all-rounder Walter Knox and the Scottish sprinter Alfred Downer both worked with a number of backers throughout their careers, the results being financially beneficial for both parties.

It is likely that Jimmy's work as a barman was set up by a backer, someone who would reap the financial benefits that a physically healthy Jimmy could provide. Serving beers to locals would not put the same physical pressures on his body as mill work. It would also allow shifts to be easily covered to allow him to train and attend meets. This flexibility would have been necessary when he turned professional and was, often, running more than one meet a week. Such arrangements were common with the best athletes. Alfie Shrubb was able to buy a tobacconist's shop after his backers arranged finance for him.

If Jimmy did work with backers then he would have been aware that these were not men to be messed with. His childhood friend, William Torrie, was a good enough runner to have backers. Legend had it that he once beat a heavily-backed runner, refusing to bow to the calls of 'steady up, Wull' from the betting men. So enraged were they that Torrie had to scarper up the nearby hills. Another individual who passed on his tales of backers and their willingness to protect their investments by means fair or foul, was a fellow Galalean called James Lee, who was Jimmy's first trainer. Years before the two met, he was reputedly drugged by backers when he refused to lose a race.

Many runners, both amateur and professional, were more than willing to comply. Why compete for a watch or a few shillings, damaging one's handicap in the process, when trailing in behind the winner could bring vastly richer rewards?

As such there were, over the years, repeated attempts by the various amateur bodies in Scotland to outlaw the presence of bookmakers at sporting events, usually through legal means. The committee of the Alva Games, for example, banned bookmakers in 1904, likely due to one bringing a roulette table into the park the previous year. But each attempt to limit their intrusion was met with abject failure. In 1906 the Street Betting Act attempted to address the issue, and the effect of this was seen in 1907 when bookmakers were banned from the Hawick Common Riding, a lowland equivalent of the Highland Games. The result was a lower than usual crowd, and a local reporter argued that should the ban continue it would lead to the ruin of sports events in the Borders. The athletes concurred, one lamenting 'Weel, Johnny, if there's tae be nae mare baitin' we may gang and seek a job the morn.'

Much to the chagrin of the amateur authorities, the bookmakers and backers retained their places at Scottish athletic meetings. And the amateur and professional athletes alike continued to fix races on their behalf.

When Jimmy returned from South Africa he was faced with a choice – run as an amateur or a professional? The decision was not a difficult one to make; he was still learning the tricks of the athletics trade, and many of his friends were members of Gala Harriers, the local amateur athletic club. The club had been formed about a year before Jimmy had returned home, and enthused by his successes of the past years, he wanted to test himself against the best amateurs the town of his birth could throw against him. Over the next few months he took part in many of the training sessions they ran on the roads around the town. His first known race in the Harrier colours took place on the cinder of Fred Lumley's famed Powderhall track in Edinburgh. Running off a handicap of 90 yards in a mile race against a field of 57, Jimmy took the lead in the final straight and won 'in fine style' by two yards in the time of 4.28. In the next six weeks Jimmy ran at three more Edinburgh athletic meets. A win in a half-mile at Tynecastle, the home of Heart of Midlothian Football Club, was followed by a victory in a mile at Powderhall in which Jimmy beat the legendary Scots-Irish runner John McGough, who two years later would win a silver medal at the Intercalated Olympic Games, albeit with a 70 yards handicap in his favour. As the bell rang for the final lap McGough had eight men firmly in his sights, and by the final stretch had only Jimmy to pass. But Jimmy had too much for him. It was the fastest McGough had ever run a mile in Scotland. Notably this was the first meet where Jimmy came across the Olympic sprinter Arthur Duffey. Their paths would cross again. A further Powderhall race finished in disappointment for Jimmy. It had been run without heats and a large field meant it was almost impossible for the backmarkers, of whom Jimmy was one, to work their way through the field. The newspapers were scathing of his tactics, but offered some hope for the future. One noted that 'Curran ran here with little judgement, but he impressed onlookers with his quality, and the Border youth should come to the front if his heart is in the game.' Another commented on how 'the graceful running of [Jimmy Curran] at once caught the eyes of the cognoscenti, but, lacking in judgement, he ran too fast in the early stages, and had nothing to do with an exciting finish.' But these races, along with an unsuccessful outing in Berwick, were a precursor to the event that Jimmy had his sights set on – the illustrious Border Mile Championship at Hawick.

The Championship was first run in 1899 when Samuel Strang Steel of Philiphaugh presented the silver Strang Steel Challenge Cup to the SBAAA. This was given to the winner for one year, along with the Craig-Brown medal. Jimmy was entered for two races – the mile open handicap and the Border Mile Championship. His main opponent in both races would be J.B. Cowe. Cowe won the less important handicap race in 4.26 for a prize worth £2. But Jimmy had played a tactically brilliant game. Cowe started the race with a handicap of 40 yards, 15 yards behind Jimmy, and as a result was forced to extend himself in order to pass and beat him. But Jimmy's aim wasn't to win, it was to ensure Cowe pushed himself. Jimmy saw the Border Mile Championship ahead – Cowe saw the prize. As a result Jimmy was the fresher of the two come the second race and won easily in 4.31, the fastest time in the race's five year history. Some years later the *Border Telegraph* would note that at the time of his victory he was 'as fine a half-miler as there was amongst amateurs in Scotland.'

In early August, in preparation for an international meet in Glasgow, Jimmy ran at the Primrose League event in Galashiels. As was the case the year before, he failed to win any of his races, placing second in both the mile and half-mile races to men with superior handicaps. His conqueror in the mile was fellow Harrier and good friend, William Torrie.

Jimmy's athletic star had been rapidly rising up to this point. It soon took another massive fillip. Each year Glasgow Celtic Football Club held an athletics event at their 40,000 capacity stadium that attracted the finest athletes in the world.

On an overcast day interspersed with showers, athletes from across the United Kingdom and the United States, including several Olympians past and future, descended on the east of Glasgow to test themselves against some of the finest athletes in the world. These included the trio of American sprinters, Arthur Duffey, Harry Hyman, and J.S. Westney, the Scottish distance runner John McGough, and the Irish high jumper Con Leahy.

Jimmy was entered in the half-mile handicap, against a field of 88. Running off 18 yards he won his heat before coming third in the final behind J. Regan of Cork and M. Hyman of Dublin. Regan was later revealed as a professional, and disqualified. Jimmy had announced himself to the world's greatest athletes, and the press were quick to make it known to the wider public, calling him a 'very promising athlete' and a 'splendid runner.'

A week later Jimmy took part in the mile and half-mile at the final track event of the season, the Leith Flower Show Sports. He walked away defeated, despite running his fastest ever half-mile time of 2.02 seconds, leading the *Field* newspaper to note that his 'fine running [was] the feature of the afternoon.'

In September Jimmy attended a meeting of the Gala Harriers at the Abbotsford Arms Hotel. After an announcement that membership had risen to over 100, he was elected as club captain. He spent the following months running cross country with the team including some competitive races such as those at Portobello where he beat 127 others, Hawick in mid-November where he beat a group of 45 runners over six miles in 49.5 minutes, and a Harriers team race where he won the three mile race in 17 minutes 20 seconds. Often he would act as whip, donning a dark vest with the word 'WHIP' stitched into it in large white lettering, and ensure the pack stayed together and no-one fell too far behind.

These local runs were a lead in to the most important cross country race of Jimmy's career – the Eastern District Championship of the National Cross Country Union of Scotland at Ochilview Park in Stenhousemuir in February 1905, and by this time Jimmy was clearly making a name for himself. The *Edinburgh Evening News* noted that he was the 'best known' in the field of 132 runners, and that he was probably the favourite. Despite such faith, Jimmy finished, disappointingly, outside the top 12.

Jimmy's first race of the track season took place at Melrose in April. He was beaten into second place in the 440 yards, and retired from the mile. Then came a mile loss at Powderhall, followed by a run at the annual Edinburgh Harriers' Sports in June. Jimmy placed second in the 440 yards and failed to place in the mile (in a huge field of 83) or the two miles. And then it was over. Jimmy never again ran an amateur race. Almost a year to the day after Jimmy had joined the Gala Harriers, the lure of the professional circuit, with its financial benefits and stronger opposition, proved too great. Strangely his move to the professional ranks was announced in the *Southern Reporter*, a small paragraph noting that he was to be known on the professional circuit as G. Gordon. It is unclear why Jimmy would make it known that he would be running under a pseudonym. Taking on a name was generally a way of hiding one's true identity, allowing professionals to run in amateur races. Jimmy had no intention of doing this.

During the winter the men raced on cinder tracks, housed within permanent venues (usually football grounds). And as the sun began to burn through the crisp Scottish spring, the athletes made their way to a plethora of summer games and gatherings across the country, often held in local parks and grass fields, stretching from the north of Scotland, into the central belt, continuing through the Borders and south into England.

In June he turned out at the Hawick Common Riding, his first outing as a professional. He came first in the one mile, running off scratch. Days later, at Selkirk, he took the honours in the mile, and at Jedburgh, the following Saturday, he finished second in the mile, and in a three-way tie for first place in the 800 yards, making up 32 and 60 yards on his opponents. He followed this up with a hugely successful meeting at the St Ronan's Games in Innerleithen, where he walked away with two first places in the two mile race and the steeplechase. He also took third place in a speed, stamina, and strength event called 'basket and stone.'

Jimmy's first foray into the world of professional athletics had been more successful than he could have hoped for. It is unknown how much his winnings were, but the types of events Jimmy was competing in generally drew around £8 for the winner and £3 to a few shillings for the lower places, although high profile meets could attract much higher offerings. Compare this to the average weekly wage of a coal miner in Scotland, 25/-, or an agricultural labourer, 15/-, and it is clear that

THE BEST HALF MILER IN SCOTLAND

Jimmy was able to supplement his income substantially through his successes, with one win equating to two months' wages for a miner.

With the 1905 summer season complete the races returned to the track, and Jimmy headed for Edinburgh on a much-reduced schedule. It is likely he took part in a number of races from September onwards, but his only known race in the latter part of the year was in a sprint at Edinburgh's famous Powderhall track. Fighting against strong winds which put paid to any thoughts of fast times, Jimmy ran against 138 runners in the half-mile. In a heat of 12 runners, Jimmy, running off 20 yards, strode to a win in 2.02 seconds. The final took place just as darkness was descending. Lining up as the backmarker, Jimmy was unable to reel in the men in front of him and finished out of the top three places.

The turn of each year was a momentous time for professional athletics in Scotland. The world famous Powderhall Sprint, on New Year's Day, was immediately followed by a New Year Handicap race at the Royal Patent Gymnasium, both situated in Edinburgh. At Powderhall he finished second in the 880 yards, and the following day he ran off 30 yards in the half-mile at the Gymnasium, turning in the fastest time of the day at 1.57 seconds, but couldn't maintain this form and turned in a poor time to finish second behind the winner in the final, who started 40 yards ahead of him. The following day he made the final of the mile, racing as one of a field of 13, including the talented Irish runner George Tincler. Things looked good after Tincler withdrew after about a lap, but Jimmy, for reasons unknown, followed soon after.

A week later he took part in a half-mile handicap at Powderhall. Running off 25 yards he judged his 11 opponents well and won by three yards. He entered the final as third favourite against such luminaries as Tincler, but was beaten out of the top three by men whose handicaps exceeded that given to Jimmy by 40-45 yards.

The summer months brought with them the Common Ridings and Highland Games. Jimmy's first known appearance of the year was at Selkirk, just south of Galashiels, although he had likely run at Hawick the previous week with no success. He placed second in the 215 yards handicap and third, behind Bill Struth, in the hurdles. In the following two months he criss-crossed the country, from the Borders and the Lothians, into Fife, and as far west as the Isle of Bute. At Armadale, Johnstone, Kelso, and Greenlaw he could only manage multiple places. The highest profile race he competed in during this period was at Alva when he took on J.S. Duffus and George Tincler in a 1,200 yards race. On a day ruined by poor weather, Jimmy ran a good second behind Duffus. Other outings proved more successful. He strode to first in the mile and second in the mile and a half at Jedburgh, won the 120 yards at Lochgelly, and in 'magnificent weather' at the end of August took first place in the steeplechase at Innerleithen's St Ronan's Border Games, whilst at the Bute Highland Games he took two first places, in the half-mile and 440 yards. A day later he took part in the Cowal Highland Games in Dunoon, where he finished 3rd in the half-mile. Jimmy no doubt attended many other meets, and certainly ran in more races than are accounted for in the newspapers. But he had completed his first professional season with decent results. And he was learning more with each passing race. In 1940 he would tell the Waynesboro Rotary Club that top American runners such as Glenn Cunningham were of the belief that racing at Madison Square Garden tested their mettle, 'but let them try their skill in a Scotch race with Scotch runners as competitors when there are three cash prizes for the winners, and they will know what running means.'

After the annual summer round of Common Ridings and Highland Games, it was back to track athletics. Jimmy would hop on the train at Galashiels and head into Edinburgh to take part in meets at Powderhall and the Royal Patent Gymnasium. September and October saw him take part in a series of half-mile and sprint races at Powderhall. But his reputation was growing with each race and he was often the backmarker, chasing down those ahead of him. In one half-mile race he reached the final to find himself 45 yards behind his nearest opponent. In December he appeared in various national newspapers, listed as a runner in an upcoming 125 yards handicap sprint at Byker Racecourse in Newcastle. Unfortunately he was drawn against the strong favourite, a black Canadian called Elbridge Eastman. There was so little doubt that Eastman would win the huge prize of £100 that betting on the event was virtually non-existent. It would, Jimmy surmised, be a wasted trip, and so did not attend. Eastman, as expected, won his heat, semi-final, and the final with ease. The two would meet several times in the coming months.

As 1906 turned into 1907, he returned to Powderhall for the New Year sprint series. Avoiding the Blue Riband event – the 130 yards – he entered into the 300 yards race. On a cold, windy day, in front of a crowd of 7,500, he won his heat in 33 seconds, and came second in the final, 'vigorously challenging' the eventual winner and scooping a prize of £2, beating Eastman in the process.

Two days after the Powderhall meet, with the weather having turned frosty, he ran a half-mile race at the Royal Patent Gymnasium before an attendance of 3,000. In his heat he made up 65 yards on A. King of Musselburgh to take the win. In the final he took the lead with 30 yards to go, having taken the bell in last place, and went on to win relatively easily in a 'well-judged race' to walk away with the £8 prize.

Jimmy's successes were starting to bring attention from the press, and the following months saw much praise. The most glowing came in the wake of his New Year races: 'When Curran ran as an amateur it was generally admitted that he had few equals as a distance runner. To-day one of our leading sporting papers voices the opinion that he is one of the best runners over half-a-mile in Britain.'

*****

In the quiet period immediately after the New Year races in Edinburgh, Jimmy's life changed forever. He had been courting a local girl called Janet Mabon, a bobbin worker in one of the town's woollen mills. The fourth of eleven children she had lived near the Curran family her whole life. By late 1906 Janet was pregnant, and having a child out of wedlock at the beginning of the 20th century was a social taboo that few were willing to break. The reaction varied from family to family, and from town to town, but could end in the mother and illegitimate child being ostracised. The answer was to wed. Their impending matrimony was complicated somewhat by the religious mores of the time, which meant that marriages between Roman Catholics, as Jimmy was, and Protestants, as Janet was, were frowned upon, especially by the Catholic Church. In order for the Church to agree to the nuptials, Jimmy approached Canon Edmond Rooney of Our Lady St Andrew Catholic Church for dispensation to marry a 'heretic' and agreed to fulfil three conditions – that he would continue to freely exercise Catholicism, that all children to come from the union would be brought up as Catholics, and that he would do all possible to convert Janet to his religion. On 12th February Jimmy and Janet stood before Rooney and were married.

In many ways the two would prove well matched, with a shared appreciation of fine clothes (perhaps borne out of growing up in a town where clothes were so central to everyday life) and a love of walking in the mountains. They also enjoyed a more sedentary lifestyle: they had a television as early as the 1953, and were serious Canasta players in later years, taking part in games with the couple in the apartment below theirs. But in other ways they were opposites: Janet was exceedingly frugal (in later years she was at pains to tell her family that she had saved enough money to cover the cost of her funeral), whilst Jimmy was more extravagant. When he purchased an expensive table Janet threatened to have it fashioned into a coffin when the time came. But it worked. Their relationship was, throughout their lives, a loving one, playing off one another; him telling stories and her feigning offence.

Whether their marriage and pregnancy was the catalyst for another major event in Jimmy's life will never be known, but in early 1907 Jimmy and Janet decided that he should make his way to America and, when he had raised money through work and running, send for Janet and their as-yet-unborn child.

*****

Jimmy was well aware of his talents, and just how much the limitations of the foot-racing scene in Scotland constricted them. There were many races to be had, and as long as the handicapper gave him a fair mark he was capable of winning a good number of them, and placing in many more. But Jimmy was a man driven by challenge. In later years, when his athletics career was over, he would set physical goals for himself time after time, simply to prove to himself that age was not getting the better of him. But while he was still young he needed stiff competition to make his winnings seem worthwhile. Occasionally he would come up against athletes of the quality of Bill Struth, J.S. Duffus, George Tincler, or John McGough, but he was mainly running against journeymen, and that wasn't enough. On top of this, the returns for the time and energy he was expending, compared to those on offer in America, were relatively low, rarely exceeding £10 and more often than not only a few shillings, plus anything his backers gave him.

The question Jimmy was asking himself was whether or not he could leave. His parents were becoming less capable of looking after themselves – two years earlier his mother had had a bad fall down stairs at the family home in Bank Court. She was found unconscious with a severe head wound, and taken to the Cottage Hospital in the east of the town. She would eventually recover. But he felt he had to strike now. Physically he was at his peak, and capable of holding his own against the best runners in the world. And others were heading across the Atlantic to avail themselves of the money on offer. The Welshman Percy Smallwood was already plying his trade, and J.S. Duffus was said to be heading over. So Jimmy paid the £6 for a ticket to cross from Liverpool to New York on RMS *Lusitania*. He would leave Galashiels in early October.

It is likely that others had persuaded Jimmy of the benefits. One was the famed American sprinter Arthur Duffey. The two had first met at Powderhall in 1904. Three years later Duffey was deeply embedded in promoting professional athletics on the American east coast. The best runners in the world competed through much of the year, using indoor tracks when the weather dictated. And in order to draw athletes of such stature, the prize money could reach levels far beyond that on offer in Scotland.

But Jimmy had some months of Scottish racing left. The period of around four months after the New Year races was generally a quieter time for racing, and Jimmy is only known to have run four races from March to May, all on the track at Powderhall. That he was widely considered one of the finest athletes in the country at his favoured distance of the half-mile is clear when, in March, he was made the backmarker, considered the finest runner, in a field of over 120 entries. Making it through to the final, he found his mark just too much to make up against the best of his opponents and finished unplaced. In early April he finished fourth in the final of the 130 yards, well beaten by men behind him in the handicap. Later in the month he ran his last Powderhall race of the spring, a half-mile, but failed to win.

In May the annual round of Highland Games, Common Ridings and smaller local meets scattered across Scotland and the north of England began. Jimmy had one goal – win as much money as was possible. The season began at Powderhall with a loss in the mile. A month later he was at the Vale of Leven Highland Games where, despite average results, one reporter noted that 'perhaps it is safe to say that a more versatile athlete than Gordon never toed his mark.' Days later he ventured into Fife for the Cowdenbeath Annual Games where a third place in the 300 yards was followed by victory in the 220. The Lothians and Fife, two of Jimmy's main sporting battlegrounds, were separated by the Firth of Forth, a body of water that cuts deep into the right flank of Scotland. Jimmy commuted between the two by train, crossing the Forth Bridge, a structure made famous some years later for its prominent role in Alfred Hitchcock's adaptation of John Buchan's *The*

39 Steps. This would become almost a daily occurrence as Jimmy followed the events around central Scotland, and occasionally beyond.

Cowdenbeath was followed by the illustrious Hawick Common Riding. Jimmy had been favourite to win the sprint, but a stumble cost him. The *Border Telegraph* noted that favourites 'knuckling down to a dark horse belonging to Hawick' was not uncommon, implying that those expected to win, in this case Jimmy, were paid to lose in order to guarantee a local winner. But Jimmy wasn't always paid to lose, which freed him up to show his true colours. A win at Selkirk Common Riding was followed by a highly successful day at the smaller Swinton Games where he walked away with four wins, his only defeat coming to Bill Struth, and two wins at Dalkeith. His schedule was relentless: the birth of his first child, Mary Davidson Curran, jammed between meets at Musselburgh and Jedburgh.

Jedburgh marked the beginning of perhaps the busiest period of racing of Jimmy's entire career, travelling by train almost daily over the Forth Bridge. A small meet in the south at Airth was followed by two in quick succession at Dunfermline and Thornton. Little more than a village, Thornton's Highland Games had nevertheless grown to become 'the greatest athletic meet in Scotland', and around 50,000 spectators looked on as Jimmy stepped into the arena. With a strong field making it to the final of the 120 yards sprint, Jimmy was, unusually, near the front of the handicapped race. It wasn't enough, and most of the backmarkers passed him. His only success was winning the 300 yards consolation race.

The following day he was back in the Borders, for a moderately successful outing at Kelso's annual games. Two days later he was back north once again, picking up a second place in the 300 yards handicap at the Kinross Games. And so ended ten days that had seen Jimmy travelling up and down the country to attend six meets. His hectic schedule was certainly not at an end, but it would slow down in the coming months.

On 27th July Jimmy appeared at the Langholm Games, just a few miles north of the Scotland-England border. It proved a profitable outing with three first places, and one second place. A week later he was once more on a train as he headed to Bridge of Allan in Fife for the Strathallan Games. Like many annual Games in Scotland the size of the event far exceeded what could reasonably be expected given the small size of the town. With origins dating back to the mid-19th century the Strathallan Games had grown exponentially until, by 1907, the crowd exceeded 15,000, aided by the weather, and it being held on a Trades Holiday. Another defeat to Jimmy's old rival Bill Struth in the 440 yards hurdles was followed by a win in the 110 yards handicap.

He continued to zigzag north and south with his greatest success coming on a wet day at Alva when he defeated a strong field, including the highly-rated J.S. Duffus, in the 1,200 yards race, exacting revenge for the previous year's defeat. At one of his final races in Scotland, at the St Ronan's Games at Innerleithen, the suggestion of deliberately losing a race emerged again, with one reporter noting that he was 'content to take seconds.'

With the Scottish games largely over, Jimmy headed south into Cumbria, in northern England, for a number of final races before his journey across the Atlantic. First up was the games at Workington on 24th August, when he lost out in the 120 yards handicap. A week later he was at Pooley Bridge for the Ullswater Sports, winning both the quarter and half-mile, with one reporter salivating at his performance, noting he was 'probably the best man in the country over the distances [and] simply spread-eagled his opponents in the scratch quarter and half-mile.' A sprained ankle temporarily halted his relentless schedule, but he was able to fit in some final races at Powderhall in Edinburgh. A 130 yards race ended in defeat at the semi-final stage, but two weeks later he 'was in fine form' and, as a mist so thick that spectators occasionally lost sight of the runners descended, he strode to a win in a 300 yards race, winning £8 in the process.

Exactly how much money Jimmy won in 1907 is unknown, but he competed in at least 30 meets, winning 19 events, with 15 second places, and eight thirds.

In the four years since returning from the war, Jimmy had risen from virtual obscurity to become an athlete who drew the plaudits of the country's finest reporters. John James Miller of the *Aberdeen People's Journal* called him 'the best all-round, over any distance man at present on the track', whilst the *Border Telegraph*, always quick to promote Jimmy, noted he 'is a jumper a good bit above the average, and his success in this direction is another tribute to his all-round athletic ability' and that his 'all-round ability as an athlete has already stamped him as one of the best which our Borderland, or even Scotland, has ever produced.'

*****

Over the years Jimmy had built up a large circle of friends. Those he had known since he was a child, those he had run with, worked with, and those who had made money off his wins and losses. In late September, a farewell dinner was held in his honour, at the Abbotsford Arms Hotel. In the chair was Jimmy's long-time friend A.D. Lawson, president of the Gala Harriers, who presented Jimmy with a 'well-filled purse of money subscribed by his friends and admirers,' before eulogising Jimmy's achievements, both as an amateur and professional. He finished up by making clear his belief that, over sprint or distance, he was 'one of the finest runners in the country.' He set out Jimmy's plan to take on the best America could muster, before Jimmy offered a reply and thanked the assembled well-wishers for their generosity. The room spent the remainder of the evening in that most Scottish of ways – eating, drinking and singing. By the time the *Border Telegraph* printed an extended piece detailing the evening, Jimmy was already part way across the Atlantic Ocean.

Chapter 6 • Ameriky Bound

At the beginning of the 19th century travel between Britain's cities and towns was a long and arduous undertaking. A coach journey from Edinburgh to London could take three days, with the additional rigours that wood and iron wheels and rutted roads inflicted on weary passengers. From the late 18th century, as men such as James Watt and George Stephenson made titanic technological advances, the way was paved for a railway network that would see 6,000 miles of tracks laid in the decade up to 1850, criss-crossing the country from north to south, and east to west. Vast quantities of people and goods moved at speeds that just decades earlier seemed unimaginable. Journey times were slashed. The three days from Edinburgh to London was reduced to less than 18 hours.

Once the country's major towns and cities were connected, a labyrinthine network of branch lines was laid to incorporate outlying smaller towns. And so, in 1849, Galashiels, Scotland's primary wool town, became part of the nation's rail network, connected to Edinburgh, London and the country's largest ports as the tips of one's fingers and toes are connected to one's major organs.

On a cold day in early October 1907 more than fifty years had passed since those connections had been made. In that time hundreds of thousands of Galaleans had passed through the station, readying themselves in times of peace and war for journeys short and long, some to return, some never to do so. And in their shadows stood Jimmy, 27 years old, attired in his finest plaid suit, and holding a carpet bag. Janet and Mary, and numerous family members, were there to see him off. Kisses were exchanged, tears wiped, hands shaken. And then the family were left standing on the platform as the rear of the train pulled ever further away. And then it was gone. When the family would be reunited was wholly dependent on how quickly Jimmy could forge a life in America.

JIMMY CURRAN

Harbouring the dreams that millions before him had carried with them on their journeys to the New World – gazing up at New York City skyscrapers, driving west towards the promise of verdant farmland, and fortunes of Rockefeller-esque proportions – he headed south, bound for Liverpool, an industrial port on England's west coast. Jammed up hard against the River Mersey, the city had just finished celebrating its 700th year of existence, an event that had drawn not only the great and good of the north-west of England, but also the country's full naval prowess, which sat observing proceedings from the river. The city had an industrial grace, with ships big and small endlessly pulling in and out of the 1,600 acres of docks and 35 miles of quays, alongside which ran the Dockers' Umbrella, a seven mile long overhead railway. In the wake of the Industrial Revolution industries large and small sprang up across the city; alongside one small section of dock, immediately east of Victoria Tower, were a tannery, a gas works, a sugar refinery, a bottling store, a bone manure works, a brewery, a distillery, a coal yard, and mills and warehouses galore. In contrast to this great industrial landscape sat an array of impressive architecture, such as Liverpool Town Hall, St George's Hall, a plethora of museums, libraries and galleries, as well as the recently-opened Dock Office which would soon find fame as one of the Three Graces. On the outskirts of the city sat two extensive parks – Toxteth and Stanley – offering Liverpudlians designed landscapes and peaceful walks, around which were constructed a bowling green, a fishing pond, a cricket ground, and palm houses.

But Jimmy's visit was limited to the city centre and docks, where he was confronted by a vibrancy that could not be found in Galashiels, and was only hinted at on the streets of Edinburgh. Newspapers vendors called out the latest local news, dominated not by the western journey of the *Lusitania*, but by the first football derby of the season between Everton and Liverpool at Goodison Park.

Horse-drawn carts and trams trundled over cobbled streets, past wide pavements bustling with orange sellers, shoe-shiners and all manner of traders, looking to make a quick penny from the thousands of sailors and emigrants passing through daily. Like the street urchins who skimmed and danced between the legs of the buyers, often barefooted and always painfully thin, some wearing cloth caps handed down by their fathers, poverty and degradation oozed through the city's streets and alleyways, its houses and workplaces, infusing disease and sickness into the food and water, the skin and hair, killing and maiming as it went, indifferent to social status, but discriminatory against the very young and the elderly. The carnage it wrought was accepted, a part of life.

Arriving in the city Jimmy and his fellow Cunard Line passengers were met by the company agent, who split them into their various nationalities, loaded them onto busses, and transported them to the Cunard Hotel system in the centre of Liverpool; Scandinavians, for example, would stay at the Goteborg Hotel. The system provided rooms for around 2,000 second and third class Cunard Line passengers. The complex was sanitary and provided good quality meals for those about to embark on their journey. Jimmy was housed in a dormitory with around 10-15 other men, and revelled in the luxuries of steam heat and electric lighting. The tiled toilets and bathrooms were sanitary with running water, soap and towels. The two dining rooms provided good quality food and great care was taken to cater for those about to travel – kosher food being provided for Jewish passengers. Jimmy enjoyed his last night in Britain.

Most importantly the stopover at the hotel provided a chance for the health of passengers to be assessed before they set off for Ellis Island, America's busiest immigrant inspection station. Whilst at the hotel Jimmy was checked by the Cunard Line's physician for any infectious or contagious disease. On 5th October he boarded a bus and headed to the docks, bound for the company's newest liner, the RMS *Lusitania*, several hours before it left port.

The dock before departure was a heaving mass of bodies, young and old, fit and decrepit, some silent, most chattering in a babel of mainly northern European tongues. They weaved around the horse-drawn carriages, their vast array of bowlers and boaters bobbing on the dockside like the tugboats surrounding the behemoth upon which they would soon start their new lives. Jimmy made his way to the gangplank and boarded. He found a spot on the rail and looked down upon his old life.

The hours spent on the ship before its departure allowed time for three final physical checks of each of the passengers – the ship's doctor, a British Board of Trade medical officer, and once again by a Cunard Line physician. As a steerage passenger Jimmy was required to submit to all medical checks. Not for the last time in October 1907 a thousand butterflies danced in his stomach. He passed.

Living conditions on transatlantic liners ranged from sumptuous to sybaritic, dependant on both which liner a traveller was on, and on which class of ticket they had purchased. Conditions and food aboard the SS *Kaiser Wilhelm II* were so bad that passengers occasionally came close to mutinying. On the SS *Fürst Bismarck* the bread was of such poor quality that the passengers threw it overboard, whilst on the SS *Statendam* thirsting steerage passengers had to steal water from the second class area. Such failings prompted Edward Steiner, a member of the National Conference on Immigration, who would often travel incognito on these ships, to describe steerage as 'often indecent and inhuman', and 'responsible for not a little imported anarchy, and the sooner it is abolished the better.' Fortunately for Jimmy the British shipping companies generally treated their steerage passengers better than their continental counterparts. And travelling on a brand new ship meant that if nothing else the dirt and shabbiness that pervaded many older ships had not yet had time to become embedded.

Only a month past its maiden voyage the *Lusitania* was a mammoth, by far the largest vessel crossing the Atlantic, capable of carrying 1,993 passengers and 800 crew, with a passenger on its maiden voyage noting that when he climbed to its highest deck it felt like being atop the Lincoln Cathedral. And the physical presence that met one's eye as it sat in the water was matched by the grandiosity of the interior.

AMERIKY BOUND

It was decorated in an array of styles, and any passenger passing through its public rooms could not escape the sumptuous designs of its Scottish architect James Millar. Walls of mahogany and walnut rose from plush carpets – each room with its own colour and design – whilst Rose du Barry silk curtains and upholstery were scattered throughout. But Millar's greatest achievement was to be found in the first class dining room, where Corinthian-styled pillars surrounded the plaster, gold-leaf, and mahogany panels. The room was topped with a plaster dome bearing frescos in the style of François Boucher.

Its 25 Scotch boilers, four Parsons steam turbines, and four funnels capable of emitting the smoke of 1,100 tons of Welsh coal daily, saw it reaching speeds over 25 knots, and led to it being hailed The Greyhound of the Seas. Eight years later the ship would steal the headlines away from the battlefields of the First World War when it was torpedoed by a German submarine, with the loss of almost 2,000 lives. But in 1907 it was the jewel of the Cunard crown. As a result the ship was stocked with the great and the good – Senator Eugene Hale, George Marks MP, the concert pianist Mark Hambourg, the actor Bransby Williams, and the playwright Robert Courtneidge, fresh from the opening of his opera *Tom Jones* in Manchester and London. Also on board was Julia Rice, who had just founded the Society for the Suppression of Unnecessary Noise, to campaign against the horns and whistles of ships, a campaign that would eventually prove successful.

On leaving the dock, the ship rounded the New Brighton Pier and headed south to Queenstown in Ireland where it picked up mail and more passengers. At 10.25am it left the harbour and passed the Daunt Rock Lightship before speeding out into the Atlantic. There were fears that it would encounter the poor weather that had dogged ships crossing in the previous week – the RMS *Umbria* had been tossed around the Irish Sea as it if were a toy in a bathtub, emptying the dining room and sending seasick passengers running for the toilets – but the weather turned and Jimmy and his fellow travellers were met by mainly tranquil oceans. The journey itself promised to be riven by boredom, but the passengers attempted to make the best of their lot by forming micro communities; friendships were forged, love affairs blossomed, savings were bolstered and lost at card games, and dancing abounded as the more musically-inclined accompanied with violin, guitar, and the ship's piano.

Not quite five days after setting sail from Liverpool, with the ship's bow forcing white waters upwards from the dark oceanic stillness, and its four funnels exhaling furiously out into the early evening sky, Jimmy and his fellow passengers, already enjoying a party to celebrate what they were aware was about to become a record-breaking journey, crowded along the starboard railing, peering out into the oncoming darkness for a glimpse of Nantucket, only a mile to starboard. And they were soon at the eastern end of Fire Island, passing its full length in 45 minutes. Just after one in the morning the ship passed Sandy Hook, a peninsula jutting out from the New Jersey mainland, in the fastest average speed ever recorded on a westbound journey (a feat for which it was awarded the Blue Riband). Jimmy, his fellow passengers, and around 800 crew, had just crossed the Atlantic Ocean westbound faster than any other human beings.

Celebrations in steerage were tempered somewhat by the fear of being refused entry, but amongst first class passengers the revelries reached their height as Mark Hambourg gave a concert in the ship's drawing room, followed by imitations of the rich and famous by Bransby Williams. There followed a speech by George Marks MP. Pointing towards a number of German engineers, his voice shaking, he harnessed all his oratorical skills and proclaimed 'England once more rules the sea' before going on to praise the stokers working in the bowels of the ship. In response, first class passengers raised $125 for them. This inspired Williams to put on a stoker's raiment, an engineer's overall, and a greasy cap. To top off the disguise he smeared his face with oil and coal dust, before making his way into the drawing room and, in the 'husky tones' of 'Garry the Irish stoker', thanked the passengers for their kind words about the men below decks, before lighting up a pipe. After much cheering, the passengers, many no doubt having drunk a good share of spirits, handed over the purse for the man and his mates. But Williams almost didn't get the last laugh – when a purser was informed that a stoker was mingling with first class passengers, and promptly had him taken back below by two 'burly' officers. Williams eventually informed the men who he was, but not before they had roughly manhandled him down some flights of stairs and left him gasping for breath. He handed the $125 over to the ship's stokers.

That same purser, 'Jolly Jo' Lancaster, his talents clearly not equal to those displayed by Williams, poked fun at Germany, the now former record holder:

> There was a young man from Westphalia
> Who had charge of the Kaiser's regalia
> To his sweetheart he said
> "My dear, when we're wed
> We'll call our first girl Lucy Tania".

Subsequent events would give Germany the last laugh.

The liner remained at anchor off Sandy Hook until dawn began to break. The first medical and quarantine examinations of the day, of first and second class passengers, lasted an hour. Soon after, the ship proceeded upriver, passing between Staten Island and Brooklyn, flanked by a vast array of ships, steamers, and launches. Passengers flocked to the port side as the Statue of Liberty appeared, the oxidation process well on the way to turning its deep brown copper to a light green, with flame held high and welcoming the tired, the poor and homeless, the wretched refuse, the tempest-tost and the huddled masses. As the ship approached Pier 54 in Manhattan, New Yorkers lined the shore, cheering the record breaking ship.

Once docked the first and second class passengers, and American citizens, were disembarked, their examination having been conducted aboard ship. But travelling in steerage offered no such comforts, and there was no way for Jimmy to avoid Ellis Island Immigration Station, opened only seven years previously, emerging from the waters of New York Bay like a red-brick crannog, where so many dreams would soon hang in limbo.

And so Jimmy and the third class passengers loaded onto barges, herded there by aggressive dock employees, mainly Germans speaking only broken English, who had little compunction at using brutality to force the immigrants to bend to their will. The journey across the Hudson River was a short one before the barges docked in the wharf of Ellis Island. And here the new arrivals waited. And waited, often for hours on end. After Jimmy eventually disembarked the barges, he passed through a gauntlet of attendants whose verbal and physical abuse mirrored that of their colleagues at Pier 54. On reaching the baggage area he left his luggage behind, to be reunited, or quite often not, at the end of the Island process.

For some it would be their fifth inspection, and the most feared of all. A year before Jimmy entered America Edward Steiner wrote:

> Let no one believe that landing on the shores of
> "The land of the free, and the home of the brave" is
> a pleasant experience; it is a hard, harsh fact,
> surrounded by the grinding machinery of the law,
> which sifts, picks, and chooses; admitting the fit and
> excluding the weak and helpless.'

From the baggage area he walked up a set of stairs, all the while being observed by numerous doctors – the six-second medical – checking for some physical or mental defect. And then came the Great Hall, vast, officious, and iconic; huge arched windows on the ground and first floors pouring light upon the new arrivals, and the American flag draped from the balcony, serving as a metaphorical barrier between what many perceived to be the injustice and oppression of the Old World, and the liberty and equality that lay beyond. The cavernous hall magnified the desperate, sometimes hysterical, cries by parents and children as they were separated in the throng, the fear and confusion tangible, the dehumanisation complete as, like cattle, they shuffled through their pens awaiting their fate. The room was divided by iron railings, and Jimmy sat on one of the wooden benches provided, where he and his fellow immigrants awaited the physical probing and intrusive questions of the Immigrant Inspectors. Jimmy's heart pounded against his chest as the tests were conducted. He didn't fall into any barred group – convicted criminal, pauper, polygamist, anarchist, nor was he likely to become a public charge – and had no reason to lie to ease his passage, but still his thoughts were filled with visions of what would befall him should he fail some aspect of the examination. Should an Inspector suspect him of any indiscretion he would be sent before the Court of Inquiry for a final determination. And even if he passed the morality test, his obvious fitness and strength were by no means a gauge as to how he would fare in the physical tests. Even the most outwardly healthy travellers could be harbouring a hidden ailment, the most notorious of which was trachoma, a highly contagious eye disease, the diagnosis of which would see immigrants immediately refused entry. A chalk mark on one's clothing was an indication of a problem – E for eyes, H for heart, S for senility, Ct for trachoma, and so on. Most diseases were not enough to see immigrants sent home, but could have a lasting effect on their lives. In 1929 a young Jewish boy called Alvin Garrett entered the Station and was found to have ringworm on his scalp. After a treatment of electrolysis his hair fell out, and his family were warned it would never re-grow. It did, but he was left with a bald patch.

But, after around five hours of waiting, questioning, and testing, pass through Jimmy did, one of just over one million who did so in 1907, the largest single year influx of immigrants to America. So as Bransby Williams headed off to Broadway, where he would star opposite Jimmy's fellow Scot, Harry Lauder, and Mark Hambourg began a seven-week tour that would pinnacle at Carnegie Hall, Jimmy exchanged his pounds for dollars, purchased some food and, landing card in hand, stepped onto another barge, this time to be transported to the Central Railroad of New Jersey Terminal. Here he boarded a train and headed west, through Trenton, into Pennsylvania with its great forested mountains, passing a endless juxtaposition of steel mills and swaying cornfields, and was finally able to bathe in the beauty and vastness of the New World.

*****

In the early 1880s Jimmy's uncle, Michael Curran, and his family, had emigrated and made their home in Harrisburg, Pennsylvania. Here his oldest daughter, Christina, married a railroad clerk called Alvin Stacks and started her own family. And so Jimmy's first nights in the United States were spent in the house of his cousin on Peffer Street in Harrisburg, one block from the Susquehanna River. But his stay was short-lived. He was soon headed east where a job was awaiting him at Reading Iron Works.

That job was as a puddler, or actually as a puddler's assistant, which earned him a weekly wage of around $13, or almost $700 a year. A puddler needed to be strong with tremendous stamina, for the job was a physically demanding one, and life expectancy was low, often in the 30s. In oppressive temperatures Jimmy relentlessly shovelled brittle 'pig' iron into a roaring furnace until it reached the optimum temperature, at which point he would stir it until it transformed into malleable wrought iron. As protection he wore heavy clothing, and the resultant sweat caused a greasy film of dust to cover him head to toe.

But Jimmy could never have known the storm he was about to enter. Just two miles from where he first set foot in America, a copper mine owner turned banker called F. Augustus Heinze was in the midst of plans to corner the stock of the United Copper Company. Heinze had arrived in New York 18 months previously with $25m and a dream of emulating the J.P. Morgans and John D. Rockefellers. With success after success, Heinze appeared well on the road to achieving his goal. But the United Copper Company takeover, in the midst of an already jittery market, was a step too far and within two days of setting his plan in motion he had lost $50m. The Knickerbocker Trust Company went to the wall, and was followed by a number of others. The dominoes had begun to tumble; regional banks began to withdraw funds from New York banks, while citizens began to withdraw savings from the regional banks.

With the situation rapidly deteriorating, it seemed that a miracle was needed to reverse the trend. That 'miracle' came in the form of J.P. Morgan, financier and banker, who persuaded the US Government to inject the considerable sum of $25m into the New York City banks. In its footsteps followed John D. Rockefeller who added an additional $10m of his own money. Over the next few days the banking system swung precariously between rescue and collapse. Finally, after repeated interventions by Morgan, which included the browbeating of senior trust company presidents and bankers in order to persuade them to invest their money to rescue struggling trusts, the situation began to take a favourable turn. Total collapse had been averted. But if the crisis was akin to an electric shock for New York's bankers and financiers, their pain was nothing compared to how the wider country suffered, as Gross National Product fell by 11%, industrial production by 16%, imports by 22%, exports by 16%, and the unemployment rate almost doubled.

Heinze's folly was like a stone thrown in a pond, and the resultant wave soon found its way into the steel communities of Pennsylvania. Jimmy had barely lifted his tools when companies began to lay off employees – in the six months after the panic, the number of employees at, for example, Steelton Mill, fell 44% from 6,789 to 3,809. Being one of the last men employed by the Reading Iron Company, he stood little chance of avoiding redundancy.

But as much it may have seemed like Jimmy's world was collapsing around him, his lack of employment was to prove a blessing in disguise. On weekends he attended running events. At one of these, at the

JIMMY CURRAN

University of Pennsylvania's Franklin Field in Philadelphia, Jack Roden, a sports promoter, introduced him to a fellow Borderer called William Renwick. Renwick was a long-serving groundskeeper and masseuse, or rubber as they were called, for the University's sports teams. Known as Scotty he, in turn, introduced Jimmy to a slight gentleman wearing a suit and a bowler hat, whose handsome features were part hidden by a drooping moustache. The man was Mike Murphy. He was the head coach of the University of Pennsylvania's athletics team, and had coached the 1900 and 1908 Olympic teams. He was revered in the world of college athletics. Jimmy asked him for a job.

If Mike Murphy had any qualms about whether he should hire Jimmy, they were quickly dispelled. A swift circuit of the track made clear that this down-on-his-luck Scot knew the rudimentaries of running, and had the speed and stamina to back it up. Furthermore, his coaching résumé, namely his work with Wyndham Halswelle (a runner Murphy was aware of due to his having participated at the Intercalated Games of 1906 in Athens) was evidence that he could dissect and analyse the technical aspects of the sport, and use that understanding to improve the performances of others. But if running and coaching were Jimmy's fortes, self-promotion certainly wasn't. Murphy asked him if he had ever worked as a rubber. Jimmy said he hadn't and the wily coach offered some sage advice: 'Always say yes when asked if you can do something. The worst that can happen is they'll fire you.' He then offered Jimmy the job.

Born in Westboro, Massachusetts, in 1861, Murphy spent his youth striving for athletic greatness, mostly in pedestrianism, but also sprinting and baseball. Realising that greatness did not necessarily equate to financial security he moved into coaching. And he soon acquired the customary quirky back-story that would, in later years, only enhance his legendary reputation: he worked for some time as the trainer of the champion boxer John L. Sullivan, before spending a year scouring Canadian lumber camps for a fighter who could defeat his previous charge. His failure to uncover Sullivan's conqueror did not deter him from further pursuing coaching and his hiring by Yale, in 1887, was the genesis of a career that would mark him out as the 'dean of American coaches.' For the next decade he moved back and forth between Yale, and the Athletic Clubs of Detroit and New York until, in 1896, he was hired by the University of Pennsylvania. Although he would briefly move back to Yale he would eventually return to Pennsylvania and spend the remainder of his career there. And it is easy to see why he was in such demand. In the 21 intercollegiate championships his teams entered, they walked away with 15 first places, and never placed lower than third.

By 1907, when America was choosing its Olympic team, there were no dissenters when Murphy was chosen to train the athletes, as he had done with his University of Pennsylvania athletes at the successful 1900 Games. When asked who had nominated Murphy, James E. Sullivan, president of the Amateur Athletic Union (AAU), and Commissioner of the US Olympic Committee, noted 'No-one in particular. We all nominated him at once. He was the only man we considered.' Four years later, when deciding who should train the 1912 team, the Committee was once again determined to get their man, even though Murphy was in extremely poor health with an illness that would eventually kill him. His athletes were a stunning success at both Games – in 1908 they took 16 athletics gold medals, from a possible 27, and almost half of all the athletics medals available, and four years later returned home with a similar haul.

But Murphy did not simply train athletes, he discovered them and he developed them. He took them from raw runners, worked on their techniques, and turned them into champions. In 1889 he watched the 28-year-old John Owen play tennis and saw a potential that had evaded less pioneering coaches. Owen was soon the fastest man in the world, the first to break 10 seconds for the 100 yards. Likewise with the New Zealander, Guy Haskins. Haskins was well beaten in a scratch 600 yards race at the University of Pennsylvania, but Murphy liked his effortless style and in 1907, with some training, he broke the intercollegiate record for one mile. Others who trained under Murphy included the quadruple Olympic gold medallist Alvin Kraenzlein, Walter Tewksbury who won two golds, two silvers and a bronze at the same 1900 Games, and Don Lippincott who won a silver and bronze at the 1912 Games.

With this résumé Murphy hardly needed to hire any old athlete who asked him for a job (and it is probable that many did). Jimmy could not have asked for a better mentor. Walking into a post in one of the premier athletic programmes in the country, under arguably the finest coach, was the equivalent of a lawyer passing the bar and starting work the next day with one of the top law firms in New York City. What he also got was access to Murphy's impressive coaching staff – men such as George W. Orton, winner of gold and bronze medals at the 1900 Olympics, and coach of Penn's cross country team, Mike 'Doc' Dee, later trainer with the Phillies baseball team, where he was considered the best trainer they had ever had, and also the University's Director of Physical Education Randolph Faries, author of the ground-breaking book *Practical Training for Athletics, Health and Pleasure*.

A coach without a support team was bound to lose, because one of the primary factors that separated winning teams from losing ones at the turn of the century (as it still is today) was not just quality of squad, or tactics – it was the ability to keep a squad healthy and allow athletes to compete as many times as possible in a season. If injuries depleted a squad of athletes the possibility of success became ever more distant. Bring on Mike Dee! If Murphy was the 'dean of coaches' then Dee can perhaps be considered the 'dean of trainers.' If Murphy was the man to teach athletes how to win, Dee was the man to keep them in a physical state to do so. Dee put in place a programme to ensure that the likelihood of injury for those under his charge was reduced, as much as was possible. He ordered his athletes to warm up slowly, to stay warm between workouts, and to avoid chill winds. Stories of his miracle cures abounded – whether it be injecting antiseptic to avert blood poisoning, setting a broken thumb, or simply treating strains, wrenches and charley horses. But it was not a one-man job. During the 1909 baseball season

AMERIKY BOUND

Bert Semmons, trainer of the Chicago Cubs, averaged 11 massages a day as well as treating the usual cuts, bruises and sprains. Dee was rubbing the kinks out of the muscles of 40 athletes each day. Indeed, Murphy had so much faith in rubbers that in 1894 he doubled the number under his charge.

The rubber was the lowest rung on the coaching ladder. The aim of the coach and trainer was to bring success to their school. And the rubber was an important cog in the wheel that drove towards that goal. A rubber had to be an 'expert masseur, something of a medical practitioner, surgeon, nurse, osteopath' and be willing to undertake a multitude of random jobs. Jimmy's fellow Scottish coach, Lawson Robertson, would say of Mike Dee that '[he] is more than a mere trainer. He's a physician, who can give a prescription and diagnose a case. He's also a mental and physical adviser.'

In 1913 the Finnish distance runner Hannes Kolehmainen, still basking in the glory of three gold medals and a silver at the 1912 Olympics, brought his own rubber with him to America, and in 1911 Harry Andrews, trainer to the South London Harriers, noted that he used rubbing with every one of his athletes and that its use was the primary reason for American dominance on the athletics field. After a game or meet, athletes would make for the rubbing tables where they would be met by the Mike Dees and Jimmy Currans who would produce their oils and liniments, the ingredients of which were often guarded like a state secret by the amateur alchemists who brewed them, but often included alcohol and basil. With the skin suitably oiled up they would, with hands and elbows, employ a 'tortuous kneading' to remove the sprains and bruises.

So Jimmy went to work under Dee, and grabbed the opportunity with both hands. He had much to learn. He had gone from being unemployed to earning upwards of $500 annually, on top of his race winnings. Jimmy had used his not inconsiderable talents to find work. But he had also struck lucky, being in the right place at the right time. This mixture of talent and luck would serve him well three years later.

For now all that was required of him was to prove he could work within Murphy's system.

Chapter 7 • A Race Like No Other

In the years since he had raced against and trained Halswelle at Port Elizabeth in South Africa, Jimmy had followed success with success in, first, amateur, and then, professional races. Halswelle's star, however, had risen at an even more astonishing pace, eclipsing all around him. And behind Halswelle's success was his old friend, who had followed his progress and was absolutely sure that 'he could defeat any man running in England from 100 yards to the half-mile.' Jimmy had initially attempted to attach Halswelle to a running club but one after another refused due to Halswelle's 'blue blood.' With possibilities running out, Jimmy approached Edinburgh Harriers, and his luck changed. Here was a club whose ethos was of egalitarianism, a club devoted to amateur sports, but accepting of members regardless of their social background – be they from 'the regiment, the office, or the workshop.' Jimmy's training schedule brought almost immediate success. In 1904 Halswelle won his first Army Championship at the half-mile. Over the next two years he settled on the quarter-mile as his preferred distance and won event after event at the very highest level, as well as representing Scotland. In 1905 he won this distance at the SAAA and AAA Championships. His most successful outing was at the SAAA championships of 1906, when he claimed victory at 100 yards, 220 yards, the quarter-mile and the half-mile in a single afternoon. Two weeks later he entered and won the 440 yards at the English Championship in London. He rounded off the 1906 season with a Scottish record in the quarter-mile, and was picked to represent Great Britain at the Intercalated Games – an event organised in an attempt to re-inject some popularity in the failing Olympic Games. Halswelle had everything needed to be chosen to represent his country – the speed to challenge for a medal, and the social background and etiquette that the selectors were wholly at ease with. The latter wasn't an overriding necessity – John McGough, who ran in the 1,500 metres at the 1906 and 1908 Olympics, was a postman – but it certainly didn't hurt one's opportunities or chances of selection.

Halswelle was to run in three events – the 100, 400 and 800 metres. First was the shortest, his least favoured. After a mediocre showing in the heats, he finished third in his semi-final and was out. The same day he took part in the heats of the 800 metres. After storming through his heat he would line up in the final as one of the favourites. But first he had the heats and final of the 400 metres to contend with. He looked impressive in his heat, finishing first in 54 seconds. In the final, three days later, he set the pace alongside the Australian Nigel Barker, but was passed on the final stretch by the unfancied Paul Pilgrim from the USA. He was forced to settle for silver, but still had the 800 metres final. The 800 metres was viewed as his most likely victory, but he underperformed, finishing third by 10 yards, behind Pilgrim and his fellow American James Lightbody. Halswelle's Games had been a disappointment. He had failed to live up to the weighty expectations placed upon his shoulders.

An injury in 1907 put his place at the 1908 Olympic Games in jeopardy, but he recovered in time, running a world record for the 300 yards and a British record for the 440 yards, which would stand for 53 and 26 years respectively, to take his place in the 400 metres.

But before the London Games even started, the relationship between Britain and the US was already strained after a series of incidents that began with the British failure to display the American flag at the White City Stadium, an oversight that would soon elicit a British apology. The American retort was, supposedly, to refuse to lower their flag when marching past King Edward VII. What followed was a series of refereeing decisions that, the Americans argued, were unfavourable to the American team – they questioned rules in some field events and refereeing decisions in others. The high jumper Harry Porter complained that 'in nearly every event the boys had to compete not only against their competitors, but against prejudiced judges. The judges may not have been intentionally unfair but they could not control their feelings, which were antagonistic to the Americans.' And even the crowd got in on the act, booing the American long and high jumper, Frank Holmes, so vociferously that an official had to warn them to desist. Tempers frayed and boiled ever hotter until they finally found an outlet in the final of the 400m race. A 536m long track meant that the race was run only around a single bend. Lining up were three Americans – John Carpenter, John Taylor, and William Robbins – against the sole Briton, Halswelle. He had breezed his way through the rounds, running a time of 49.4 seconds in the heats, the fastest of the day. The semi-finals, run the following day, were a relatively relaxed affair, with Halswelle winning his heat by 1.4 seconds in an Olympic record of 48.4 seconds. The final took place the following day.

The starter, Harry Goble, prior to firing his pistol, warned the runners that English rules would be applied; 'any competitor wilfully jostling or running across or obstructing another competitor so as to impede his progress, shall forfeit his right to be in the competition', reiterating a rule that was printed at the head of every programme, and was also relayed to every competitor before the Games started. As the gun went off, Carpenter stormed into a lead and Halswelle settled in at the rear of the four. Coming off the bend he began to move onto the shoulder of Carpenter. At this Carpenter, it has been argued, moved out, driving Halswelle to the periphery of the track. Halswelle later noted that he was so close to Carpenter that he could not cut inside without chopping his stride. Carpenter was clear that he kept a straight line from the final end to the finish line. Seeing what he believed was an infringement of the rules, one of the race judges, Dr Arthur Roscoe Badger, rushed on to the track and ended the race with around 40 yards left to run. On seeing Badger on the track, Halswelle slowed up. Carpenter did finish, in what would have been a world record time of 47.6 seconds, but it was to no avail as the decision of the officials to end the race stood. He was subsequently disqualified.

The decision of Carpenter to run Halswelle wide, if indeed he did this, may have been a deliberate one, informed by a belief that the Scot was liable to buckle under pressure. Indeed, after the race James E. Sullivan accused Halswelle of 'quitting as I have seen him quitting before.' Sullivan may have been referring to Halswelle's three races in the Intercalated Games of 1906, when he failed to live up to expectations. It is unknown whether Jimmy spoke to Murphy about Halswelle's strengths and weaknesses.

The final was re-run on 25th July, but Sullivan refused to sanction Taylor and Robbins taking part in what he perceived to be a charade. This left Halswelle to complete the circuit alone, running in a roped off lane. He finished in 50 seconds dead. Of the Americans, only Taylor, who had trained under Murphy at the University of Pennsylvania, ever tasted Olympic success, winning a gold medal in the 400m relay on the same day as Halswelle's solo run. Four months later he would be dead, succumbing to typhoid pneumonia at the age of 26. Halswelle later lamented the decision of the Americans not to run, wishing he could have had opposition in the final.

And if Taylor's loss to the sport was not enough more was to come. Just when Halswelle was at the very top of his game, just when he could have perhaps moved on to begin capturing more world records, he retired, disillusioned with the sport which appeared to have placed success before gentlemanly conduct. The British press mourned the loss of their great champion, whilst the Americans, still smarting from what they saw as underhand dealings at the Olympics, gave grudging praise. Jimmy summed it up succinctly, refusing to bow to nationalistic pride or the bitterness caused by a contentious defeat, calling him the greatest quarter-miler he had ever seen run. It wouldn't be long before he would be forced to re-assess this belief.

Chapter 8 • A Roller Skater, Two Indians, a Welshman and the Great Alfie Shrubb

Jimmy's American adventure had never been predicated on a life of toil in Pennsylvania's steel fields. Graft and grime had always been a means to an end, a stopgap, to allow him to pursue his running career. Almost immediately upon arrival on American shores he began to immerse himself in the world of east coast professional racing.

One evening he turned up at Philadelphia's Third Regiment Armory before the evening's race, which had been organised by the promoter Jack Roden, and was to feature Alfie Shrubb. On arriving at the venue Jimmy spoke to the doorman who, in turn, spoke to Roden: 'There is a skinny looking bloke outside and he says he wants to see Jock Roden – I think he means you.' Roden ventured out to meet Jimmy, who was clutching a carpet bag in one hand and a letter of introduction from Frank Morley, a *Sporting Life* journalist, in the other. 'I'm a runner', explained Jimmy in his broad accent, 'and I want a trial.' Amused at the cheek of this diminutive Scot, Roden invited him in, where he quickly proceeded to regale Shrubb with tales of the old country. Immediately taken by the young Scot, Shrubb turned to Roden and said, 'Give him a chance Jack, I think he's all right.'

Jack Roden was a fast-talking, wide-shouldered Irishman. After emigrating to America when he was barely 16 years old, he began building a pot of money from professional racing and used this to set up as a promoter. He was soon one of the most prominent on the east coast. In 1907 he brought Alfie Shrubb across the Atlantic for the first time, and utilised his skills so adeptly that Shrubb never earned less than $6,000 on this or any subsequent US trips. By the 1930s no-one in America had promoted more sporting events than Jack Roden.

And so Roden, without having seen Jimmy run, immediately entered him in a race before the Armory crowd. It was a race like no other Jimmy had ever run before; Roden knew how to please his audience, and they liked something a little unusual thrown in amongst the high quality races. Jimmy lined up against a female roller skater called Nellie Brookmeyer in a 1,000 yards race. He won, in the fast time of 2.23, picking up his first winnings in America - $15, more than a week's wage in the steel mill. The following day Jimmy worked out with Shrubb at the Point Breeze Park track. With a best mile time of 4.20 and the ability to run a half-mile in two minutes flat, he had more than enough in his tank to impress Roden, who immediately saw his great worth – he could challenge Shrubb, and few men in the world could do that. He was a marketable commodity. So Jimmy joined Roden's 'troupe', a group of athletes and novelty acts that he used to draw in crowds. A typical Roden-promoted race took place in Philadelphia in February 1908 when Jimmy ran against Al Nash, occasionally known as Blackhawk, an Indian runner out of the Carlisle Industrial School, who was variously described as a 'hustler' and 'as graceful as a deer', in a 1,000 yard race. Such races were no doubt fixed, to some extent, in order to give the crowd their money's worth. The two ran side-by-side until the finish line loomed, at which point Jimmy strode away to victory. Interestingly a big Scottish contingent came down from the Kensington area of the city, boosting the crowd to around 2,000. Had the crowd been dominated by supporters of Nash it may have led to a different result.

Another Jimmy contacted on his arrival in America was his old friend Arthur Duffey, who was soon acting as his promoter. Within weeks of his arrival, Duffey made it known, through the *Boston Herald*, that his man wanted to race the best the east coast had to offer. And if Duffey's pedigree was not enough to draw out opponents, the article also noted that Alfie Shrubb thought highly of Jimmy.

Organised athletic competition had been taking place in America since the first half of the 19th century. But support at that time was stuttering at best, and it struggled to reach the high levels of participation attained by football, baseball, and crew. When it did finally begin to gain a foothold, in the latter half of the century, it was on the back of increasing popularity in the elite English universities of Cambridge and Oxford. Perhaps naturally, given the tradition of foot-racing in Scotland, when track eventually started to gain traction it was at the Scots-founded Princeton University, where immigrants founded Caledonian Games. Slowly but surely the number of track athletics meets began to increase, led by students at the Ivy League universities. By 1894 competitions began to take on an international flavour when Yale competed against Oxford, and this laid the foundation for American participation in the first modern Olympic Games, held in Athens two years later.

The growth in cross country was not quite so seamless, and colleges struggled to maintain annual events. It had had its adherents at Harvard since the 1820s, when Dr Charles Follen would lead his students on hill runs. But it was the publication, in 1857, of Thomas Hughes' novel *Tom Brown's School Days*, featuring an early incarnation of cross country running, known variously as the 'paper chase' or 'hare and hounds', which was the catalyst for a rise in student participation in this pastime in the major east coast colleges.

Hand-in-hand with the growth in the popularity of sports came, naturally, the overwhelming desire for success. And many colleges believed the way to attain this success was through the hiring of professional coaches. Their introduction was a turning point in American sport. Professional-coached teams stood head and shoulders above their amateur-coached rivals. In 1864 Yale hired William Wood, its first professional coach, and a swathe of smaller east coast colleges, spurred on by the University's almost immediate success, followed suit. But for some the main objective of sport was simply taking part. This view was epitomised in author Caspar Whitney's assertion that the professional coach was 'the most serious menace of college sport today.' Leading the institutional fight for the retention of the amateur ethos was Harvard University. In the late 19th and early 20th centuries, Harvard was being routinely beaten at crew and football by its biggest rival, Yale; from 1884 to 1905 the two met 21 times in both crew and football –

Yale won 18 times in both sports. But still Harvard clung steadfastly to the amateur ideal, casting itself as a New World equivalent of the universities at Oxford and Cambridge. In 1905, Harvard's resolve finally gave way and Bill Reid was hired to coach its football team. And as if to assert this new-found allegiance to professionalism, Harvard decided to pay their new coach the staggering sum of $7,000 per year, twice as much as the average professor's salary, and almost as much as the college's long-serving president. In the 11 years following the hiring of Reid, Harvard won seven of the crew races against Yale. A year after Reid took up his post, he noted that if Harvard was to return to the amateur coaching era his team would be 'wiped off the field every time we compete.' And so they embraced professionalism with the fervour of a born-again, and college sport's march into the modern era was assured.

But whilst the insertion of professional coaches was grudgingly accepted, any attempts by *athletes* to insert themselves into the wider professional athletic arena were met by a phalanx of administrators whose puritanical zeal at protecting their domain could be viewed as bordering on the pathological. Jimmy, fresh from the bitter stand-off between amateurs and professionals in Scotland, had fallen headlong into an equally fractious battle between those demanding change, and those defending the status quo. At the forefront of the conflict were two men – James E. Sullivan and Arthur Duffey. When Jimmy first met Duffey in 1904 the American was still one of the finest sprinters in the world, having previously pulled up injured in the Olympic Games 100m final of 1900 and set numerous sprint records, most notably, in 1902, a world record of 9.6 seconds for the 100 yards. But on his retirement in October 1905 he admitted to having run professionally for the past seven years. Duffey's professionalism had long been suspected, indeed was even investigated – how can an amateur athlete with little discernible means afford to travel to Europe and Australasia to compete? – but never proven.

Duffey wanted change. He believed that the AAU was, at best, autocratic and, at worse, corrupt. In May 1907 he laid out his arguments at a meeting of the Protective Basketball Association of the Eastern States (PBA), an organisation set up in 1905 to 'promote and safeguard' basketball which, its members believed, was falling into disrepute due to some of the decisions made by the AAU. In a move that put it at odds with the AAU, it did not require its members to divulge their amateur or professional status. In addressing the group's second annual dinner, Duffey proceeded to rail against the AAU's apparent hypocrisy (and more specifically that of its president), which saw many of its officials employed by the Sporting Goods Trust, and required its members to wear only the apparatus of that Trust, but at the same time demanded complete amateur status for all its athletes:

> What a pitiful example is presented the American athlete when we learn that the president of a so-called amateur organization is employed by the Sporting Goods Trust. The disgusting example of a staff of athletic grafters who order you to use a certain sporting goods concern's apparatus has gone far enough.

On hearing of the threat from a rival to break up the AAU, Sullivan's reaction was to mock: 'Far be it from me to say that that association is not a good thing. It rids the AAU of a class we have been trying to keep out.'

Duffey's admission of professionalism and the threat to set up a rival organisation opened the floodgates for those favouring amateurism to launch a concerted attack, not only on Duffey's character, but also on his achievements. If the reaction of Sullivan can be taken as a bellwether, his 'crime' was at heinous levels. Sullivan spent much of his time at the AAU promoting what he considered the wide-ranging benefits of amateurism. His other favourite pastime appears to have been his penchant for vehemently denouncing the 'evils' of professionalism. He was livid at what he saw as Duffey's deceit, declared his records 'fraudulent' and, in an act that reveals much about Sullivan's character, had Duffey's times expunged from the AAU record books. Indeed, Duffey was effectively removed from the history of amateur athletics when, in a 1938 booklet celebrating the 50th anniversary of the AAU, he does not deign a mention despite being the premier sprinter of the late 19th and early 20th centuries. As the spat between the two continued, Sullivan began liaising with other organisations in America, Britain and Australia to enquire whether they too would remove his records. And if the removal of Duffey's records was not enough to sate Sullivan's vindictiveness, the AAU began investigating whether or not legal action could be taken. The 'seal of amateur condemnation' had been placed on Duffey.

He was not, however, the type of man to buckle under the barrage of criticism and meekly accept his fate as an outcast. Initially he fought back in print, and the following year in the courts. But Duffey's aim was not simply to poke, prod, and annoy the AAU. He intended to challenge its hegemony. He set out to form an organisation similar to the PBA which would oversee athletics but, unlike the AAU, put professional and amateur athletes on an equal footing. He called on fellow professionals for support. As someone who was working closely with Duffey at this time, and had experience of running in both the amateur and professional ranks, it made sense for Jimmy to lend his voice. He also had nothing to lose – he had no intention of running in amateur races, and any subsequent press would highlight the fact that this top Scottish athlete was in America and looking for races. On 21st January 1908 Duffey, Jimmy, and others met in Philadelphia to discuss the setting up of the National Protective Athletic Association (NPAA). Jimmy spoke to the assembled group, arguing that the creation of the NPAA would encourage athletes from Great Britain, both amateur and professional, to visit the United States for competition. Many British athletes, he noted, would relish the opportunity to test themselves against the finest runners in America. But Jimmy was being somewhat disingenuous. While the opportunity to challenge oneself against quality athletes may have added a little spice to the idea of crossing the Atlantic, it was by no means the primary reason. The single most important factor for athletes was, quite simply, financial reward. For men capable of putting on the best athletic shows huge pots, ranging from around $10 to hundreds of dollars, were available. Jimmy knew he didn't have Alfie Shrubb's ability, but that was irrelevant. There was no benefit from Shrubb beating his opponents with no fight. What the crowd wanted was a close run thing, where Shrubb had to dig deep. Athletes capable of competing with Shrubb, at least for part of a race, could command substantial sums of money. Jimmy fit the bill.

In January 1908 Frank Kanaly accepted a challenge from Jimmy to race anywhere between 1,000 yards and one mile, with each man putting in between $500 and $1,000. Kanaly plumped for 1,000 yards for $1,000 for the winner. The race was set for June, but it is unknown whether it actually happened. Later in the year, Al Nash, the Indian runner, who was another acting as a promoter for Jimmy, made it known in the *Boston Herald* that he wished to set up a half-mile race between his man and either Frank Kanaly or Bart Sullivan, or a mile race with Samuel Myers. Both runners were to receive between $250 and $500.

Jimmy's first known serious race in the United States, on 16th January at Boston's Park Square Coliseum, was organised by Duffey. There was no attempt to continue the charade of running under a pseudonym, and G. Gordon disappeared, never to return. Jimmy once again lined up under his real name. He was the fourth man in a relay team to take on Shrubb in a 10-mile race. Shrubb was so dominant that promoters were forced to put him up against relay teams in order to create a competitive race. Still he won most of his races. And this occasion was by no means different; he won the race by five laps. Jimmy, however, more than held his own, taking 50 yards out of Shrubb's lead. A week later the two lined up against each other once again, this time in Philadelphia in a six-mile race. As the second runner in a four-man relay team Jimmy initially fell behind, but came back strongly and, as he passed over to the third runner, was ahead, the only one of the four runners to best Shrubb. But the other runners didn't have Jimmy's talents and Shrubb again won by five laps (wearing only tennis shoes).

With a settled job and no family commitments, other than sending money back to Scotland, Jimmy was free to attend race meetings, and compete against the best runners in the country, and sometimes the world, for cash prizes. In the following years he would travel around the east coast, mainly in Philadelphia, New York and around New Jersey, with an occasional foray north to Boston.

His showing against Shrubb brought with it much-needed exposure, highlighting his significant talents to east coast promoters and laying the foundation for a busy athletic year. Conversely it meant that the handicappers were now fully aware of his talents, and this became apparent on 22nd February at Philadelphia's Third Regiment Armory when he ran off scratch in the one mile race against a big field which included the well-regarded Indians Al Nash and Tall Feather, as well as two lightweight boxers in Jack Cottman and Jack Blackburn. His nearest opponent at the start was running off 25 yards. The result is unknown, but clearly Jimmy had his work cut out if he was to make a sizeable profit.

Races were limited during the spring months, but, as the summer racing season began, Jimmy starred in some races for Jack Roden's touring athletes. The first was in Tamaqua, and this time it was Al Nash who raced a local skater, while Jimmy took on, and beat, Tall Feather in a 1,000 yards race. Next he headed to Mahanoy City, and then to Washington Park on 26th and Allegheny Avenue in Philadelphia for his first outdoor race since arriving in America. He would compete here several times over the next few months. With a crowd of 3,000 looking on he started a strong favourite, after a rumour, albeit false, circulated, perhaps as a means of influencing the betting odds, that he had not lost a half-mile race in five years. He lined up in the mile and half-mile races, easily winning the longer race and finishing a close second in the other.

Over the next month he took part in a number of events at Washington Park, competing against the two Indians Al Nash and Tall Feather, the Welshman Percy Smallwood, as well as George Seaman, Bobby Hallen, Frank Kanaly, and Billy Paull, all vying for bragging rights and financial glory. He had a reputation to live up to – one newspaper called him 'the best that Scotland ever turned out at the middle distances.' He walked away from four race meetings with at least four wins and two second places. How much he won is unknown, but it was likely substantial; at one meet when he was twice beaten into second place he ended the day $20 richer.

On 29th August, at the Annual Games of the Journeymen Bricklayers, held at Washington Park before a crowd of 5,000, Jimmy ran in two races, both of which included two of his frequent opponents – Paull and Nash. In the mile Jimmy entered the final lap 50 yards behind Paull. All appeared lost until Jimmy put in an incredible burst of speed. But it wasn't enough and Paull crossed the line a few inches ahead. In the half-mile, the best race of the day according to the *Philadelphia Inquirer*, a spurt by Jimmy on the final straight beat out Paull by roughly the same distance he had lost by in the earlier race. He returned home with $13 prize money.

On 7th September, Labor Day, Jimmy began a hectic day at Hill's Grove in Trenton, taking part in a 120-yard sprint and a one mile race. He won one of the sprint heats, but lost out in the semi-final. In the mile he defeated Billy Paull for a large purse of $50. After the race he and Paull made their way south, along the Delaware River, to White City to take part in a 10-lap, two mile race. The evening start, demanded by the two runners in order that they could compete earlier in the day at Hill's Grove, meant that it was run under electric lighting. Running off scratch, both men reeled in the rest of the field and were neck-and-neck until the last 10 yards, when Jimmy pulled away to take the purse of $15, making it a profitable day.

Five days later Jimmy was at Fairmount Park in Philadelphia to take on Alfie Shrubb in a mile race, the first time the pair were to meet head-to-head outside a relay. But Shrubb's main race was the five mile, and with a new world record on the cards, the crowd swelled to at least 15,000, the vast majority of whom were there to see Shrubb. Feeling conditions were in his favour to oblige the crowd, Shrubb withdrew from the mile. Jimmy finished third of four runners. In the five mile race Shrubb shaved two seconds off the world record.

Jimmy's exhausting racing schedule was briefly interrupted when he was finally reconciled with Janet and Mary who, at the end of September, arrived in New York on the SS *Furnessia*. After less than a year apart, the family was reunited. His running successes had clearly been profitable – the pair travelled second class, thus avoiding the most invasive immigration tests. Unlike Jimmy's first foray to America, however, the family did not head for the house of another. Jimmy was renting a property at 1583 Ogden Street in Philadelphia, only three miles from Franklin Field.

But the year still held two more races for Jimmy. The first was at the Tri-State Field in Trenton on 26th November, when Jimmy took on New York's Bobby Hallen as part of a three-race card that included Alfie Shrubb against Percy Smallwood. The result of Jimmy's race is unknown, but as soon as the card was complete the four caught a train to Philadelphia, where they took part in their third relay of the year. Joined by Percy Wharton, and on a heavy and hilly course over eight miles, the four men each ran two miles and gave Shrubb the toughest race he had faced in America. Still he won out.

The year had begun with Jimmy in the doldrums. Out of work and with a massive downturn in the economy, any chance of turning his American adventure into a success seemed a remote possibility. But early in 1908 he had secured a job that offered a steady wage and distinct opportunity for career progression. And simultaneously his success on the track marked him out as one of the first runners promoters turned to when they needed to fill an undercard. And to attract him were substantial cash offers.

THE GREAT ALFIE SHRUBB

Jimmy's first event of 1909 took place on 11th February in Philadelphia's Third Regiment Armory before a crowd of around 2,000; a 1,000 yards race against Al Nash. This was a curtain raiser for a 12 miler between Percy Smallwood and Dorando Pietro, the latter being a massive draw after his controversial disqualification from the Olympic Marathon in 1908 after crossing the line first. Pietro triumphed in the main event after Smallwood withdrew mid-race. Jimmy took the honours in the race against Nash, with a fast time of 2.30. Two weeks later the pair repeated the race in the same venue, with Jimmy once again walking away the winner.

What followed was one of the busiest racing periods of Jimmy's time in America. On 5th March Jimmy stood on the start line of a dirt track built within the smoke-filled 69th Regiment Armory in Manhattan. In what was, for him, an unusually long race of five miles, and warming the crowd up for a marathon with a massive prize of $1,000, Jimmy lined up against six others including his old adversary, Percy Smallwood. Sitting in behind Smallwood, with half a mile to run, he burst into the lead and won by 50 yards in a time of just under 29 minutes, taking home $50 in the process.

Three days later he and Smallwood teamed up. The Celtic duo, competing as a Scottish-Welsh team, lined up against 27 international two-man teams in a six-day race at Madison Square Garden, with only one of the men running at any one time. The total prize money was $5,000, with $1,500 going to the winners. In the two hours leading up to the race, a band played in the clay and cinder track's central area. At five minutes past midnight, Jimmy cruised from the start line as the gun was fired by the actor William Collier Sr. The two started well, and by the end of the ninth hour were in second place. But the end was nigh; Jimmy was 'seized with cramps' and the pair pulled out at the end of the tenth hour. It is possible they were simply there to make up the numbers and had no intention of finishing the race.

Two days later, Jimmy made his way to the Essex Troop Armory in Newark. He ran in another five mile race, which preceded the main event of Dorando Pietro against Bobby Hallen and Samuel Myers over 12 miles. He finished third. The following day he returned to the Garden. Interspersed throughout the six-day race were a number of smaller events, aimed at boosting the crowd. Jimmy took part in two of these. The first was a relay with Jack Sapsford, against Hallen. Sapsford ran the first two miles and was two laps down as he passed over to Jimmy, who reined in 30 yards. It wasn't enough and Hallen won by almost two laps. Next was a two-mile handicap race against Smallwood and Ettore Ferri, and running off scratch Jimmy took first place. But so many distance races in such a small period of time took its toll. He strained the ligaments in both his calves and would not see action again for three months.

Jimmy was never one to allow such constraints to bring him down. Curious as to whether the handicappers in Scotland still rated him, he began entering himself into races back across the ocean, albeit with no intention of actually taking part. The results no doubt pleased him. Most of these were New Year races at Powderhall, where, much to his delight, he was placed on scratch in most races.

But if, upon his return from injury, his opponents expected him to reduce his schedule, they were sorely mistaken. With his ligaments fully healed, Jimmy made his comeback in early June at the annual Scottish Games of the Northeast Burns Club. As the sound of bagpipes skirled across Philadelphia's Central Park, and girls competed in Highland dancing competitions, Jimmy beat Al Nash in a close mile race.

In early July he took part in Philadelphia's Irish Games, winning both the mile and half-mile races. A fortnight later he moved on to White City, an amusement park just outside Philadelphia. In a 1,000 yard race he started 25 yards behind the Indian runner Tall Feather and after reeling in yard after yard passed him in the home stretch to win in 2.25. In the two mile relay he teamed up with a runner called J.D. Murphy to defeat Tall Feather and his partner.

And the races continued to pile up. The following weekend he headed to New York where he won another mile race, but finished third in the 440 yards, behind fellow Scottish trainer Lawson Robertson in his maiden professional run. The defeat, however, was a blip. A week later he ran in three races at the Loom Fixers' Games in Gloucester City, New Jersey, walking away with first places in the mile, half-mile and 1,000 yards, beating out Tall Feather in all three of the races.

On 14th August, at the Foresters of America event in Philadelphia, before a large crowd of 5,000, he captured the one mile from his old rival Tall Feather, and even found time to place third in the potato race. By 6th September, when Jimmy took part in the New York Caledonian Club's games, he hadn't lost a mile or half-mile race all year. With the mile race being the last of the year he was aware that a win would see him go the year undefeated in his two main events. He strode to an easy victory.

Jimmy's 1908 season had been impressive. Where a result is known, he won eight out of 14 half-mile to two-mile races. But the following year he took his running to a different level, with 12 wins and only two losses – both these losses being outwith his preferred half-mile to two miles distances. On his arrival in America in 1907 he had been a virtual unknown. Two years later promoters were falling over themselves to attract him to their events, secure in the knowledge that the paying audience would be witnessing one of the finest runners on the east coast, if not the world.

Chapter 9 • Mercersburg

Making the transition from great athlete to great coach does not always prove an easy task, a point adequately proven each and every year in professional sports worldwide; the careers of former players littering the coaching fields of the world. And even in Jimmy's day this was the case. Alfie Shrubb, who can reasonably lay claim to being the greatest runner of all time, coached Oxford University Athletics Club after his retirement, but after some years in charge was considered 'useless' and eventually sacked. Alvin Kraenzlein, quadruple Olympic gold medallist, also struggled to make the transition, and his time at Mercersburg Academy was patchy at best.

Only time would prove if Jimmy had the talent to become a coach, but his commitment to the cause was soon beyond doubt. One story, apocryphal or otherwise, is of the day the Carlisle Indians travelled to Philadelphia to play the University of Pennsylvania at football. The day before the game, Mike Murphy lamented the fact that the only way to stop the Indians was to stop Jim Thorpe, the Indians' halfback, who would go on to win Olympic gold medals in pentathlon and decathlon, and is widely considered one of America's greatest-ever athletes. Jimmy took Murphy at his word and, early in the game, with Thorpe tearing up the sideline, he grabbed a water bucket and made to take him out. Jimmy was held back before any damage could be done. Jimmy was undoubtedly embellishing the story for effect – as one of Jimmy's athletes, Jef Evans, put it, 'Thorpe would have crushed the bucket and Jimmy too without losing his stride.' But it was the first widely-told story in a life of stories that cemented his place as a legend amongst those who knew him.

Jimmy spent 1908 learning his trade with both the track and cross country teams, soaking up the knowledge of Murphy and his coaches, Mike 'Doc' Dee and George Orton. For two years he bided his time, waiting patiently for an opportunity. It came in October 1909. With the intercollegiate cross country championships approaching in Boston, Orton, the team's coach, passed the reins over to Jimmy. Before Boston, chances arose for Jimmy's team to prove itself in races at Mercersburg and Haverford. A freshman team was sent to the former and, despite low expectations, they stormed to victory, much to the surprise of Mike Murphy. Less than a week later an embarrassing defeat was inflicted on Haverford and the prospects for success at Boston were good. Jimmy had repaid Murphy's confidence in both training and competition, and his successes had not escaped Murphy's attention. The team travelled to Beantown in a weakened state, with captain Billy Paull missing, and the result was a poor performance.

By autumn 1910, Jimmy had served under Murphy and Dee for three years. And then a chain of events left a door open. The resignation of Val Flood as track coach at Princeton saw Keene Fitzpatrick resign as coach at the University of Michigan to replace him. Fitzpatrick's place was filled by former Olympic champion Alvin Kraenzlein, leaving vacant the coaching post at Mercersburg Academy, a preparatory school in southern Pennsylvania. Murphy had always worked closely with the coaches at Mercersburg. Indeed, he had trained both Kraenzlein and his predecessor, Johnny Mack, in their running days. And he was aware that getting his own man into the school would have a knock-on benefit for his University of Pennsylvania team, as athletes passed from school to university. In effect, he wanted Mercersburg to become a feeder school for the University.

But in order for this to happen, Murphy needed Kraenzlein's place filled by someone he trusted, someone who could nurture raw athletes and ready them for college athletics, specifically his University of Pennsylvania programme. On top of this, Murphy was a man known for returning favours, so much so that his friends called him the 'reciprocity kid' – just months before, he had been instrumental in Mike Dee being offered the post of trainer at the Philadelphia Phillies baseball team.

To be recommended for a coaching post was not, however, simply a case of working under Murphy and putting in the time. Murphy needed to know that anyone he recommended could be trusted to properly nurture the hundreds of young boys under his charge. He would tell those he refused to recommend: 'Knowing about athletics is not everything a coach ought to possess.' They had to be able to 'show something', to display an intelligence that would allow them to interact with athletes across the emotional spectrum, from the modest to the egotistical, from the passive to the aggressive. In Jimmy, Murphy saw this quality. He was accepted into the inner circle – that group of coaches and trainers, at the very core of which was Murphy, a coterie of Massachusetts-born men such as 'Pooch' and 'Piper' Donovan, Johnny Mack, Keene Fitzpatrick, Jack Moakley, Bernie Wefers, and a handful of others. To gain the acceptance of the core group hugely increased one's chances of gaining employment as a coach at one of the top prep schools or universities. But this was not an 'old boys' club' – subsequent events at Mercersburg would prove that Murphy was as adept at discerning talent in coaches as he was at discerning it in young athletes.

Approached by the headmaster at the Academy, Dr William Mann Irvine, he recommended his protégé, Jimmy Curran. Irvine was fully aware of Murphy's standing in the sport, and that any recommendation would be well thought out and beneficial to both parties. And so, on the back of it, Irvine offered Jimmy the role of head coach on a salary of $700 a year, plus a house. Jimmy didn't have to think twice. He snapped up the opportunity to take the step up. His role would be to take raw, untested schoolboys and turn them into athletes capable of competing against the very best the east coast's prep schools could throw up, and to build within the boys, athletes and otherwise, a strong moral fibre and character that would guide them in later years. Many years later he would recall the appointment as the outstanding event of his life.

Mercersburg Academy was a young school, founded in 1893, having been formed out of an earlier college. But it was no backwater institution where Jimmy would tumble into a well of obscurity. In 17 years it had risen to become one of the premier prep schools in the country, and it used its athletics programme to attract the progeny of America's elite families, with one reporter calling it 'the Oxford of America.' The sons of presidents and industrialists walked its lawns like the sons of kings and queens walked the lawns of Eton.

The school placed great stock in athletics, considering it a central tenet of its teaching programme. 'The pursuit of athletic prowess' it was noted 'rounds out the full development of a man. Striving to improve his record the Mercersburg boy plays hard, clean, and fair to establish a record commensurate with that of his predecessors.' But whilst there is little doubt that there was a desire within the school for a rounded educational experience, it also ran a scholarship programme, albeit a discreet one, bringing outstanding athletes from less affluent backgrounds to the school, where they would be educated for a reduced fee, and in return represent the school in their chosen sport. As a result, the school began to produce some of the finest young athletes in America. By early century, guided by the legendary coach Johnny Mack, the school was becoming virtually unbeatable at cross country and on the track, rivals getting used to trailing in behind this new athletics powerhouse as athlete after athlete lifted honours in the school's blue and white uniform. The 1903 season ended with wins at Yale, Princeton and Pennsylvania, and two world interscholastic hurdles records for Robert G. Leavitt, who would later go on to win a gold medal in the 110m hurdles at the 1906 Intercalated Olympic Games. Equally good seasons were recorded up to 1907, when the former Olympic gold medallist Alvin Kraenzlein took over from Mack. Kraenzlein lasted only three years before leaving to take up the coaching post at the University of Michigan.

On arriving in town, the expanding Curran family – their second child Ellen, born on Jimmy's birthday, was not yet a year old – moved into a property called the Justice William Smith House (known locally as the Smith House), an impressive property on North Main Street, best known as the birthplace of the second amendment. Jimmy was now free to focus his energies on his new post.

It was an opportune time to arrive, with William Mann Irvine intent on rapidly expanding the school. Just one year after Jimmy took up his post, the building of a new gymnasium was underway, with a new running track opening, just to the south of it, two years later. It was a time of change for both coach and school. The partnership would flourish quicker than either imagined.

*****

Since his discovery of Wyndham Halswelle in 1902, Jimmy had been involved in training athletes in some form for almost a decade. In his early years, the techniques he employed to help an athlete to progress were based purely on what worked for him, and from watching others in action. But it was the input of men such as Murphy and Dee, from 1908 onwards, which saw his education formalised. From them, students of the history of athletic training, came a century of knowledge and understanding.

In 1813 Walter Thom, a Scottish journalist, noted the age-old reliance of athletes on a good diet, temperance, celibacy, fresh air, massage, regular evacuation of the bowels, and how these should be employed by the modern athlete. In the following decades, others latched on to these types of ideas and produced a wealth of material detailing how an athlete should train and treat his body to extract the optimum performances from it.

But by the end of the 19th century an in-depth dissection of training had still to happen. This changed in 1897 with the publication of Randolph Faries' *Practical Training for Athletics, Health and Pleasure*. Faries was the Director of Physical Education at the University of Pennsylvania and he gave a sweeping exposition of how an athlete should prepare, both physically and technically, in order to achieve his maximum potential. His insight into how to condition the body far exceeded previous works, focussing not only on the preparatory aspects of conditioning but also injury prevention and treatment. He covered many of the issues touched on by his predecessors but went much further, delving into the deepest recesses of an athlete's life – sleeping, bathing, even skin care – as a means of helping him achieve his full potential.

Murphy read works like those by Thom and Faries and used them as a foundation upon which to build his own understanding. In 1913 his *Athletic Training*, the final pages of which were relayed to his editor whilst he lay on his deathbed, was published. None of those who had previously championed athletic conditioning in print carried the gravitas and respect afforded Murphy by his peers. Widely accepted as the finest athletic trainer in America, he took all his years of first-hand experience and knowledge and wrote a book that transformed the way athletics was approached. He described, in intricate detail, how each event should be approached technically and, although not as wide ranging as the work by Faries, he also placed great weight on just how an athlete should treat his body in order to fully augment the technical aspects of the sport.

But many coaches still baulked at pushing athletes to their limit. By the late 19th century many physicians, coaches and trainers, informed by the arguments of men such as Benjamin Ward Richardson and Friedrich Wilhelm Beneke, believed that those who trained excessively left themselves susceptible to what would later be termed 'athletic heart' – cardiac hypertrophy – which weakened the organ beyond repair, occasionally leading to premature death. In 1899, studies by Eugene Darling at Harvard and Salomon Henschen, a Swedish physician, argued that the 'athletic heart' was indeed a medical condition – the heart did expand with training – but noted that this was not a life-threatening occurrence. Although scepticism in the Darling and Henschen theories persisted – as late as 1927 Austrian physicians Felix Deutsch and Emil Kauf noted that 'athletics brings about changes in the heart in a not inconsiderable number of cases which, in the present state of our knowledge cannot be looked upon as harmless' – support was forthcoming, and one of these supporters was Mike Murphy. 'The dangers of the so-called athletic heart', argued Murphy, 'have been terribly exaggerated.' So, whilst some around him clung stubbornly to antiquated ideas that had been all but debunked by science, Murphy forged ahead and thought through the arguments, instituting his own exhaustive studies in which he worked with 'one of the most famous heart and lung specialists in the United States', measuring the hearts of athletes and non-athletes after a period of intense athletic activity. Murphy's conclusion was one where scientific findings took precedence over age-old thinking based on spurious evidence – hard training had no detrimental effect on the heart, and indeed strengthened it. He was an innovator, employing pragmatism where others remained chained to the ways of the past, like a physician practising modern medicine whilst those around him clung stubbornly to the four humours.

Murphy's place at the summit of the coaching pyramid was forged by advances he made in athletics training that fundamentally altered how events were approached. It is said that he was the first to introduce the crouching start and passed it to Charles Sherrill (although Sherrill himself claimed its invention, as did a number of other sprinters). The crouching start measurably reduced athletes' times. But most advances were small. The difference between success and failure on the athletics track, especially in short races, is often tenths, sometimes even hundredths, of a second, or in the days before finishing line technology, the width of a vest. Many athletes, at schools such as Mercersburg, had never run track before and could quickly make huge improvements to their personal bests. But once they were running at a good level, the extra seconds, or even tenths or hundredths of a second, were difficult to find.

To shave them off, far-sighted coaches such as Murphy began to move beyond the basics of an athlete's start, his arm movement, his breathing and the range of other technical aspects that took the raw teenager to competent athlete, to bore down into the specifics that were, at the time, considered virtually irrelevant. He began to consider the notion that athletes should not be viewed as a homologous group that would slot into a generic training regimen, but individuals who required to be treated in isolation. All around him coaches struggled to shake off antediluvian training regimes and diets that varied little between sprinter and middle-distance runner, between football and baseball players. Murphy baulked at this. Surely, he concluded, it is ridiculous to attempt to create a single regime that encompasses a sprinter and a miler. Indeed, even the regimes of two sprinters should differ. And so, Murphy's athletes were studied in order to ascertain a bespoke training and dietary regime tailored to that individual, aimed at building on his strengths and addressing his weaknesses.

And where a trend could not be held up to scrutiny, Murphy was quite often at the forefront of those attempting to buck it. At a time when coaches were determined to force their best players to stay on the field until the bitter end, regardless of whether they were injured or not, Murphy saw the bigger picture – physically exhausted players were far more susceptible to injury than fresh ones, and so weakening a team during a match actually increased a team's chance of success over the course of a season. And when players did sprain an ankle or pull a muscle, Murphy rigged up ingenious 'athletic paraphernalia and devices' to aid his men, such as a liniment that he went on to sell through Spalding & Bros, and elastic bandages.

But the academic dissection of training was a learning process and outlandish ideas and errors of judgement were part of that process. Randolph Faries noted that 'profanity is [a] bad habit that interferes with physical as well as mental harmony.' George W. Orton, a Canadian steeplechase gold medallist in the 1900 Olympics and trainer at the University of Pennsylvania, warned that athletes should avoid masturbation at all costs. This 'self-abuse', he argued figuratively, would be 'fatal.' Even the great Mike Murphy succumbed to the occasional bizarre thought on training, advising any athlete running in cold weather to 'protect the chest with a piece of newspaper or brown wrapping paper.' And Jimmy was by no means immune from outlandish and frivolous ideas, arguing that one shouldn't stay in the shower for too long as it has a weakening effect. He also subscribed to the widely-held theory that the speed of black runners could in part be attributed to long heel bones. When asked what was the secret to the success of Allen Woodring, a white runner, he attributed it to 'the shape of his foot. He has a long heel which gave leverage to the muscles of his leg ... it gave him a long stride.'

*****

The foundation of Jimmy's career at Mercersburg was his ability to look beyond the barely discernible talents of new athletes, to scrape beneath the surface and find a boy with the makings of a sprinter, middle-distance runner, jumper, or weights man. Whilst Jimmy was able to headhunt a handful of athletes each year, the majority were chosen from those who were enrolled at the school. The selection of talent from the annual group of freshmen was made at the school's Field Day, held annually in November. The students would compete for the Williams Cup, awarded to the best all-round athlete, but for Jimmy it was about unearthing boys who, in many cases, were not aware of their own talents. In 1915 Elmer Smith arrived as a sprinter. But Jimmy detected something that Smith himself apparently could not, and, displaying what one reporter called 'the wizard's tip', moved him up to the 440 and 880 yards, where he would prove a standout athlete. Larry Lattomus, who would run for Jimmy in the 1950s, noted how Jimmy worked out what his natural distance would be:

> One day he called me over and told me to run one full lap, 440 yards. My usual distances were 60, 100, 220, and 300 yards. When I got ready and he had his stopwatch, I lined up and as I started I noticed there were several teammates spread out 25, 50, 75 and 100 yards in front of me. Later I learned he wanted

to see if I could catch up and pass them. Afterward he said, "Larry, you might consider the quarter-mile as your race." He was right, of course!

Lester Cagle had a similar experience when Jimmy was trying to work out which event to place him in. Aware that Cagle had been a quality high jumper in high school, Jimmy had him run a 110m high hurdles. As he crossed the line, Jimmy looked at his stopwatch and a 'quizzical' look came across his face. He asked Cagle to do it again, 'fast as you can.' As the youngster crossed the line for a second time, Jimmy told him, 'that was two tenths off the school record. You're my high hurdler.'

Once he had built a nucleus of athletes, he set out bespoke training regimes aimed at improving their technique and physical conditioning. He would begin working on an athlete's technique as soon as he arrived at the school, passing on tips about how to start, how to breathe, how to pace oneself, how to run on one's toes, and how to run through the line, placing emphasis on each as required. In the 1911/12 season Albert Robinson's slow start was addressed with daily drills. A decade later Frank Conway was 'a notoriously weak finisher' when he arrived at Mercersburg; Jimmy improved him to such an extent that he was soon capable of running a 49 second quarter-mile, and in the months leading up to the 1924 Olympics defeated that event's star performer, Eric Liddell. In the 1950s, Henry Thresher arrived as a raw 17-year old. Jimmy set in place a program to work on his weaknesses – his start, arm movement, and breathing techniques. And a long jumper called Andy Anderson was told, 'don't spring for distance, spring for height.' He went on to become one of the school's finest-ever athletes. Jimmy's relay teams were always recipients of his knowledge. According to Paul White, a sprinter in Jimmy's 1960/61 team, he would 'not only ... stress the importance of speed in the relay, but more importantly, the mechanics of the baton handoff and the ultimate meaning of teamwork. We practiced with the same sprinters, again and again, perfecting our speed and handoffs within the 20 yard exchange zone.' This relentless baton hand-off practice was something also noted by Larry Lattomus, who added that Jimmy would not accept 'sloppiness.' Indeed, in his desire to instil how much he hated batons being dropped, he would tell students, somewhat harshly, that, 'it is better to die in infancy than to drop the baton.'

There *were* those who felt he hadn't been as great a help to them. Charles Hill, a cross country runner at Cornell in the 1950s, bemoaned Jimmy's use of him on the track team rather than cross country. 'I'm convinced' he argued 'that the experience I could have gotten as a schoolboy [cross country runner] would have been of great help today.' And Bob Batdorf, a high quality weights man, felt that 'the only time he gave me advice was to put the shot higher! I liked him, but he knew nothing about the throwing events.' Batdorf went further, noting that he believed Jimmy was 'living off laurels from his early years. The athletes during my time there trained themselves.' But by and large the feeling about Jimmy's training techniques was overwhelmingly positive.

So respected was Jimmy's understanding of training methods and technique, and how to utilise them in order to extract rapid improvement, that he was almost certainly involved in the authorship of a mid-1920s athletics training booklet called *Middle Distance and Relay Racing* produced as part of the *Spalding's Athletic Library*. Officially it was written by Ted Meredith, but in all likelihood Meredith provided the name, whilst Jimmy offered his previous charge the benefit of his knowledge. This standing as an unofficial trainers' trainer, of sorts, is further proven in the 1940s when Roberta Ranck Bonniwell, coach of the female athletics team, the Turner Maids, adopted Jimmy's relay technique which required the baton receiver to face the inside of the track. And his intimate knowledge of relay technique is given further weight when we learn of an exchange with two of his relay runners. Having trouble passing the baton, they informed Jimmy they would pass from right hand to right hand, rather than left to right. 'You'll get spiked' said Jimmy. After the race one of the athletes sought out their mentor and told him 'you were right,' as he displayed his wounds.

But Jimmy was not one to limit himself to training minutiae. He was more than happy to occupy himself with answering bigger athletic questions. In 1942 he laid out how he would train an athlete to run the four-minute mile. Track coaches, he argued, had to re-evaluate their training regimes. Rather than alternating mile runners between speed and distance work, they should be trained to run three quarters of a mile. Only when they dipped below three minutes would they have the tools to break the four-minute mile. Jimmy thought it unlikely that the four-minute barrier could be broken. It would be only 12 years before Roger Bannister would prove him wrong.

So great was his reputation that top athletes called on him to act as a personal trainer. When the Scottish athlete Syd Williams travelled to the US in 1912, to race Billy Queal and Hans Holmer, it was to Jimmy he turned. And Jack Green, whilst aiming to qualify for the 1932 Olympics, was taken under the wing of Jimmy during that year's Easter break.

But perfect form would almost certainly be for nought if an athlete did not treat his body with respect. Jimmy's over-riding mantra was simple: 'When I'm not with you, you need to be sensible – treat your body and mind with respect.' His training regime consisted of a number of central tenets. Foremost was his strident belief that an athlete's performance would be affected, advantageously or adversely, by what he ingested. An athlete was dependant on his body. If he abused that body it would fail him when put under pressure.

Food, he told his athletes, should be chewed thoroughly, and shouldn't be eaten too fast, in order to allow the stomach to rest, and as a means of avoiding the dreaded stitch that affected so many athletes. From his early years Jimmy created designated training tables for athletes in the Commons area, where they would eat three times a day. He would sit with athletes and ensure they were sticking to their set diet. And don't smoke, he continued. Tobacco is hurtful to the body; it inflames the linings of the nose, throat and lungs, making them dry and causing short-windedness, it injures the heart, damaging blood corpuscles and interferes with the absorption of oxygen into the bloodstream, and it impacts digestion, causing upset stomach.

Despite an ever-increasing knowledge about the benefits and ills of what one ingested, many athletes failed to pay heed. On a trip to England in the early 20th century Arthur Duffey could not conceal his amazement at the attitude taken to tobacco, noting that English athletes 'smoke continuously while training. They do not believe in denying themselves such fancies.' But if some European runners refused to change their lifestyle, others placed great emphasis on doing just that. In 1913 Hannes Kolehmainen, the Finnish distance runner, in America to compete in a series of athletics events, outlined to a reporter his precise daily routine – his early rise and walk, how he cooked his own food, his wearing of women's stockings to keep his muscles warm, and how he brought his own rubber with him.

But a strong, athletic body was not the only requirement of the top athlete. 'A boy does not necessarily have to be big and strong', explained Jimmy, sounding decidedly like a preacher. 'The essential necessity for every fellow who someday hopes to develop into a strong and vigorous man,' he proclaimed to a group of Academy boys, 'is a clean mind. There are many men whose minds are so degraded, that they fell to the wayside of life before thirty.' It is unclear exactly what a 'clean mind' entailed, but Jimmy offered up athlete-turned-evangelist Billy Sunday as an example that the boys should aspire to.

Jimmy had long been an adherent to the belief that a fit athlete will almost always run faster and longer than an unfit one. So he instituted a training system of long runs to build stamina. As he had in his Gala Harriers days, he would pace the runs himself. But he made certain not to work the boys *too* hard. His faith in their ability was such that he felt one of the greatest threats to their success was not their opponents, but over-training. He had learned not to push his athletes too hard from Mike Murphy who, in 1895, before the International Games between the New York Athletic Club and the London Athletic

Club, rested the high jumper Michael Sweeney for three days before the event. When the time came to compete, 'he was so full of ginger he could hardly stand still' and jumped to a new world record height. Gus Ormrod, an athlete in one of Jimmy's teams from the late 1940s, would later recall that Jimmy 'never wanted his boys to leave their best time in a time trial.' Before one meet, as the boys were in full flow, he wrapped up the session early, telling them they were in great shape. 'Saturday', recalled Ormrod, 'we were like roaring lions. The other team didn't stand a chance.'

And this belief in the recuperative power of resting the body carried over into race days. As well as urging his athletes to sleep for eight hours each night, he had them nap between races at meets, an early incarnation of a technique that would later gain prominence as 'transcendental meditation' and the 'relaxation response.' He had employed this technique with Wyndham Halswelle at the 1903 Port Elizabeth New Year's Day Sports, and he was still using it almost 60 years later, at the tail end of his career. Sprinter Paul White later recalled:

> [Jimmy] actually trained me to lie down under the bleachers and rest (take a nap!) between events, which sometimes added up to 3-5 per meet. He perfected the response so that I would reduce my heart rate and wake up unassisted and refreshed after 10 minutes. This system helped me through many stressful meets.

But taking a boy from raw, untested youngster to high-achieving athlete is not simply a case of working on his athletic technique, or conditioning him to a point where he is fitter than any opponents. Of equal importance is an athlete's psychology. By the late 20th century the benefits of sports psychology were well known and for teams and individuals they were an accepted and necessary part of sporting life. In 2015 the British swimmers Rebecca Adlington and Mark Foster discussed the importance of the sports psychologist. Adlington noted having 'used a sports psychologist throughout my career, and I wouldn't have been able to carry on without him', whilst Foster argued that 'you can have the best body in the world, the most fit body and fastest body in the world, but if your mind's not right at the same time, that's when things go wrong.' But 100 years previously psychology in sport was, at best, a burgeoning idea. Studies on the effect of the mind on sporting achievement took place from the late 19th century, but were few and far between. In 1898, Norman Triplett wrote a paper outlining how the introduction of a pacemaker could enhance sporting performance. But it wasn't until the post-First World War period that academics began to place far greater emphasis on the importance of the mind on sporting achievement. In 1920 Robert Werner Schulte founded the Deutsch Hochschule für Leibesübungen (German University of Physical Education) which had its own psychology laboratory. And the next few years saw intensive study by Coleman Griffith, now recognised as the father of sports psychology. Theirs was an exceedingly complicated science, but paradoxically it revolved around a simple premise – if two athletes of equal ability faced one another, the one who was best prepared, not just technically and physically, but also mentally, would almost always emerge victorious.

Jimmy's mentors subscribed heart and soul to the belief that an athlete's state of mind had a hugely positive impact on the quality of his performance. Mike Murphy was, according to his colleague Robert Tait Mackenzie, 'a combination of a professor of applied psychology and an evangelist.' Mike Dee was equally supportive of the benefits of psychology. The rubbing of joints, he argued, was hugely important to an athlete's conditioning, but it had to be utilised in conjunction with getting an athlete in 'the proper frame of mind.' Their embrace of the powers of sporting psychology did not fail to rub off on Jimmy. From his first days at Mercersburg he was ahead of the curve in the techniques he employed to help his athletes squeeze every extra second or inch out of their performance. Jimmy's opening mantra was simple: 'Don't worry about [your physical condition]. Let the coach do that. Worry has killed many a man, but has never done any one any good.' Charles Moore Jr would later expand on this tenet. Speaking of all his coaches, he said that 'I learned to concentrate only on what I could control. I learned to rely on myself – largely because my coaches had faith in me.' Andy Anderson later recalled an incident where a particularly good high jumper had badly missed his first two jumps. Jimmy walked up to him 'in a private sort of way' and walked the 'morose' boy down the track. Jimmy began talking calmly to him, no doubt telling him that he was the finest jumper in the competition and that he would easily clear the height on his next jump. As they reached the end of the track they turned, and the boy was now laughing with his coach. He went on to easily clear the height.

But preparing an athlete mentally was not just about removing stress factors. On one occasion a half-miler called Albert Watson Jr noted that 'Jimmy was a tremendous psychologist long before that word ever became popular.' He was matched to run a practice mile against the school's best miler, but as it was longer than his usual distance, and it was against a quality athlete, Jimmy handicapped the miler several hundred yards. He complained the distance was 'grossly unfair' so Jimmy, ever mischievous, flipped them and gave the miler the head start. He was fully aware that Watson would relax, expecting to be defeated, and his opponent would tighten, fearing the profound embarrassment of defeat. He was absolutely correct; Watson went on to win the race.

Jimmy would build his athletes' belief in their ability, sometimes just by giving praise where it was due – Paul White would later recall that Jimmy 'never got excited, but was always consistent in his praise of a good efforts.' Jef Evans also remembers Jimmy praising those who had done well, in his own 'quiet way.' After one meet in which he won a cross country race against Hill School, Jimmy headed straight to him to offer his congratulations and shake his hand. In 1957, after failing a couple of long jumps, apologetic Andy Anderson was walked down the track and told 'You are fine, I've expected you to jump in the 23s since you started jumping.' He went on to break the school record with a jump of 23' 5 ½". On occasion he would tell his athletes they were top class, more than capable of beating the opposition. He boosted their egos to such an extent that when they walked on to the track they had absolute faith in their ability to win. He would talk to local reporters and tell them that this boy or that boy was a champion. And he would tell the boys themselves that they were unbeatable. Ted Meredith, he boasted, was the best in world, and then, when Albert Robinson was his prime runner, he declared that he could beat Meredith at any distance from 50 yards to 440 yards. After winning Olympic gold and silver medals, Charles Moore Jr would say of him – 'Jimmy believed in me. So I began to believe in myself.' Jef Evans agreed. When he arrived at Mercersburg he did not consider himself a good athlete, but that changed because 'Jimmy believed in me. His belief gave me confidence that I had never had before.' By the late 1940s Jimmy would end training sessions early, telling his teams that they were more than ready for a coming meet. And if a private talk was not enough to massage the egos of his winning athletes, then this was remedied each post-meet Monday, when Jimmy would rise before the school assembly and, in his own inimitable, colourful way, outline the previous meet. His greatest praise was reserved for those who had performed at the highest level, and in his strong Scottish burr, he would glorify the athlete before his peers:

He r-r-run a go-o-o-od r-r-r-race.

Until this point only Jimmy's positivity towards his teams and individual athletes has been shown. But he was strident in his belief that athletes were representing the school at meets, and as such should comport themselves in a befitting manner. He would tell his teams that he had sent boys home in the past and would not hesitate to do so again. But he was not oppressive in the enforcement of his rules (and those laid down by the school). Rather, he was fair. If a runner's behaviour warranted a scolding, he would be scolded. If Jimmy believed a transgression was prompted by an underlying issue, he would attempt to burrow down and find out what the problem was. And he was always quick to offer support. He never got upset with an individual or team when they lost. Or at least he never outwardly showed it. But he was quite willing to show his displeasure when he felt a situation demanded it. Jef Evans remembers one cross country race where the top finishers were all from the Academy. Flushed by success, they clasped hands and crossed the line as one. Jimmy 'rushed up to us and said that was not to be done. It was not sportsmanlike to come in looking like a "daisy chain".'

On another occasion Evans was part of a group which approached the Director of Athletics and argued that cross country should be a Varsity sport, and this request was granted. He remembers Jimmy meeting the team in the locker room and asking why they had not simply asked him as he was the coach. As Evans recalls, 'he seemed less angry and more hurt. Whatever part I had in our petitioning, I wish I had had none.'

And very occasionally this displeasure spilled over into downright anger. Whilst at a meet at Cornell, Andy Anderson and two others were invited to a fraternity party by a former Mercersburg student. Despite being aware of Jimmy's rule that they be in bed by eight, and the school having a strict 'no alcohol' policy, the three boys decided that they would attend the party. Sneaking to the bathroom in their pyjamas, they changed into their clothes and snuck out. Arriving back around three in the morning, they returned to the bathroom and were standing naked when Jimmy appeared in the doorway: 'I'll be giving you five minutes to get into your bed.' The next morning Jimmy wouldn't accept their apology, telling them 'you've violated my rules.' He then sent them to the back of the bus, where no other students were allowed to speak to them on the six hour return journey. On arriving back at Mercersburg, they were, according to Anderson, 'sweating bullets' as they knew they could be thrown out of school for breaking the 'no alcohol' rule. They attempted to apologise again, but Jimmy simply held up his hand and refused it. Their futures at the Academy rested on Jimmy's actions. He didn't say a word, but the incident was never mentioned again.

This was not, however, always the case. On at least one occasion, boys were dropped from his team, Jimmy telling listeners at a dinner, that in 1946 he had taken this course of action with three athletes, as 'no boy is bigger than the team.'

Whilst perfect technique, top physical conditioning and mental strength were central to the success of Jimmy's teams, there was a final factor that Jimmy utilised in order to extract the very top performances from his athletes – over the years he built up a camaraderie with the boys. He was their coach, but he was also their guide, their mentor, the surrogate father figure to whom the boys, many who, as boarders, did not see their parents for months on end, could turn when they needed advice. When the boys came to school he was the teacher with the strange rolling accent; when they left it was Jimmy, of all the teachers at the school, who would leave an indelible mark on their lives, remaining with them in spirit many years after they had left him behind – a Mr Chips, Glenn Holland and John Keating rolled into one. In the 1920s a young man, already given the sobriquet Elmer by his classmates due to his 'gawky, small-town qualities', tried out for the high jump at Mercersburg. He wasn't an important part of the team – Jimmy would later joke that he was a far better accordionist than he was an athlete – but his coach left a mark, and 40 years later, upon Jimmy's death, he sent a telegram of condolence to the Curran family. The boy was Jimmy Stewart, world famous actor. That he had taken time out of his schedule to actively remember a man he had seen only intermittently in the past 40 years is testament to the mark Jimmy left on those he trained and how much they respected and trusted him. Gus Ormrod also remembers how, when he was a freshman living in an off-campus farmhouse, Jimmy would visit him one evening a week and the two would sit and chat for an hour. It was Jimmy's subtle way of telling Ormrod that he cared.

There are numerous stories that highlight the building of the relationships between Jimmy and his athletes. One of the most revealing involved Gus Ormrod. In the early 1950s, the young athlete made his way to the bar after a meet in New York City. After ordering a beer he looked up to see Jimmy sitting having a drink. Nothing was said, and the incident was not reported, but a simple warning was left hanging in the air – don't do it again!

It was not just his athletes that he left his mark on. In the 1950s, for several weekends of the year, Jimmy and Fred Kuhn, the school's football, baseball and wrestling coach, took advantage of the school's proximity to an array of south Pennsylvanian rivers, creeks and caves. The boys would be piled into station wagons and, under the guise of the verbosely-named Mercersburg Mastless Marine and Marching Society, also called the Pneumatic Tube Navy, they would head to the Conococheague Creek where they would go tubing, explore caves and walk around the area, eventually covering the creek's 60 miles. One former student, Christopher Montgomery, who openly railed against what he saw as the school's authoritarian attitude towards students, remembered these trips well. It brought a respect for the two teachers that he never held for the school. 'Both men', he later recalled, 'treated us like we were special. They both had a way of making me feel safe. Getting away from the school seemed the point. Both of them seemed to care about the students they took on trips. To show us something other than the norm. Something other than the school.' Again Jimmy had watched, and learned from, Mike Murphy's interactions with his students. It was said of Murphy that '[he] has the faculty of winning the love and confidence of those who work under him to a remarkable degree. Any man he trained would do anything for Mike.' And Jimmy was fully aware that if a coach could get his runners wanting to succeed for him, driving themselves into the ground to please their coach, then it added an extra dimension to their performance.

Jimmy endeared himself to his students through his self-deprecating personality, often portraying himself as a stereotypical frugal Scot, revelling in telling reporters how he, and Scots generally, had saved money in one way or another. He appeared to have a bank of these jokes. In 1930 he provided one for the school magazine, about the Scotsman who got so excited when a filling station was giving away free air that he blew out all his tyres. Five years later he told one about Scotty, out walking at night. The only other person out and about was a fellow Scot who was developing film. And in 1957 a light-hearted exchange between Jimmy and Emil von Elling, the coach of New York University, was published in the *New York Times*:

Von Elling:	It is true that you use only one golf ball when you go out on the links?
Curran:	Why sure I do. I don't need any more than one. When I hit a ball it sails fair and straight – right down the middle.
Von Elling:	It does, huh? Why don't you tell me about the time you lost your ball on the first hole and then broke your three clubs over your knee in disgust?
Curran:	That's a lie. A true Scotsman never would do that. Clubs cost money.

On his retirement in 1947, Lawson Robertson, fellow coach, also got in on the act, noting that the slowest race he ever saw was when Jimmy and another Scotsman reached for the cheque after lunch.

And Ed Pollock, sportswriter at the *Philadelphia Evening Bulletin*, told a story upon Jimmy's death of the time he had asked him if he intended spending the night with a friend. 'I do' came Jimmy's reply,

JIMMY CURRAN

'and that's all a Scotsman should be expected to spend.'

Spurred on, his students 'good-naturedly chided him on his deep brogue and his tartan sport coat with matching tam', and jokingly used his stereotypes against him in the school's magazine, *The Karux*:

> We wondered why Jimmie joined the Scot's [sic.] Thistle until we saw a copy of the Society Bulletin. One paragraph read as follows:- "The Society owns a beautiful lot in Mount Moriah Cemetery, containing 3,000 square feet for the burial of friendless Scots, free of charge".

But he was also genuinely quick-witted. Soon after the end of the Second World War, he and Janet were walking deep in the Appalachians when they came across a Scottish couple who were somewhat cut off from the outside world. The man asked if the war was over, to which Jimmy replied, 'which war?' In 1957, on the occasion of his being celebrated at the Penn Relays, the oldest and largest track and field competition in the United States, first run in 1895, for reaching 50 years as a coach, Jimmy walked up to the gate only to find he had forgotten his badge, and had no time to go back to his hotel to recover it. Turning to the guard, he said 'I forgot my badge, but I am Jimmy Curran and I am being honored today.' 'And I, by God' came the reply 'am the Pope.' How Jimmy eventually got into the event is not known, but on returning to the Academy he regaled students with his version of what followed. One student, Hank Spire, later recalled Jimmy saying, initially, he didn't quite know what to do, but then realised the guard wasn't too bright so he said, 'I just turned around and walked in backwards and he thought I was coming out.'

And just a couple of years later a minor incident again brought much merriment for his students. Harry Pickle III recalled:

> Jimmy asked me what distance I had trained for and

134

I told him 440, 200, and no one can beat me out of
the starting blocks in the 100. So he decided to have
me just run through a 440. I took off with a couple
of other runners and lo and behold I saw a ten-year
old kid running twenty or thirty yards ahead with a
shoe under each arm. I recognized them as my street
shoes and I took off after him like I was lit on fire.
The little bugger was smart enough to throw one in
the woods on his left side and keep on going with
the other under his arm. I pulled up and got the first
shoe and then took off after him again with one shoe
under my arm. Well, he threw the other shoe deep
into the woods on the other side of the field. Again
I stopped and retrieved the other shoe and by that
time he was out of sight when I came back to the
open field. I trotted back to the track and Jimmy
came up to me and said loud enough in his Scottish
brogue "Laddie did I not tell you, there are four
turns to this race". Everyone had a big laugh or two
and then I returned to running on the track.

And even when he felt the need to put a student in his place, he often
did so in such a jocular way as to leave the student sporting a wry smile.
In 1960 a visiting cross country runner questioned the positioning of a
marker flag. Harper Girvin, a Mercersburg student at the time, recalled
Jimmy eyeing the young man and asking him, 'Dae ye expect tae be
leadin' the whole bloomin' bunch.' By now struck with a sudden
sheepishness, the student replied, 'Eh, no, sir.' Jimmy looked at him and
said, 'Aye lad, then just follow the rest', before turning and striding
towards the start line.

In Jimmy his students saw someone who had been there and done
it. He was not simply a dilettante who was interested in athletics and
had drifted into training without having competed at a high level. He

had raced against the best athletes in the world, he had competed in the highly competitive Scottish Borders racing circuit, he had won celebrated titles, and he had run for amateur glory and the professional purse. When Jimmy had left Scotland he was considered by many to be the finest athlete at his distance in the country (no small accolade), and in his early years at Mercersburg he was still at the top of his game, and considered one of the best on the east coast. When Alfie Shrubb needed an opponent he called on Jimmy. Few in the world could boast such an impressive athletic résumé. The boys on his teams were aware of his achievements and, in his early years as a coach, witnessed him race on a number of occasions. Indeed, they had watched him take on two of his finest athletes, Ted Meredith and Albert Robinson – Meredith, Olympic champion, could not reel in the handicap given Jimmy. In the years after taking charge, he also set the pace for them in training sessions, and his desire to win no doubt meant that he often showed his charges a clean pair of heels. He would continue to do so until around the Second World War. The raw athletes stepping onto the Mercersburg track heard the stories of the diminutive coach winning championships in South Africa, Egypt, Ireland and Scotland, holding his own against Alfie Shrubb, and defeating the best that America could throw at him. Whilst Jimmy was never outspoken about his accomplishments, he no doubt added a little spice to the tales that he did impart. How could these young boys not look at Jimmy in awe? He was, in sporting terms, what they aspired to be.

Just how much he was respected by his students is highlighted in three stories. In 1923 Jimmy accepted the request of a former student, Charles Mason Fairbanks Jr, to be the Godfather to his daughter. And in 1927 another former student, Albert Watson Jr, along with his bride-to-be, eloped from Yale and made for Mercersburg, where Jimmy would act as his best man. For Jef Evans, one of Jimmy's athletes from the 1950s, it was important that his wife-to-be, Marty, met, and was accepted by, Jimmy. So, after both sets of parents had met the prospective couple, the next stop was Jimmy's apartment on Linden

Avenue (they had downsized from the Smith House in 1947) – fortunately Jimmy and Marty got on well.

Furthermore, Jimmy's students were aware that he was wholly devoted to them, and the school. His first four years as athletic coach at Mercersburg had brought spectacular success, and with it the widespread respect of his peers. He had already risen to be one of the finest athletics coaches in all of the United States, and the natural career move for a successful high school coach was into college coaching. Johnny Mack, Amos Alonzo Stagg, Lawson Robertson, and a number of other prominent college coaches, began their careers coaching high school athletics, taking the step up when the depth of their talent became apparent. Jimmy was offered several high school and college coaching posts, including that at Harvard, and was on the shortlists for numerous others, including the University of Pennsylvania in 1916, and even went as far as being interviewed for the head coach role at Phillips Exeter Academy in 1924, but he turned down all that would have seen him leave Mercersburg. And there is no doubt he could have made a financial killing if he had taken one of these posts. In 1906 Mike Murphy was earning between $4,000 and $5,000 annually, as well as having free use of a house. In 1910 Keene Fitzpatrick took the Princeton coaching job for an annual salary, albeit larger than the norm for a coach, of $8,000. The average annual wage for a male employee at this time was around $600, whilst a US Senator earned around $7,500.

A fellow teacher at Mercersburg, Archibald Rutledge, would no doubt have approved of Jimmy's decision to forego the money to remain at Mercersburg, having, in one of his many books, bemoaned that 'some coaches, for a few weeks' easy outdoor work, are paid more than some college presidents.' The boys under his charge saw someone for whom loyalty came long before any thought of financial gain, who was there for the love of the sport, and the thrill of taking raw schoolboys and turning them into quality, sometimes world class, athletes. And they loved him for it. Examples can be found throughout Jimmy's career of his former students presenting him with some reward.

In 1924 and 1960 he was presented with trips to the Olympics, whilst for his 40th anniversary as Mercersburg coach his former athletes presented him with a set of golf irons.

One final factor in Jimmy's success was his ability to build a team from what, at the start of each school year, was little more than a disparate group. Whilst most of his athletes hailed from lives of great privilege, many of his scholarship athletes came from more straitened backgrounds. Jimmy, his own upbringing at the forefront of his mind, attempted to instil in the former group a humbleness and egalitarianism, a lesson taught no better than the day he had John Coolidge, son of the then-President Calvin Coolidge, rake out the long jump pit:

> When John had finished I said, 'John do you know why I asked you to do that?' John said no. 'Well' I replied 'I came over here an immigrant and I just wanted to see what it would feel like to order around a President's son.' I understand John told his father about it and he gave a wry smile.

He was aided by his sport; athletics is a great leveller – the poor man and the rich man compete side by side and the one with the greater skill, endurance, power, speed and mental strength usually wins out. This simple fact, likely unspoken, instilled in the boys that they had to work for everything in life, as someone was always waiting in the wings to take it from them. For the less privileged, it was a daily reminder that if they applied themselves to a task they could achieve anything they set their minds to.

But there was an external factor that threatened to stand between Jimmy's teams and success – if the success of his teams was to depend only on those boys who came to the school for academic reasons, then the success would be reliant on a massive slice of luck. And so, with the express consent of William Mann Irvine, the school's headmaster, he set out to track down and attract potential athletes and bring them to the school on athletic scholarships. It was a controversial policy, and one that the school conducted surreptitiously. Within two years the arrival of two teenage athletes, one headhunted by Jimmy, the other discovered by Mike Murphy, would prove its worth.

*****

Jimmy's team, inherited from Kraenzlein, took their first steps at a cross country dual meet against Princeton Freshmen. The result is unknown, but just days later the team took part in the 5th Princeton Interscholastics cross country run. Cross country events were decided on a points system; the first placed runner would receive a single point, the second-placed, two points, and so on. The team collecting the lowest number of points would emerge the winner. Mercersburg finished fifth, but its captain, Reuben Warner, won the individual honours. A week later they were defeated in a dual meet against Cornell Freshmen, with Warner once again victorious. The track season began with defeats at Johns Hopkins indoor meet, and a fourth place in the mile relay at the Penn Relays. But improvements did come. Victories at the Franklin and Marshall College meet, and in a dual meet over the University of Pennsylvania Freshmen, sandwiched a second place at the large Princeton meet. The season hadn't been a soaring success, but equally it hadn't been a flop. The pressure on Jimmy would now increase as he was able to build his own team.

Chapter 10 • The Greatest Year

In 1908, a 16-year-old of Irish and Welsh descent from the south-eastern Pennsylvanian town of Media dove into the sports section of the local newspaper and devoured stories about the exploits of athletes at the Games of the Fourth Olympiad in London. The written words exploded into visions of what was transpiring 3,000 miles to the east, providing an inspiration that would, in time, evolve into a dream, and that dream into an ambition – an ambition to stand in the shoes of the athletes he was reading about and to return home, four years later, with a gold medal. His name was James Edwin Meredith, known as Ted.

His family had strong links to athletics. His grandfather, William, had been a successful professional runner in England, before emigrating to the United States. James Meredith, Ted's father, a horse trainer, had started a track and field programme at Williamson Trade School in 1906, and it was there, after graduating high school, that Ted enrolled to become a bricklayer.

His own introduction to athletics had come early, when he ran alongside the colts bred and trained by his father. He then went on to represent Media High School at the Penn Relays, where he was first spotted by Jimmy, and in the following years he continued to excel at running and football.

In the summer of 1911 his father brought him to Mercersburg and the pair met Jimmy. Three years earlier Ted had no doubt marvelled at the wondrous running and incredible times of Wyndham Halswelle, and baulked at the treatment of his American opponents. Now the man who had coached Halswelle wanted to coach him. What he did not realise, however, was that his time at the school would be spent under a coach who was soon to become widely recognised as one of the best in America and, based on results, one of the finest in athletics history. Jimmy could not have failed to notice the young boy. Meredith's neatly trimmed dark hair was swept back and parted in the centre, revealing thick eyebrows and pugilistic features that wouldn't have looked out of place weighing up Jack Dempsey. In an age when weight training amongst athletes was largely frowned upon, Meredith, physically, was a beast, an 'ox' the *New York Times* would call him, 'the strongest individual who ever essayed to gain fame on the cinder track.' At 5'8" tall and weighing 155 pounds, he was straight backed, his chest and shoulders bulged against his running vest, and his powerful thighs stretched his shorts. His running style was unorthodox, his head thrown back, his chest protruding, and his arms flailing like windmill blades as he ran. But unorthodoxy can be overcome when countered by immense natural speed. And then there was his spirit. When an average man would long have surrendered to the lactic acid screaming in his muscles, Meredith continued to fight on, performing beyond the pain, in a realm where humans usually only venture when running from certain death.

But in an age when communication was conducted at an at times sedentary pace, few were aware of Meredith's prodigious talent, and the potential he possessed. Jimmy Curran was. He knew exactly what he was bringing to the school in the shape of Meredith. Mike Murphy had taught him well. At this time Meredith's best for the quarter-mile was 52 ⅖, and 2.03 for the half-mile. 'From the first day he arrived', crowed Jimmy, 'I knew I had the boy who, with a little careful training, would lower all the Interscholastic records from the 440 to the mile.'

Jimmy was effusive in his praise of the young man to William Mann Irvine. The two men determined to bring the youngster to the school. It was clear his family would not be able to afford the school fees, which stood at $425, so Irvine offered 'working scholarship terms' which reduced the fees to $175. But even with this reduction the Merediths were not in a position to pay. Jimmy made a 'very impassioned plea' to Irvine asking him to find a solution to the impasse. Irvine sent a letter in reply, beginning 'My dear Jimmie.' It told him to 'go see Meredith immediately and tell him that we will give him extra work so that he can earn all of his tuition. Jimmy headed to see Meredith, snatching him from under the nose of Muhlenberg College, where he had agreed to attend. During his time at Mercersburg he would perform a number of menial tasks, such as manning the school switchboard and trailing the dormitories selling photographs of sports events. But the demeaning nature of his financial situation was worth it. As well as attending one of America's premier prep schools, he was a top athlete in one of the finest athletics programs in America. If he lived up to expectations he could guarantee to be snapped up by an Ivy League university, and that virtually guaranteed a successful future career.

The school's drive to attract the best athletes through scholarships was highly controversial. As such, it was very much kept under the radar, discussed only between headmaster and coaches. To the outside world Mercersburg was producing the very best athletes through the very best coaching. In 1916 William Mann Irvine addressed the National Collegiate Athletics Association, denouncing the practice:

> In persuading boys to enter school or college there is a legitimate form of proselyting, but proselyting takes objectionable form when a boy of limited financial ability is helped simply because he is an athlete.

At best he was being disingenuous, at worst, telling a bare-faced lie as, privately, he was fully supportive of the practice. Meredith being a case in point. Charles Tippetts, when he became headmaster of the school, recalled the use of scholarships to attract 'ringers' during his time as a student when Irvine was in charge:

> No use kicking dirt under the rug. When I was a student here as a young boy, I had for a roommate a 26-year-old man who had been brought in from Maine to play football. He had no chance of getting into college and no desire to either.

143

And if Meredith was not enough to sate Jimmy's desire for success, he began to build a fine support team in the shape of Albert Robinson, Eugene Hammitt and Theodore Dale. Robinson was the cream of this supporting trio. A good-looking youngster with a shock of blond hair, he had come to Mercersburg on Mike Murphy's recommendation. Towards the end of 1911 Murphy attended a picnic in his hometown of Westboro, and witnessed Robinson take on all-comers, including Murphy's son Thorne. Murphy was effusive about his speed and finishing, but told Jimmy that he would need to work on the boy's strength and a slow start. On arrival at the school, also on a scholarship, he stood 5'8" tall and weighed in at 125 pounds. Jimmy put in place programmes to counter both weaknesses and with some months of intensive training he added 25 pounds, but his start was still proving a problem and despite daily drills it was taking him 30 yards to build up real speed. But in early 1912, even with these teething problems, and when both Meredith and Robinson were still only raw bundles of emerging talent, Mercersburg had one of the finest relay teams in America.

The track season began at the Barnard School Games in New York City on 3rd February 1912. Travel to away meets was a great adventure for athletes, especially freshmen, tempered somewhat by pre-race nerves. Some years later Ted Meredith's son, also called Ted, recalled one trip to New York:

> Jimmy accompanied us, entertained us, lectured us, fed us. His favorite cost-saving act was to stop at one of those Pennsylvania Dutch country inns where you could eat all you wanted for $1.00 … tables laden with roasts, turkeys, hams, every kind of vegetable, potatoes and gravy, bread and butter, cakes and pies.

The fun stopped when we got to the hotels and the

pre-race apprehension grew and our nerves became taut. Jimmy checked us in our rooms, but after bed check one night in New York City, Ed Beetem and I ventured out into Times Square to see the sights, including a stint at a ten-cents-a-dance emporium. Jimmy was never the wiser until I told him about it ten years later.

But his father's first trip lost much of its sheen when the result, and his performance, did not go to plan. It was a baptism of fire, and Meredith failed to place in any solo events. Of the Mercersburg runners only Robinson, in the 220 yards, claimed victory. The team placed second in the one mile relay. Two weeks later, at a Johns Hopkins meet, the roles were reversed. Robinson trailed in second in the 100 yards, and Meredith, running off scratch in the 440 yards won his race in 53 ⅗ seconds. The team won the one mile relay.

It was two months before they took to the track again in earnest – at the illustrious Penn Relays. It had been two months well spent. Competing in the one mile relay, under skies heavy with rain and a crowd thick with umbrellas, Meredith, taking over from Hammitt, Dale and Robinson (who had limped the last 15 yards to record a time of 50 ⅕ seconds), closed out the last quarter of the race, in 49 ⅘ seconds. On a sodden, slow track the team posted a new world interscholastic record of 3.27 ⅕, beating the old time by three seconds, with Mike Murphy and others positing that another five seconds could have been shaved off in dry weather. One of the stopwatches captured Meredith's time as 49 ⅖ and he was hailed as the stand out runner of the day. Indeed, the team was only three seconds behind the time posted by Syracuse in the college race. Indeed, so impressive was the run that not one of Jimmy's teams would better it over the next 49 years, and exactly 100 years after it was posted the team would be inducted into the Penn Relays Wall of Fame. The onlooking James E. Sullivan, referee of the event, couldn't have failed to be impressed on a day when he was seeking potential athletes for the 1912 US Olympic team. But if Sullivan required further proof, he need only have waited a week when Meredith competed at the Princeton Interscholastics and promptly broke two more world interscholastic records, taking a second off the quarter-mile record, and four seconds off the half-mile, posting times of 49 ⅕ and 1.55 respectively.

Over the course of May, Meredith's performances continued to impress, sweeping aside all before him in the quarter and half-mile events at both the Pennsylvania Middle States Championships and the Cornell Interscholastic Championships, equalling one intercollegiate world record in the process, and helping Mercersburg to three first places. The newspapers were beginning to take notice, commenting enthusiastically on his star potential, and talk of his competing at the Olympics was increasing in volume.

Meredith was rapidly repaying Jimmy's faith in him, but still he did not fully believe he could make the Olympic team, constantly asking Jimmy if he thought it was possible. Jimmy had none of his student's doubts, telling him that all he needed to do was keep up his training. '[He] does not know how fast he can run', opined Jimmy, 'but I know he is the fastest runner the world has ever seen, and, if he goes after any record from 600 yards to cross country, he will lower every one.' His faith was bound up in the letter sent to the Olympic trial committee, containing Meredith's entry.

On 8th June, the finest athletes on the east coast met at Harvard Stadium in Cambridge, Ma., to compete for the privilege of representing America at the Olympic Games. In 1900 and 1904 the Olympics was viewed as sideshows to the World's Fairs which ran alongside them, whilst the 1906 event did not generate the recovery that was envisaged, but it was transformed into an athletic meeting of international importance at the 1908 Games in London. By 1912 it stood centre stage as the premier track and field meeting in the world. Inspired, the athletes at Cambridge put on one of the greatest athletic displays America had ever witnessed. World and American records tumbled, Olympic records were bettered, and numerous personal bests achieved.

Days before the trials, Jimmy dropped into Arthur Duffey's *Boston Post* office to impart his views on Meredith: 'Take my word for it', he said, 'Meredith should show some of his greatest form in the contests Saturday. I have prepared the boy especially for the [Olympic] tryouts, and as he has done everything I have asked him so far, there is no reason why he shouldn't repeat Saturday.'

Jimmy travelled north with Meredith – ready to unleash a plan for success which had been brewing in his head for some weeks. There were questions asked when Meredith's name was listed amongst those competing in the 800m, at the expense of the 400m, against the strongest crop of middle-distance runners ever, but Jimmy believed Meredith could win either distance. In the 800m, Jimmy told him to lead from the start in his heat, and he stormed home first in 1.53 ⅘. In the final, he lined up against athletes that were the finest he had ever competed against, men such as 'Peerless' Mel Sheppard and David Caldwell. Meredith led early in the race, but ended up in third, unable to repeat the time he had run earlier that day. The third place was a disappointment, and Jimmy took a ribbing from fellow coaches who were firmly of the belief that the quarter-mile was Meredith's distance, but Jimmy, and Mike Murphy, learned much from the race, and knew that to run the race from the front against men of Sheppard's quality would once again lead to defeat. Future races would bring a different approach.

Two days later the list of athletes chosen to represent the United States was released – Meredith had his place, in the 800m, and interestingly, given he had declined to compete in the 400m in the trials, the 400m and the 1,600m relay (4x400m) – and three days after this he was marching down 6th Avenue, along 23rd Street, to the strains of *Yankee Doodle* and *Dixie* with stars and stripes in hand, towards New York's piers, where he mingled with cheering crowds before boarding the SS *Finland* bound for Stockholm. Only two months earlier the survivors and corpses recovered after the sinking of the *Titanic* were brought to the very same landings. But the mood on this warm summer day had a less sombre tone.

The ship had barely passed Sandy Hook when a stowaway was found on board. Harry Naughton was a 16-year-old from Toledo who had hidden beneath the tarpaulin of one of the ship's lifeboats. The captain resolved to send him back to New York, but Colonel Robert Thompson, president of the US Olympic Committee, agreed to pay his passage and promptly installed him as the team's mascot.

Every attempt was made to ensure the athletes could train on the two-week journey, so the ship was turned into a 'veritable floating gymnasium.' Some sports, such as distance running and fencing required little modification to the ship to enable training. But the sprinters, including Meredith, had a two-man 70-yard long cork track constructed on the ship's top deck, whilst the discus and hammer were attached to a rope, allowing them to be hurled into the ocean and then retrieved. And if training was not enough to drive athletes towards victory, a number of Native American athletes attempted to sway the odds in their favour by performing war dances on deck. After a short stop in Antwerp, where the athletes trained at the stadium of Beershot Antwerpen Club, the ship headed north to Stockholm. In four years he had graduated from reading newspaper reports of distant Olympic victories to standing on the cusp of his own personal athletic glory. The only hurdle between his passing into legend or obscurity was his own ability.

The 19-year-old Meredith almost didn't make the final team at the Olympics. Unable to accurately judge him on the short track on the ship, where he was looked upon as a training partner for big name runners, Murphy took him to a track near the Olympic stadium and faced him off against John Paul Jones, the world record holder for the mile. Meredith won by a wide margin. His place in the 800m was sealed, and his first heat came on 6th July. He was confident of doing well – since September 1911 he had, with Jimmy's help, shaved over seven seconds off his best time for the 880 yards, and three seconds off the

440 – and placed second in his heat behind the Canadian, Mel Brock. He returned the following day for his semi-final race and won comfortably, ahead of the two men he considered the best in the world – Hanns Braun and Mel Sheppard. Despite his success, gained with the fast time of 1.54.4, his rivals likely still believed that his lack of experience would be his downfall in the final.

On the day of the final, Meredith stepped onto the short 383m track, almost overcome with nerves but with a plan in mind to stay close to Sheppard in the hope he could snatch silver. A letter to William Mann Irvine's wife revealed he was in excellent physical shape, but despite this he didn't think he was good enough to win. Elsewhere, belief in him wasn't overwhelming – Mike Murphy, the US coach, thought he would not reach his peak for some years – and so, despite the belief that he couldn't beat Sheppard if setting the pace, he was told to do so in order to 'kill off' Hanns Braun, the German considered Sheppard's main threat. Sheppard, however, had other ideas. As he stood waiting for the gun, he was determined to lead from the off, having struggled to qualify from the semi-final due to a slow start. He took an early lead, with Meredith and Braun sitting in behind. Three times on the first lap Meredith challenged Sheppard for the lead, and each time Sheppard powered away, leading to a fast first 400m time of 52 ⅕ seconds. In the last 200m, Meredith fought off challenges from, first, Hec Edmundson, and then Braun. The race continued like this until the final stretch during which an 'all in' Meredith dug into some hidden reserve and pulled ahead, barely beating Sheppard and Ira Davenport to the line. In 1912, the 880 yards distance was still formally recognised and Meredith, aware of this, ran on for the extra few yards in order to be timed at this distance as well as 800m. His times were 1.51.9 and 1.52.5 – both new world records. The 800m time would stand for another 14 years. Meredith viewed his win with typical humility. He was simply overjoyed at having beaten Sheppard and Braun, who he considered the best in the world. Word of Meredith's win was soon plastered across the pages of the nation's newspapers – with headlines hailing him the 'boy wonder' and focussing on the fact he was still a schoolboy. On receiving a cablegram from Meredith, William Mann Irvine, sought out Jimmy to break the news. He was working a summer job as part of a maintenance crew on campus and Irvine called for him to come down from the ladder he was working on. Jimmy would later call it the greatest thrill of his coaching career. His fellow Scottish coach, Lawson Robertson, called it the greatest race he ever witnessed.

And Meredith wasn't finished yet. On 12th July he was back on the track for the 400m. He qualified second from his heat behind Hanns Braun, and later in the day won his semi-final, knocking out Mel Sheppard. The following day he lined up against the winners of the other four semi-finals. Tapes had been added to the track to separate the lanes after a semi-final incident, and Meredith started on the inside. But the form he had shown in the 800m didn't carry into the final of the shorter event. He was able to reel in only four men, and finished in fourth place. He wrote to Jimmy after the race. Racing in lanes, he admitted, was confusing, and he had gone out too fast, causing him to 'blow up at the finish.'

The day after the 400m final, Meredith returned to the track as part of the 1,600m (4x400m) relay team. With only seven teams in contention, the racing started at the semi-final stage. The British team won the first race in a new Olympic record time. The second race saw the Americans qualify ahead of Braun's German team, but with a time four seconds slower than that posted by the British team. In the third race the French also bettered the American time. The gold medal was by no means done and dusted. On 15th July the Americans lined up against the British and French and stormed home in a world record time of 3.16.6. Meredith had his second gold of the Games, and his third world record. Ted Meredith was 19 years old when he won two gold medals at the Olympics. He had taken on the best in the world and emerged victorious. He had repaid the faith placed in him by both Jimmy and Mike Murphy, and cemented his place in history.

As the Games ended, the US team sneaked to the top of the medal table with 25 golds to Sweden's 24, with a grand total of 63 golds, silvers and bronzes. In a letter to the *Glasgow Herald*, a month before the Games, Jimmy had predicted the team's success, highlighting the strength in depth at all distances from 400m to two miles, as well as the pole vault, high jump and broad jump – he was correct in all but the 1,500m, where Abel Kiviat was beaten into second place by one-tenth of a second. After the disappointment of four years earlier when it had trailed far behind Great Britain in all three medals, the country was ready to celebrate. And those celebrations started almost immediately the athletes arrived back on American soil, with a parade through New York City. Around 100,000 Americans, including Jimmy, thronged a route resonating to the sound of martial music and hung with stars and stripes, and banners, stretching from the newly-built New York Public Library down to City Hall in Lower Manhattan.

At 10am a group of mounted police led off the parade, followed by members of the Coast Artillery Corps, United Spanish War Veterans, and Boy Scouts. The medallists were put into pairs and seated in around 30 cars mounted with placards bearing their names. In the lead car were manager Matt Halpin and assistant Paul Pilgrim, whilst Meredith travelled with the sprinter Alvah Meyer. They were followed by the impressive United Swedish Societies, and then an array of various amateur athletic clubs such as the New York Athletic Club, Irish-American Athletic Club, plus 38 others. And the parade went on and on, snaking through Manhattan, taking an hour for the last participant to pass the point of the first. But amongst all the pomp and ceremony, the gold medallists and national heroes, the star of the show was double-gold medallist Jim Thorpe, chewing gum and resplendent in a Panama hat, oblivious to the fact that perhaps he wouldn't have made it this far if Jimmy had not been held back from hitting him with a bucket some years earlier!

On reaching City Hall Park, the city's Mayor, William Gaynor, who two years earlier had survived an assassination attempt that would eventually kill him, addressed the crowd in fulsome terms – 'You have shown the whole world, and particularly Europe, what the American stomach, the American heart, the American muscle, and the American man can do.' The athletes reciprocated with appreciative cries of 'Rah, rah, ray, USA', and when it was all over the crowd rushed forward and mingled with their returned heroes.

But the day was not finished, and the athletes and officials made their way to Terrace Garden for a celebratory banquet, followed by more speeches. And in a nice touch, the athletes made their way onto the menu – Meredith became Sauce Meredith, accompanying fresh beef tongue, and followed by Sorbet Jim Thorpe.

Two days later, Meredith was one of a small group of Pennsylvanian guests of honour at another parade and banquet in Philadelphia. Jimmy was in attendance. The following day he was honoured by his hometown of Media. Jimmy travelled west to Media to attend this final celebration. The evening kicked off with a march and fireworks display. Later, at the town's Armory, telegrams of congratulation were read out: Mike Murphy praised Ted's character, whilst William Mann Irvine, apologised for his non-attendance as he had just returned from holiday, but noted 'we join with the citizens of Media in feeling great pride in his record.' Jimmy then came to the platform to 'hearty applause' before making a brief speech during which he relayed that Meredith was the best athlete he had ever trained and 'the most popular boy in the school.' Meredith was later presented a three carat diamond ring, upon which was inscribed 'Citizens of Media, 1912.' This ring would be accompanied by a jewel-encrusted sword presented to him by Sweden's King Gustaf V. Several Mercersburg athletes had competed (and one had won gold) at the Olympics before Meredith, but the London Olympics four years earlier had turned the event from a minor one on the athletics calendar to the greatest gathering of sportsmen on the planet. To win Olympic gold in 1912 one had to be a supreme athlete.

Soon after Meredith's victory, William Mann Irvine commissioned the artist Edwin Blashfield to produce a painting depicting the school's ideals and aspirations – hard work, fair play, and clean living. In the centre is an athlete – the Victor – holding the school flag and a javelin, and wearing the Mercersburg athletic uniform, surrounded by Hermes, Athena and the Angel of Victory, each of whom extend an offering. The Olympic Games was highly influential in settling on the theme of the painting, and as a nod towards the school's own real-life victor, Ted Meredith's body was used as a model. Like those he had read about four years earlier – Wyndham Halswelle, Mel Sheppard and Johnny Hayes – he had passed into legend.

*****

Jimmy significantly reduced his exhausting racing schedule after taking on the coaching role at Mercersburg. In the late summer of 1912, just prior to his appointment, he ran two events in Washington Park, Philadelphia, taking two first places in the first (for a total prize of $24) and one first place, two second places and two third places at the second, including stepping outside his usual events to compete in the pole vault. A month later he headed to a different Washington Park, this one at Maspeth in Long Island, for the annual meeting of the New York Caledonian Club, in what proved to be the largest-ever gathering of professional athletes at one games. Against formidable opposition, Jimmy came away with a second place in the 440 yards and a win in the one mile. His winnings aren't known, but as a rough guide Hans Holmer walked away with the huge sum of $125 for winning the five mile race.

The following year, 1911, Jimmy is only known to have competed in one race, at the annual jubilee of Philadelphia's Foresters' courts. Roared on by 25,000 spectators, he stormed home in the one mile race for a prize of $8.

The summer of 1912 again brought with it another restricted race card. At the Scottish Games in Philadelphia in August, Jimmy appeared out of sorts, trailing in second in the mile, leading the *Philadelphia Inquirer* to imply he wasn't trying. He took third in the 220 yards hurdles, but did win the hop, step and jump. The following day he took part in the annual games of the New York Caledonian Club, but failed to place in any races, taking only a second place in the pole vault.

*****

The 1911/12 season at Mercersburg had proven two things to Jimmy – that headhunting athletes was a sure route to success, and that a team didn't have to be strong from top to bottom to court success, it only needed a couple of good athletes. The following year he instituted a lesson he had learned just months before when the Carlisle School arrived at Lafayette College for a dual meet. Only two athletes – Jim Thorpe and Lewis Tewanima – stepped off the train, and when asked where the rest of the team were, their coach, 'Pop' Warner, replied 'Tewanima runs the half, mile, two mile and on up. Thorpe does the rest.' Thorpe won seven events, and his achievement was immortalised in the film *Jim Thorpe – All-American*. The bottom line was that a good sprinter generally could only win two events, the 100 yards and the 220 yards, whilst a good distance man might win the half-mile and the mile. A weights man, however, could make a relatively easy transition from discus to hammer to javelin to shot put, and if he had good speed then all the better. A dominant field athlete could build a solid foundation for the track men.

And so, with Thorpe in mind, Jimmy set out to bring such an athlete to the school. That athlete was a giant of a boy called Wallace Maxfield, known as Pete. With Meredith having departed for the University of Pennsylvania, he had big shoes to fill. He did so admirably. At the National Interscholastic Championship at Travers Island, New York, in June, he won the javelin, shot put and discus, alongside two victories each for Robinson and hurdler Thomas Fields. Such was the importance of athletics at this time for the school, that when Maxfield was injured playing basketball, just after his triple victory, the sport was banned on campus. The season overall proved a good one, with

Robinson and Maxfield being particularly impressive.

Of the hundreds of meets Jimmy's athletes took part in, most quickly descended into obscurity, remembered only by those who took part. Only a handful made it into school folklore; Penn State Interscholastics meet of 1913 was one of these.

Jimmy had expected Albert Robinson to make the Olympic team alongside Meredith. He had built up his strength and his starts were improving. But his first season was plagued by a snapped tendon, forcing him to run with his leg bandaged from ankle to hip. By the time of the trials he could barely walk. Jimmy was in no doubt that Robinson was a phenomenon, and by early 1913 both he and Mike Murphy were lauding him in the most glowing terms; Jimmy arguing he could beat Meredith at any distance from 50 yards to 440 yards, whilst Murphy believed him to be the only sprinter in America capable of beating the 100 yards world record of 9 ⅗ seconds recorded by both Arthur Duffey and Dan Kelley.

And in the space of one month he rewarded their faith. At Penn State Interscholastics he ran the 100 yards in 9 ⅗ and the 220 in 20 ⅘. A poor quality photograph exists showing Jimmy, stopwatch in hand, looking on as Robinson crosses the line. His opponents, including a youthful Charles Tippetts, future headmaster of Mercersburg Academy, are distant, competing only for second place. His times were so fast that they were questioned by the timekeepers, and even though the track was found to be full length, his times, at the behest of James E. Sullivan, were reduced by one-tenth of a second. Sullivan's reasoning was based on nothing more than his belief that 'it's impossible for an 18-year-old boy to run that fast.' Jimmy accepted this reduction in order that the times could be recorded. The following week the team was at the Cornell Interscholastics where, in a snowstorm, Robinson ran a time of 21 ⅕ in the 200 yards, and a week after this, in a downpour at the Penn Relays, he ran 21 ⅘. The incessant racing led to an injured ankle, which saw a slower time posted at the Princeton Interscholastics. These slower times gave officials more ammunition to further question the times posted at Penn State.

Jimmy wanted to get as much out of Robinson as possible. By May 1913 he was planning a return to Galashiels and plans were afoot to bring along Robinson to run at the Scottish, English, German, French and Irish championships. Within a week, Robinson's sojourn, at the expense of the school, had been cancelled by William Mann Irvine amid accusations, likely well-founded, that he was crossing the Atlantic to go 'pot-hunting' in professional meets. In later years Jimmy would show he hadn't lost this hankering to pit his students against professional athletes when he attempted to facilitate a race between Henry Thresher and the Harrisburg-born professional Barney Ewell, with the monies raised to go to Mercersburg Academy. He thought better of it and advised Thresher to wait until college was finished or he would disbar himself from running in college and also at the Olympics.

But Jimmy had every intention of still returning home. He had never intended to make a clean break from his past life, and this was evident from his participation in a cultural organisation called the Scottish Border Club of Philadelphia, where he rose to the position of chairman. He had remained in touch with family and friends since leaving Scotland. In 1910 he had sent a set of three medals – gold, silver and bronze – to the Gala Harriers committee, with the instructions that they be competed for over a mile distance. He would later send a golden shoe, to be competed for over 350 yards, and would present the Burgh School with an impressive athlete-topped trophy. But before he headed back across the Atlantic, he had a more sombre event to attend – the funeral of his mentor, Mike Murphy. Murphy, only 53 years old, had never had the strongest constitution, and since watching Pennsylvania play Detroit in a blinding snowstorm, he had caught a severe cold that he could not shrug off. Over the next year his health gradually deteriorated further, until the inevitable occurred. So revered was he that flags at the University of Pennsylvania were lowered to half mast, and all athletic activity suspended until after his funeral. His body was to be laid to rest in his home state of Massachusetts, but a funeral service held in Philadelphia drew a roll call of famous coaches and athletes, as well as a vast crowd of mourners.

After the funeral he headed to New York, where he boarded the RMS *Caledonia*. Three years later the ship, like the *Lusitania* before her, would be sunk by a German submarine. Galashiels was waiting for Jimmy, his imminent arrival having been announced in the local newspaper. Travelling second class, he arrived in Glasgow on 23rd June and headed to his parents' home. It would be the last time he would ever see them. In March 1916 his father, John, 74 years old, suffered a stroke and passed away, his mother, Ellen, 77 years old, following just over a year later after a bout of acute bronchitis. With America's entry into the war coming only months before his mother's death, and the sinking of the *Lusitania* still fresh in the memory, there was little chance of returning home. Jimmy would grieve from afar. When he returned in future years he would stay at the home of Janet's parents, 152 Halliburton Place, looking down on Galashiels from its elevated position on a ridge to the north of the town. In future years, when it passed to Janet's sisters, he would often continue to list it as his destination whenever he returned to Scotland, a trip he would make at least 17 times. It is likely, however, that he was nomadic, and bunked down wherever a bed was available.

Two trips list Overhaugh Street, the home of his brother, John, as his destination. John was a somewhat eccentric character. Fond of a drink, he would frequent the town's pubs, most notably the Waverley Inn, dressed in a yellow waistcoat with cravat, holding a cane, and all topped off with a checked bonnet. The Inn was known locally as the Gluepot, having gained this rather indecorous sobriquet due to John complaining about his shoes sticking to the floor. It is unclear whether the floor or his shoes were the culprit. It is likely, however, that the two ventured out for a few pints in this pub, as well as other haunts around town. Many years later, a student called Jef Evans would recall that Jimmy liked to frequent the bars in Mercersburg, although was never to be seen inebriated.

JIMMY CURRAN

The Galashiels Jimmy had known was changing. Just a month before he arrived, an impressive fountain had been erected in Cornmill Square. It had been preceded by the opening of a new sewerage works in 1912, the town's first cinema a year previously, and a year before that had seen the demolition of King's Temperance Hotel.

But his return home, whilst driven by the desire to see his family again, was dominated by travelling around Scotland and northern England to take part in a series of professional running events, often competing alongside men of the stature of Walter Knox, Hans Holmer, William Kolehmainen, and Jack Donaldson. Indeed, in his first month after landing at Glasgow, he met up with two others who had crossed the Atlantic to challenge the British racing circuit – Frank Kanaly, athletics coach at Massachusetts Institute of Technology (MIT), and Nate Cartmell, quadruple Olympic medallist and coach of the North Carolina Tar Heels basketball team. The threesome headed for the coastal town of Portobello, just east of Edinburgh, where they no doubt practised on the sands before the tourists arrived.

With no need to hide his identity, he ditched his professional name, Gordon, and reverted to Curran. His first race was the 800 yards Lothian Handicap at the Jedburgh Border Games. He had won the race previously, in 1905, that time running off scratch. But even a six-year absence was not enough to pique the goodwill of the handicappers, and once again he would run from the rear of the field. Once the race began he quickly picked off his opponents, took to the front, and led throughout, scooping up the Calgary Cup as his prize. A week later he won both the half-mile and the half-mile handicap at the Kelso Games, winning £2 in the latter. He then travelled across the country, taking first places in Forfar and Blairgowrie, plus a third place at the Clyde F.C. Sports in Glasgow where he beat Hans Holmer and William Kolehmainen (albeit with a 70 yards advantage). His intent had been to then attend a major athletics meet in Manchester, which was to be graced by a top quality field including the great Australian sprinter Jack Donaldson, as well as Kanaly, Cartmell, Holmer and Kolehmainen. But in what was likely a tactical move to avoid a strong international field, Jimmy headed to the other side of the country to take part in an event in Morpeth.

In 1873 a wrestler called Edmund Morgan, wanting to create a competition that would attract the nation's best wrestlers, founded the Morpeth Wrestling and Athletic Games, later known as the Morpeth Olympics. Before the coming of the railway, Morpeth had been a successful market town on the east coast, 15 miles north of Newcastle on the road to Edinburgh. Its geographic situation made it easily accessible for spectators and the event quickly grew with crowds reaching several thousands. Races in the early years were often won by local men, but this became less common as the event prizes grew, attracting runners from further afield. By 1913, when Jimmy took part in the half-mile handicap, he was one of three runners who hailed from outwith the north-east. With the sun beating down, 6,000 spectators looked on as Jimmy, starting from 15 yards, and with his opponents ranged from 10 to 35 yards in front of him, stormed through the field and won by 10 yards. His fellow interlopers, from Carlisle and Jedburgh, took the other two places. He walked away with a prize of £8 10s.

On his return to Scotland, Jimmy continued on where he had left off south of the border, with two wins in Innerleithen, including a race around the town. He then headed to Carnwath to take part in the world's oldest road race. The winner of the three mile race, which is still held today, was presented with a pair of red hose, or stockings, into the tip of which was sewn a gold sovereign. Even more impressive was that for one year the winner would become heir to the lands of Lee and Carnwath, and thus a seat in the House of Lords, should all members of the landowner's family die of natural causes. Jimmy's second place, and therefore failure to put himself in the hunt for ownership of the lands, was tempered by a win in the half-mile. Years later he would argue that he was slightly too old to win it, but would have done so in his younger days.

Two days after Carnwath, he headed south once again to compete in the mile handicap at the Whittingham Games near Alnwick. Running off scratch he won the race by three yards from a runner who had started 90 yards ahead of him. An injury ended the chance of squeezing in any final races before he returned home.

How many races Jimmy competed in isn't known. He was home for two months and attended at least 10 meetings, running in multiple races at most. By the time Jimmy boarded the RMS *Celtic* at Liverpool on 4th September, he had won at least 12 events, and taken two second places and a third place. How much money he had in his pocket as he journeyed west across the Atlantic is also unknown, but it would have more than covered his travel costs, and allowed him to bring back an array of goods from Scotland. In later years his granddaughters remembered him bringing back fine woollens which would be fashioned into clothes such as kilts and coats, as well as shortbread, a 1953 Coronation coin, and records of the Royal Edinburgh Military Tattoo. Christmas of 1913 was a good one for the Currans.

The enormity of Jimmy's feat should not be underestimated. The handicapping system is an attempt to ensure that no one runner can dominate a racing season. Jimmy did just that. He was so good he beat the system.

*****

The 1913/14 season began with a sense of unbridled optimism. Meredith had moved on to the University of Pennsylvania, but Robinson had been joined by one of the finest athletic prospects in America, an all-rounder from Oak Park, Illinois, called Harry 'Dutch' Goelitz. Goelitz had been an outstanding all-round athlete at Oak Park High School, his finest moment being victory in the decathlon in the 1913 International Games in Chicago. It was only the second time the event had been held in America. Jimmy was aware that an all-round athlete of Goelitz's stature, could virtually guarantee victory at multiple events, and so offered up a scholarship. The next intake of students at

THE GREATEST YEAR

Oak Park High School saw the arrival of a budding literary giant, rather than a sporting one – Ernest Hemingway.

At the annual Field Day, Robinson and Goelitz battled it out for the Williams Cup, split the honours, and the trophy was engraved with both names. Soon after, a Faculty-Student Dual Meet was set up, with Jimmy to race Robinson over 50 yards. As good an athlete as Jimmy was, he had no answer to the weapons in Robinson's armoury.

On his return from Scotland, Jimmy, along with some of the finest college and high school coaches in America, was invited to attend a meeting of professional coaches in New York City in the office of William 'Sparrow' Robertson, a sports journalist who had spent much of his career writing for the Paris edition of the *New York Herald Tribune*. The aim was to create a coaches' organisation to protect athletics from the views of theorists, such as the Physical Research Society, whilst promoting practical training methods. On 30th December, the Professional Trainers' Association of America was founded and its committee members elected – Harry Hillman of Dartmouth College as chairman, and Lawson Robertson of the Irish-American Athletic Club as secretary-treasurer – and a discussion saw strong support for the continuation of the Amateur Athletic Union rule prohibiting amateurs and professionals competing against one another. Although a further meeting was to be held in Boston two months later, the organisation appears to have faded into obscurity without achieving a great deal. It would be another four years before coaches and trainers would again attempt, this time successfully, to create a formal body to oversee the profession.

The following day, with Jimmy barely back from New York City, and the family preparing for their traditional Scottish Hogmanay, it was announced that Albert Robinson had been expelled from Mercersburg Academy. The school had a strict rule that students had to be back on premises by 6pm, and around Christmas he was spotted in town by a professor and failed to return until 8pm. The strictness of the rule was brought into stark profile when he was euphemistically 'excused from further study.' The day he was caught, two other athletes, Barry Cantwell, and future Olympic decathlete Harry Goelitz, were given the same punishment, for leaving the Academy without permission. William Mann Irvine, refused to allow them back into the school. But were these transgressions enough to warrant expulsion, even in the face of the more repressive mores of the early 20th century? The answer will likely never be known. However, one must ask whether William Mann Irvine, a man for whom a successful athletics team was a driving force, and who was more than happy to flout scholarship ethics in order to achieve that success, would threaten his vision in order to punish what can, at best, be described as misdemeanours?

In later years Jimmy would always mention Robinson as one of the two greatest runners he had ever coached, but would often lament his departure. In an effort to retain Robinson's dignity, he never revealed the full story, always noting that he had met a girl, moved north to Detroit, and quit athletics altogether. For a short time Robinson did compete, along with Harry Goelitz, for Keewatin Academy in Wisconsin and, in what was to prove an ironic twist of fate, Mercersburg faced Keewatin on 9th May 1914 at the Cornell Interscholastics. Fully aware that his team was no match for Robinson, Jimmy, in a sly attempt to tire him out, kept him up to 2am playing pool and drinking Coke. But the two-man Keewatin team destroyed all before them, walking away with the team trophy. The defeat summed up Mercersburg's season; wins in a few dual meets, but defeat at all major ones.

Soon after, Robinson entered the University of Michigan, but by February 1916, a severe bout of rheumatism had ended his university career. By August he had married and, in a move that was Rimbaudesque in its finality, ended his athletics career whilst at the very pinnacle of his powers.

But despite this unfortunate saga, Jimmy's first three years at Mercersburg had been a success, surpassing the feats of his predecessors and building a foundation for his own legacy. His teams had brought home first and second places in the Penn Relays, and had won the majority of meets they had entered, whilst Ted Meredith had returned from Stockholm with two gold medals, three world records, and a reputation as one of America's greatest ever athletes. Furthermore, he had, importantly, endeared himself to William Mann Irvine, who would address him in letters as 'my dearest Jimmie.' This was no doubt, in part, due to his engaging personality, but Jimmy was also an incredibly hard worker. He threw himself into school events with gusto. In addition to his athletic duties Jimmy also served, for several seasons, as the manager of the Academy's soccer team. It is likely that he wholeheartedly embraced the role, perhaps in part because it was he who introduced the sport to the Academy after returning from his trip to Scotland in 1911. He also frequently kept time at football games, as well as taking on the role of coach to the school's boxers, whose opponents were warned 'not [to] molest them or they may demonstrate, to your sorrow, some of the graceful motions which Coach Curran has taught them.' But Jimmy was not merely a sports coach with a limited skillset. The school's YMCA was a regular recipient of his wisdom, with one talk declaring that boys should live 'clean lives, towards which the best influence is our participation in athletics.' Others included *Training Experiences* and the intriguingly-titled *The Vicissitudes of a Coach*. For the rest of his life he continued to give diverse talks to equally diverse groups, his eclectic repertoire perhaps best summed up in a talk given to the Mercersburg Woman's Club titled *Problems of a British Housewife*. Jimmy continued to spread his wisdom far and wide throughout his career. His largest audience likely came when he was interviewed on the WNEW radio station in New York City in 1950. And he even tried his hand at acting. Soon after the start of the First World War he even took part in a school play, squarely aimed at Germany, called *Kaser Vilhellum Der Grocer*. Jimmy, appropriately, played the role of Scotland, no doubt created for him. He had laid a foundation for himself. Now he had to build upon it.

Chapter 11 • The Master Mechanic

There were certain benefits to working at a school. As well as the decent, regular wage, it also offered a free summer. In 1912, when the news arrived of Meredith's Olympic victory, Jimmy was working on a paint crew at the school. In later years he would use his time equally well – undertaking summer coaching jobs, travelling home to his native Scotland, or taking in sporting spectacles such as the Olympics or the Open golf. There was one thing he had no intention of doing – lounging around Mercersburg.

Within months of the 1912 Olympics ending, Jimmy's name was being promoted as coach of both the British and American Olympic teams to compete at Berlin in 1916; a sportswriter called Francis noted that Jimmy's name was in the frame for the US coaching role, whilst Jimmy's old promoter Arthur Duffey was touting him for the British role. But the most effusive promotion came from a reporter at the *Sporting Chronicle* who noted, 'I have no acquaintance with Curran, never spoke to him, never "ground an axe" in my life, but if Great Britain is in earnest as to [the 1916 Olympics], here is the name of the master mechanic.'

The role of British team head coach never came his way, but on the back of his trip to Europe in 1913, an offer was forthcoming. At many of the events he took part in, one of those who also competed, although never against Jimmy, was a Canadian all-rounder called Walter Knox. The enigmatic Knox was a fine athlete, perhaps the best all-rounder in the world. His slight build – in his youth he weighed only 150lbs – belied his speed and strength, and, placing great emphasis on technique, he was considered one of the finest shot putters in the world. He competed against the best the world had to offer, both in officially-sanctioned events, and in ones cobbled together with huge prizes at stake. By March 1914 he had been hired as head trainer of the British team for the 1916 Olympics, and was in search of nine assistants. Each would be assigned a geographic region of the country, and work with the athletes in that region. He offered Jimmy one of these posts, covering the Scottish region, on a £3 per week contract lasting three months running from June to August in 1914 and 1915. Jimmy accepted the post on the provision that his expenses across the channel would be paid. It is unclear if Jimmy's expenses request was a step too far for Knox, but he never took up the offer. Within months, in light of the unfolding conflict in Europe that would descend into the Great War, Knox would be paid a lump sum of £400 to terminate his employment. Jimmy's offer, if it was still in place, was withdrawn.

And so, free from this international undertaking, he had, by early May 1914, accepted a summer coaching job at the Meadowbrook Club of Philadelphia. It was an offer he accepted each year until 1920, due in great part to the fact that it didn't impinge on his work as coach at Mercersburg.

The Meadowbrook Club was the brainchild of John Wanamaker. Born in Philadelphia in 1838, he opened his first clothing store in the city in 1861, and thereafter continued to expand his empire. It was his purchase of an abandoned railroad depot, in 1875, that heralded his transition from successful merchant into world-renowned businessman. Aided by a fine understanding of the burgeoning art of advertising, he began to expand outwards, first to New York, and on to London and Paris. But Wanamaker was not simply obsessed with making more and more money with little thought for those who undertook the menial tasks that helped him achieve his goals. He cared deeply for his employees. And so, in a philanthropic effort to improve their education and health, he founded the Meadowbrook Club in 1909. Those seeking a healthy outlet could join Meadowbrook's athletic club, which had grounds built at 23rd and Market Street on the Schuylkill River in Philadelphia. Wanamaker then built the world's most expensive gymnasium, complete with running track and tennis courts, known as Wanamaker Field, on the roof of the company's new 12-storey store at Juniper and Market Streets. All employees of the John Wanamaker Store were eligible to become members. But whilst the motive of the Club was to 'promote sport for sport's sake' and forge 'good health and sound body', Wanamaker had an overwhelming desire to compete with the country's great athletic institutions in New York, Chicago and Detroit. His employees alone were no match for these clubs, so he headhunted established athletes to turn out in the Meadowbrook colours, and brought in experienced coaches to train them. It is unclear whether Jimmy was offered the Meadowbrook head coach role full-time, but it is a distinct possibility. If this was the case, he turned it down, and the role went to Clarence Foster, physical instructor at Mercersburg Academy, and formerly a Major League baseball player with the New York Giants and the Chicago White Sox. Foster (later replaced by Louis Spealler) grabbed the opportunity. But the Club was determined to acquire Jimmy's skills and knowledge in some way, and he was offered the role of trainer during the summer months. Jimmy, always looking to fill his free time, jumped at the chance. The choice of a coach from Mercersburg was no chance occurrence – Rodman Wanamaker, son of John, had attended Princeton University with William Mann Irvine, and he was fully aware that through this link he would have access to numerous former Mercersburg athletes. Jimmy's addition as trainer only made the prospect of attracting former Mercersburg athletes more likely, and that it was successful is evidenced by many of Mercersburg's finest athletes from the 1910s – Meredith, Eddie Shields, Allen Woodring, and Allen Swede are but four – pulling on the Meadowbrook vest. Mercersburg was now, effectively a feeder school for the Meadowbrook Club, in much the same way as it was for the University of Pennsylvania.

The Club's athletes competed at events across the east, as far south and west as St Louis, breaking records wherever they went. Each year the Club held its own sports carnival in Philadelphia, attracting some of America's finest sports clubs, and some of the world's best athletes. World records fell like dominoes, as did a number of smaller records, many times at the hands of men trained by Jimmy. Ted

Meredith was the most prolific, breaking the world indoor record for the 660 yards in 1915, and the world outdoor record for the 880 yards the following year. At the 1918 Meadowbrook Games athletes and teams trained by Spealler and Jimmy won event after event – the one mile handicap and two mile relay races won by Meadowbrook and Mercersburg respectively, the one mile interscholastic by Mercersburg, the long jump and 660 yards race all went to Meadowbrook runners, whilst Allen Swede, formerly of Mercersburg, won the half-mile in the fastest ever indoor time at that distance by a schoolboy.

*****

In July 1914 Europe was thrown into turmoil. A murdered Archduke and two out-dated alliances saw fears and tensions, simmering for decades, finally boil over. Foes dug into the mud of Flanders and waited for a Christmas victory that never came. The months stretched into years, as new recruits replaced old soldiers, and men suffered mental trauma that would haunt them for the rest of their lives. And America waited, determined to avoid burying the hopes and dreams of its sons in the blood- and sinew-infused mud of Europe. It was a country filled with first generation immigrants and many had immediate family serving in the conflict, on both sides. There was little doubt as to where Jimmy's loyalties lay. As well as his ties to Scotland, he was also a veteran of the British Army, and many of his old friends and colleagues, including his former protégé, Wyndham Halswelle, were dodging bullets and artillery and disease in the Flanders hellhole.

Despite the self-imposed distance the war began to impact recent immigrants, and Jimmy was no exception – his cousins John and Thomas Mabon died in the last two years of the war at Gaza and Arras respectively. Halswelle also fell. Ironically, for a man for whom fair play was paramount, at the hands of a sniper's bullet. Stateside, life went on much as it had before, and athletic competitions continued without interruption.

THE MASTER MECHANIC

In the early years of the First World War many Scots returned from America and Canada to sign up and fight for their homeland. With America's entry into the war in April 1917, driven by the re-introduction of unrestricted submarine warfare, and the Zimmerman Telegram, there were opened across the country a number of recruiting stations whose primary aim was to mop up those America-based Britons who had not already returned home across the Atlantic. In August 1917 Jimmy headed to Philadelphia to take part in the Scottish Games. The day before the event he made his way to 23 South 9th Street and entered the recently-opened British Recruiting Mission, which was bedecked with posters dominated by a Union flag and bearing the words 'Britishers Enlist To-Day.' He may have been in his late 30s with a wife and five children (the Mission accepted men between the ages of 18 and 45), but he wanted to play his part – he was supremely fit and had experience of warfare. But even an overwhelming desire could not trump army regulations; since he was a young man Jimmy had been plagued by chronic varicose veins, and they put an end to any dream he had of fighting for his country. The following day he attended the Scottish Games and witnessed a rousing speech by Colonel St George L. Steele in which he pled for young men to sign up to the flag. He then went on to win the mile and half-mile races, and even tried his hand at the hammer, finishing third with a throw of 70' 9". Witnessing this display of prowess, one of the recruiting officers, quite possibly Steele, approached him and asked if he had considered enlisting. Jimmy relayed the story of the previous day, and the officer was apologetic, promising to see what he could do to have this particular regulation changed.

As Jimmy's former Mercersburg athletes crossed the Atlantic, schemes were being organised whereby men and women on the home front could play their part. In April 1918 he and 100 other college and high school coaches, including 'Pooch' Donovan, Johnny Mack and Keene Fitzpatrick, attended a meeting in Philadelphia at the behest of Walter Camp, formerly a successful football coach at Yale and Stanford. Camp had been asked by the War Department to bring together, under the auspices of the recently-organised Commission on Training Camp Activities, the finest trainers, coaches, and athletic directors in America, with a view to travelling to Europe and ensuring America's aviators were provided with recreational activities, and to further reduce the spread of sexually transmitted diseases and alcohol abuse, normally rampant in army camps. Jimmy listened as Colonels Theodore C. Lyster and George H. Crabtree outlined why the men were needed, and what would be required of them. Inspired, eight of the attendees signed up, including Jimmy's friend Arthur Duffey, and his old adversary Percy Smallwood. Jimmy remained non-committal.

But he did eventually sign up, albeit when he was required to do so. Three registrations took place over the course of the war with the earliest birth date covered in the first two being in 1886. In September 1918 a third registration was instituted encompassing all men, whether naturalised or not (Jimmy was not), who had been born any time from September 1872. Jimmy fell well within the boundaries and so, on 9th September 1918, the 38-year-old Scot, still considered an alien in the eyes of the US Government, headed to the Post Office building in the neighbouring town of Greencastle and signed on for service in the US Army. After the US entered the Second World War, in 1941, Jimmy was also part of the 'Old Man's Draft', used to determine the 'industrial capacity and skills of men' aged between the ages of 45 and 64.

*****

But despite the news coming from Europe, life in America had to go on. Beginning in 1914 the Curran family began attending the Caledonian Games in Philadelphia. A traditional Scottish gathering, it saw new immigrants mingle with the descendants of early Scots settlers, bringing the hills and glens of Scotland to a tartan-bedecked south Philadelphia. In 1916 the day began with a parade through the city, as 1,500 Scots marched down Kensington Avenue to Glenwood, their woollen kilts swishing from side to side as they walked, before catching trolleys to Central Park. And the revelrous atmosphere was no doubt aided by the imbibing of vast quantities of Scotch whisky (at least until the introduction of prohibition in 1920). The Curran girls competed at Highland dancing competitions and young Jimmy, resplendent in full Highland dress – coatee, kilt, sporran, sgian-dubh – won a special prize in the best dressed boy category on at least one occasion. But the gathering was not simply an opportunity for those of Scots descent to openly display their ancestry; included in the day's events was a sporting programme that drew the best from not only the east coast, but across the world.

For the next six years it would prove a happy hunting ground for Jimmy, winning a number of mile and half-mile races. In 1916 the reporter at the *Philadelphia Inquirer* took great delight in Jimmy's victories, noting that his 'mercurial heels still possess the old dash and vigor in the mile and half-mile runs', whilst the following year his half-mile time of 2.11 was highlighted as 'exceptionally fast when the poor condition of the track is taken into consideration.'

*****

After four seasons at Mercersburg, Jimmy's record was patchy, from the highs of the Meredith and Robinson successes of the 1911/12 season, to the lows following the Robinson and Goelitz controversy of 1913/14. It is unlikely Jimmy's job was on the line, but his own personal pride would have been smarting. The school needed success, and so did Jimmy. The 1914/15 season brought control back into Jimmy's hands, but if he hoped the cross country runs at the end of 1914 would provide some stability, then his hopes were about to be dashed, at least initially.

On 14th November, Mercersburg strode out at the Columbia University meet, held on the streets of New York City, confident and capable of victory. But they hadn't counted on a powerful runner called Alvin Robertson, the sole representative of Evander Childs High School. As the 200 starters made their way up Riverside Drive, Alster

Schunk, who Jimmy had brought on board through a scholarship, and Harvey 'Beck' Reed, were in contention with a handful of boys as they turned into the hill of 116th Street. The incline, however, proved to be the downfall of all but Robertson and he strode to victory with the two Mercersburg boys just seconds behind. The team placed a disappointing fourth, due in great part to the captain, William Merriam Stevenson, falling ill mid-race.

If the boys were crestfallen after this unexpected defeat, Jimmy rallied them for the Thanksgiving American Interscholastic Cross Country Championship. In the days following the defeat in New York he had unearthed a new secret weapon. Eddie Shields had been a star on the school's swim team, but only a week before the race he tried his hand at the mile in the school's Field Day, emerging victorious. Three days before the cross country meet Jimmy had Shields jog five miles. The next day he pushed him harder over three miles. On race day he finished in sixth, one of four Mercersburg boys in the first seven places. The low placing of the team's fifth runner, who trailed in in 26th place, almost cost the team victory, but they eventually defeated Philadelphia's Central High School by a single point.

In the New Year the track season began, first indoor and, as the weather improved, it passed into stadia. Essentially a coach had to build two teams if he wanted success in both disciplines. And that is just what Jimmy did. Reed and Shields transferred from the cross country and were supported by a strong group of runners, notably George Meredith (Ted's brother), Elmer Smith, and William Stark. An author in the alumni magazine highlighted why, in his opinion, Jimmy had built such an outstanding team:

> By careful, slow, conscientious work, molding his men, training the distance men into middle distance, developing new field material, and again training the men back to other events as he weighed the opponents in the next meets.

THE MASTER MECHANIC

In February 1915 the school was abuzz with the news, announced by Jimmy in the school dining room, that Ted Meredith would return to the school and run a special race – against his former coach. The two lined up against each other on the track sitting atop the gymnasium, as the students, including Ted's brother, stood enthralled and cheering below. The race was handicapped – Ted to run ten circuits of the short 80-yard track, Jimmy to run nine. Ted would have to lap Jimmy to win. As the two set off Ted took an early lead of four yards, but Jimmy stayed tight on him and the lead never extended. When Jimmy finished his ninth lap, Ted still had almost a lap to go.

In February the team strode to victories at Brooklyn and Baltimore. Another easy win followed at the New York University Interscholastics in April, where, as well as Ted's brother George, the crowd were also witness to the talent of his cousin, Bob Meredith, running for Peddie Institute.

A week later Jimmy and his boys travelled to Franklin Field in Philadelphia for the Penn Relays. On a day dominated by Ted Meredith, when he ran a 48 ⅖ last leg for the University of Pennsylvania relay team in the college mile, breaking the world record in the process, the Mercersburg team dug deep to win the prep school mile. Starting the last lap seven yards behind Phillips Exeter, Elmer Smith made up the deficit, and then added an additional 10 yards to win easily in 49 ⅗.

With three months of the season down and only one to go, Mercersburg had run its way to a perfect track record. But the schedule in May was the year's busiest, with three major meets, plus a dual meet with the Penn Freshmen. On the 1st of the month came the Cornell Interscholastics, and the team's spectacular form continued, with five Mercersburg runners walking away with first places in the sprints and middle distances. A week later, in preparation for the Middle States Interscholastics, the team faced up to the Penn Freshmen, a home meet designed to test the Prep School boys against college opponents. The college team was roundly beaten, with Smith winning three events, finishing second in one, and Shields and Reed winning the one and two miles respectively, the latter breaking Mercersburg's two mile record.

The penultimate race of the season was the prestigious Middle States Interscholastics, held at Franklin Field. The standout event was the mile race, where Eddie Shields, who had already proven himself throughout the season, and his twin brother, Larry, of West Chester High, battled it out. The two ran neck and neck, outclassing the rest of the field. In the final stretch Eddie took a two-yard lead, but his brother closed and they couldn't be separated as they approached the line, where Eddie, likely using a technique taught him by Jimmy, flung himself at the tape, winning by less than a foot. The paths of Jimmy and Larry would soon cross again. Reed also won the two mile race. But overall the Hill School athletes were just slightly better and took the meet.

A week later came the season's last event, at Princeton, and again Eddie Shields would prove his class. Running in a downpour that laid a pool of water over the track, he emerged victorious from the mile and two mile races, whilst the school also recorded victories in two more events, exacting revenge over the Hill School on the way by a margin of 14½ points. Any thought from William Mann Irvine that Jimmy might not be a good fit with the school was dispelled by a season that was one of the very finest Jimmy would put together in his 51 years as Head Coach. The team hadn't contained the stars of his 1911/12 team, but it was his most rounded. Jimmy had found a formula: build a team capable of competing in every event and you give yourself the chance of victory. Dependence on one or two track stars left success reliant on variables such as injury and form.

The omens seemed good for the 1915/16 season. The previous season had been an overwhelming success, and all the major athletes in that team – Reed, Shields, Schunk, Meredith and Stevenson – had returned to the school. At the Columbia cross country event, held again on the streets of New York City, Shields and Reed proved the class of the team and, with the previous year's winner, the supremely talented Alvin Robertson, not competing, placed first and third respectively. The team also emerged victorious, with its best five runners all finishing in the top 12 places, putting together a low score of 30, compared to the previous year's 126. 'The Mercersburg boys', according to the athletics administrator Gustavus T. Kirby, 'ran like one man.'

Two weeks later the team was at the American Interscholastics meet. Shields showed his class, winning easily and leading Mercersburg to victory. As well as an interest in his own athletes, Jimmy was always on the lookout for others he felt might strengthen his team the following year. And at this meet he no doubt had his eyes set on Allen Swede and Alvin Robertson, finishing in second and third respectively. His pursuit of Swede would prove successful. Robertson would remain at Evander Childs.

*****

In an effort to lighten the boys' mood during wartime, albeit with America not having yet joined, a cross country race was set up in December 1915 between Jimmy and two students of German descent – Donald Hellfrich and Harry Smock. Jimmy won – his prize being the desserts of the two losing students – and the joke around campus was that Hellfrich has lost his hyphen and Smock had stumbled over it.

*****

The track team began where the cross country team had left off, with wins in the Wanamaker Games and the New York University Interscholastics. On 29th April they made their way to Philadelphia to defend the prep school mile championship at the Penn Relays, in what Jimmy knew would be a major test: Phillips Exeter Academy boasted a team that was considered one of the best ever, and St Albans School was known to be a quality outfit. As the gun fired, the lead-off man for St Albans, Untz Brewer, a future NFL quarterback, false started. He was pulled back one yard, and this saw him boxed in over the early part of the race. Once he broke free, he charged to a two yard lead by the time he handed over the baton, with the *Washington Post* asserting that if he had run from his original starting point he would have been ahead by five yards. By the time the teams got to the anchor legs, Mercersburg had fought back, mainly through the efforts of George Meredith who had overcome a deficit to lead the field by three yards. With the ever reliable Reed running as anchor the crowd must have thought the title was sewn up. But they had overlooked the not inconsiderable talents of St Albans' Bob Maxam. Starting in third place, he kept his powder dry for around 300 yards before putting his foot to the floor. He won by five yards. Jimmy's hope for a perfect season was gone.

But if the season was not to be perfect, it still had the potential to be exceptional. In the following fortnight the team posted wins at the Cornell and Princeton meets. And then, in early May, Shields ran a two mile race at a meet on the Mercersburg track, knocking 13 seconds off the previous world interscholastic record. Mercersburg students now held the world interscholastic records for the 440 yards, the half-mile, and the two miles. This sparked the mischievous side of Jimmy, and he resolved to take the missing record, the mile. So, on 20th May, just a week after his two miles record was set, Shields stepped onto the track at the Tome School meet and ran 4.23 ⅗, taking three seconds off the previous record.

The final major meet of the season was the Middle States Interscholastics Championship at Franklin Field. The team's performance would have raised a smile on Jimmy's face, with five wins from the 13 events. But on a personal level it was the performance of Beck Reed which made his day. He won the mile and two mile races at a canter, but it was in the former where his performance really raised eyebrows. He fell at the beginning of the race, picked himself up, chased down the pack, and won by a good distance.

For the 1916/17 season, Jimmy had continued to work hard to bring in quality athletes across the disciplines: Harold 'Boots' Lever in the sprints, Allen Swede in the longer distances, and Bob Angell, described as a 'whale' among the schoolboys, in the throwing events, would prove to be the foundation of Jimmy's success over the coming seasons. And they were soon to prove their worth. But occasionally fate intervened and did Jimmy's job for him.

Allen Woodring was a slight, quiet and studious boy with thinning blonde hair, the son of a lawyer from Hellerstown, Pennsylvania. He first pulled on a Mercersburg vest in the autumn of 1916 and initially saw his athletic future as a cross country runner, until he was beaten in a race and ended up on the receiving end of some light-hearted banter. He bet his tormentor that he could beat him in a 100-yard race. Jimmy looked on as Woodring broke away from the start and won by a distance. But it wasn't simply Woodring's victory that impressed Jimmy – it was the form with which he won. In that 100 yards, Jimmy was able to deduce, as his mentor Mike Murphy had done three decades earlier with John Owen, that Woodring, with his 'beautiful easy stride', had a natural and largely untapped speed. It is this intuition that sets the great coaches apart from the good ones. Jimmy had proved, once again, that he could look upon those with little more than raw talent and discern that with some coaching they could be capable of extraordinary athletic feats. His track team had a new sprinter. Over the years he fell back on this talent many times to build his teams.

Swede impressed early. As he had done the previous year, when a student at Central High, he finished second in the Columbia Interscholastics Cross Country Championship. In the New Year, as part of the track team, his form continued, and on the track at the Central High Games he won both the mile and half-mile, the former in an American interscholastic record. At the end of April the team won the New York University meet, and days later the mile relay team finished second in the Penn Relays. In May, at the Princeton Games, the whole team showed its potential emerging victorious from seven events, with wins for Lever, Swede, Angell and Woodring seeing the school defeat Hill School. A week later the school was found at the Middle States Interscholastics meet, and the boys must have arrived at Franklin Field feeling particularly positive, having defeated their main challengers, the

Hill School, just a week previously. But despite two wins for Lever, and one each for Angell and Woodring, it was not to be. Hill School walked away with the honours, Mercersburg's day summed up by a rare defeat for Allen Swede in the two mile race. Whilst the season had not attained the heights of the previous two, the strength in depth was enough to bring decent success across the season, never finishing below second place in the relays or team events.

After two second places in the American Interscholastics Cross Country Championship, one with Central High and the other with Mercersburg, Allen Swede finally registered a win at the start of the 1917/18 season, finishing the 4½ mile course in 22.30, one of the fastest ever times, a display described as 'one of the greatest triumphs ever achieved in scholastic circles.' For once Jimmy took some of the plaudits alongside his athletes, one newspaper noting that 'Jimmy Curran's name once more stands out in a blaze of glory when compared with the names of other American schoolboy coaches.'

The track season began with a return to Allen Swede's old school, Central High. And Swede delivered devastating performances in the mile and half-mile, breaking the interscholastic indoor record in the former, and the meet record at the shorter distance. Jimmy's team was solid across the board and the meet ended with Mercersburg victorious. The following months saw defeat at the Wanamaker meet, and second place in the mile relay at the Penn Relays. But victories came at a dual meet against the Carlisle Indians, and at the Middle States Interscholastics and Princeton meets in late April and May. Against Carlisle they proved dominant, while at the Middle States meet they walked away with six wins, six second places, and a host of thirds and fourths. Woodring set out Jimmy's stall early in the 220 yards heats with a time that was a mere fifth of a second outside the world record. He failed to repeat his time in the final, but still won the event. And then Allen Swede did what was becoming commonplace for him, he broke another record. This time it was the interscholastic world record for the two miles, despite contending with strong winds and showers that left the track muddy. Indeed, so fast was he that his first mile was four seconds faster than the winning time in the mile race. Mercersburg was absolutely dominant. And this dominance continued on into the Princeton meet just a week later, which once again saw Woodring and Swede wins secure victory. The individual performances of men such as Woodring and Swede marked out Mercersburg as having perhaps the finest high school athletics programme in America, and Jimmy as perhaps the finest coach.

So successful was the team that Woodring, Swede, Angell, and Frank Davis all made the All Scholastic Team, made up of the finest high school athletes on the east coast. Mercersburg athletes regularly made this team, and occasionally the All-American Team, but this was the only occasion that four boys made a single team.

As the new term approached, sad news made its way to Mercersburg. Former athlete, Eugene Davis, just weeks away from entering the University of Pennsylvania, was killed while earning tuition money doing summer work on the Philadelphia & Reading Railroad. And Jimmy lost a number of the other stars who had been central to the school's recent success, albeit in less tragic ways. Woodring was off to Bethlehem Prep, whilst Swede headed to the Line Officers' Training Camp at Camp Lee, Va.

Jimmy's 1918/19 team faced their first test at Fairmount Park in Philadelphia at the American Interscholastic Cross Country Championships, and it did not end well. A number of low placings saw the boys gain only fifth place. But the day was about to get much worse. With the race over, Jimmy needed to take his boys to eat. On checking for the $100 assigned him for this task, he found his pocket empty. A light-fingered opportunist had ended the day significantly better off than he or she had started it. Jimmy had to borrow the fare home from the University of Pennsylvania.

The season was to prove a mixed bag, with wins against Harrisburg Tech, and in the one mile prep school relay at the Penn Relays. But the meets at Princeton and the Middle States did not end so well, finishing third in the former, and a close second behind the Hill School in the latter.

There were few positive signs in the early part of the 1919/20 season, with a mixture of wins and losses, including a third place in the one mile at the Penn Relays. But all was not completely lost. Harry Bigelow broke the interscholastic indoor high jump record at Newark with a leap of 5 feet 9⅝, and this was followed by victories at the Wanamaker Games, the Cornell Interscholastics meet, and the Pennsylvania Middle States Championships.

The quality of Jimmy's athletic programme over the previous decade was clear to all who took an interest in the sport. He had produced a double Olympic gold medallist, and a string of quality teams and individuals. Had the First World War not erupted, it is likely that many others, not least a returning Ted Meredith, would have paraded their talents on a world stage at the Berlin Olympics of 1916. But some did get their chance in the wake of the war. With the conflict over, hundreds of thousands of American servicemen were based in France awaiting transport home. In order to keep them occupied, the General Staff of the American Expeditionary Force (AEF) organised a series of sporting championships, drawing together the best European-based athletes from the Allied countries. A broad range of sports were organised from company level, through battalion, regiment, division, corps and the whole army, leading to the AEF Championships, and culminating with the finest athletes competing at the Inter-Allied Games at Stade Pershing in Paris. In terms of numbers of competitors, this was a competition on a grand scale, with an estimated 1.2m soldiers taking part in at least one event. A number of Jimmy's former students – Harold 'Boots' Lever, Eugene Hammitt and Pete Maxfield from Mercersburg, and Eddie Meehan, Harold Barron and Eddie Shields from the Meadowbrook Club – took part.

From March the events moved around France and Luxembourg, allowing thousands of soldiers to compete. The quality of the field is evident in the fact that even Jimmy's two future Olympians – Shields and Barron – failed to record a solo win at the Inter-Allied Games. The best results recorded were a 4.27 ⅗ mile by Shields at the AEF Championships, and relay wins for both Shields and Meehan at the Inter-Allied Games. Shields also looked nailed on for a bronze medal in the final of the 1,500m – he was 'trotting' towards the finish line when the Canadian, H.E. Lapierre, used every last ounce of his strength to pip him at the line. The event was not overly important, but it paved the way for the following year's Olympics, to be held in Antwerp.

The most well-known of Jimmy's students looking to take part in the Antwerp Olympics was Ted Meredith. Upon the announcement of the Games, several newspapers requested that Ted cover the events for them. The best way to gain access to the athletes, he concluded, was to qualify and become one himself. After eight years that had witnessed him set further world records at 440, 500, 880 yards and the mile relay, and then retire from athletics to become an aviator in France in 1917, this was Meredith's opportunity for a final resurrection. He began to hit the track, and finally returned competitively at a meeting on 12th June at Travers Island, home of the New York Athletic Club. All did not go to plan. In a handicapped quarter-mile race, running off scratch, Meredith showed his old form in the early stages but weakened late on and failed to qualify from the heats. A week later he turned up again, this time at Pershing Field in Jersey City. Again he was defeated, but this time only by the width of a vest, and in the relatively fast time of 52 seconds.

The Olympic trials were held in June and July, and Jimmy's former charges were well represented with five who had attended Mercersburg – Ted Meredith, Allen Woodring, Harold Lever, Eddie Shields and Harry Goelitz, as well as at least three, Eddie Meehan, Harold Barron, and Larry Shields, he had worked with at Meadowbrook. Allen Swede would almost certainly have taken part, and probably have qualified, but was in England competing for Princeton against Oxford University.

At the first trials, held at Franklin Field, Philadelphia, the sun flooded onto the running track, with the heat tempered by a light breeze blowing in from the northwest. Conditions were perfect. Jimmy's boys performed well, but paled next to those travelling from New York. Woodring performed best with a win in the 220 yards, whilst Meredith struggled with a fifth place in the 880 yards.

From Philadelphia, the trials moved on the following month to Harvard Stadium, where the best of the best competed once again. Once more, Jimmy's former charges had a chequered day. The most unfortunate was Harold Lever. One of the finest sprinters in America, he had been fully expected to make the Olympic team but fell during his race.

Another who came close was Eddie Shields. Being skilled in running, swimming, horse riding and shooting, Shields took part in trials for the modern pentathlon. He failed to make the team, losing out to two West Point graduates.

The numbers were whittled down and Ted Meredith's qualification in the 400m and the 400m relay, according to one reporter, was enough to 'warm the cockles of Father Knickerbocker's heart.' Allen Woodring took a place in the sprints and sprint relay, and both Larry Shields and Harold Barron made it. And to add to the small coterie of Curran trainees was one of those who had left Mercersburg under a cloud in 1913: Harry Goelitz qualified for the decathlon.

And so, on 26th July, these five, along with around 250 others, attended a farewell program at Manhattan Opera House before parading along a confetti-strewn 34th Street where they boarded ferries that were the first part of a journey that would see them arrive in Belgium, 12 days later, aboard a former troop ship called SS *Princess Matoika*. The conditions aboard the *Matoika* were poor. Ted Meredith, in a letter home, wrote of conditions being a 'disgrace', the food being 'mediocre' and that he was aware of two athletes being bitten by rats. Athlete-led protests began almost immediately. By the time the team neared Antwerp they had issued a series of complaints, railing against the poor standard of onboard accommodation, quality of the food, and a number of other points. Signed by a significant number of athletes, their ire would, in years to come, be known as the Mutiny of the *Matoika*.

THE MASTER MECHANIC

Much of the time on board was spent training as best as was possible within the limited confines of the ship's deck, much as had happened eight years earlier on the Olympic team's journey to Stockholm. The team's fencers and rowers faced few problems, while the middle- and long-distance runners pounded their way around the outer deck of the ship. For others, such as the swimmers and weights men, ingenious methods, first employed in 1912, were used to aid their training – the swimmers wore a belt and swam in place in a miniature canvas pool, while the javelin and discus were attached to ropes allowing them to be thrown into the sea and then reeled back on board. The sprinters made use of a 70-yard cork track. Strangely, the team's 1912 stowaway, Harry Naughton, was again found hiding on board, and again accompanied the team when it reached its destination.

A delay in the trip, due to a leaky boiler on board the *Matoika*, meant that the athletes didn't arrive in Antwerp until 7th August. After settling into their rooms in a schoolhouse in the Rue Oudain, they were finally able to train in the Olympisch Stadion.

The first of Jimmy's athletes to take to the track was Harold Barron. Entered in the 110m hurdles, he was considered a real medal possibility. In his first heat he was pitted against, and beat, the fancied Canadian Earl Thomson. With the two men having the fastest times in the heats, they were split up in the semi-finals. Barron came out in the first semi and equalled the 12-year old world record of 15 seconds flat. Minutes later Thomson strode on to the track and replicated Barron's feat. The scene was set for an incredible final – joint world record holders, the pre-Olympic favourite against the man who had beaten him in the heats. Both camps played up the chances of their men, and when the race started Thomson soon trailed Barron. But by the sixth hurdle Thomson was level and it was then his race to lose. He finished like a 'hurricane', bursting through the tape in a new world record. Barron took silver. Two years later Jimmy would give Barron an opportunity to learn the art of coaching at Mercersburg.

Larry Shields was entered in two events – the 1,500m and the

3,000m team race. On 19th August he lined up for the final of the 1,500m, after breezing through his heat. The race favourite was Shields' team-mate Joie Ray, but he faded badly, leaving Shields to fight it out with two Britons – Albert Hill and Philip Baker – for the gold medal; Hill took the honours with Baker close behind. Shields had to make do with bronze, after a 'courageous effort' that saw him pass a number of opponents in the closing yards.

Two days later he was back on the track for the semi-final of the 3,000m team race. Each competing team has six runners with the first three to finish awarded points according to their finishing place: the winner receiving one point, the runner up two, and so on. The team with the lowest number of points wins, much like the cross country scoring system. In the final the US took three of the top six places to easily win gold. Shields finished in eighth, the fourth-placed American. Outside the three top Americans, he wasn't entitled to a medal.

Harry Goelitz was an all-rounder who, seven years earlier, had been thrown out of the Academy. Unlike one of those who accompanied him out the door, Albert Robinson, Goelitz continued with his athletic career. And the pay-off was a chance to compete in the decathlon at the 1920 Olympic Games. His first step towards selection took place on 10th July at Travers Island. He finished fourth, and took his place in a team that also consisted of the eventual silver medallist Brutus Hamilton, and Eugene Vidal, father of the writer Gore Vidal. At the event in Antwerp he competed well until the end of the fifth event, ending the first day in 11th place, but only 131 points off the bronze medal. But on the second day of events his scores began to drop. Why is unclear, perhaps injury, or simply a run of his less-favoured events. The fact he pulled out of the event before the final race suggests the former.

For Meredith things did not go particularly well: he had clearly suffered at the hands of time. Reaching the semi-finals of the 400m he was beaten into fourth place, fully three seconds outside his world record set at the slightly longer distance of 400 yards. The rest of the

400m runners barely performed better, with only Frank Shea reaching the final. This all-round mediocrity was never clearer than in the final of the 400m relay, against equally mediocre opposition, with the team finishing in fourth, fully seven seconds slower than the 1912 Olympic and world record breaking team.

But as a Jimmy Curran-trained Mercersburg boy had been one of the stars of the 1912 Olympics, eight years later he was about to be eclipsed by another. By the time of the Olympic trials, Allen Woodring was running for Syracuse University and the Meadowbrook Club. So unprepared was he after arriving in Antwerp, his running shoes fell apart and he was forced to borrow a pair from a fellow athlete.

Woodring had only been the team substitute, sixth in line behind Charley Paddock, George Massengale, Loren Murchison, Morris Kirksey and Jackson Scholz. Massengale, however, was struck down by a bout of rheumatism, and when Scholz declared himself too tired after his exertions in the 100m, Woodring grabbed his somewhat unexpected chance.

In the semi-final the British West Indian runner Harry Edward, impressive in his previous races, tweaked a muscle as he rounded the final bend, and spent much of his time between crossing the line and starting the final on the massage table. Woodring won his semi-final ahead of the fancied Charley Paddock. Paddock allowed Woodring his victory, but feared his main opponents lay in Edward and Murchison. In the final Woodring received a favourable draw in the third lane, with Paddock, Edward and Murchison outside him. As the home stretch appeared Paddock was five metres ahead, but with 20 metres remaining Woodring had come up to his shoulder. They crossed the line in a conjoined blur, but, despite both men running 22 seconds dead, Woodring was given the decision. Barely able to comprehend his victory he believed Paddock had let him win. Paddock soon disabused him of this notion. Woodring had won the 200m on his own merits. If Woodring was surprised, those who knew him certainly weren't. Both Jimmy and his coach at Syracuse University had him marked out as a star runner.

A week after the Games, a vast triangular athletic meet against Sweden and France called the Colombes Games brought together many of those athletes that had represented their countries. A number of Jimmy's athletes took medals – Barron a silver in the 110m hurdles, Shields a silver in the 1,500m, whilst Woodring took gold as part of the 400m relay team.

As he had done eight years earlier to celebrate Ted Meredith's success, Jimmy attended a dinner, this time at the Bellevue-Stratford Hotel in Philadelphia, to honour the 26 Philadelphia-area athletes, including Allen Woodring, who had competed at the Olympics.

Chapter 12 • Ru-u-un Laddie

Jimmy had not been home to Scotland since his glorious visit in 1913, largely as a consequence of the war. In late 1920 he returned. The intervening years had seen monumental changes in his personal life. He and Janet had added two more children to the family group – Margaret in 1914, and Jean in 1919 – joining Mary, Ellen and James Jr.

The children would all call Jimmy 'father', and the relationships were loving ones. He rarely lost his temper with his children, but it did happen. Jimmy Jr would, in later years, recall playing baseball with his father in the backyard. He threw the ball, and Jimmy swung the bat and blasted the ball straight through one of the windows in the house. On running in and seeing his mother standing over the broken glass, Jimmy Jr began wailing in the high-pitched voice of a panicking child, "'I didn't do it, I didn't do it!'". Then BAM, I was on the floor looking up at my father who had knocked me down, wagging a finger at me saying "NEVER talk to your mother that way".' Jimmy Jr would then laugh at this childhood memory.

In July 1920, Janet took the children back to Scotland, and would remain there for just over two years. Why she returned to Scotland for such a long period of time is unknown, but it was almost certainly the reason why Jimmy crossed the Atlantic three times in 18 months, starting in December 1920. Little is known of this short trip ending in January 1921, other than he took part in a half-mile race at Powderhall on Christmas Day, in which he placed second in his heat, not good enough to make the final.

*****

As the thrill of Woodring's Olympic success gave way to the realities of school life once again, Jimmy began to bring together a number of potential stars to his team for the 1920/21 season. Middle-distance runner Marvin Rick had come from Erasmus Hall High School at the tail end of the 1919/20 season, and at the start of the new term was joined by sprinter Frank Conway, and an all-rounder called Henry Charles Taylor, known as Chuck.

Conway and Taylor soon proved they were prospects of the highest standard, posting victory after victory throughout the following two seasons, often multiple times at each event. Rick appears to have been less successful, but did produce two second places against the Penn Freshmen, a college team, in the mile and half-mile races. They were joined in their second year by a hurdler called Charles Moore, later known as Crip due to an accident that saw him lose four fingers on one hand, who was equally successful. So impressed was Jimmy by Taylor – he wrote to the boy's hometown paper espousing the belief that he could make the next Olympics – that when the season ended Jimmy crossed the Atlantic for the second time in six months and brought Taylor along. With tickets paid for by Taylor's father, a bank president, the two boarded the RMS *Cedric* in New York, bound for Liverpool. Before he began an abbreviated summer tour through the various Borders games, he and Taylor made their way to the Amateur Athletic Association's Championships at Stamford Bridge in south west London. Taylor was entered into two events – the pole vault, and the long jump. Aided by some good-natured ribbing about America's late entry into the war, a second place in the former was followed by a win in the latter, with a jump of 22' 1". Jimmy had his first Amateur Athletic champion since Wyndham Halswelle had won multiple events at the Scottish and English championships in 1905 and 1906.

Jimmy was aware that the years were catching up on him. For a man of his determination and drive, age would normally have been no barrier, but he had also been plagued by chronic varicose veins since his youth. His mind was willing, his body less so. But he was determined to put his skills on display yet again, challenging the next generation of Borders athletes. It was, effectively, his farewell tour. He had slowed, of that he was fully aware. But in handicap races that simply meant he would be given a better mark.

The first chance to prove himself came at the prestigious Jedburgh Border Games. It had always proved a good hunting ground, with wins in the 800 yards in 1905, running as G. Gordon, and then again eight years later in 1913, running under his real name. And now it was a further eight years on. The stars were aligned, and Jimmy stepped up against some of the finest half-milers in the Borders and took first place.

A week later he was in Dumfries, where he likely still had friends from his time based there in 1898. Once again he took the 800 yards, and topped it off with a second place in the mile, and a win in the hop, step and jump. Over the next month he undertook a mini-tour of the Borders Common Ridings, turning up at Langholm, Greenlaw and Innerleithen, and taking two first places. He likely ran at several more events than are evident in the local newspapers.

Jimmy returned to Scotland again in 1922, and for the first time took part in no events, although he did act as steward, alongside old friends A.D. Lawson and John Torrie, at the Selkirk and Galashiels Agricultural Society event. And he also looked on as one of his daughters, Ellen, tied for second place in the 100 yards for 12-13 year old girls while representing Glendinning Terrace School at the Selkirkshire Inter-School Sports. When he travelled back to America, this time he brought with him the whole Curran family, who had been living in Scotland for two years.

Taylor and Conway moved on at the end of the 1921/22 season, but a youngster called Bill Cox stepped into their shoes. Cox was a rangy but powerful boy, with dark hair parted in the centre. He would go on to become one of America's finest athletes, come within eight seconds of Paavo Nurmi's 1923 world mile record, and eventually compete at the Olympics.

Cox's first tests came on the cross country courses at Yale, Columbia and Philadelphia. He passed with flying colours with wins at all three, leading the school to victory in each. It was an incredible start to his time at Mercersburg, and as the track season began in February his victories continued – first a 4.38 ⅖ seconds mile at the Erasmus Games, and then a 4.33 ⅗ seconds mile at the National Interscholastic Track and Field Championships at Newark. A one mile relay win at the Penn Relays was sandwiched between the first and second halves of the Cox show. His 25ᵗʰ win in a row came at the Carnegie Tech Interscholastics. This was followed by mile wins at Princeton with the fast time of 4.30 ⅗, and Philadelphia's Annual Interscholastic Games with a time of 4.29 ⅖. At this final event the school won six of the 13 events, and was so dominant one reporter noted that it 'literally left the other dozen prominent Eastern [and Canadian] schools in the lurch.'

In November of the following school year, Mercersburg won cross country races at Yale and Columbia, with Cox emerging as victor in both. The National Cross Country Championship saw another Cox win, although the team could only manage third place.

And on the track Cox was easily the standout athlete. He stepped up in class at Millrose, running the mile against a top-class field that was led home by Joie Ray. He didn't place. Thereafter he won at Newark and Princeton, topping the season with a 4.24 mile. But Cox was not alone. At the Millrose Games the school's one mile relay team ran the fastest ever schoolboy mile relay in a time of 3.33 ⅘, and two months later won the medley relay at the Penn Athletic Club meet. And as the season progressed a high jumper called Gail Robinson began to record notable victories.

In late April, Jimmy, along with his various teams, attended the Penn Relays. Success came, as expected, in the one mile relay, but there was one other race Jimmy had an interest in; the Relays were attended by the famous Scottish runner Eric Liddell, who would re-enter the public consciousness, many years after his death, upon the release of the Oscar-winning film *Chariots of Fire*. Jimmy likely went out of his way to meet Liddell, but it is unclear whether Janet attended the Relays to see him. For Liddell, and many others, the Penn Relays was one of the final warm-ups before the Olympic Games – he finished a disappointing fourth in the 100 yards. The season was rounded off at the Penn

Interscholastic Games at Franklin Field, where Cox ran a 4.26 ⅖ mile, and Robinson excelled at the high jump.

For all Jimmy's success in training athletes to a point where they could compete, and often defeat, the best in the world, he had never attended an Olympic Games. By 1923 he was considering attending the 1924 Games, to be held in Paris, taking a number of students and alumni with him as part of the annual schoolboy tour. The school trip never came to fruition, but at the Alumni Dinner, held before the Penn Relays, the Alumni Association, headed by H.B. Swoope, introduced an unsuspecting Jimmy and announced that to repay the time and faith that Jimmy had invested in them they would be sending him to the Olympics. William Mann Irvine was clearly touched by the gift, sending a note apologising for not attending, but adding, 'Your dinner to Mr Curran is a beautiful tribute and one that is fully deserved.' Irvine would later present him with a cheque for $450.

A good selection of current and former Mercersburg athletes entered Olympic trials in both the US and Canada. For Jimmy it was his most well-attended US trials, with several current and former Mercersburg students attempting to book their place on the boat to Paris. Frank Conway was unsuccessful, but high jumper Gail Robinson and Chuck Taylor both made it through initial qualifying before losing out. Holding up Jimmy's end were Bill Cox who ran a good second to John Romig in the 5,000m, Marvin Rick who achieved the same result in the 3,000m steeplechase, and 'Crip' Moore who, despite only achieving fifth place in the U.S. trials due to an injured ankle, was given his place on the strength of his past performances. Rounding out Jimmy's athletes was George 'Buck' Hester, a sprinter from Canada.

In mid-June the team left New York on the SS *America* bound for Cherbourg. As in previous Olympic years the ship was converted to aid the various athletic training regimes. Once in France the team made its way by train to St Lazare Station in Paris where they were loudly cheered by a waiting French crowd. The majority were then bussed to the Rocquencourt estate, where entertainment was organised by stars of stage and screen such as Mary Pickford and Douglas Fairbanks Jr. Training continued well, with the only hiccup being a widespread fire in a local town which saw athletes rushing to provide help, and then collecting $200 for the victims.

In July, Jimmy crossed the Atlantic on the RMS *Majestic*, accompanied by some fellow teachers, students, and Johnny McHugh, a race starter, who would start some of the races at the Games. Arriving in Cherbourg, they journeyed to Colombes, on the outskirts of Paris, where the athletics was due to take place in the Stade de Colombes. At the time of the Games it was capable of holding 45,000 spectators.

Jimmy's early battles with the French language did not end well. He and McHugh ventured out to eat and requested bacon and eggs, to be presented with plates of sardines. Things clearly did not improve, when a further request for meat saw them served up a salad.

As well as his own athletes, Jimmy had other interest in the Games. Janet's nephew, the highly-rated Scottish athlete Eric Liddell, was also taking part. Liddell's story has been oft told, but its telling is often erroneous and based on the version given in the film *Chariots of Fire*. In reality he was handed the event timetable several months before the Games and, due to the devout Christian beliefs that precluded his running on a Sunday, immediately withdrew from the 100m, his strongest event, and the 4x400m relay. That left the 200m and the 400m. After taking bronze in the 200m he worked his way through the rounds of the 400m. In the final he shot off at what some considered a suicidal pace, but when the challengers expected him to wilt he surged on, eventually defeating the second placed American, Horatio Fitch, by almost a second. Jimmy celebrated the victory of his nephew, and fellow Scot.

On 5th July news began to filter through that one of Jimmy's students, Calvin Coolidge Jr, son of the President, was gravely ill after a blister, suffered whilst playing tennis, turned septic. Three days later, just two days after the start of the athletics competition in Paris, newspapers reported his death. Jimmy was distraught. So too was Bill

Cox, who had roomed with Coolidge at Mercersburg. Almost a year later Coolidge's mother, the First Lady, would visit Mercersburg and Jimmy looked on as she unveiled a portrait of her son. William Mann Irvine gave Coolidge's eulogy:

> Today we honor youth – beautiful youth, consecrated youth, ideal youth, youth that won our admiration and deepest love. This hour may be colored by regret and sorrow, but our spirits rise in joy and exaltation because this, our dear boy whom we delight to honor, although only in his teens, glorified many of the most noble qualities of the human soul.

But the Games had to continue for the Mercersburg contingent. Jimmy's greatest hope at the finals was 'Crip' Moore, a 110m hurdler who was one of the finest in his event in the United States. At the US trials he had made the team as an alternate. The IOC/IAAF rules laid out that an alternate could only be used when one of the other team members could not compete due to injury or illness (a rule that had allowed Allen Woodring to replace George Massengale four years earlier). But trials in France had seen Moore beating the other US hurdlers, and team manager, Lawson Robertson, saw an opportunity to strengthen his team by slipping Moore into the starting four. However, on the day of the event, Robertson walked up to Moore, who was stripped to run, and said, 'Get dressed, you're not running'; a French protest, citing the IOC/IAAF rule that only the first four finishers in a country's trials could take part, was successful. Moore's dreams of a gold medal were dashed in the cruellest of circumstances.

Moore could take a small crumb of comfort when he attended a post-Olympic competition in London on 19th July and was part of the American team that won the 480 yards hurdles relay race. But his proudest moment was still 28 years away.

RU-U-UN LADDIE

A number of other Mercersburg athletes stepped up. George 'Buck' Hester was competing for Canada in the 100m, 200m and 4x100m relay. Despite some good runs, most especially a time of 10.7 in the 100m quarter-final, Hester was unable to convert his talent into a medal.

Marvin Rick came close. Winning his semi-final of the 3,000m steeplechase he took on the mighty Finns in the final, finishing a worthy fourth.

But the real star of the Games, from Jimmy's perspective, was Bill Cox. He had qualified as a member of the 5,000m team, having achieved second and fourth places in the trials at Yankee and Harvard stadiums. Considered the weakest of the five Americans he transferred into the 3,000m team race. This event was featuring at the Games for the third, and what would prove to be the last, time. With only nine teams competing, the competition started at the semi-final stage, and the US team avoided the fancied Finnish and British teams. In a race won by the flying Swede Edvin Wide, Cox finished second, followed by his team-mates in third and fourth, allowing the team to progress to the final.

Two days later the team stepped out onto the track for the final, but barring injuries to the best of the Finns and Brits it was unlikely that they would get better than third place. But Cox's opportunity almost never came. Like Liddell, he was deeply religious, and running on a Sunday was not something he was comfortable with. It is not known if he spoke to Jimmy when the schedules were announced, but it is likely. He decided he would run, and in later months noted 'I have competed only once on a Sunday, and that was for my country at the Olympics. Any minor challenge Cox and the American team thought they could muster disappeared when the best of the Americans, Joie Ray, who had finished down the semi-final field after having his shoe kicked off, attempted to keep pace with the two legendary Finns, Paavo Nurmi and Ville Ritola. His challenge petered out and he finished well down the field and out of the top three Americans. The Finns stormed to victory and the US team finished 11 points behind the second-placed British. Cox, the day after his 20th birthday, finished in eighth place, second of the Americans, and as he crossed the line a 'Mercersburg cheer rang out over the field' courtesy of the teachers and students who had travelled to Paris. No doubt this cacophony was underpinned by Jimmy yelling 'ru-u-un laddie!' The team won a bronze medal.

After the Games Jimmy travelled north to Scotland. He had been booked to return to the US on 16th August, but for an unknown reason he cancelled his trip and remained in Scotland for a further two weeks. That reason may have been to allow him to travel throughout Europe, or to take in the much-anticipated farewell appearance of his nephew, Eric Liddell, just five weeks after his Olympic triumph, at the Gala Harriers' Sports. It is likely that Jimmy presented some winners with the prizes he had gifted the club – medals, and a golden shoe which would be competed for in the coming years over the distance of 350 yards. Days later Jimmy travelled south to Liverpool, where he boarded the RMS *Baltic* and headed home.

*****

The Mercersburg cross country team had a good start to the 1924/25 with a victory at the Columbia University event, although they couldn't stop former student Bill Cox, now running for Penn State and fresh from his Olympic success, from emerging the individual victor.

The following two track seasons proved erratic, with a few excellent team and personal victories interspersed with mediocre performances. Ralph Shotter, a quarter-miler, and George Stollwerck, a hurdler, stood out as the individual stars. The team occasionally delivered on its promise, coming to the fore at the Penn Relays in both years; in 1925 it won the mile relay, and the 440 yards relay in a world interscholastic record, and in 1926 they again took the 440 yards relay.

But the stand-out athlete of this era was a 6' 1", 190lbs weights man called Bernard Ernst Berlinger, known as Barney. Jimmy first saw

Berlinger in early 1925, competing for Penn Charter. Naturally strong, he bulldozed his way through the strength events, often amassing enough points to take on whole teams himself. He was, as many a reporter noted, 'a one man track team.' He enrolled at Mercersburg later that year.

But Jimmy had no intention of putting all his eggs in one basket. Besides his new heavyweight star he also had one of his finest-ever track teams, one capable of sweeping all before it. And in a perfect athletic storm all this came his way. Despite a slow start the team took the meets at Princeton and Penn Interscholastics before their talent was brought into sharp focus at the Penn Relays.

In the quarter-mile relay the Lawrenceville School, from just north of Trenton, New Jersey, broke the existing world record set by the 1926 Mercersburg team. The Mercersburg team promptly took to the track and lowered the record again. Due to some timekeepers forgetting to wind their watches, the races had to be re-run. 'All right', said Jimmy 'we'll run it again and beat our own time'. Lawrenceville ran first and once again broke the old record. Undeterred the Mercersburg team hit the track and beat the Lawrenceville time, although it didn't quite meet Jimmy's expectations – it equalled the previous time they had run. The school magazine called it 'one of the most successful seasons in the history of the school' and the press concurred, with one reporter calling the relay squad 'a brilliant quarter-mile team.'

Berlinger was so dominant throughout the season that Mercersburg frequently steamrollered its opponents. According to a fellow athlete at the National Academy Championships in Chicago, 'it is doubtful if many *college* athletes could have equalled [Berlinger's] performance.'

His rise to prominence could not have come at a more opportune time, with the 1928 Olympics just around the corner. The 1927/28 season would determine whether he was Olympic material; whether the best on the east coast could compete with the best in the world.

Arriving at the school was a 'slender, square-jawed' young distance runner called Terrell 'Tex' Cobb. He immediately signalled his intentions when he lined up for the Columbia Interscholastics cross country race in Van Cortlandt Park. As a field of 174 rushed from the gun, Cobb, a relative newcomer to the sport, grabbed the race by the scruff of the neck, set the pace, and won by 12 seconds.

Cobb's success on the cross country fields paved the way for similar success on the track. And he would have assistance from a sprinter and long jumper from Arkansas called Bill Carr. Carr had arrived at Mercersburg in a poor physical state, his legs having been terribly burned in an accident, and with both ankles still recovering from being broken in a high jumping accident. Despite this he won the Williams Cup in his first year, and would repeat the feat the following year. But the season did not reach the expected heights. Cobb placed well in several mile races, but could only garner one win, at the Princeton Games. Carr was also defeated in the season's first meet, at Newark, but thereafter won multiple races and jumps, including breaking the meet record for the long jump at the Penn Interscholastics.

The 1928 Olympic trials featured at least three former Mercersburg students. In June the high jump national champion Gail Robinson, and Bill Cox, turned out at Yankee Stadium to attempt to make the ship to Amsterdam. Robinson did not reach the required height. Cox entered the last lap of the 1,500m in front, but was overtaken by a number of athletes in the closing stages and was 'badly beaten.' The school's run of having a student, or former student, at every Olympic Games since 1906 was now reliant on Barney Berlinger.

At the final Olympic trial at Franklin Field in Philadelphia in early July, Berlinger placed third in the decathlon with a point score of 7,362, enough to guarantee him a place on the boat to Amsterdam. And so on 12th July he boarded the SS *President Roosevelt*, 12lbs underweight after performing in unbearably hot conditions in Philadelphia.

The decathlon was one of the first events at the Games, the competition taking place under heavy downpours that left the track like an 'Irish bog.' But this did not halt the charge of the world record holder, Paavo Yrjölä, as he became the first man to break the 8,000 point barrier. Berlinger's challenge was schizophrenic, ranging from inspired to insipid, with no apparent middle ground in his performances. With 38 athletes starting the events, Berlinger finished between second and ninth on five occasions, and between 19th and 30th on the other five. These five low placings contributed to his finishing the event in 17th place, on 6,619 points, well below his personal best. In the 1,500m, for example, widely known as his weakest event, where he finished last of the 25 finishers, his points total was almost 450 behind the race winner. It was disappointing for Berlinger. His fellow Americans finished in third, fourth and fifth, and his points total in the US trial would have earned him sixth place. Three years later, at the Penn Relays, he would score 7,735, enough to have won him bronze in Amsterdam. But regardless of his finishing place Berlinger's feat was remarkable. The decathlon is the toughest of all events, and with Jimmy's training, Berlinger had risen to become one of the finest all-round athletes in the world. In 1931 he won the Sullivan Medal for outstanding amateur sportsperson, and had he chosen to compete in the 1932 Olympics he was more than capable of putting in a top five display.

In the conspicuous wake of Berlinger, who had moved to the University of Pennsylvania in 1927, Jimmy saw Cobb and Carr as the foundations of his cross country and track teams. Cobb continued on in late 1928 where he had left off the previous year, starting with a win in the Scottish Clans' Games Cross Country, followed by victory over a field of almost 400 at the Columbia University Interscholastics cross country in November, more than double the size he had beaten a year previously.

At the first meet of the track season at the Meadowbrook Club, the team was second in the mile relay, setting the scene for the season. The Penn Relays saw a win in the 440 yards relay, and losses in the two miles and medley. The final two meets of the season, at Princeton and the Penn Interscholastics meet, saw two victories, with Cobb and Carr winning a combined total of five events, the finest of which was Cobb's mile win in the time of 4.25.4.

The following year the team was strengthened further. Jimmy brought in Bill Estes, a sprinter from Woodhaven, Queens. The team meandered between wins and losses. A victory at the Meadowbrook Games was followed by defeat at the National Interscholastic Championships. Victory in a triangular meet against the Navy Plebes and William & Mary was followed by a narrow defeat at the Princeton Games, and a win at the Penn Interscholastics. But the team's finest moment came at the Penn Relays; victories came in the 440 yards relay, the mile relay, and the medley relay, with Bill Estes featuring in all three races. 'Mercersburg', noted one reporter, 'did all the winning of interscholastic relay titles there was to be done at the Penn Relay Carnival here yesterday, annexing the [three championships] at stake.' He went on to note that 'many and frequent have been Mercersburg triumphs at the Penn carnival, but never has it had a day of triumph such as this.' It was a fitting way to celebrate Jimmy's 20th year as Mercersburg's head coach.

The Mercersburg athletic teams of the late 1920s were of the very highest quality. So much so that Jimmy's son was unable to make a significant impact. To put this in perspective – when he took the step up to the Ivy League splendour of Princeton, he became a central member of the Tigers' track team. Despite an uneventful early athletics career at the University, generally running in the sprints, but occasionally taking part in the long jump, his 'faithful work and … improvement' in the 200m saw him awarded a medal in June 1934. This preceded the finest moment of his track career when, in July 1934, he travelled to England as part of a joint Princeton-Cornell track squad which was to take on a Cambridge-Oxford team at London's White City Stadium. Before a crowd of 15,000 Jimmy came third in the 220 yards. He then journeyed north to Scotland with some members of the American team and on 4th August he took part in the Rangers Sports at Ibrox Stadium. Around 25,000 spectators looked on as America took on British and Finnish teams. In the 220 yards his mark of two yards proved too much to overtake the two men, running off 17 and 15 yards, who would finish ahead of him. By April 1935 he had 'attained the honour of being perhaps the fastest man in college.' Later that year, with his study at Princeton drawing to a close, he was presented with the Bonthron Cup in recognition of his 'sportsmanship, ability and effort.' So, failing to make it on to a Mercersburg team during the late 1920s – the golden era of Tex Cobb, Bill Carr and Bill Estes – was no disgrace.

*****

Jimmy's time at the school had coincided with an equally successful period for the swim team, under the equally charismatic Coach John Miller. As such, it was decided to build a new trophy room to house the school's ever-growing collection of silverware. Ironically, victories in the 1930/31 and 1931/32 seasons were few and far between, with the most notable coming in the prep school mile at the Meadowbrook meet in 1931, and the 440 yards at the Penn Relays in 1932. It isn't known if Jimmy suggested filling it with his own personal trophy won in December 1931 – the head of a deer he killed (his first in 22 years), apparently having run it down before administering the fatal shot – but knowing his sense of humour, it is quite likely.

As the 1931/32 season ended, the Olympic Games approached. And one former Mercersburg star looked like a sure thing for at least a silver medal; in 1929, Bill Carr had moved on to the University of Pennsylvania, where he was trained by Jimmy's fellow Scot Lawson Robertson, and over the following three years, after a series of astonishing runs – he was part of the Penn team to break the one mile relay record, and then shattered the long-standing 440 yards world record set by Ted Meredith in 1916 – he put himself in the running for the Los Angeles Games. After an injury to his knee in 1931, one newspaper called him the 'hard luck story of all time.' But despite a seemingly endless list of injuries, stretching back beyond his studies at

Mercersburg, his class shone through. He was, according to Robertson, 'the fastest Carr in America.'

Carr's assault on the Olympic 400m race began at the trials in Palo Alto in California on 15th July. He set the bar high from the very beginning, equalling the Olympic record in his semi-final. The following day he lined up against world record holder Ben Eastman. The two ran side by side for much of the race, but closing in on the finish Carr stepped up a gear and 'Eastman's head came back and his form was lost.' Carr crossed the line in a world record time.

The Los Angeles Games was held in somewhat odd circumstances, with the world still suffering the effects of the Wall Street Crash. As a result only 1,332 athletes competed, compared to 2,883 in Amsterdam four years earlier. If an athlete was to prove he was the best in the world he would, in many events, have to break records. Carr set about doing just that.

He cruised through the early rounds of the 400m, breaking the Olympic record in the semi-final. The final was watched by 70,000 in the Los Angeles Memorial Coliseum as Carr and Eastman raced for the third time in 1932. The race was billed as east v west, Carr of Penn v Eastman of Stanford, and it lived up to the hype. As they rounded the last bend Eastman was three yards ahead, but Carr quickly closed and crossed the line two yards in front, breaking the world record by almost a second, with Eastman also breaking the previous best. Sparrow Robertson called Carr's performance the best of the Games.

In the last days of the competition came the 4x400m relay. Carr didn't take part in the heats when the United States team shaved almost a second off the world record. In the final he stepped in to fill the last leg. And he was needed. The British upped their game for the final and although the United States team led all the way they were pushed by their Old World rivals until Carr pulled away from Godfrey Rampling to win by 20 yards, in a time that took a further three seconds off the world record. The time would stand for 20 years until it was beaten by Jamaica at the 1952 Olympics.

RU-U-UN LADDIE

*****

With the Olympics only a cross country drive away, and with the added draw of seeing his former student take part, it would have seemed an obvious choice to make for Jimmy to attend. But he had other plans – he returned to Scotland, with his son Jimmy in tow. In June the two made their way to New York and boarded the RMS *Transylvania*. Eight years later the ship would be sunk by a German U-Boat, mirroring Jimmy's experience with the *Lusitania*. Travelling Tourist Class, the equivalent of third class, they arrived in Glasgow on 27th June. From there they boarded a train and headed east to Edinburgh, and then south to Galashiels, where they attended a civic reception for overseas visitors, along with around 500 others. It was the first time Jimmy had visited Scotland as an American, having been naturalised on 26th March 1929.

The trip was timed to coincide with the Braw Lads' Gathering, an event incorporating aspects of Highland Games and Common Ridings. In only its third year the events included a mass fording of the River Tweed by Galaleans on horseback, led by the Braw Lad and Lass, who then headed to Abbotsford House where they were met by the great-great-grandson of Sir Walter Scott. The entourage then made their way to the Mercat Cross where, in brilliant sunshine, before a vast crowd, they re-enacted an age-old ceremony called Sod and Stone, that saw Margaret Tudor take possession of the lands of Ettrick Forest. The ceremonies ended with a rousing rendition of Burns' *Braw Lads o' Gala Water*.

But for the two Curran men, the main draw was the athletics to be held at Raid Stane Park. Jimmy was now 52 years old, struggling with chronic varicose veins which had plagued him since his youth, and decided not to participate, choosing instead to act as a judge.

Jimmy Jr, however, had no such limitations, and entered himself in the 100 yards, eager to compete against the finest the land of his ancestors could offer up. But being an unknown quantity, and perhaps with memories of his father's skills still lingering in the mind of the handicapper, he was given a mark of only 6½ yards. If he was to win he would have to reel in the majority of the field; it proved too much and, as a crowd of 14,000 roared the boys on, he was beaten by inches in his heat.

It would not be Jimmy Jr's last visit to his father's home town. In 1934, on his trip to London and Glasgow to represent Princeton, he made his way to Galashiels, and no doubt bunked down in the house of a relative, before travelling ever northwards, through Edinburgh, Stirling, Inverness, and an array of smaller towns, until he reached Durness, where he spent some days studying rock formations for his degree. A year later Jimmy and Janet travelled to Princeton where, on the lawn in front of Nassau Hall, they watched their only son graduate with a Bachelor of Arts degree.

Left: The earliest known photograph of Jimmy, likely taken in the mid-1890s.
Copyright: Curran family

Below: An Ordnance Survey map, surveyed in 1897, depicting the Eastlands Cemetery in Galashiels. The gravel path on the upper left quadrant measured 452 yards, just longer than the standard track size of 440 yards. Jimmy trained on the paths prior to emigrating, and then again in 1953 when recovering from an operation to address his varicose veins.
Courtesy of the National Library of Scotland

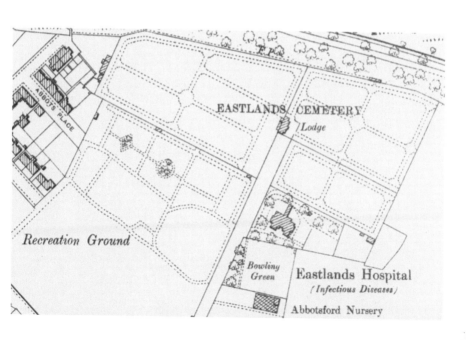

Left: A photograph of Jimmy taken in Plymouth in 1899, shortly before he made his way to South Africa. *Copyright:* Curran family

Below: HM Troopship *Kildonan Castle*, 1901. Jimmy travelled to the Boer War on this ship. It is possible that this photograph was taken on the day Jimmy and his comrades left Southampton.

When Jimmy went off to war in South Africa, it was with the Highland Light Infantry. As his service neared an end he transferred to the 11th Hussars, in order to be close to home when his enlistment ended. This colourised photograph, taken in 1903, shows Jimmy in his Hussars uniform and wearing the King's South Africa Medal. It is the only known photograph depicting Jimmy with a moustache. A second, full-length, image of Jimmy in his Hussars uniform exists. This also shows crossed rifles and crossed swords badges on his arm, awarded for his having attained a high degree of marksmanship and swordsmanship. *Copyright:* Curran family

The two known photographs of Jimmy's short-lived football career.

Top: Gala Hailes Villa players sit with the Paul Shield after winning the Border Senior League. Jimmy is second from left in the second row from the front.

Above: The players invited to trial at Mossilee, Galashiels, to decide who would play against Celtic, Heart of Midlothian and Rangers. Jimmy is far right in the front row.

Left: Jimmy posing in a Galashiels photographic studio, around 1905-07. The varicose veins on his legs are evident.
Copyright: Curran family

Below: Jimmy showing off his slight, but muscular, build, around 1905-07.
Copyright: Curran family

Top: Jimmy showing his skills extended beyond track athletics, 1916.

Above left: Jimmy poses with Hans Holmer and Walter Knox at Powderhall, Edinburgh, August 1913. *Copyright:* Curran family

Above right: Jimmy stripped for a Scottish Games meet at Central Park, Philadelphia, August 1916.

The Justice William Smith House (top), where the Currans lived from 1910 until they downsized to an upper flat in Linden Avenue (above) in 1947. *Copyright:* Curran family

A portrait photograph of Jimmy published in the
Meadowbrook Year Book, 1916. *Copyright:* University of Indiana

Top: Jimmy, with whistle in mouth, acts as referee at a Meadowbrook Club meet on their sports field at 23rd and Market Street, Philadelphia, 1916.
Copyright: Craig Statham

Above: Jimmy (back row, centre) with coaches and athletes of the Meadowbrook Club at a meet in St Louis, September 1918. The two coaches at the far left of the back row are Louis Spealler and Lawson Robertson, and the athletes include Eddie and Larry Shields, Allen Woodring, Elmer Smith, Harold Barron, Ted Meredith, and Joe Berry, who would go on to become second baseman for the New York Giants in 1921 and 1922.
Copyright: University of Indiana

Photographs depicting the days that saw Jimmy twice entered into *Ripley's Believe It Or Not*.

Left: Dropkicking a football 50 yards, barefooted, in November 1930.

Above: Walking around Mercersburg Academy's golf course in August 1938, on his way to completing 290 holes in one day.

Copyright of all images: Curran family

Left: Jimmy with Bill Cox, c1922. Cox would later win a bronze medal as part of the three-man US 3,000m team race at the 1924 Paris Olympics.
Copyright: Curran family

Below: Jimmy with three Mercersburg Olympians at Franklin Field, Philadelphia, c1932. From left are Barney Berlinger, Ted Meredith, Jimmy and Bill Carr.
Copyright: Curran family

Bust of Jimmy, created by the Spanish sculptor, Fernando Valero, when, in 1935, the two were employed at the MacJannet summer camp in Angon, France. It still resides with the family.
Copyright: Curran family

Above: On his visits to Galashiels, Jimmy often acted as a judge at local sports events, as depicted by the badge on his lapel. Here he stands with his long-time friends William and John Torrie, during the 1948 Braw Lads' Gathering. *Copyright:* Curran family

Left: Photograph depicting Jimmy, on what is believed to be his last trip to Galashiels in 1957, presenting Rob Renton, a local athlete, with the Strang Steel Challenge Cup for winning the Border Mile Championship. Jimmy had won the same trophy over 50 years before.
Copyright: Curran family

Left: Around 1960, Jimmy's son-in-law, Tom Danaher Sr, bought a Rolleiflex camera, and took a number of family photographs. The one of Jimmy was used as a basis for a painting by Danaher, that would eventually be hung on the walls of Mercersburg Academy. *Copyright:* Curran family

Below: Jimmy's son, Jimmy Jr, standing beside the painting of his father in the 1990s. *Copyright:* Curran family

Left: Jimmy in the Mercersburg trophy room, January 1950. *Copyright:* Curran family

Right: Jimmy and Janet in the living room of their house on Linden Avenue, Christmas 1946. *Copyright:* Curran family

Left: Telegram of condolence sent by Jimmy Stewart to the Curran family after Jimmy's death. *Copyright:* Curran family

Jimmy's first and last discoveries.

Above: Lone runner Wyndham Halswelle crossing the line in the re-run 400m final at the 1908 Olympic Games in London.

Left: Paul White, last leg of the 440 yards relay team, taking the honours at the 1961 Penn Relays. Courtesy of Paul White.

Chapter 13 • Highs and Lows

By early 1933 Bill Carr was still trying to decide the direction his life would take. He announced that he would probably retire after the US track and field team completed a tour of Europe in that summer, in order to concentrate on his career. But only two months later the decision of whether or not to retire was made for him. He was thrown from the running board of a car and broke both ankles and his pelvis. His running career was over.

Some months earlier in September 1932 Jimmy and son arrived back on American soil, having travelled across the Atlantic on the *Tuscania*. Refreshed after his trip to Scotland, and basking in Bill Carr's double Olympic glory, Jimmy returned to a talented team, one he believed contained his fastest mile team since 1912. Charles Mutchler and Bob Cowan were joined by Jack White, a miler with great potential, and sprinter Alfred 'Bud' Mills. The 1932/33 season rarely progressed beyond mediocre, but two performances at the Penn Relays made it clear that this was a team with some serious potential. The 440 yards relay team, made up of Cowan, White, Mills, and Mutchler, equalled the meet record of 42.8 seconds in its heat, and then broke it in the final with a time of 42.5 seconds, eclipsing the time of the Mercersburg team of 1927. It was the school's seventh victory in nine years.

The team's talent did not take long to emerge in the 1933/34 season, kicking off with victories at the Millrose Games, and the National AAU Championships at Madison Square Garden. The team entered the Penn Relays undefeated on the track, and they emulated the previous year's team with victory in the 440 yards relay, albeit with a slower time of 44.4 seconds. With just the Princeton Games to go to close out the season, Jimmy was well aware that victory would mean an undefeated season. Despite the Hill School having won the Games the four previous years, Mercersburg won comfortably, with Bill Bradway the star of the meet with two first places, in the javelin and discus, and a second place in the shot put. Despite having no Merediths or Carrs or any future Olympians in the team, the season had proved to be one of Jimmy's most successful, comfortably winning each and every track competition entered.

In the fall of 1934 Jimmy brought the highly-rated Steve Szumachowski of Mont Pleasant High School of Schenectady to the school. The distance runner was widely considered the best on the east coast, a two-time national champion, with 17 wins in a row, establishing records in 15 of these. The school's first race of the 1934 cross country season took place on home soil against the almost unbeatable Navy Plebes. Despite Szumachowski taking the honours, and slashing 36 seconds off the course record, the Plebes proved too strong overall and walked away victorious.

From the race against the Plebes it was on to the National Interscholastic Championships at Newark, where Szumachowski had won the previous two years. With a field of 300 it was never going to be easy, and so it proved. For much of the race it looked like Szumachowski was going to win, but Syracuse Central's Len Dauenhauer came strong in the last half-mile, setting a new course record and edging out Szumachowski by a yard.

The track season began in February 1935 at the Eastern Interscholastic Championships in Madison Square Garden. Szumachowski, entered in the mile, again suffered defeat, to St Benedict's Vinnie Braun, with the school's only victory coming via Edwin Salter in the 440 yards. The remainder of the season proved erratic, jumping between victory and defeat. It started well with victory in a dual meet that saw multiple wins for both Charles Mutchler and Bill Bradway. A further victory followed at the Penn Relays when the team won the 440 yards relay in the fast time of 43.2 seconds. But just when things were looking up, again the team fell below the standard Jimmy expected. At the Princeton Games, Szumachowski was once again bettered by Vinnie Braun in the mile, and Mercersburg was beaten out for the title by Hill School.

In the summer Jimmy headed back across the Atlantic, landing at Cherbourg. From there he made for Paris, where he met up with the journalist Sparrow Robertson, now working for the *International Herald Tribune*. Robertson was accompanied by Emory Foster, the brother-in-law of an educator called Donald MacJannet. MacJannet was a 41-year old of Scottish descent who, in 1924, opened a school for American children just outside Paris. The following year he opened another school at St Cloud, and two summer camps, one for boys, the other for girls, at Angon, a French town in the Alps sitting on the banks of Lake Annecy, about 25 miles south of Geneva and roughly the same distance west of Mont Blanc. So esteemed were MacJannet's schools and camps that they drew visits from some of America's greatest personalities, including Amelia Earhart and Babe Ruth. Foster and Jimmy headed for Angon, where they met up with around 20 coaches, educators, missionaries and all manner of people who would impart their wisdom on the camp attendees. These included Gustav Kalkun, an Estonian Olympic discus thrower, Wilfred Grenfell Jr, an American missionary, Val Bouryschkine, an American basketball player and soon-to-be one of the leaders of the French resistance, and Fernando Valero, a Spanish sculptor. For a fee of 1,000-1,500 francs per month, which equated to US \$40-\$60, Jimmy spent the next two months teaching boys MacJannet's philosophy of education, with an 'emphasis on individual achievement, the pursuit of individual interest, tolerance, teamwork and mutual respect.' But there was some down time: Jimmy posed for Valero, and the result was a stunning sculpted bust, which Jimmy transported back over the Atlantic. The bust still resides within the family.

He arrived back in New York in September 1935. The new term at Mercersburg was his 25th as coach. The commemoration of his quarter century had actually begun at the end of the previous season. On the eve of the Penn Relays he was fêted at the school assembly, with headmaster Dr Boyd Edwards declaring an honorary holiday for the school. That same evening the Alumni Association held a testimonial dinner in his honour. The stature of the attendees says much about the respect in which Jimmy was held. Fellow Scottish coaches Lawson Robertson and Tom Keane were there, alongside an array of former students including Bill Carr, Barney Berlinger and the baseball pitcher 'Bump' Hadley. After a speech by Jimmy, the answering of some questions, and his acceptance of a travelling bag, others, including H. Jamison Schwartz, director of the Penn Relays, and Edwards, lauded his coaching career.

This triumvirate of coaches, alumni and peers was joined by Jimmy's students on the pages of the school magazine, where they honoured him with an eloquent paean:

> A Scotchman with the best qualities of a great race
> Soldier in South Africa in youth
> For all his manhood years a good American
> True sportsman, philosopher, humorist and teacher
> Gifted in discovering hidden powers in boys:
> Forever afterward inspiringly interested in them
>
> "Mens sana in sano corpore"
> [A sound mind in a sound body]

If Jimmy's stock was at a high amongst those at Mercersburg, then it was just as high in the wider community. In the 1930s the Mercersburg Police Department, made up of only two men, was having an issue with drivers speeding on their way out of town. The means of catching speeding drivers in 1930s small town America was not yet advanced and local police departments had to come up with ingenious ways to catch their prey. In Mercersburg the police brought on board the man with the most accurate watch in town – Jimmy (who himself was a non-driver). A policeman would stand off-road at the bottom of the hill with a light, with Jimmy 200 yards away at the top of the hill, also with a light. The policeman would judge the speed of the car by eye, and if he thought it might be speeding he would flash the light at Jimmy, who then set his stopwatch in motion. If the car reached him in fewer seconds than it could at legal speed, Jimmy flashed his light back at the policeman, and the speeder was charged.

Plaudits were all well and good, but for Jimmy the important business was the athletics, and it kicked off in November with the team's almost annual defeat by the Navy Plebes, the pain alleviated somewhat by individual honours being taken by the Academy's team captain Ed Powers.

The early track season proved tough, with defeats at the Millrose Games and the AAU Championships. But as the season progressed, the team grew in stature. At the Penn Relays they took part in the two mile relay, an unusual event for Jimmy's teams which normally focussed on the mile and the quarter-mile, and broke the world interscholastic record (the only time they would win this event under Jimmy). A week later, at the University of Maryland Championships, Jimmy's team won seven of the 10 events, strolling to victory. And a further week on, the team again tasted victory, this time at the Princeton Games.

*****

Since 1908 Jimmy had been 'represented' at each Olympic Games by at least one athlete he had trained, as well as at the 1906 Intercalated Games. But as the controversial 1936 Games in Berlin approached it became apparent that for the first time since 1904 no athlete who had passed through Mercersburg would be in attendance (other than Ted Meredith who was training the Czech team). Why the school had no athletes at the 1936 Olympics may well be down to chance. But a number of factors may have contributed. By the 1930s the school was struggling to recover from a number of major projects and events costing the school both financially and emotionally. From 1922-1926 William Mann Irvine brought in the finest architects and builders to erect his dream, a Gothic chapel on land looking down over the school. It was the pinnacle of his vision, but so expensive was the erection – the intricacy of the adornments included an 8 by 6 feet, 14 carat gold leaf-covered cross weighing 600 lbs, 36 stained glass windows created by the finest artisans in America and Britain, and a 43-bell carillon containing metal from Admiral Nelson's HMS *Victory* and a shaving from the Liberty Bell, with the largest bell weighing 7,168 lbs – that by the time it was completed, at a cost of $750,000, the school was in a difficult financial position. With no project demanding further expenditure it was envisioned that time would be spent replenishing the financial pot. But just three months after the dedication of the chapel, the Great Hall was razed to the ground, the victim of faulty wiring. It needed to be replaced. A year later William Mann Irvine, the driving force behind the school for 35 years, died of a stroke. His impact on the school should not be underestimated. Under his stewardship the school estate had grown from four to 120 acres, with $2m raised and expended on land and buildings. The faculty had risen from four to 46, while 7,000 boys, representing every state and 30 countries, had passed through its halls. His replacement Boyd Edwards arrived at a time when the faculty, students and alumni must have believed the school was at a financial and emotional nadir – they were sorely mistaken. If Edwards envisioned a decade of consolidation, building a new era and strengthening the school's now-precarious financial situation, he was in for a rude awakening. On 28th and 29th October 1929 stock prices on Wall Street plummeted, losing $30 billion in value on those two days alone. And thus began the Great Depression. For a decade America fought its way back to stability, but the impact on the country was like nothing it had experienced before. The crisis wound its way into every nook and cranny of life, and Mercersburg Academy was not immune: once-affluent families of potential students suddenly found themselves barely scraping together the money for necessities, whilst the school could ill afford to be spending its reserves on funding sports scholarships. Indeed, so serious was the financial situation that, when things were at their lowest ebb, faculty members were not guaranteed to be paid. But they were grateful for the fact they were fed at the school each day.

The school's lack of impact on the 1936 Olympics cannot be solely blamed on a temporary downturn in the school's fortunes. Quite simply, athletics in America had moved on, and the bar had been raised, partly due to a greater willingness to utilise black athletes. In the sprints, for example, Eddie Tolan, Jesse Owens, Ralph Metcalfe and Eulace Peacock, four black athletes, had all bettered the 100m world record between 1932 and 1936. And they were the tip of the iceberg. Prior to 1932 only one black athlete, Harry Edward, had won Olympic sprint medals. In 1932 they won four of the nine medals (two golds, a silver and a bronze) and four years later upped this to five (three golds and two silvers).

But while the school had no Olympians to cheer on, a celebration was underway. In 1936 the town of Mercersburg celebrated 100 years of educational enterprise, and to commemorate this achievement the Academy commissioned H.H. Saylor to design a memorial, titled *Dreamer and Scholar, Worker and Builder*. His work took the form of a seat, built of concrete and stretching in a crescent in the school's Quad. Within the seat were set three bronzes, created by the former Director of the Physical Education Department at the University of Pennsylvania, Dr R. Tait McKenzie, who was also a sculptor of great note. The main bronze was of Dr William Mann Irvine, founder of the school, and this was flanked by two smaller ones: of Robert Michelet, a high-achieving academic and sportsman who had trained under Jimmy, gone on to become a Rhodes scholar, and died in his final year at Dartmouth in 1934, and of Bill Carr, the school's recent double Olympic gold medallist. The two students were chosen as they were considered 'the best types of American boyhood.' The cost of the Carr statue was underwritten by Boyd Edwards, the school's headmaster.

The Carr bronze had actually been sculpted some years previously. McKenzie had been looking for a 'small-boned slight figure with ... well-balanced, muscular development.' He was aware of Jimmy from his time at the University of Pennsylvania and contacted him regarding an athlete who fit the bill. Jimmy proposed Carr, who posed for McKenzie in both a relaxed position and in 'full stride', and from this collaboration was created a sketch and three bronzes. When McKenzie was commissioned to create the three bronzes for the school, he had one of Carr ready-made.

The dedication ceremony at the Academy took place the following year and began with an alumni reception followed by a march to the site of the memorial. Carr's three-foot high bronze was the first to be unveiled. With Bill Carr looking on, Jimmy, having been at least partly responsible for his rise to Olympic glory, stepped up to complete the honours, pulling away a banner bearing the seal of Pennsylvania.

And as if inspired by the events, the cross country team rose to the occasion. The Navy Plebes team had proved, and would continue to prove in later years, that they were an elite cross country team, older, stronger and faster than Mercersburg. But in the fall of 1936 Mercersburg showed its mettle, winning the dual meet for the first time since its inception in the late 1920s. Ed Powers once again took individual honours, winning the race as he had the previous year. It would be a lonely victory over the Plebes amongst a deluge of defeats lasting many decades.

The track season saw Jimmy fall back on a technique that had served him well in the past – relying on the talents of a dominant field athlete. In the 1920s the role had been filled by Barney Berlinger and Bill Bradway, and now Jimmy's faith was placed in Ed Beetem, a 6' 8" tall, 270lb mountain of a man.

He laid down a marker at the school's annual Field Day, breaking the school's long-standing shot put record. He kicked off the season proper at the National AAU Championships at Madison Square Garden and repaid Jimmy's faith with a new meet record in the shot put. He followed this up in May with a double win in Maryland and a triple win at Princeton. The track team failed to rise to the challenge, with the only bright lights being Ed Burrowes and Ted Meredith Jr, who contributed to a mile relay win at Baltimore's Fifth Regiment Armory, 25 years after the latter's father had won his first Mercersburg race in the same venue.

Jimmy's attempts to build a top team in the early- to mid-1930s had been a mixed bag of success, with a spattering of good athletes, and a multitude of average ones. But by the beginning of the 1937/38 season Jimmy once again had the foundation of a solid track team in place. Joining Beetem, Burrowes, and Meredith Jr, were Jack Watt, Jack Milne, Paxson 'Pax' Gifford, and Bob Ufer. A first equal place at the National AAU Championships at Madison Square Garden was followed by a number of good performances, rounded out by solid wins in the 440 yards relay at the Penn Relays and the Princeton Games. The season ended at the Harvard Interscholastics, and it brought home just how much of the loss Beetem and Burrowes, both headed to university, would be, with the weights man taking two first places, a third and a fifth. Burrowes took the 800 yards time trial with a record time of 1.57.5.

Into the team came the miler, Ed Morgan, and all-round speed man, Austin Kellam. Added to the remnants of the team from the previous season, Jimmy now had a group of athletes capable of sweeping all before them. But they were at the foot of a learning curve.

Since returning from Christmas recess, the mile relay team of Gifford, Morgan, Milne and Ufer had been training, like every one of Jimmy's relay teams that had gone before them, on speed, endurance, and baton hand-offs. Their first chance to shine came at the Millrose Games in Madison Square Garden. The team finished fourth in the mile relay, behind an excellent La Salle team who took four seconds off the interscholastic record. Indeed, the time was so fast it was one of the fastest miles ever run by any class, including college, in the history of the Games. Fourth place was a major disappointment for a team upon which great hopes had been placed. They soon had the chance to prove themselves again, against the University of Pennsylvania freshmen. This they did in spades, the team turning in a mile relay time of 3.28.7 seconds, with further individual victories for Kellam, Watt and others. The Penn freshmen won only one event, with the victor being, ironically, Mercersburg's former mainstay Ed Beetem. It was clear that this was a team capable of great things, but its biggest test would come two weeks later at the National AAU Championships at Madison Square Garden. Things, once again, did not go to plan – the top athletes from Seton Hall exposed them, with only Kellam winning in the long jump. But Jimmy was aware that they were raw, and this made for erratic performances. Improvement, he knew, would come. As the season progressed, the team did indeed improve: Jimmy's training led to advances in technique and strength, whilst his motivational skills saw them gain in confidence and self-belief. Strong results in the 70 yard dash and 1,000 yards saw the team win prep honours at the University of Maryland meet. And to top off this success, Jack Milne won a special 660 yards race in a meet record time of 1.25.2.

If Jimmy's fellow coaches doubted the quality of his team, they were quickly disabused of this notion at the Penn Relays. All the pain of the previous two months' defeats disappeared in one stunning afternoon. In the 440 yards relay the team of Watt, Kellam, Ufer, and Gifford, flew to a time of 42.2 seconds, astonishing not only because it broke the interscholastic record held by the 1932/33 Mercersburg team, but also due to the rarely-achieved feat of bettering the time posted by the winning college team. Jimmy felt that with better weather they could have run 41.8 seconds. It was an incredible time, and good enough to earn the team, 58 years later, a place on the Penn Relays Wall of Fame. But Jimmy and the boys had little time to celebrate their victory as later in the day the team was back to try for the medley relay record, with Watt and Kellam replaced by Milne and Morgan. The time was fast enough to win the title, but nine-tenths of a second outside the record.

The final meet of the season, the annual Princeton Games, allowed the boys a chance to further show off their individual talents. Of the seven track events, the team won six, whilst in the field events they won three out of a possible seven. Austin Kellam gave a dazzling display, winning three events, cementing his place as a serious contender for a place on the next Olympic team. Jimmy had put together a team that was one of the finest of his career, filled with boys who would all go on to success at college level. And most still had a year to go.

It was to be a busy summer. First up, just a month after the Princeton meet, Jimmy made his way to Washington DC to attend a Royal Garden Party at the British Embassy. Part of the itinerary of King George VI and Queen Elizabeth, during their American visit, Jimmy was invited on the strength of his being a former British soldier. He joined a wealth of famous and wealthy attendees, from political leaders to financiers. A roll call of American royalty was led by Mrs Cornelius Vanderbilt and Mrs Woodrow Wilson, as well as well as John D. Rockefeller and J.P. Morgan.

Just a week later Jimmy returned to Princeton Stadium to watch what was being dubbed the 'Mile of the Century' – the world record holder, Englishman, Sydney Wooderson, taking on some of the finest runners in America. Jimmy arrived at the stadium some days before the event and met up with those in the know. Joe Binks, former British mile record holder, was not sure Wooderson was in the best of form. Wooderson's trainer, Albert Hill, the man who had broken Binks' record, believed his man would win easily. Jimmy was also reunited with his old nemesis, Bill Struth, former professional athlete in Scotland, and now manager of Glasgow Rangers Football Club.

So impressed was Jimmy by the wiry, bespectacled English runner that he gathered together his team and traipsed the group to New Jersey to witness the man known as the Mighty Atom. In the run up to the race Jimmy lionised his speed to his runners, warning them that they were about to see what 'a good miler looks like.' He had reason to be confident: Wooderson was indeed a special athlete. Six years later he would run the mile in 4.04.2, infinitely quicker than Jimmy, or any of his students, or opponents, ever ran the distance. Unfortunately for the Scot the Englishman let him down on this occasion. Taking intermediate times at the 220 yards mark, Jimmy saw the Englishman give too much too early, and he was well beaten in the last 50 yards, trailing in last of the five runners. After all Jimmy's hot air, his runners took their revenge – they sent him a note, on funeral stationery, and after the message of condolence, which read, 'Extending my sympathy to you at this time of sorrow', they added, 'Defeat of Wooderson – fifth too. Ha, Ha!' The wily old coach was clearly amused by the boys' joke – he sent the details to a Scottish newspaper for publication.

As students began arriving at school in September 1939, Neville Chamberlain, the British Prime Minister, was standing before his fellow MPs in the House of Commons and annunciating Britain's obligation to Poland by declaring war on Germany. And with this announcement it became clear that any thoughts that students, former and current, had of making it to the 1940 Helsinki Olympics had all but disappeared.

But Jimmy still had the school season to consider. It started well. His students stepped up at the school's annual Field Day, the highlight of the event being Jack Milne's 4.25 mile, a run that Jimmy noted as being the 'fastest mile ever run on the Mercersburg track.' Milne followed this up with an impressive cross country win against the Navy Plebes, although the team suffered its almost inevitable annual defeat.

The school's success in the 1939/40 season initially rested on the experienced shoulders of boys such as Kellam, Milne, and Morgan. At Baltimore in early February Jack Milne's phenomenal form continued when he took the 1,000 yards race, and he followed this up two weeks later at the National AAU Championships at Madison Square Garden with a victory in the mile race in a fast time of 4.24.1 seconds. He was joined on the rostrum by Austin Kellam who retained his long jump title with a meet record. As the season progressed, the core of Jimmy's team continued to provide his best results. In April, Morgan ran a time of 4.30.5 seconds to set an indoor mile record at the Middle Atlantic Championships.

The remainder of the season was a success. There were blips, with defeats against the freshmen of Cornell and the Navy Plebes, and a loss to Seton Hall at the Penn Relays, but the wins were frequent. In early May the Penn State Freshmen were beaten, with Kellam setting a new 220 yards hurdles interscholastic record in the process. A week later, Kellam shone once more, taking four wins in a victory against the Penn Freshmen. The following month he went one better, taking five first places in a win against Yale.

Unlike 1914, when Jimmy attempted to enlist in the British Army, he was aware that fighting was not an option for a 59-year old. Instead he focussed his energies on raising money to send back to his homeland. In October 1940 he sponsored a two-night film showing of the Tyrone Power vehicle, *Brigham Young*, at the Star Theater in Mercersburg to raise funds for the Soldiers' and Sailors' Comforts Fund in Galashiels. Staff and students were encouraged to buy a ticket, for 37¢, and did so with gusto. And no doubt he had a chuckle at his offer of a 'Scotch Special' of three tickets for $1.15. Indeed, virtually every boy in the school attended the event. A bank draft for $108 ($1,930 in today's money) was sent across the Atlantic, but had to be re-sent after the ship it was on was torpedoed and ended up at the bottom of the ocean. In a letter to the local Galashiels newspaper he noted that 'all exiles in America feel proud about the way you are taking it over [there], and we feel it is not only a privilege but a duty to help you', adding jokingly that he doubted he could return to Galashiels if he did nothing to help.

The torpedoed ship served as an appropriate metaphor for the 1940/41 season where Jimmy's team, now missing its two finest athletes – Jack Milne and Austin Kellam – who had both left for university, lacked any great quality and struggled to impress. A lone victory at the University of Maryland Games was one of the only high points in a season of defeats. A fifth place at the AAU Championships was perhaps the low point, but no doubt Jimmy would have been greatly pained by the ending of one of his finest accomplishments – in 1939 he had been interviewed by Cy Peterman, sports reporter at the *Philadelphia Inquirer*, noting proudly that his teams had, in his 32 years of coaching, never dropped a baton. Fate did not take long to intervene – just over one year later, in the final of the 440 yards relay at the Penn Relays, his prophecy came to pass, when the Mercersburg lead-off man, C. Harry

Barber, dropped the baton soon after the gun.

The season, one of the worst in Jimmy's coaching tenure, was not a complete loss. At several meets Jimmy's team had been put to the sword by a sprinter from La Salle Military Academy called Paul Cowie. In February Jimmy had looked on as he ran 60 yards in 6.3 seconds at the National AAU Championships, and was on the winning relay team that beat Mercersburg at the Penn Relays.

And so, in an effort to turn around the team's mini slump, Jimmy set out to attract Cowie to the school. This he did. But as had so often been the way, great athletes came to Mercersburg in batches. And so it was in 1941. As well as Paul Cowie came perhaps an even greater prospect. Jeff Kirk was a young, bespectacled divinity student. His father, who had once beaten Ted Meredith in a race, had presented him with his first spikes when he was only six years old. Lawson Robertson would later say of him, 'he's tall, strong, and has a long powerful stride and plenty of endurance. He's one of the most promising boys I've seen, and when he reaches his peak in another two or three years I won't be surprised if he's among the best of all time.' On the day after the attack on Pearl Harbor, a newspaper reported Jimmy as saying they were the best pair he had coached since Meredith and Robinson. Praise indeed.

Despite the school opening two weeks late, due to an epidemic of polio in the state, Cowie impressed early with a storming victory in the Annual Field Day, winning the Williams Cup after taking five of the six events.

But things quickly began to unravel. An injury to Cowie saw the relay team forced to withdraw from the Millrose Games, and he missed much of the remainder of the season. And the school's other great hope, Kirk, struggled to impress at the AAU Championships which were once again dominated by Seton Hall.

At the Penn Relays, the team finally proved its quality. With Cowie fit again, the boys ran the fast time of 43.1 seconds as part of the 440 yards relay team, and this was followed up with a victory at a mud-ridden 'C' Club meet, where Kirk showed his talents with victories in the 440 yards and as part of the mile relay team.

But the loss of Cowie and Kirk at the end of the 1941/42 season did not augur the slump that some might have envisaged. Jimmy had a wealth of young athletes waiting to fill their shoes.

As America began readying itself for war, Jimmy had another potential champion on his hands. Dick McFadden was an all-rounder from Lemasters High School near Mercersburg. He was an outstanding athlete; at the end of his rookie season Jimmy believed that with a year's training McFadden could be the next Barney Berlinger – a weights man with good speed. His time at the school started well, winning the Williams Cup. He followed this up in the Penn Relays, with a win in the 440 yards relay. The time of 44.2 seconds wasn't particularly fast, until one considers that one of the team, Irvine Condon, was suffering from measles. Aware he had them two days before the race, he was afraid to tell Jimmy, so kept them secret, and went ahead with what proved a winning run.

But Jimmy's job was being made increasingly difficult by the fact that athletes began to leave the school to join the war effort. By 1945 around 2,400 current students, alumni, and faculty had boarded ships for various theatres of war. Jimmy likened the departure of these young American boys to his experiences in Scotland at the turn of the century, when boys were rushing to sign up to fight the Boers. One of those who headed across the Atlantic was McFadden. His sporting skills transcended the track, so much so that in 1943 he was offered a contract to play baseball for the New York Yankees. But he never returned home to take up this opportunity – he was killed in Germany in 1944, just before the Battle of the Bulge.

The next two years saw the team held together by a clutch of athletes, notably Maurice Brewton, Byron Kellam (brother of Austin), and Bob Black who took the first three places in the Williams Cup. The strength of this core meant that a handful of wins were forthcoming, but the order of the day was usually a loss.

In 1944 the team registered four victories to win the National

AAU Championships at Madison Square Garden, with only a stray Bob Black elbow robbing the team of a fifth win due to disqualification. And the following year, with Brewton and Kellam both gone, Black stepped up and dominated all races he took part in between 220 yards and 880 yards.

The 1945/46 season saw the arrival of a youngster called Charles Moore. Moore's father, 'Crip', can perhaps be said to hold the crown of Mercersburg's most unlucky Olympian. He had been part of the US Olympic team in 1924, failing to start his race after a protest from the French team on a technicality. But at the lowest of ebbs he had made a vow: if he was to ever have a son he would complete at the Olympics, and that he would be such an outstanding athlete that no technicality could deprive him of his place in history. Moore Jr was over 6 feet tall and 170 pounds. As a child he had broken his femur in an automobile accident, eliciting a dread in his father that his desire for his son to win Olympic gold was about to be scuppered before it had advanced beyond the realms of a dream. But the bone had been secured with kangaroo gut, and the surgeon who performed the procedure would later delight in explaining that it was the kangaroo in Moore that made him the hurdler he was. But when Moore arrived at Mercersburg he was by no means a prodigy. Indeed, he later argued that he had never run before arriving at the school and Jimmy, seeing the father in the boy before him, said, 'Here, let me help you.' And Moore grasped this opportunity with both hands, taking on board every piece of advice passed him by his new mentor.

Mercersburg's season was an average one with few highlights. Of greater interest is Charles Moore's season. He began it in the Williams Cup, taking a first place in the 120 yards hurdles. He followed this up with a second place in the 60 yards hurdles at the National Interscholastic Championships, and places in a dual meet against Woodberry Forest, and as part of the 440 yards relay team at the Penn Relays. He closed the season with two wins against the Navy Plebes.

While Moore's first season had been a learning one, his second saw him begin to make inroads towards becoming one of America's greatest ever hurdlers. Within days of the school term starting, he strode away with the overall Williams Cup honours. At the evening assembly he was presented with the cup by his father, as Jimmy looked on from the back of the dais. At the Inquirer meet he took the Prep School mile, followed it with third place in the National Interscholastic Championships, and was part of the winning 440 yards relay at the Penn Relays.

*****

In the summer of 1947 Jimmy returned to Scotland once again, this time with Janet. The trip coincided with a royal tour of several Borders towns by King George VI and Queen Elizabeth, their two daughters, Elizabeth and Margaret, and Elizabeth's fiancé, Lieutenant Philip Mountbatten. They arrived in Galashiels in July, and interest in the momentous event was given a boost by the recent engagement of Elizabeth and Philip, soon to become Queen Elizabeth II and Prince Philip. To allow the gathering of the largest possible crowd the welcome of the royal party was made by the Burgh Chambers. Thousands looked on. Jimmy's childhood friend, John Torrie was a Bailie, and was central to the proceedings.

*****

The 1947/48 season was one of few stars, but much success with mile relay wins at the Inquirer meet, the National AAU Championships, and the Spiked Shoe meet, as well as a win in the 440 yards at the Penn Relays. But while his team met with reasonable success, Jimmy had his eyes on an opponent that he believed would herald the rise of one of his finest teams. Gus Ormrod was a miler from Atlantic City, excelling in track at Holy Spirit High School. In 1947 he won the state championship in cross country, and the following year won the Spiked

HIGHS AND LOWS

Shoe for his High School, and was awarded the outstanding athlete award. This was followed by a win in the mile, in a time of 4.29, at the Penn Relays. Such was his talent that Jimmy offered him a scholarship.

*****

By the summer of 1948 Jeff Kirk hadn't quite met Lawson Robertson's expectation of becoming the best of all time, but he was clearly an exceptional athlete. Along with Cowie he took part in the trials for the first post-war Olympics; Cowie was eliminated at the preliminary stage, but Kirk took third place in the final of the 400m hurdles and was on his way to London. Also crossing the Atlantic was his former coach, Jimmy, bound for Scotland, but determined to take in the Olympics at Wembley Stadium. All did not go well for Kirk. He injured his leg during a workout on board the team ship, the SS *America*, and then exited at the semi-final stage, after miscalculating the steps to the last hurdle. He had the dubious distinction of being the first American athlete to be eliminated from the Games. Jimmy had much else to cheer on, but undoubtedly his loudest praise was reserved for the 17-year-old Bob Mathias, no older than most of his own students, winner of the decathlon. Jimmy's thoughts on the quadruple gold medal performance by Fanny Blankers-Koen are not known, but his opposition to women's athletics was, according to David Emory Jr, 'Victorian.' So much so that his granddaughter, Laurie Danaher, had to be trained by David Emory. She would later recall: 'Papa wasn't keen on me running. He said he'd buy me a tennis racket, golf clubs, anything but not running. [However] Papa used to brag about me when he went down to visit Uncle Jimmy in Texas and he used to secretly watch me running on the Academy's indoor track.' Further to this she would later recall that her grandfather was a great admirer of Wilma Rudolph who, 12 years later, he would watch winning three gold medals. After the Games Jimmy headed back up to Scotland where he made his way to Abbotsford, home of Sir Walter Scott, and visited with the writer's descendants. Another trip

223

complete, he was soon headed home, this time on the RMS *Queen Mary*.

*****

The start of the 1948/49 season gave Jimmy an opportunity to test Ormrod. And the youngster repaid Jimmy's faith by dominating the cross country races. First place against the Navy Plebes saw him lop 31 seconds off the course record, although the team was subjected to its usual defeat. Three weeks later he took second place against an extremely strong University of Pennsylvania Freshmen team. In January 1949 he ran as part of the mile relay team at the Inquirer Star meet, recording a time of 3.34 seconds, and then went on to dominate the University of Pennsylvania's Spiked Shoe Club meet at Franklin Field, striding away with the 880 yards and the mile, and was awarded the Spiked Shoe Trophy for performance, sportsmanship and team spirit.

But the team performances were erratic, due in great part to a weakness in the field events and a lack of depth on the track. Jimmy was well aware that one dominant field athlete could virtually win events single-handedly, a fact he had exploited in previous years with men such as Pete Maxfield, Barney Berlinger and Ed Beetem. The strength of this tactic was amply demonstrated when Jimmy's team travelled to take on the Kiski School. Kiski was a small prep school from Saltsburg, PA. Its star athlete was Bob Mathias, who 10 months earlier Jimmy had watched being crowned Olympic decathlon champion at the tender age of 17, a feat he would repeat at the 1952 Games. Jimmy's team was on the receiving end of a one-man thrashing. Mathias won six events and Kiski won by two points.

But this blip did not deter Jimmy from the task at hand – building a track team that was the best in America. He now had his eye on a teen sensation from Garden City, New York, called Henry Thresher. Just three months after Ormrod's stand-out performance at Franklin Field, Thresher 'put on a one-man show' for the Garden City Trojans at the Nassau County Track Championship. On 4th June he ran a time of 9.9

seconds for the 100 yards, and followed this up in the 220 yards with a time of 20.9 seconds, just 0.2 seconds off Jesse Owens' 16 year-old scholastic record. A week later he recorded two more wins, including a New York state record in the 220 yards.

And so, at the start of the 1949/50 season, Thresher arrived at the school, joining Gus Ormrod, the hurdler Dewey Lee Yoder, and a group of sprinters including Larry Lattomus, Gordon Follett, Reed Donnelly and Joseph Albanese. Jimmy had a team that could seriously aspire to being the best he had ever had – although only time and results would tell.

By the time he competed in his first race for Mercersburg, at the Washington Star Games in January 1950, Thresher was 17 years old. He turned in first places in the 70 and 80 yards, and a second in the 100 yards, with an overall performance that was described as 'out of the ordinary', and already he was being talked about as the successor to Jesse Owens. A loss in early February to Andy Stanfield, who would go on to win two Olympic gold medals and one silver, was followed by victory in the 60 yards in a time of 6.4 seconds, and a six-lap relay victory with Lattomus, Yoder and Follett, at the Millrose Games. Days later he ran a dead heat against Ben Kreitzberg in the semi-final of the 60 yards at the New York Athletic Club games. A mix up saw Thresher showered and dressed before he could run in the final.

Just weeks later, he captured the National Interscholastic 60 yards championship at Madison Square Garden, with the time of 6.4 seconds. And he continued to better his own performances. At the Spiked Shoe Club meeting in March 1950 he broke the world record for the 60 yards with a time of 6.2 seconds, while Ormrod secured the mile and the school's relay teams steamrollered all before them.

The following month, in a dual meet against Woodberry Forest, Thresher excelled once again, as did Ormrod and Yoder. He won the 100 and 220 yards, Ormrod put in an exceptional time of 4.24 to win the mile, whilst Yoder took the 220 yards low hurdles, and the relay team also emerged victorious.

JIMMY CURRAN

A week later at the Penn Relays, Thresher, Lattomus, Yoder and Jim Sutton ran a time of 42.9 seconds, only 0.7 seconds outside the world interscholastic record, set by the Academy in 1939, and 25 yards ahead of the second-placed team. Lattomus and Yoder then took a step up to the mile relay and again walked away with the honours.

The following week, Mercersburg had its chance to exact revenge on Kiski School for the thrashing it, or more accurately Bob Mathias, had handed out a year earlier. With Mathias now gone the natural order was restored. Ormrod ran a 4.25 mile. But once again it was Thresher who was the stand out, with a 19.2 second 200 yards, and a 9.5 second 100 yards. One timer clocked him at 9.4, equal to Jesse Owens' best, and only a tenth of a second behind Mel Patton's world record, leading Jimmy, psychology to the fore as always, to posit that Thresher was the 'fastest schoolboy athlete in the world.'

Thresher's summer was spent running for the New York Athletic Club, beginning with wins in the 100 and 220 yards at Brooklyn's Red Hook Stadium. A week later he lined up against the talented Ira Kaplan at Randall's Island in New York. The honours were split with Kaplan taking the 100 yards, and Thresher the 220.

Things didn't go quite as well at the start of the 1950/51 season, with two third places, in the 70 and 80 yards at the Evening Star Games, both behind Art Bragg and England's MacDonald Bailey. The elation of victory at a 50 yards race in Philadelphia lasted just a matter of seconds after he broke the tape, when he found that his clothes had been stolen. It may have been a harbinger of things to come; eight days later he lost to Andy Stanfield in the 60 yards at the Millrose Games.

But a runner of Thresher's stature couldn't be kept down for long. Just weeks later he won the 60 yards at the National AAU Interscholastics in 6.4 seconds. And he went from strength to strength, starting with a 6.4 seconds 60 yards at the Spiked Shoe meet, and a 9.6 seconds 100 yards in a dual meet against Woodberry Forest. Further wins were forthcoming against the Navy Plebes, and at the 16th AAU Track and Field Championship at Randall's Island, as well as taking part in a 2,900m medley team, along with Charles Moore, that finished just over one second outside the world record on a rain-sodden track. A blip had to come, and it did with a fifth place in the 200m at the National AAU Track and Field Championships in Berkeley. But Thresher's season had been phenomenal. With the Olympics only a year distant, Thresher was now a serious contender for not just a place on the team, but for Olympic gold – indeed Bill Carr had noted his gold medal potential as early as February 1950. But then it all began to go wrong. In August, just as he was entering college at Yale, just as he looked as if he had the world at his feet, he was struck down by polio. He was sent to the Sister Kenny Institute in Jersey City to recuperate.

But in a reflection of his track career, Thresher emerged victorious, beating the disease. By June 1952, with the US Olympic trials looming, he was readying himself for a comeback. In dual meets he was running close to his personal bests in the 60 and 100 yards. But with an overcrowded field in the short sprints, and Thresher's start never the best, it was decided he would concentrate on the 200m in the lead up to the Olympic trials.

But it was not only Thresher amongst Jimmy's athletes that had the Olympics in their sights. Dewey Lee Yoder, Gus Ormrod and Jack Milne also attended the US trials, as did the long-graduated Charles Moore. The two great qualification hopes were Thresher and Moore, with Yoder, Ormrod and Milne real possibilities. The feeling amongst coaches was that Thresher was likely to win a place in the US team. But before he could test himself against the best in America at the US trials he suffered a muscle pull, and his Olympic dream was ended. Jimmy had high hopes for Moore, noting that 'He's a serious trainer and he possesses the will and determination to win. I look for him to set new world marks in both the 400 meters and the 400 meter hurdles.' If evidence is needed that this was indeed the case, one need only consider the recollection of Moore's room-mate, Lester Cagle, that Moore had him hold a thread suspended in their room, while he breasted it, in an effort to perfect his technique. He was also a deep thinker. While other hurdlers implemented miniscule changes to shave microscopic distances of their runs, Moore considered how he could turn his rangy physicality to his advantage. And, in an event-changing decision, as revolutionary as the introduction of the crouching start in the sprints and Dick Fosbury's introduction of the flop into the high jump in the 1960s, he threw out the accepted convention that hurdlers take 15 steps between hurdles, and reduced it down to 13.

Moore fulfilled his promise, winning the 400m hurdles at the Olympic trials, in a new American record of 50.6 seconds. Yoder took second place and would join him in Helsinki. Ormrod and Milne failed to win places.

And so, 28 years after 'Crip' Moore had vowed his son would win an Olympic gold medal, the elder Moore he sat in Helsinki's Olympic Stadium awaiting his son stepping onto the track for the final of the 400 metres hurdles. Yoder had been eliminated in the semi-final, but Moore, unbeaten at the event, had stormed through his heat, quarter- and semi-final, breaking the Olympic record in the quarters. In the final he saw off a strong challenge from the Soviet Union's Yuriy Lituyev, equalling the Olympic record he had broken the day before. Less than a week later Moore was back on the track, after he was unexpectedly chosen to be part of the 4x400m team; so unexpectedly that his family had already returned home. In the final they bettered the 20-year old world record, set by a US team including Bill Carr at the 1932 Olympics, by four seconds. But they came up against an inspired Jamaican team. Early on it had all looked good for the US team with Ollie Matson and Gene Cole running them into a 10 yard lead, but Moore came up against the 400m silver medallist Herb McKenley who was leading by the time he passed the baton to the gold medallist in that event, George Rhoden. Even 'Marvelous' Mal Whitfield, double gold medallist at the 1948 Games and recently-crowned 800m gold medallist, could not pass an athlete of Rhoden's talents, and the US team lost the race by one tenth of a second. Moore has admitted he was devastated, feeling that he had cost the team the gold medal. But he has since attempted to put the defeat into perspective – the US team ran four seconds faster than the previous world record, and the time they ran was almost a second faster than the winning time at the next Olympic Games.

*****

Jimmy's desire to remain fit never left him. He continued to run with his athletes into the 1940s, play golf, and was an avid handball player – around 1940 he played a doubles game, along with swimming coach John Miller, against two students. The two staff members won 21-10. Ten years later he celebrated his 70th birthday with a game against Miller. In 1949, Cy Peterman called him 'that monument to physical condition.' Jimmy was proud of his fitness, noting, 'I'm in better condition than [my athletes] are when they first report.' His desire to continually physically push himself prompted Michael Strauss of the *New York Times* to note that Santa Claus might consider bringing 'the Academy's hike-loving track coach ... some six-league boots' as a Christmas present.

This wasn't strictly true. Since his youth Jimmy had been plagued by chronic varicose veins. Then, in 1929, after walking to Chambersburg and back, a distance of 34 miles, he was unable to raise himself from the dinner table due to a stiffness in his legs. Any doubt that he would try again was dispelled when the Academy's doctor warned him off, telling him he was too old. And so he set off on the shorter 20 mile round trip to McConnellsburg. Again, his legs stiffened on return. Jimmy loved walking, the longer the distance the better – he and Janet had once hiked to the summit of the 2,000 feet Mount Parnell in the Appalachians.

In 1951, 22 years after the problem arose, Jimmy underwent an operation to resolve the varicose veins in his legs, and was readying himself for a 34 mile walk to Hagerstown to test whether it had been effective. But Jimmy was no fool. He had no intention of pushing his legs to the limit without first giving them some softer tests. And where better to find his running legs again than on the gravel paths around Eastlands Cemetery, while on a trip home to Scotland, two years after the operation. And so, 50 years after he had pounded around the stone testaments to Galashiels' past, he returned. This time he walked, but as with all Jimmy did, he would have pushed himself. This he followed up by shadowing Ben Hogan for 36 holes around Carnoustie during the Open golf. And finally, he played the hallowed course at St Andrews, the home of golf, with E. Aldin Lakin, president of his local golf club in Hagerstown. His legs suitably tested, in November 1953, Jimmy walked out of Mercersburg bound for Hagerstown. A blister almost ended his trek, but a passing friend drove him to a filling station where he bought a sticking plaster. After lunching in Hagerstown he caught a bus to Greencastle in order that he would arrive home before the sun set, and he walked the final 11 miles.

*****

The early- to mid-1950s were, it could be argued, a lost period for the school, much like the mid-1930s had been. Even the odd victory at the Penn Relays were in some of the slowest winning times the school had ever recorded. There were highlights. Some good cross country seasons were tarnished only by the expected annual loss to the Navy Plebes. There were some outstanding meets, such as the Spiked Shoe in 1955, which saw wins in the 440 yards, 880 yards, the mile, mile relay and pole vault. But by and large the track performances were mediocre. Two shining lights split the darkness – weights man Bob Batdorf and sprinter Malcolm 'Andy' Anderson. For the duration of their time at Mercersburg the two men dominated events, Anderson often winning multiple races at meets, and Batdorf doing likewise in the weights events, breaking a number of records along the way.

But if the mid-1950s had not quite met Jimmy's expectations, his wit was not dampened. In April 1956 he attended a meet where he came across Art Jackson, coach of the Hill School. On seeing a large stopwatch around Jackson's neck, Jimmy enquired as to where he came across his 'awfully big locket.' Jackson proceeded to tell him that a major watch company was permitting his coaches to use them, each valued at $500. Jimmy pointed at his little pocket watch and said it had served him well. Nevertheless, he ordered one that very night. The three levers initially caused him problems, but he quickly grew attached to it, until what appeared to be a bill for $500 arrived. After questioning anyone in authority he could find as to whether there was a way out of paying, he learned that the bill was actually a memorandum sent for the purposes of inventory. Jimmy, smiling, noted 'I knew all the time a misfortune – a $500 one – couldn't ha' happened to me. After all, this is America!'

And the Olympics had rolled around once again. In 1952 Henry Thresher had lost out on a trip to the Helsinki Games through injury. Had he made it he would have been amongst the favourites to medal. Four years later he was still dreaming of shining on the world's biggest stage – this time in the warmer climes of Melbourne. In the intervening years he'd continued to race, first for Yale, and then for the US Air Force. He was originally assigned to jet training but his talents were well known and he ended up training for the Olympics at Sheppard Air Force Base. But once again his body let him down – in the Air Force Olympic qualifying event he ruptured his Achilles tendon, ending, once again, his Olympic dream, and this time his track career. The boy who Jimmy would rate as one of the finest two athletes he ever trained had gone the same way as the other one, Albert Robinson, thwarted by injury from attending an Olympics.

Despite the disappointment of Thresher's injury, Jimmy was represented in Australia. A recent arrival at Mercersburg was a young Puerto Rican pole vaulter called Rolando Cruz. At just 17 years old, 5' 10" tall and 145 lbs, he didn't have the typical build of a vaulter, causing Jimmy to later comment that 'once Cruz gets a stronger body, there's no telling how high he'll go … he's a fine boy.'

Had he been from the United States it is unlikely Cruz would have qualified for the Melbourne Games, but in Puerto Rico, with a far smaller pool to choose from, he was a stand-out vaulter. The experience wasn't a good one for Cruz: 'I couldn't speak English. I didn't have any friends. It was no good.' This was reflected in his competition, where he failed to qualify for the final, despite being one of only two vaulters using the new fibreglass pole.

But those around him continued to rave about his potential. Two years after the Melbourne Olympics, Jimmy noted 'I don't want to go overboard on this kid, but I wouldn't be surprised if he did 14 feet at the Inquirer meet. I'd say this kid is so good that he will go 16 feet if [Boo Morcom, the University of Penn's track coach, and former Olympic pole vaulter] gets him.' Jimmy did see some flaws in Cruz's character, telling him 'You're stubborn like the Scotch. Maybe I ought to learn to speak Spanish. Then maybe you'd listen. But better still, maybe you ought to study Scotch instead of English. Then I could really teach you the tricks of the trade.' But such shortcomings were not insurmountable.

In April 1957, the night before the start of the Penn Relays when he was an honorary referee, a number of Jimmy's former students, including Bill Carr, Charles Moore, 'Crip' Moore, Barney Berlinger and Dewey Lee Yoder, as well as the swimmer John Macionis, Admiral John H. Brown, and Admiral Roger Heimer, gathered at the Academy's alumni banquet, where they were regaled by an AAU official, who recalled tales of Jimmy's 50 uninterrupted years of attendance at the Penn Relays.

A ringing endorsement also came in the *Philadelphia Inquirer*, from sports writer Don Daniels: 'You will [have] to dig around a long time in the sports world to find a more fabulous character than the cagey and ageless little Scotsman who has produced more and better runners than practically anyone anywhere.' In the stadium he caught the eye of old friend Michael Strauss, reporter for the *New York Times*. Strauss would write of Jimmy: 'If energy, enterprise and enthusiasm by a coach are the necessary ingredients, Curran is still young enough to produce another champion… he appears sprier than ever these days.' But he was not being entirely honest. Years later he would recall being shocked at Jimmy's appearance, telling his readers that the seated coach 'seemed extremely weary.' As was his way, Jimmy attempted to make light of the situation – 'I'm not sitting here because I'm tired. I jus' dinna want to get in anybody's way.'

In May the school received an illustrious visitor – Arnie Sowell. Sowell was a middle-distance runner who represented the United States at 800m in the 1956 Olympics. He was widely considered one of the finest runners in the world. A former Mercersburg student, studying alongside him at the University of Pittsburgh, asked him if he would be willing to spend a day with the Academy's track team. He agreed. After chatting to the team for a short time he took to the track with them for a half-mile run. For much of that 1.59.4 minute race he sat in behind Jef Evans, passing on tips as they ran. Evans won, but held no illusions who the quality athlete was.

Just six months after the celebration of Jimmy's half century as a coach, another gathering took place. This time it was a more sombre occasion. At a funeral home in Haddonfield, New Jersey, Jimmy attended the service to his most famous athlete, Ted Meredith. In March he had suffered a massive stroke, likely brought on by alcoholism, and in November he died following an operation to repair a broken hip. He was only 65 years old. Mourners at the Haddonfield Methodist Church were a roll call of Olympians and star athletes, from Don Lippincott, Larry Brown, Earl Eby and Sherman Landers to Wallace McCurdy, Joe Lockwood, Ed Harter, and the sculler Paul Costello. The minister read from Corinthians:

> Know ye not that they which run in a race run all, but one receiveth the prize? So run, that you may obtain.

Whilst the 1957/58 season was similar to its predecessors in terms of lack of success, it was marked by the emergence of Cruz as a real prospect. In May, at the Stevens Trade International meet, he jumped an impressive 13 ¼ feet. Days later at the school's Field Day, moved from fall to spring the previous year, he won the Williams Cup, winning two events and placing in all the others. Jimmy wanted to test him at two meets – the intercollegiate meet in Philadelphia, followed by the Meet of Champions in Houston, the hometown of Jimmy's son, on 7th June. All seemed well until his family found out that the 1,400 mile trip to the latter would be undertaken by bus, not aeroplane. To appease them he had his son-in-law, Howard Dovey, drive him to and from a track meet in Annapolis, a 230-mile round trip, to test whether the trip to Houston was going to be too much. Some middle ground was reached – Jimmy could go if two of his daughters, Margaret and Ellen, travelled with him, driven by his granddaughter Jeannie. The family group, with Cruz in tow, his pole roped to the side of the car, headed for Jimmy Jr's house in Houston, via a stopover in New Orleans.

The family had reason to worry. On another trip to Houston around this time, his varicose veins were once again proving bothersome. By the time he reached his son's home he was in a bad way. So bad was it that his daughter-in-law, Nathalie, Jimmy Jr's wife, was shocked enough to try and work out how she could bring him back to health. The solution, she decided, was to be found in the seemingly innocuous form of Bing cherries. The cherries, it is claimed, aid the prevention and treatment of varicose veins. She bought in large quantities of them, washing them off and having everyone eat them freely. Jimmy's health began to gradually improve, and he began taking eight-block walks, with his young grandson Stephen, to the Tanglewood Pharmacy. There he would take a seat at the lunch counter and trade stories with the locals. He would then leave Stephen at his counter seat, while he took off for a short walk. But as the days passed, Stephen was left at the counter for longer and longer periods until, on the last day before Jimmy returned to Pennsylvania, Stephen sat there through lunch and beyond. Jimmy's strength was growing by the day. When he had left Mercersburg, he was ailing. On his return, his family called the

Currans in Houston, marvelling at his transformation.

The trip to Houston with Cruz proved worthwhile – he placed first, albeit tied with two others.

The 1958/59 season was not one of overarching success, other than the Spiked Shoe meet where Mercersburg athletes took a number of events. And again, Batdorf and Anderson were standouts, as was Rolando Cruz, who was now competing at a world class level. At the Millrose Games in late January, accompanied by Jimmy and assistant coach David Emory, he placed second to Don Bragg with a jump of 14½ feet, and then he jumped so high against Kiski in a dual meet that makeshift props had to be used to raise the bar. And at the end of the season he once again won the Williams Cup.

The following year was again rather mediocre, Cruz being one of the few bright spots.

On 7th January 1960 Jimmy attended a celebration, in the Academy's assembly room, a double celebration of his 80th birthday and his 50 years as Academy coach. For the first time, Charles Tippetts introduced him with the epithet Sir James Michael Curran. Two members of the Philadelphia Alumni Association of Mercersburg Academy, Lawrence S. Warren and former crack athlete Jack Milne, then took to the stage and reminisced about the wily Scot, before presenting him with a trip to the Olympics, to be held in Rome. Jimmy had crossed the Atlantic at least four times in the 1950s, at least two of these on an aeroplane, and he used this mode of transport again in 1960, stopping first in Scotland, his last ever trip to the land of his birth. As was his way on visits home, he stayed with relatives and took in the town's eateries, such as Galashiels Café, and presented pencils to each winner in the girls' school relay race.

Cruz returned to the Olympics for the second time in 1960. Despite his gold at the Central American and Caribbean Games, as well as bronze at the Pan-American Games, both a year earlier, he wasn't considered a real medal hope in Rome, and certainly no major threat to the two Americans, Don Bragg and Ron Morris. In the qualifying round he easily jumped the required height, eventually posting 4.40m. Thirteen men progressed to the final, but one by one they fell by the way. By the time Cruz equalled his 4.40m from qualifying, the field was down to ten. Ten centimetres later a further two had dropped out, and only Cruz and Günter Malcher of Germany had flawless records. The height was raised to 4.55 and took its toll, with four vaulters failing all three attempts – Cruz failed his first but made his second. Four men remained – Cruz, Don Bragg, Ron Morris and Eeles Landström of Finland. As Jimmy looked on from the stands, a medal looked a distinct possibility, although gold appeared unlikely as Bragg appeared to have it sewn up. Crux found 4.60 a step too far, having already beaten his personal best. He failed all three attempts. Landström also failed all three, but the rules of the pole vault in 1960 meant that he took bronze as he had jumped 4.55m at his first attempt. When Bragg eventually took gold, with an Olympic record, the competition had been going on for over six hours. Cruz had come within one single fail of a bronze medal, and was more than pleased – 'Oh, I cared because I just missed a third place medal, but not too much. I was happy I did so well. I knew I was not ready to beat Bragg.' Jimmy, no doubt, was filled with pride for his young charge, albeit tinged with a hint of 'what could have been.' Four years later he would attend the Tokyo Games, but fail to progress past qualifying.

After Rome he flew home to America, met at Idlewild Airport by three of his daughters.

Entering his final year as Mercersburg coach, Jimmy was first faced with a series of cross country races. And as if to set up a final season of success, the team went out for seven races and won them all.

Before the track season started, Jimmy headed to the Sheraton Hotel in Philadelphia to receive an honour from the Philadelphia Sports Writers Association. Before a crowd of almost 1,000, the main honours went to Mike Ditka, future first round draft pick and Super Bowl winner as a player and coach, recently retired football player Norm Van Brocklin and swimmer Jeff Farrell. Most notable of the other honourees was Sonny Liston.

Chapter 14 • He run a good race

Jimmy had intended to retire in 1960, but decided against it for unknown reasons. This was not just an opportunity to work out his final year. Jimmy's eyes were always peeled for the next new talent. And in 1960 he found one. During the summer holidays he came across a youngster called Paul White, keeping in shape by running on the Mercersburg track. White hailed from Maryland, and was studying as a summer school student at Mercersburg, in an attempt to gain entry to Cornell University. Jimmy thought he saw something in the tall, good-looking youth. White remembers a 'mild-mannered gentleman' asking if he could time his run. The next few seconds would change his life – Jimmy offered him a place at Mercersburg the following term. White initially baulked, thinking about the cost of being a student, but Jimmy told him not to worry as he would sponsor a scholarship.

Jimmy had been a coach at the school for 51 years. In that time he had become adept at spotting a talent, and in Paul White he saw something special. The next weeks and months were spent working on his speed and technique at the 100, 220 and 440 yards, as well as the long jump. White also remembers well Jimmy teaching him the 'relaxation response' – short naps between races – a technique he still uses today, calling it an 'ole man's nap.'

White would later recall that Jimmy would offer up a double incentive at the Penn Relays – he had invited the coach of Cornell to see White with the possibility of a scholarship on the table, and also reminded the team that the winners would be awarded the world-famous Penn Relays gold watches. And if winning a Penn watch was not enough incentive for White, then the possibility of attending an Ivy League school on a scholarship certainly was. He won his scholarship, and topped this off with the Williams Cup, the Bob Black Trophy for sportsmanship and the Varsity Trophy for being the best all-around athlete of the year. For Jimmy, it was 'a good going away present.'

HE RUN A GOOD RACE

But it could not last forever. For 51 years Jimmy had been a faithful servant to the school and its athletes. Prior to that he had spent three years as a rubber and coach at the University of Pennsylvania. But, as Chaucer noted, 'time and tide wait for no man' – even Jimmy Curran. His mind was that of the lad who had stormed to victory in the Border Mile Championship in 1904, and the young man who had twice in a week taken a chunk out of Alfie Shrubb's lead against relay teams in 1907. As late as 1958 he told one reporter 'It seems like I started yesterday.' His body, however, was beginning to let him down; for eight years he had suffered from arteriosclerosis, and his varicose veins were still hugely problematic. But it could not stop him – his granddaughter, Laurie Danaher, remembers him taking her sledging on the roads of the Academy after his retiral. The time to retire had arrived. In May 1961 his track team took part in a dual meet against Gettysburg. Appropriately, his grandson, Tom Danaher, now a student at the Academy, rose to the occasion and won the mile race. The rest of the team did likewise, winning the meet with ease. A month later, at the Franklin County Track and Field meet, competing against local schools, Mercersburg won the event with six wins from 13, four of which were records. Tom Danaher was again dominant, winning the mile race and being part of the successful 880 yards relay team.

And so, one week after the County Track and Field meet, after 51 years as Head Coach of athletics at Mercersburg Academy, Jimmy finally retired, at the age of 81, and was given his final handshake. To thank him for his service he was presented with an honorary diploma as a member of the Class of '61 and an engraved silver tray. One might imagine that after such a long period of time with one employee, doing the same job day in, day out, that Jimmy would find his retirement an exceedingly difficult step. And he may well have, but if he did, he did so discreetly. Outwardly he was philosophical, telling one reporter, after his 31st win at the Penn Relays, 'It's a great one to go out on. We won this one, we're undefeated in cross country and haven't lost in track yet this year. It's time to retire when you have a good year like this one.'

JIMMY CURRAN

While his job had demanded he focus on the boys with the greatest athletic talents, his retirement showed that he was just as happy, perhaps more so, training those with limited skills. Before his retirement he had lamented 'I just want to coach the four-foot jumper, the seven-foot pole vaulter and the boy who runs the 100 yards in 13 seconds. I just didn't have time to do anything with them before, but someone should help them out.' He was as good as his word, continuing to train boys until a week before his death. And he still joked with reporters about schemes he had dreamed up. 'What I would like to do' he told them, 'is go over to Africa and get some of those Watusi warriors that are seven feet tall. They can all jump, too. I figure that with about two weeks of training, they could beat any basketball team in the world.' And then there was Willie Mays, the baseball player. Jimmy delighted in outlining his scheme to teach Mays how to throw the javelin. But for all of his training of lesser athletes, and his athletic dreaming, Mercersburg Academy was still in Jimmy's heart, and he continued to offer his support by attending track meets, replete with stopwatch hanging from his neck, especially those where his grandson Tom was competing. He was, however, always respectful of the new coaches, never offering advice or attempting to impose his views. But he did like to indulge in a little 'philosophizing with the athletes.'

On 3rd February 1963 Rolando Cruz became the eighth 16-foot pole vaulter, winning the Philadelphia Inquirer Games in the process. The following day, around lunchtime, Jimmy left his home and started walking towards town. On the way he passed David Emory Jr, son of a former coaching colleague, and they said hello to each other. Later that day he collapsed, victim of a heart attack, and an ambulance raced him to Chambersburg Hospital, the very hospital where Janet had been recovering from a broken hip for the past six weeks. It was quickly clear he wouldn't recover. The nurses took advantage of the fact Janet was so near – they dressed her, did her hair, sat her in a wheelchair and took her to Jimmy's bedside. The couple had one final kiss. He died three days later.

HE RUN A GOOD RACE

*****

By the time of his death, Jimmy had outlived virtually all of the legendary coaches that had revolved around Mike Murphy. Murphy himself had died in 1913, and was followed within 20 years by Johnny Mack, Walter Camp, Alvin Kraenzlein, 'Pooch' Donovan, 'Piper' Donovan and Steve Farrell. Harry Hillman, Jack Moakley, Lawson Robertson and 'Pop' Warner were all dead by 1955, and Dean Cromwell preceded Jimmy in death by half a year. Most of those who did outlive him tended to enjoy exceedingly long lives – Emil von Elling was 90 when he died in 1973, and Amos Alonzo Stagg was 102 years old when he passed away two years after Jimmy.

*****

Jimmy Curran came from a life of great poverty, growing up in the shadows of the mill chimneys in Galashiels. He was blessed with a divine talent and an unyielding appetite for a challenge, bound together by a work ethic that would put men half his age to shame. This combination offered him the opportunity to escape a life that trapped most others, and grasp a success that very few would know. He worked at one of America's premier prep schools where he trained the sons of Presidents, bankers and industrialists, within 20 years he sent his only son to Princeton University, and was widely lauded as one of the finest coaches in the country. He had realised his own slice of the American Dream. But despite plying his trade amongst the future captains of America, he always retained all sense of who he was; he returned to Galashiels regularly and his thick Scots brogue was still evident as he lay on his death bed.

In his time as a coach in Scotland and the US he had trained 16 Olympians, five of whom had won gold, with a total haul of eight medals from ten Olympic Games (only Berlin in 1936 being bereft of a Mercersburg track and field athlete). At the time of his death he was believed to have trained more US track and field Olympians than any other high school coach in history. But his significance transcends the medals his students brought home, or his athletic and coaching prowess; his legacy is his athletes. The impact on the lives of those who knew him is clear from their eulogies and memories.

In the days following his death, messages of condolence flooded in. William Fowle, headmaster of his former school produced a simple, yet powerful, epitaph:

> In the life of every schoolboy there is often one man who stands out above all others as the strongest influence for hard work, fair play, and clean life. In the past half century for literally hundreds of Mercersburg boys Jimmy Curran was that man. His record as a coach is unmatched in preparatory school annals. But Jimmy was more than a great coach. His keen wit, canny understanding, and contagious desire to do his best brought forth the best in his pupils, building in them traits of character which would be essential and beneficial throughout their lives. His influence, so helpful for the development of the school from 1910-1961, will be felt for many years to come. He has left us a heritage worthy of our best efforts in every way.

Former students, colleagues, opponents and newspaper reporters all wanted to pay their respects. The *Harrisburg Patriot-News* kept it simple, noting that Jimmy was 'one of America's most colourful sports figures.' Ed Pollock, of the *Philadelphia Evening Bulletin*, noted that 'his death [has] cast a long shadow over the world of sport. Ron Smith, sports reporter at the *Philadelphia Inquirer* painted a more vivid picture: 'When an integrity like Jimmy passes on, it is more than just the loss of a man. It is the loss of the things he said and did. Jimmy said many things – some worth remembering, some that need forgetting – and he did some things that will take a lot of forgetting.' And his impact on school sports was stressed by the James Buchanan Joint School Board in a message relaying its 'sincerest feelings of remorse':

> You may rest assured that this almost unprecedented request by the board springs from a heartfelt appreciation of Mr. Curran's contributions to the Academy, the boys under his direction, this community and, indeed, to the program of our own school system. May the inspiration of his many worthy accomplishments give you strength; and may the esteem and respect in which his memory is held serve to sustain you in future happiness and well-being.

Some of the finest words describing Jimmy were written some years before his death by Cy Peterman, sports reporter at the *Philadelphia Inquirer*, who noted that Jimmy was 'the sort of character found between the covers of boys' best sellers; more than likely he'd be called "Pop" instead of "Coach".'

But the most telling remembrance came from a student who had left southern Pennsylvania 35 years previously. Telling not just because a former student who played no great part in his team remembered him after almost four decades, but because that student was one of the most famous men in the world. Jimmy Stewart had left Mercersburg and gone on to attend Princeton University. Thereafter his star rose, film by film, until he became America's doyen of the big screen. But despite his fame he remembered Jimmy. And no doubt Jimmy would have allowed himself a wry smile each time he watched George Bailey, Elwood P. Dowd or Jefferson Smith grace his television. He was driven to send a telegram to Janet, via the local funeral director. The message he sent was simple:

JIMMY CURRAN

= I SEND YOU MY DEEPEST HEARTFELT SYMPATHY =
= JIMMY STEWART =

Two services were held for Jimmy. The first was during the Academy's regular Sunday morning service. Jef Evans remembers it well. Jimmy and Jef had always had a close relationship, and Jef attributes his decision to apply for a coaching position at Mercersburg was due to being encouraged to do so by Jimmy. A prayer was made by the school's headmaster, William Fowle, whilst the minister, Rev. Herbert W. Stroup, drew on Jimmy's career as inspiration for his eulogy. Evans was on the teaching staff and was overcome by grief, openly crying, a reaction that drew the attention of some students who likely had never before witnessed an emotional teacher.

The next morning a Requiem High Mass was held at the Chambersburg Corpus Christi Catholic Church, with mainly family invited. The family asked that in lieu of flowers contributions be made to the Academy Development Program. The few flowers on the altar were paid for by the Alumni Association. He was buried in the Fairview Cemetery in Mercersburg, the second last of John and Ellen's children to die – his elder sister Ellen, who had emigrated to Australia, outlived him.

Time did not diminish the memories of Jimmy. Former students recalled him to this writer, and almost to a man were praiseworthy. Paul White noted 'the effort that Coach Curran put into me changed my life, as he taught me the worth of hard work, ethics, and character. Jimmy Curran will always have a special place in my heart as one who inspired me to greatness.' Henry Thresher noted that he was 'an outstanding track coach and an outstanding person.' Christopher Montgomery, who baulked at the school's strict rules and rebelled against them at every opportunity, considered Jimmy one of the few bright points in his time there: 'Mr Curran and Mr Kuhn showed me that all others at the school were not enemies.' In 2008, Charles Moore noted, 'I owe everything in my track career to Jimmy Curran, who simply turned to this kid who had never run – ever – and said, "Here, let me help you",' and in his book, *Running on Purpose*, dedicated a chapter, titled 'Mentor, Legend', to Jimmy. And, for this book, Jef Evans recalled Jimmy as 'kind, intelligent, sharp witted, and dedicated to every boy who stepped on the track. He had the sense of what we could do and inspired us to reach it. He believed in me. I learned to do the same. Running for Coach Curran was a pleasure and an honor.'

But what should be remembered is that his students who went on to athletic greatness were only a tiny portion of the thousands who passed through his teams, and on who he had a lasting impact. After Mercersburg, many went on to top universities, often Ivy League, and thereafter to successful careers in every imaginable field. Those that survive remember their mentor well, and in some cases still implement his teachings. They remember Jimmy being a good man, a man who was strict, but never used his authority to lord over or demean those he coached. A mentor, willing to proffer his guidance to those who desired it. A man who was funny, using his sense of humour to endear himself to his students, and using levity to defuse difficult situations. But most of all a man who cared deeply about his students, who wanted what was best for them, not just in school, but outside its walls, and in the years afterwards. In short, he was that rare teacher that impressed himself so deeply upon his charges that he remained with them in later life. In all of them was instilled the philosophy of Mercersburg's founding headmaster, William Mann Irvine – lofty ideals, great faith, noble integrity, and a ceaseless devotion to a mighty task.

*****

In February 1980, 17 years after Jimmy died, Janet passed away, aged 94. She was buried beside her husband in Fairview Cemetery. The last surviving of their five children, Margaret, died in 2007. Their grandchildren and great-grandchildren are spread throughout America (most in Pennsylvania and Texas) and the United Kingdom.

JIMMY CURRAN

*****

While most of his contemporaries had only a fleeting dalliance with fame Jimmy's legend saw him remembered in tangible form, in some quarters, long after his death. Through the years Jimmy was presented with a number of gifts from students, alumni and those who admired and loved him, with typical praise coming from his 1918 team, whose gift was presented due to Jimmy's 'devotional service towards the track team.' These ranged from loving cups to golf clubs to free trips to the Olympic Games. But more permanent posthumous legacies were put in place, mostly by the school at which he worked for so many years, but also his home town of Galashiels.

In the wake of Jimmy's passing, a committee of former Mercersburg students, mostly athletes, was set up, and called The Friends of Jimmy Curran. It was made up of a who's who of Jimmy's finest surviving athletes. Its primary goal was to contribute to the Academy's development plans by building a 'suitable physical memorial' in the form of an all-weather track. Led by Charles Moore Jr, those involved no doubt believed that they would create their memorial within a relatively short period of time. But it was not to be; Jef Evans remembers approaching the Academy's headmaster, William Fowle, and although he listened, may not have viewed the track as a priority. And as months turned into years, rising prices and difficulty in raising funds saw delay after delay. In light of this lack of commitment from those holding the purse strings, it perhaps comes as little surprise that it took nine years from Jimmy's death to put a new track in place. But in May 1972 an all-weather track was finally built, at a cost of $80,000. Jimmy's family, led by its matriarch, the 86-year-old Janet, made their way to the school to watch as former crack athlete, Jack Milne, and the Academy's athletic director, Leonard Plantz, unveiled a stone memorial with plaque, presented by members of Jimmy's 1929 team, at trackside.

Things did not, however, go exactly to plan. In a sport often decided by the thickness of a vest, the track was built six inches too long, amounting to an extra two feet for every mile run. It is unclear whether this error was ever rectified, but in 1994 a postcard sent to alumni noted that the Curran Track was, 'badly in need of repair and out of date with its non-metric calibration, [and] must be resurfaced and renovated this summer.' By the time the postcard was sent, $150,000 had been raised from the Moore family and others, of a required $300,000. Moore was the chairman of the campaign.

The Jimmy Curran Track is the most visible legacy of Jimmy's time at the school. But there are others. In the basement of the Academy's library, leaning against a wall, is a portrait, finely painted in oils. It depicts Jimmy, sitting in profile, looking austere, very much the 1950s teacher. Exactly how it came into being isn't absolutely clear, but it appears likely that the artist, his son-in-law Tom Danaher Sr, was paid to produce it. The painting was then presented to the school by Mario G. Nevarez, a Puerto Rican alumni.

In 1999 Jimmy was finally recognised at a state level, being introduced into the Pennsylvania High School Track & Field Hall of Fame.

For 45 years Jimmy was largely forgotten in his hometown of Galashiels, remembered only by a few family members. But in 2007, whilst doing research for the Scottish Borders Sporting Hall of Fame, a local government officer called Neil Renton, who fortuitously also happened to be a member of the Gala Harriers, Jimmy's former athletics club, came across Jimmy and started to dig into his past. He was intrigued that such a successful important figure had descended into obscurity, so in an effort to find out more he contacted Mercersburg Academy's archivist, Jay Quinn, requesting information on Jimmy to tie him unquestionably to the Scottish Borders. Once this was proven beyond doubt Jimmy's name was put forward as a possible inductee of the Hall of Fame. Accepted, he was inducted in 2008, and the few remaining Scottish Curran family members were presented with a glass plaque to honour his inclusion.

Perhaps the greatest honour that could be bestowed upon Jimmy would be inclusion in the Scottish Sports Hall of Fame, accompanying a plethora of legendary sports men and women including Eric Liddell, Chris Hoy, Kenny Dalglish, lesser known inductees such as Bobby Thomson – 'the shot heard around the world' – and Jimmy's old friend Wyndham Halswelle. In 2019 his name was forwarded to the selection committee by this author, with the support of Jimmy's family. We await a reply …

Biographies

Mike Murphy (1860-1913)

After parting ways with Jimmy, the two remained in close contact, with Murphy suggesting athletes that Jimmy could bring to Mercersburg Academy on scholarship. He had a weak body, and had suffered physically throughout the first decade of the 20th century. By 1913, in the midst of writing a second book outlining training techniques for athletes, he was confined to bed. It soon became clear he would not pull through, and he relayed the final pages to a friend in his final hours.

Mike Dee (1868-1954)

Dee became a trainer after a successful boxing career. After leaving the University of Pennsylvania in 1911 Dee worked for the Philadelphia Phillies until 1919, where he was the highest paid baseball trainer in America. In 1914 he was 'borrowed' by the Boston Braves to raise their physical condition on the way to winning the World Series. He then returned to his former employer, working there until 1933. He also spent time at Penn Athletic Club and the Philadelphia Eagles.

BIOGRAPHIES

James Lee (1874-1939)
Jimmy's first known trainer was a respected athlete in his early years. He worked for many years at a factory in Galashiels, and died in 1939.

Bill Struth (1875-1956)
After his running career Struth went on to train footballers at Heart of Midlothian F.C. and Clyde F.C. In 1914 he became assistant manager at Glasgow Rangers F.C., graduating to manager in 1920 upon the premature death of the club's manager, William Wilton. He would remain as manager until 1956, and his managerial reign saw the club amass 18 league titles and 10 Scottish Cups. He is widely considered one of the greatest Scottish football managers of all time.

Johnny McHugh (c1876-1951)
McHugh was believed to have started around 300,000 races, and 4 million runners. For 30 years he acted as the official starter at the Penn Relays, and in 1924 was the American starter at the Olympic Games in Paris. He was the first starter to stand in front of the runners, believing it made false starts less likely. He worked for the Public School Athletic League for 37 years, until around ten years before his death. He also served on the board of governors of the Amateur Athletic Union.

Walter Knox (1878-1951)
Prior to his period in charge of the British Olympic team for the 1916 Berlin Olympics, Knox had also been head coach of the Canadian team at the 1912 Stockholm Olympics, a marriage that ended in acrimonious relations between Knox and a number of team members. In 1915 he invested heavily in lands containing gold and silver, which brought with it great financial rewards. In 1920, despite the debacle of his time in

charge of the 1912 Olympic team, he was invited to once again lead it at the 1920 Antwerp Games. The issues of 1912 did not re-occur – apart from a small incident where Knox and one of the team's boxers traded blows – but the small team won only one track and field medal. In the following years he continued to train athletes, notably a number of high profile female athletes. A return to the Olympics almost came in 1940, when an offer came in to coach the Japanese team, but the offer was withdrawn (and the Second World War ended the possibility of a Games anyway).

He retired to St Petersburg in Florida, where he died of a stroke in 1951. He was buried in Ontario. As a result of his sporting exploits he was posthumously inducted into the Orillia Hall of Fame, the Canadian Olympic Hall of Fame and Canada's Sports Hall of Fame.

Arthur Duffey (1879-1955)
At the turn of the century, Duffey was considered one of the greatest sprinters the world had ever seen. A gold medal was wrested from him by a pulled muscle in the final of the 100m at the 1900 Olympics, but he would go on to break the world record for 100 yards. In 1905 he was excluded from amateur athletics in a public dispute with the AAU over his having run professionally, although it was also asserted, by the sprinter Charley Paddock, that his exclusion was due to a refusal to wear running shoes produced by the Spalding Company. In later years he worked as a columnist for the *Boston Post* and briefly coached athletes at Tufts College and Northeastern University. During the First World War he trained airmen at Camp Mills in Long Island, before returning to journalism. He retired from his job at the *Post* in 1949, and died of a heart attack whilst in hospital six years later.

Al Nash (1876-1918)
Al Nash, also known as Blackhawk, was a Winnebago Indian. He learned to run at the Carlisle Indian School, Drexel Institute and the

University of Pennsylvania. He was also a talented football player and wrestler. In the 1910s he worked as a salesman and designer in Philadelphia, designing an 'Indian play suit' that was sold by his employer, Clarence E. Miller. In 1918 he suffered intestinal problems, was rushed to hospital and, after an operation, died.

Alfie Shrubb (1879-1964)

After his running career Shrubb became a coach, first at Harvard and then Oxford University, although his success was limited. He moved to Canada in 1928 and died there in 1964, having operated a mill at Bowmanville. He is still widely considered one of the greatest middle- to long-distance runners of all time, having set 28 world records during his career, with eight of these coming in one single day in Glasgow in 1904. His place of birth and Canadian hometown both hold memorial races named after him.

Jack Roden (1881-1943)

Roden continued to promote events for many years after working with Jimmy. He also worked for the Pennsylvania Railroad, but left his employment in the early 1940s after a long illness. He died of a heart attack in 1943 whilst attending church.

Wyndham Halswelle (1882-1915)

After his Olympic win Halswelle was disenchanted, and all but gave up athletics to focus on his army career. By the time of the First World War he held the rank of captain. He died by a sniper's bullet at the Battle of Neuve Chapelle in 1915. In 2003 he was inducted into the Scottish Sports Hall of Fame.

JIMMY CURRAN

Tall Feather (1884-1962)

Tall Feather, whose legal name was Levi Parker Webster, continued running for many decades, undertaking a number of inter-city ultramarathons, including one of 90 miles, which he completed in 19½ hours at the age of 42 – for his efforts he almost died, but won $1,000. But running was not his only sport. From 1904, he played professional football in Philadelphia, until he joined the US Army during the First World War. He married in 1930 and had 14 children. He worked for 30 years as a meter reader for the Green Bay Water Department.

Percy Smallwood (1886-1955)

Whilst a runner Smallwood was also head coach of the Westinghouse Athletic Association, and then trainer for the Cleveland Indians baseball team, whose employ he was in when they won the World Series in 1920 (an achievement for which he was awarded a $1,000 bonus). Ill health apparently forced his retirement in 1922, but he was to recover enough to compete in the first Transcontinental Foot Race in 1928. Smallwood died in a Cleveland nursing home in 1955.

Jim Thorpe (1887-1953)

Having built his skills at the Carlisle School, Thorpe was, by the time of the 1912 Olympics, considered one of America's greatest ever athletes. He returned home with gold medals in decathlon and pentathlon. Soon after, he was forced to reveal having played baseball professionally, and his Olympic titles were rescinded (although they would be posthumously restored in 1983). Following the revelations of his professionalism, he took part in football, basketball and, most notably, baseball.

Outside sport Thorpe struggled to support his family, and took on a number of jobs, including acting in films, often playing native Americans, and including an uncredited role as a theatregoer in the final scenes of *King Kong*. An alcoholic, he died of a heart attack in 1953.

BIOGRAPHIES

Ted Meredith (1891-1957)

After only a year at Mercersburg, Meredith enrolled at the University of Pennsylvania's Wharton School. Whilst studying he competed on the University's athletics team, as well as for the Meadowbrook Club. In 1915 he broke the 500 yards world record, and was part of the Penn team that broke the mile relay world record. A year later lowered the world marks for the 440 and 880 yards. When he retired from athletics in 1918 he held world records in the 400 and 800m, the 440 and 880 yards, and the 1,600m and mile relays. Upon graduation he founded an import-export company with a classmate, but this was soon put on the backburner as he signed up to the Air Service and was shipped to Europe. Here he would reconnaissance missions, taking aerial photographs of German trenches. He emerged from the war unscathed despite rumours, eventually proven to be untrue, that he had been shot down behind enemy lines and captured.

After coming out of athletics retirement for his second Olympics, Meredith began working at the New York Stock Exchange, and then as a stockbroker with Paine, Webber and Company. In 1924 he worked as a reporter at the Paris Olympics, and four years later he was hired as an assistant coach at the University of Pennsylvania. After a short-lived attempt to enter politics, he returned to athletics, coaching the Czechoslovakia at the Berlin Olympics, and a year later was hired to train the Cuban team for the Central American Games.

The Great Depression had taken its toll on Meredith and his family. He was forced to sell his Olympic medals, as well as the sword and ring presented to him after his victory. He found succour in alcohol, and in 1937 his wife, Tillie, filed for divorce due to desertion and non-support, ultimately leading to his arrest. After a number of less than successful business ventures, he took a job with the Internal Revenue Service, where he would remain until his retirement in 1955. Two years later suffered a stroke in early 1957, and died later that year after complications arose from surgery to repair a broken hip.

He has been inducted into a number of local, national and international Halls of Fame.

Wallace 'Pete' Maxfield (1892-1967)

After graduating from Mercersburg, Maxfield attended Dartmouth College, then Lafayette College, before studying osteopathy at Kirksville College of Osteopathic Medicine in Missouri. In 1916 he enlisted to serve in the First World War and attained the rank of Lieutenant in the US Medical Corps. He arrived in France as part of the Whippet Tank Corps. In 1919, just as he was about to ship home, he was selected to represent the United States in the Inter-Allied Games, a sports event run along Olympic lines. He finished third in the shot put.

On return from the war he worked for the Union Oil Company as superintendent of drilling, and then in the same role in India for the Burma Oil Company. In 1939 he was still working in the oil industry in California. He died on the first day of 1967.

Eugene 'E.P.' Hammitt (1892-1972)

Hammitt, whose mother tongue on arriving at Mercersburg was Russian, studied at Penn State on leaving the Academy. After graduation he worked as an engineer in the oil and gas industry, taking leave to serve as a Lieutenant in the 319th Engineers during the First World War. After the war he continued working as an engineer and speculator in the oil industry for many years. He died of a heart attack on his way to a Mercersburg Academy reunion.

Theodore Dale (1893-1918)

After graduating from Mercersburg, Dale attended Syracuse University. He fought in France during the First World War with the 103rd

Engineers. In October 1918 he was gassed and, despite initially appearing to recover, he died of meningitis on 20th October, just three weeks before the end of the war. He is buried at the Saint Mihiel American Cemetery in France.

Albert Robinson (1893-1947)

After a severe bout of rheumatism caused Robinson's departure from the University of Michigan he continued to covet a return to amateur athletics, so much so that he turned down an offer to play shortstop for the St Louis Cardinals. After briefly running for the Young Men's Order in Detroit, he worked as a claims investigator and adjustor for the Detroit Department of Street Railways. In later life he married and had two children. In 1947, he died after suffering a massive heart attack.

Harry Goelitz (1894-1971)

After his expulsion from Mercersburg, Goelitz attended Keewatin Academy in Wisconsin and Florida. In 1914 he tied the 100 yard high hurdles world record. This result, along with a string of others marked him out as a virtual certainty for the 1916 Olympic team – he was frequently called the new Jim Thorpe – until the Games were cancelled due to the First World War. In 1917 he became national all-round track champion of America.

After competing at the 1920 Olympics, he continued to compete at a high level until his leg was badly crushed whilst working a contracting job for his father. This likely impacted his athletics career, although he did continue to compete.

In 1923 he imported a carload of horses from Kentucky, and for some years rode them at equestrian events around the country, and used them to build a polo team. He spent the remainder of his working career building the paving company founded by his father. He died in 1971 in Oak Park, the town where he was born, and lived much of his life.

JIMMY CURRAN

Harold Barron (1894-1978)

Barron served with the US Army in Europe during the First World War, and whilst there ran in many athletic competitions and attended the University of Toulouse. After retiring as an athlete, Barron was hired by Jimmy to work as an assistant coach at Mercersburg Academy, before moving to Cascadilla School in Ithaca, New York. In 1925 he took over the role of Head Coach at Georgia Tech. In 1930 he worked with Earl Thomson and Harry Hillman to design a safer hurdle with a view to reducing injuries. In the same year he took up the role of Head Coach at the University of Arizona. By 1940 he was working as a Deputy Probation Officer in Los Angeles. Little is known of his later years.

Harold 'Boots' Lever (1895-1963)

After graduating from the University of Pennsylvania's Wharton School, Lever served in Europe during the First World War. On his return to America, he became an insurance executive in New Jersey, then Connecticut. In later years he became a golf tournament scorer, and whilst scoring at a tournament in Florida he suffered a heart attack and died, just ten weeks after his former Mercersburg coach.

Larry Shields (1895-1976)

Larry Shields, whose full name was Marion Lawrence Shields, served in Europe during the First World War, achieving the rank of sergeant. When the war ended he was part of the United States team that competed at the Inter-Allied Games in Paris, winning a gold medal in the medley relay. After studying at Penn State College, Shields took up a teaching role at Phillips-Andover Academy in Massachusetts, first as an assistant track coach, and then teaching biology. In 1942, when America joined the Second World War, he was commissioned a Lieutenant Commander in the Navy, and later that same year married Ruth Noyes. Every summer, from 1930 to 1970, he hired three Eskimos and explorer the barren tundra of Labrador. After his return from the war he took up a series of non-teaching roles until he retired in 1970, spending his final years in Sarasota. He died of cancer in a hospital in Rochester, Minnesota.

Eddie Shields (1895-1970)

After graduating from Mercersburg, Shields was expected to enter Rutgers University, but instead signed up to serve in the First World War as a naval aviator. On one flight his aeroplane developed engine trouble and Shields and his two fellow airmen ditched in the ocean. For 56 hours they clung to the wreckage, with one of the men dying of pneumonia. He served again during the Second World War, attaining the rank of captain. He lived in West Chester for much of his life, but his last years were spent in Sarasota.

Harvey 'Beck' Reed (1896-1968)

During the First World War Reed served as a 2nd Lieutenant in the Air Service in Texas. After the end of the war he attended Yale, Columbia Teachers College and Yale Graduate School. In the 1930s and 1940s he worked as an English teacher at the Pingry School in Elizabeth, New Jersey, and the McDonough School for Boys in Baltimore. According to one student, 'he knew English backward and forward.' After a brief spell as a Personnel Manager with Liberty Motors & Engineering Corporation in Baltimore he worked as a teacher at the University of Baltimore. In the 1950s and 1960s he took up senior posts at the University. After moving to Daytona Beach in the 1960s, he became chairman of the language department at Daytona Beach Junior College. After retiring he stood, in May 1968, to be the Republican contender for one of the area's school board seats, losing by a small number of votes. He died in November of the same year.

Allen Swede (1897-1977)

Swede went from Mercersburg to the First World War. In the post-war years he attended Princeton, but was forced to retire from athletics after suffering from rheumatism for three years. Thereafter he worked in business in America and China, before returning to take up a post with ATT, in which he worked until retirement. Throughout his life he and his wife travelled the world. During the Second World War he reached the rank of Colonel, and was awarded the Legion of Merit.

Allen Woodring (1898-1982)
Woodring worked as a salesman for A.G. Spalding & Bros., and Sears, Roebuck & Co., before moving to Florida from Smyrna, Delaware. He died in 1982.

Elmer Smith (1895-1973)
Smith enrolled at Mercersburg after failing exams at University of Pennsylvania's Wharton School night classes. He re- enrolled at Wharton, but took three years to finish his first year of studies. He failed to graduate due to 'scholastic difficulties.' He spent some time at the Aviation School at Fort Slocum, New York, and then at the US School of Aerial Photography at Rochester, New York. Little is known of Smith's later life, although it is believed that in the late 1960s and early 1970s he ran a company in Fort Lauderdale called Samaritan Tours, providing free tours for those who could not get out of their homes. He died in 1973 in Fort Lauderdale.

Frank Ward Conway (1900-1957)
For much of his life, Conway worked for the US Postal Service in New York City, retiring in 1955. He died suddenly of a heart attack in 1957.

Henry Charles 'Chuck' Taylor (1901-1988)
By the time Chuck Taylor arrived at Mercersburg Academy in 1920, he had already excelled as an athlete at Brookville High School and Culver Summer Naval School. At the latter he set a long jump world record for an 18-year-old, of 20' 11½". After leaving Mercersburg he attended Princeton, where his athletic success continued, and he competed, albeit unsuccessfully, in the 1924 Olympic trials.

BIOGRAPHIES

After graduation, he lived for a time in Switzerland, before returning in the early 1930s and marrying Katherine Sandt. He thereafter became the managing partner of the Walter J. Sandt Co., a distributor of Pennzoil petroleum products. During the 1930s he owned and flew several private aircraft. Taylor was a highly respected community leader, serving on the Town Council, and was involved in a variety of community organisations. In the 1960s, he was named Citizen of the Year by the Brookville Chamber of Commerce and was among the first inductees into the Brookville Sports Hall of Fame.

Marvin Rick (1901-1999)

After leaving Mercersburg, Rick attended Princeton and then MIT. He pursued a career in the military, first joining the Army which saw him injured at the Battle of the Bulge. He then joined the Air Force where he attained the rank of Lieutenant-Colonel. In his 80s he began to suffer from macular degeneration and moved from his home in San Diego to St Petersburg to be nearer his son. He died in 1999, ten days short of his 98th birthday.

Charles 'Crip' Moore (1902-1983)

After Mercersburg, Moore attended Penn State and continued to run track, holding a number of hurdles world records. In 1924 he travelled to the Paris Olympics as an alternate. On his return to the US he started working at his father's boiler manufactory start-up, Lenape Hydraulic Pressing and Forging Co., prior to attending university at Penn State. While standing with his hand on a 19th century press, a faulty valve caused it to close on four fingers, which were subsequently removed. Despite his handicap, and suggestions from coaches that he should retire from racing, he persevered, and after a visit to the University of Pennsylvania that saw him fitted with a glove that allowed him to balance at the start of races, he continued on to further success, most notably at the Penn Relays. After graduation from Penn State, Moore went work at the Lenape Forge, eventually becoming chairman in 1965 when it was acquired by Gulf+Western, and remaining there until 1975. In over 50 years with the company patented a number of inventions. In retirement he began to write short stories. He died in Fort Myers, Florida, in 1983.

George 'Buck' Hester (1902-1951)

After attending Mercersburg, Hester attended the University of Michigan, where he continued his track career. For many years he worked in Detroit, until 1945 when he re-located to Indianapolis to become the Indiana sales manager for the Hinde and Dauch Paper Company. He died in 1951. In 2009 he was inducted into the University of Michigan Hall of Fame.

Bill Cox (1904-1996)

After Mercersburg Cox continued to impress at distance running for Penn State University. During the Second World War Cox served in the US Navy. He served in a number of local organisations, such as the Boy Scouts and the Red Cross, and worked as a lifeguard until he was 76 years of age. For 36 years he taught mathematics at Edison Technical School in Rochester, New York. He died in 1996.

Gail Robinson (1904-1979)

Robinson had a colourful life after attending Mercersburg. He does not appear to have attended college after his time at Mercersburg, although he did continue his athletics career at Newark and Boston athletic clubs. He worked for some years as a shoe factory superintendent, and during the Second World War he served as a chief gunner in the US Navy. During the 1940s and 1950s he worked as a stunt double for actors such as John Wayne. He was also a bit-part actor. His film credits include *The Sea Chase*, *Girl Rush* and *Ambush at Tomahawk Gap*. In his later years he worked as a bookkeeper. He lived in Hawaii for many years, and died in San Luis Obispo, Ca., in 1979.

BIOGRAPHIES

Barney Berlinger (1908-2002)
After graduating from the University of Pennsylvania's Wharton School, where classmates elected him the most outstanding member of the class, Berlinger worked for many years at the Quaker City Gear Works, retiring as president of the company. After World War II he travelled to Europe to coach track and field to troops, and was also appointed by President Dwight D. Eisenhower to work with children through the 'People to People Sports Program', encouraging them into sports. He died in 2002.

Terrell 'Tex' Cobb (1909-1970)
After Mercersburg Cobb studied at Ohio State University, eventually becoming an osteopathic physician and surgeon. He had, by 1966, risen to Chief of Staff of Osteopathic General Hospital in Rhode Island. His career was interrupted by the Second World War, when he served in the Coast Guard. He clearly enjoyed life on the water, and became an accomplished sailor, taking part in most of the major east coast yacht races, his crowning moment being a second place in the Newport-Bermuda race.

Bill Carr (1909-1966)
After Mercersburg, Carr worked as a cabin boy on an Atlantic liner. Returning a day late to register at Princeton he was told he would have to wait a year. He headed to the University of Pennsylvania where he was quickly accepted. In later years he was employed by Prismo Safety Products, and was its representative in Japan. It was here he had a heart attack and died at the age of 56. His body was returned to his hometown of Pine Bluff, Arkansas, for burial.

Bill Estes (1912-2000)
After leaving Mercersburg, Estes headed to Yale and then Fordham Law School. On graduation he worked with the Bureau of Economic Warfare, before departing for the Second World War as an Air Combat

JIMMY CURRAN

Intelligence Officer on-board the aircraft carrier Essex.

Immediately after the war he became general manager of the Navy Resale System at Quonset Point, Rhode Island, before retiring in 1974. On moving to Florida, he had an active social life, being a member of the San Carlos Bay Power and Sail Squadron, and a life member of the United States Power Squadrons and the East Greenwich Yacht Club. He was also an active member of freemason and Order of the Eastern Star Lodges. He died in 2000.

Bill Bradway Jr (1914-1987)
On leaving Mercersburg, Bradway attended the University of Pennsylvania, graduating with an economics degree in 1940. Later that year he enlisted as an apprentice seaman in the US Naval Reserve. On America's entry into the Second World War, he served in both the Atlantic and Pacific fleets. Over the next few years he worked his way through the ranks, taking command of the USS Porterfield in 1952. Thereafter he served in Korea and Vietnam, before retiring in 1967. In retirement he took an interest in the Coronado School Board, being elected to various positions within it. He died in San Diego in 1987.

Charles Mutchler (1914-1986)
During the Second World War, Mutchler served as a Flight Sergeant in the Royal Canadian Air Force. After the war he lived in Ontario, working as a plant manager for the Carnation Milk Company. After retiring he spent his summers in Daytona Beach, and was buried at New Smyrna Beach.

Steve Szumachowski (1914-2003)
Szumachowski attended Notre Dame after Mercersburg, where he continued to compete successfully. After graduating he worked at the American Locomotive Company (Alco) in Schenectady. On leaving Alco after the war, he worked for the New York Thruway Authority,

where he supervised sales of equipment. He continued to live in Schenectady, and was involved in a number of local organisations, including roles as Assistant Chief of the town's Civil Defence Organization, and coach of the YMCA athletic team. In 2002, a year before his death, he was entered into the Schenectady City School District Athletic Hall of Fame.

Jack White (1915-1983)

After Mercersburg, White attended Princeton where he was a standout track and football star, winning the Poe Award for sportsmanship, play and influence. His career started with two years as an English teacher at Pingry School, before serving for five years in the Air Corps during World War II. After the war he took up a post as mathematics teacher at Columbus Academy, and over the next 36 years taught various other subjects and sports, as well as serving as Athletic Director. In 1969 he was inducted into the Central Chapter of the Pennsylvania Hall of Fame. He retired in 1982, and the school honoured him with Jack White Day. In 1983 he died of a heart attack whilst greeting students at Alumni Day activities.

If any of Jimmy's students took on his mantle as a coach and gained a similar level of respect, it was Jack White. In 1965 he gave a speech that could have come from the mouth of Jimmy:

> I believe firmly that competitive sports have great educational value. I believe that by developing a program of sports for all within the framework of the school day we are doing the utmost for the total

welfare of your sons. The moral values derived from the constant battle with fear: fear of pain, fear of failure, fear of looking ridiculous, and fear of fear itself, is necessary for growth. I am convinced that facing these fears is the best moral training, and makes all boys better boys, better men and better citizens.

Ed Beetem (1919-2003)

Beetem attended the University of Pennsylvania's Wharton School after Mercersburg. He was not from a monied family, and was forced to pay his way through school by working menial jobs such as a painter for the Pennsylvania Railroad, for a dairy, and as a camp counsellor. In 1942 he attempted to join the US Marines, but was turned down due to his height. Little is known of Beetem's post-war life, but is thought he became a director of the Floridian Golf Course in the late 1970s. He died on St Simon's Island, Georgia, in 2003, just one month after his wife.

Austin Kellam (1919-1984)

Kellam attended Princeton after Mercersburg. After graduating he served in the Persian Gulf Command during the Second World War. He spent a brief spell working for the family coffee business, before working for the State Department in the Paris and Saudi Arabia consulates, and thereafter a government relations specialist in the oil business. On returning home he became an insurance agent, before dying in Binghamton, New York, in 1984.

Paxson 'Pax' Gifford (1919-2016)

After Mercersburg, Gifford attended the University of Pennsylvania. Such was his prowess as an athlete, especially as a football player, that he was asked to try out with the New York Giants football team. But like so many others his dreams of glory on the sports field were interrupted by the Second World War. He enlisted in the Navy, becoming an officer and flight instructor. He and his wife, Emily, had three children, and, after having started his career with the Hamilton Watch Company in Lancaster, Pa., the family moved to Connecticut in 1954 where Gifford was transferred to open a new plant for the company. After raising their children in Darien, the Giffords moved to Florida. Pre-deceased by this wife in 1984, Gifford passed away in 2016 at the age of 96.

Jack Milne (1919-1988)

After Mercersburg, Milne attended the University of North Carolina. His studies were interrupted by the Second World War, when he joined the Air Force. On returning home he enrolled at Seton Hall University, graduating magna cum laude. He then re-joined the Air Force and fought in the Korean War, eventually attaining the rank of Lieutenant-Colonel. In 1952 he competed in the Olympic trials in pentathlon, but failed to make the team. He then studied engineering at Temple University and taught classes there, before opening a general contracting company called Jack H. Milne Co. For many years prior to his death, Jack Milne volunteered thousands of hours to athletics, reaching the position of secretary of the National Indoor Track Meet Directors' Association, chairman of the National Women's Track and Field Committee, and member of the James E. Sullivan Award Committee. So respected was he in the athletics community that he was chosen to officiate at 1984 Olympics in Los Angeles. Like many of Jimmy's students he was inducted into his local sporting hall of fame – the Toms River Regional Schools Hall of Fame.

Ed Burrowes (1919-1959)

In 1944 Burrowes went to World War Two, serving in the Pacific Theatre with the 441st Counter Intelligence Corps Detachment. He worked in later years as a car salesman. At the time of his death, in 1959, he had been in ill health for some time, having received treatment at a

VA hospital for at least two years.

Ed Morgan (1918-1978)

After Mercersburg, Morgan served in the US Navy during World War II, and then worked as a Captain with the Philadelphia Fire Department. In the years after 1957 he had three heart attacks, and retired on a disability pension around 1970. However, he returned to work with his son as a manufacturer's representative for greetings cards. He died in 1978.

Jack Watt (1920-2013)

On leaving Mercersburg, Watt attended the University of Pennsylvania, graduating in 1943. Thereafter he served in Europe during the Second World War. Nothing is known of Watt's post-war career. In 2006 he was inducted into the North Penn Alumni Athletic Association Hall of Fame, due to his incredible football and athletic feats at Lansdale High School. He died in 2013 in Efland, North Carolina.

Ted Meredith Jr (1920-2006)

After Mercersburg, Meredith Jr headed to Harvard, where he sat next to John F. Kennedy in one class. As he was writing his Senior Honors thesis, the Japanese attack Pearl Harbor. Meredith immediately signed up to the navy. Before receiving his orders, he worked as a layer-out at the Sun Shipbuilding Company in Chester, Pa. When it was time to serve he was sent to New Guinea, and then the Mediterranean, as an lieutenant on a PT boat.

In later years he worked as an accountant, reaching the position of partner with PricewaterhouseCoopers, whilst also serving as president of the National Association of Accountants in the 1960s. He wrote a trilogy of autobiographical books, including one focussing on his time at Mercersburg.

BIOGRAPHIES

Bob Ufer (1920-1981)

Ufer founded an insurance company in 1947. Two years earlier he had begun broadcasting at the Michigan Wolverines football games, a role he held for 36 years, calling on every game since the end of the Second World War. He fell ill to cancer in 1981; in August he was admitted to hospital to have a blood clot removed, and died two months later.

Dick McFadden (1923-1944)

After graduating from Mercersburg, McFadden headed to Europe with the 20th Reconnaissance Division, a promise of professional baseball contract with the New York Yankees awaiting his return. But before he could fulfil his potential, he was killed, three weeks before the Battle of the Bulge.

In 1990, 46 years after his death, he was entered into the South Central Pennsylvania Sports Hall of Fame.

Jeff Kirk (1923-1976)

After Kirk left Mercersburg he served in India during the Second World War. After graduating from the University of Pennsylvania, he then received his doctorate from Temple University before working as an educator at Kimberton Farm School, Lehigh University and Adelphi University. He died in 1976.

Paul Cowie (1923-1978)

After Mercersburg, Cowie made his way to Europe as part of the US Army and was captured, spending time as a prisoner of war. On his return he attended Princeton, where he was a track and football star, despite leg wounds suffered near the end of the war. After graduation he worked in a number of senior positions, including Chief Financial Officer of the Times-Mirror Magazines Inc., his final job being as president of a public relations company. He died in 1978 of a heart attack whilst playing paddle tennis.

JIMMY CURRAN

Gus Ormrod (1929-   )

After Mercersburg, Ormrod attended Penn State on a full scholarship. However, the onset of the Korean War saw a change in his plans, and he joined the US Navy. Recognising his athletic ability he was assigned to the Athletic Department at the Naval Academy in Annapolis, Maryland after completing Naval Hospital Corps School. In 1952 he competed in the Olympic trials, followed by a further two years at the Naval Academy, during which time he competed in numerous premier athletic events. In 1954, after he was discharged from the Navy, he took up a series of government posts abroad for the following 14 years. From 1969 he took up a series of senior roles in property companies. He retired in 1995, eventually moving to Florida.

At the age of 75, he took up power walking, taking part in three one-day walks from the Lincoln Memorial to Harpers Ferry, WV. Since then he has won numerous county and state power walking championships in various age groups. In 2021 he intends to take part in the 1,500m and 5,000m at the National Championship Games.

Charles Moore Jr (1929-   )

Upon graduation from Cornell, Moore received job offers from two major companies, but decided to enter the family business at Lenape Forge. He oversaw its acquisition by Gulf+Western in 1965, and remained as its president until 1973. For the following 21 years he worked in senior positions for a diverse range of companies, creating value. In 1994 his career took on a new direction, when he was hired as Athletic Director at his alma mater, remaining in this position for five years. His career took a further deviation that same year when he was offered the role of the first executive director of the Committee to Encourage Corporate Philanthropy (CECP), an organisation created by, amongst others, the actor Paul Newman, to increase charitable efforts by large companies. He remained in post for 14 years, and even found time to serve as chair of the US Olympic Committee's 2012 bid city task force, to reduce the eight cities bidding to represent the United States to become the host of the Olympics.

Moore's sporting achievements were recognised many years after his success, with entry into the Cornell Sports Hall of Fame in 1978, and then the United States National Track and Field Hall of Fame in 1999.

In 2017 he published a book titled *Running on Purpose*, which was part biography, part motivational tome. Released alongside it was a version for junior readers, called *One Hurdle at a Time*.

Dewey Lee Yoder (1930-)
Yoder ran for the University of Arkansas after graduating from Mercersburg. He took up field hockey and in 1967, as part of the United States team, won a bronze medal at the Pan American Games. At the 1984 Olympics in Los Angeles he managed the men's field hockey team. Yoder and his wife Patricia were avid bird watchers, travelling throughout the US and the world to indulge their passion. He currently lives in North Carolina.

Bob Black (1931-2013)
Black competed as a golfer from a young age. When he left Mercersburg he studied at the University of North Carolina where he continued to play golf to a high level. He became the golf professional at Lan Yair Country Club in Spartanburg, South Carolina, where he hosted many Pro-Am tournaments. After retiring from this position, he worked as a sales rep for Regal Chemical, a company specialising in golf course nutrients. In his later years he moved to Florida, and then to Ronkonkoma, New York, with his partner. He died from heart failure in 2013 and was buried with a military honour guard.

Lester Cagle (1931-2018)
An injury ended Cagle's athletic scholarship to the University of

Pennsylvania. As a result he studied forestry at Penn State. With the Korean War in full flow, he signed up with the US Air Force. Although he never saw action, his passion for aviation remained, and for many years he attended the EAA Fly-In at Oshkosh, Wi., whilst owning his own ultralight aircraft. He then went to work for IBM, and found his calling in computer programming, and this saw him travel all over Europe.

Retirement brought the opportunity for Cagle to indulge his passions, and he learned computer languages, travelled the world, became a radio ham, taught reading and writing to convicts, and converted his Mercedes to run on biofuel made from grease procured from local restaurants.

Henry Thresher (1932-   )
After time spent at Yale and in the Air Force, where he spent time training for the Olympics, Thresher took up a role with New York Telephone, managing all telephone exchanges in Brooklyn and Queens, with a staff of 1,400, only three of whom were men. In 1980 he became National Training Director for AT&T, in Lakewood, Co. After retiring he took on a number of roles, including that of a private investigator, but didn't like carrying a gun. Around 1998 he became a volunteer at Mount Evans Home Health Care & Hospice, a facility that had cared for his parents-in-law. He offers friendship to those cared for at Mount Evans, and acts as a Eucharistic minister bringing Communion. In 1980 he was in the first set of honourees into the Garden City High School Sports Hall of Fame, and a decade later the school began presenting an annual Henry Thresher Award to its most outstanding runner. He continues to live and volunteer in Evergreen, Co.

Larry Lattomus (1933-2017)
Of all the people who make an appearance in this book, Larry Lattomus had possibly the most incredible life story. After Mercersburg he

attended Cornell where he continued to excel in track, and then served for two years as a pilot in Reykjavik in Iceland. He thereafter returned to school, attending the University of Pennsylvania's Wharton School. On graduation he took a job as a stockbroker with Dean Witter. In the mid-1960s he opened a Putt-Putt miniature golf course in Muncie, Indiana. In early 1967, he and his wife were involved in a car crash that saw the vehicle leave the road. Larry suffered damage to his spinal cord and was paralysed from the neck down. So serious was the injury that he was not expected to live beyond two years, but just over two years later, after intensive recuperation at a VA hospital in Illinois, he returned to Dean Witter, before making his way to Guadalajara in Mexico, where he lived in a wheelchair community. But Larry was not alone. His Cornell fraternity, Phi Sigma Delta, had been keeping an eye on his plight and loaned him $25,000 to help his rehabilitation, with a promise to provide the same again when needed. Although initially against the idea, his fraternity brothers persuaded him, and the money was used throughout the years to buy him a home in Tucson, Arizona, a van, and perhaps most importantly, independence. For many years Larry lived as close to a normal life as was possible, thanks in great part to a supportive family, the fundraising efforts of his fraternity brothers, but mostly to his own determination. In his later years he served on the Board of Directors of the Arizona Chapter of the Paralyzed Veterans of America. He died in 2017.

Jef Evans (1938-   )

After graduating from Mercersburg, Evans attended Stanford where he was a 'walk on' to a team made up of scholarship athletes that would eventually send three boys to the Olympics. In the Christmas of his senior year he took his fiancé to meet Jimmy. During this visit Jimmy announced he was retiring, and asked Evans if he would consider taking the role of head coach. Despite having already been accepted to a business school, Evans initially dismissed the idea, but after two months of considering his options he decided to apply for a coaching position.

He was successful, and after the summer took up the role of assistant coach. After five years as a coach at Mercersburg, he took up the role of head coach at Woodberry Forest School. His new school sweetened the offer by paying for his Masters in psychology, and he stayed there for seven years. Eventually he attended graduate school to undertake his doctorate and spent the following years building up a practice.

At the age of 54, Evans had a serious heart attack. In response he took up road running, and then track. At 65 he joined a Maine corporate track team. He has run in several National Senior Games. In corporate track he holds a number of Maine corporate records. He continues to run for the teams in his 80s and asserts he will do so as long as his health allows. He continues to live and run in Maine.

Malcolm 'Andy' Anderson (1938-   )
On leaving Mercersburg Anderson attended the University of Houston on a track scholarship. After graduation he worked at NASA's Manned Spacecraft Center as a Protocol Officer, and his time at Mercersburg helped him land the plum job of showing Jimmy Stewart around the facility on a visit. This was followed by time as Protocol Officer for HemisFair '68.

For some time he taught at an American school in Tehran in Iran. During this time he trained the athletics team, using Jimmy's techniques as his template. They beat all Iranian high schools at one meet.

Rolando Cruz (1939-   )
After leaving Mercersburg, Cruz attended Villanova University, where he continued to compete in pole vault at an international level, becoming one of first men to jump 16 feet. After graduation he returned to Puerto Rico where he became an attorney. In the 1970s and 1980s he served as the country's Commissioner of Insurance.

BIOGRAPHIES

Bob Batdorf (1940-)

After Mercersburg, Batdorf graduated from the Wharton School of the University of Pennsylvania. His career saw him holding a number of senior positions with trust institutions and investment advisors. He lives in Pennsylvania.

Paul White (1942-)

After Mercersburg White attended Cornell on a track scholarship, which saw him travel to England to take on a joint Oxford and Cambridge team. Upon graduation he was drafted into the Navy and served on its biggest destroyer, the USS Small, during the Vietnam War. The following years saw him working for a series of packaging and printing companies, including one he himself started. After selling his company he moved to Albuquerque where he again worked for a printing company, before starting his own brokerage company which creates materials for galleries. He has a son and daughter. His son, Curt, was born with a genetic defect and is Paul's hero!

Tom Danaher (1944-2015)

Tom was Jimmy Curran's grandson, protégé, and fan. After four years on Mercersburg's track team – two as captain – Tom received a full track scholarship to Syracuse University. But before completing his degree, he decided to drop out, move to Boston to join the growing folk scene, and concentrate on playing music. When that music scene expanded to New York's Greenwich Village, Tom followed, and put together a band that blended the at-the-time psychedelic sound with the Boston-based folk sound. The band – called Autosalvage after Frank Zappa suggested they use that name – released its only album in 1968. That eponymous album is still pointed to as a trailblazer, and recently was mentioned in acclaimed music-historian Ed Ward's *History of Rock & Roll, Volume II*.

The band eventually went their separate ways, and Tom made his way to San Francisco and Los Angeles, playing guitar with various musicians, and building guitars for others. He also began – like many musicians of that era – to use (and overuse) both drugs and alcohol. His habits led to the end of a first marriage, and then a second. Unlike many others, Tom recognized that he needed to leave the 'scene' in order to get his life on a better track. In the early 1980s, he moved back to his boyhood home (down the street from the original Curran household), and began to buy, refinish, and sell antiques, and continue his guitar-building work.

Almost immediately after that, he met and married his third wife, and became a hero to her and her three children when he moved the family to Pittsburgh so that he and his wife both could continue their formal educations – she to law school, and he to undergraduate, masters, and doctoral degrees in psychology.

Having reached his educational goals, Tom returned to music. In 2013, he reunited Autosalvage and, with advice and direction from Ed Ward, played three performances at South by Southwest music festival in Austin, Texas. After that, Tom became a singer-songwriter, putting together eleven songs with friends such as Irish musicians Robbie Malone and Niamh Farrell, John Sebastian of The Lovin' Spoonful, and Eric Bazilian of The Hooters. The last of the eleven songs was recorded less than a week before Tom passed away in 2015, and the album, now engineered, produced, and finalised, lives on.

Major International Games Competed in by Jimmy's Athletes

WR = World record   OR = Olympic record

DNS = Did not start   DNF = Did not finish

Intercalated Games, Athens, 1906

Date	Event	Round	Position	Time	Record
Wyndham Halswelle					
Apr, 25	100m	Heat	2nd		
Apr, 25	100m	SF	3rd		
Apr, 27	400m	Heat	1st	54.0 secs	
Apr, 30	400m	Final	2nd	53 4/5 secs	
Apr, 25	800m	Heat	2nd		
May, 1	800m	Final	3rd		

Olympic Games, London, 1908

Date	Event	Round	Position	Time	Record
Wyndham Halswelle					
Jul, 21	400m	Heat	1st	49.4 secs	
Jul, 22	400m	SF	1st	48.4 secs	OR
Jul, 23	400m	Final	2nd		
Jul, 25	400m	Re-run final	1st	50.0 secs	

Olympic Games, Stockholm, 1912

Date	Event	Round	Position	Time	Record
		Ted Meredith			
Jul, 12	400m	Heat	2nd		
		SF	1st	48.8 secs	
Jul, 13		Final	4th	49.2 secs	
Jul, 6	800m	Heat	2nd		
Jul, 7		SF	1st	1.54.4	
Jul, 8		Final	1st	1.51.9	WR
Jul, 14	4x400m relay	SF	1st	3.23.3	
Jul, 15		Final	1st	3.16.6	WR

AEF Championships, Stade de Colombes, 1919

Date	Event	Round	Position	Time	Record
		Harold Barron			
May, 30	120 yards high hurdles	Heat	1st	15 ⅖ secs	
Jun, 1		Final	3rd		
May, 30	220 yards low hurdles	Heat	1st	27 ⅖ secs	
May, 31		SF	1st	27 ⅕ secs	
Jun, 1		Final	3rd		
		Harold 'Boots' Lever			
May, 30	100 yards	Heat	1st	10 ⅘ secs	
May, 31		SF	1st	10 ⅕ secs	

Jun, 1		Final	3rd		
		Pete Maxfield			
Jun, 1	Pentathlon	Final	3rd	2,967.44 points	
		Larry Shields			
May, 30	One mile	Final	1st	4.27 ⅗	
Jun, 1	Medley relay	Final	1st	8.00 ⅕	

Inter-Allied Games, Stade Pershing, Paris, 1919

Date	Event	Round	Position	Time	Record
		Pete Maxfield			
Jul, 3	Shot put	Heat	3rd	12.806m	
Jul, 4		Final	3rd	12.873m	
		Eddie Meehan			
Jul, 3	4x400m relay	Final	1st	3.28 ⅘	
		Eddie Shields			
Jun, 23	1,500m	Heat	2nd		
Jun, 28		Final	4th		
Jul, 4	Medley relay	Final	1st	7.43 ⅖	

Olympic Games, Antwerp, 1920

Date	Event	Round	Position	Time	Record
Harold Barron					
Aug, 17	110m hurdles	Heat	1st	15.2 secs	
		SF	1st	15 secs	WR=
Aug, 18		Final	2nd	15.1 secs	
Harry Goelitz					
Aug, 20 - 21	Decathlon		DNF		
Ted Meredith					
Aug, 19	400m	Heat	1st	51.6 secs	
		QF	3rd	50.8 secs	
Aug, 20		SF	4th	50.4 secs	
Aug, 22	4x400m relay	SF	2nd	3.40.7	
Aug, 23		Final	4th	3.23.6	
Larry Shields					
Aug, 18	1,500m	SF	3rd	4.07.4	
Aug, 19		Final	3rd	4.03	
Aug, 21	3,000m team	SF	2nd (4th)		
Aug, 22		Final	1st (4th)		
Allen Woodring					

		Heat	1st	22.8 secs	
Aug, 19	200m	QF	2nd	22.1 secs	
		SF	1st	22.4 secs	
Aug, 20		Final	1st	22 secs	

Colombes Games, Paris, 1920

Date	Event	Round	Position	Time	Record
		Harold Barron			
Aug, 29	110m hurdles	Final	2nd		
		Larry Shields			
Aug, 29	1,500m	Final	2nd		
		Allen Woodring			
Aug, 29	4x400m relay	Final	1st	42.4 secs	

Olympic Games, Paris, 1924

Date	Event	Round	Position	Time	Record
		Bill Cox			
Jul, 11	3,000m team*	SF	1st (1st)	n/a	
Jul, 13		Final	3rd (2nd)	n/a	
		George 'Buck' Hester			
Jul, 6	100m	Heat	1st	11.2 secs	

		QF	2nd	10.7 secs	
Jul, 7		SF	6th	11.5 secs	
Jul, 8	200m	Heat	2nd		
		QF	4th		
Jul, 12	4x100m relay	Heat	2nd	43 secs	
Jul, 13		SF	3rd	43.3 secs	
		Charles 'Crip' Moore			
Jul, 6	400m hurdles	Heat	DNS	n/a	
		Marvin Rick			
Jul, 7	3,000m steeplechase	SF	2nd	10.11.0	
Jul, 9		Final	4th	9.56.4	

Olympic Games, Amsterdam, 1928

Date	Event	Round	Position	Time	Record
		Barney Berlinger			
Aug, 4-5	Decathlon		17th	5,499	

Olympic Games, Los Angeles, 1932

Date	Event	Round	Position	Time	Record
		Bill Carr			
Aug, 4	400m	Heat	1st	48.8 secs	

		QF	1st	48.4 secs	
		SF	1st	47.2 secs	OR
Aug, 5		Final	1st	46.28 secs	WR
Aug, 6	4x400m relay	SF	1st	3.11.8	WR
Aug, 7		Final	1st	3.08.14	WR

Olympic Games, London, 1948

Date	Event	Round	Position	Time	Record
		Jeff Kirk			
Jul, 30	400m hurdles	Heat	2nd	54.3 secs	
		SF	5th	52.5 secs	

Olympic Games, Helsinki, 1952

Date	Event	Round	Position	Time	Record
		Charles Moore Jr			
Jul, 20		Heat	1st	51.8 secs	
		QF	1st	50.8 secs	OR
	400m hurdles	SF	1st	52 secs	
Jul, 21		Final	1st	50.8 secs	OR=
Jul, 26	4x400m relay	SF	1st	3.11.67	
Jul, 27		Final	2nd	3.04.21	
		Dewey Lee Yoder			

Jul, 20	400m hurdles	Heat	2nd	55.2 secs	
		QF	2nd		
Jul, 21		SF	4th	53 secs	

Olympic Games, Melbourne, 1956

Date	Event	Round	Position	Height	Record
Rolando Cruz					
Nov, 24	Pole Vault	Qualifying	16th	4.00m	

Olympic Games, Rome, 1960

Date	Event	Round	Position	Height	Record
Rolando Cruz					
Sep, 5	Pole Vault	Qualifying	8th=	4.40m	
Sep, 7		Final	4th	4.55m	

Olympic Games, Tokyo, 1964

Date	Event	Round	Position	Height	Record
Rolando Cruz					
Oct, 15	Pole Vault	Qualifying	21st	4.50m	

Races featuring Jimmy Curran / G. Gordon

The race meets, and individual races, listed below are only a portion of those in which Jimmy participated. There are several reasons for other races he was involved in not being on this list.

It may simply be that the race was not reported in a newspaper, this being likely in early local races, during his time in the army, or as part of Jack Roden's athletic troupe. For example, a victory whilst his regiment was based in Egypt is frequently mentioned in later interviews, but was never found in documentary evidence.

The relevant newspapers may not have been digitised, or if digitised the OCR is of a poor quality, making searching difficult or impossible. Searches in the *Galashiels Telegraph*, later known as the *Border Telegraph*, for example, needed to be done manually, and as a result, it is likely that some mentions of Jimmy were missed.

I had only limited access to digital copies of the Mercersburg News. It is likely that additional information about races would have been found in its pages.

Lastly, in most cases, only those who won or placed in a race were named. So, where Jimmy finished in the lower placings, his participation would often not be noted.

DNP   = Did not place
DNF   = Did not finish
Unk.   = Finishing place is unknown

Running as Jimmy Curran, amateur

1898

Date	Games	Event/s	Place	Prize
Aug, 20	King's Own Scottish Borderers Sports, Dumfries	100 yards / Half-mile/ Long jump	1st / 1st / 2nd	

1899

Date	Games	Event/s	Place	Prize
Jul, 15	Dumfries F.C. Sports	330 yards / 440 yards	3rd / 3rd	
Aug, 10	Hamilton Garrison Sports	Throwing cricket ball	2nd	
Sep	Garrison Games, Devonport, England	100 yards / 440 yards / One mile / Hop, step and jump	1st / 1st / 1st / 1st	

1900

Date	Games	Event/s	Place	Prize
May	Queen Victoria's birthday celebrations, Modder River, South Africa	440 yards / Half-mile / One mile	1st / 1st / 1st	

1902

Date	Games	Event/s	Place	Prize
Jan, 1-2	Aliwal North, South	Unk.	Unk.	

Date	Games	Event/s	Place	Prize
	Africa			
Nov, 16	Annual Games, Port Elizabeth, South Africa	1.25 miles	1st	10s
Nov, 19	Port Elizabeth, South Africa	100 yards handicap / Long jump	2nd / 1st	5s / 10s

1903

Date	Games	Event/s	Place	Prize
Jan, 1	Scottish Society's Annual Games, Port Elizabeth, South Africa	220 yards for soldiers / 200 yards handicap run in uniform	1st / 2nd	
Jan – Apr	Cairo, Egypt	440 yards / Half-mile	1st / 1st	
Aug, 8	Primrose League Sports, Galashiels	440 yards / Half-mile / Obstacle race	3rd / 3rd / 2nd	
Aug, 29	Seventh Division Athletic Meeting, Curragh Garrison Cricket Ground, Ireland	Half-mile / One mile	1st equal / 1st	

1904

Date	Games	Event/s	Place	Prize
Jun, 8	Pharmacy Sports, Powderhall, Edinburgh	One mile	1st	
Jun, 18	Scottish Cycling Meet, Tynecastle, Edinburgh	Half-mile	1st	
Jul, 9	St Bernard's Sports, Powderhall, Edinburgh	300 yards / One mile	DNP / 4th	
Jul, 20	Leith Shamrock Cycling Club Sports, Powderhall,	One mile	1st	

Date	Games	Event/s	Place	Prize
	Edinburgh			
Jul, 25	Amateur Athletic Sports, Berwick-upon-Tweed, England	Half-mile	3rd	
Jul, 30	Cycling Club Sports, Hawick	One mile / One mile (Border Championship)	2nd / 1st	
Aug, 6	Primrose League Sports, Galashiels	Half-mile / One mile	2nd / 2nd	
Aug, 13	Celtic Sports, Parkhead, Glasgow	Half-mile / One mile	3rd / DNP	
Aug, 20	Leith Flower Show Sports, Edinburgh	Half-mile / One mile	DNP / 3rd	
Oct, 8	Portobello Cross Country, Edinburgh	Cross Country	1st	
Oct, 29	Gala Harriers Cross Country, Galashiels	Cross Country	Unk.	
Nov	Gala Harriers Cross Country, Galashiels	Cross Country	Unk.	
Nov, 12	Hawick v Gala Harriers Club Run, Hawick	Cross Country	1st	
Nov, 26	Gala Harriers Cross Country, Galashiels	Cross Country	Unk.	
Dec, 3	Gala Harriers Team Race, Galashiels	Team / Individual	1st / 2nd	

1905

Date	Games	Event/s	Place	Prize
Jan, 2	Jedburgh Harriers' Sports	Cross Country	1st	
Feb, 11	Eastern District Cross Country Championships, Stenhousemuir	Cross Country	DNP	

Mar, 22	Gala Harriers Cross Country, Galashiels	Cross Country	2nd	
Apr, 8	Melrose Annual Sports	440 yards / One mile	2nd / DNF	
Apr, 26	Powderhall, Edinburgh	Half-mile	DNP	
Jun, 3	Edinburgh Harriers' Sports, Powderhall, Edinburgh	440 yards / One mile / Two miles	2nd / DNP / DNP	

Running as G. Gordon, professional

Date	Games	Event/s	Place	Prize
Jun, 10	Hawick Common Riding	One mile	1st	
Jun, 17	Selkirk Common Riding	190 yards / One mile	DNP / 1st	
Jul, 8	Jedburgh Border Games	800 yards / One mile	1st / 2nd	
Jul, 15	Town's Band Picnic & Sports, Galashiels	120 yards	1st	
Aug, 19	St Ronan's Border Games, Innerleithen	300 yards / Two miles / Basket and stone / Steeplechase	DNP / 1st / 3rd / 1st	
Oct, 14	Powderhall Sprint, Edinburgh	Half-mile	DNP	

1906

Date	Games	Event/s	Place	Prize
Jan, 2	Powderhall Sprint, Edinburgh	880 yards	2nd	
Jan, 3	Royal Gymnasium Grounds, Edinburgh	Half-mile	2nd	£1

JIMMY CURRAN

Jan, 4	Royal Gymnasium Grounds, Edinburgh	One mile	DNP	
Apr, 6	Powderhall Sprint, Edinburgh	130 yards	4th	5s
May, 5	Powderhall Sprint, Edinburgh	Half-mile	DNP	
Jun, 16	Selkirk Common Riding	215 yards / Hurdles	2nd / 3rd	
Jul, 7	West of Scotland Highland Games, Johnstone	120 yards / 220 yards / 880 yards	DNP / 3rd / 2nd	
Jul, 13	Armadale Highland Games	440 yards / Half-mile	3rd / 2nd	
Jul, 14	Jedburgh Games	One mile / One and a half mile	1st / 2nd	
Jul, 18	Lochgelly Highland Games	120 yards	1st	
Jul, 21	Kelso Games	130 yards	2nd	£3
Jul, 28	Greenlaw Games	120 yards	4th	
Aug, 7	Alva Gymnastic Games	1,200 yards	2nd	
Aug, 18	St Ronan's Border Games, Innerleithen	120 yards / Steeplechase	2nd / 1st	
Aug, 24	Bute Highland Games, Rothesay	440 yards / Half-mile	1st / 1st	
Aug, 25	Cowal Highland Games, Dunoon	120 yards / Half-mile	DNP / 3rd	
Sep, 15	Powderhall Sprint, Edinburgh	Half-mile	DNP	
Sep, 22 & 29	Powderhall Sprint, Edinburgh	130 yards	Unk.	
Oct, 6	Powderhall Sprint, Edinburgh	Half-mile	3rd	10s

1907

Date	Games	Event/s	Place	Prize
Jan, 2	Powderhall Sprint, Edinburgh	300 yards	2nd	£2
Jan, 4	Royal Patent Gymnasium, Edinburgh	Half-mile	1st	£8
Mar, 23	Powderhall Sprint, Edinburgh	Half-mile	DNP	
Apr, 6	Powderhall Sprint, Edinburgh	130 yards	4th	
Apr, 20	Powderhall Sprint, Edinburgh	Half-mile	DNP	
May, 4	Powderhall, Edinburgh	One mile	DNP	
May, 18	Powderhall Spring Handicap, Edinburgh	130 yards / Half-mile	DNP / DNP	
Jun, 1	Vale of Leven Annual Games	120 yards / 440 yards	4th / 3rd	
Jun, 4	Cowdenbeath Annual Games	220 yards / 300 yards	1st / 3rd	
Jun, 7-8	Hawick Common Riding	120 yards / 250yards	DNP / DNP	
Jun, 10	Powderhall, Edinburgh	130 yards	DNP	
Jun, 15	Selkirk Common Riding	100 yards / 120 yards / 215 yards	1st / DNP / 4th	
Jun, 21	Swinton Games	100 yards / 300 yards / Standing hop, step and leap / Running hop, step and leap / Running spring	1st / 3rd / 1st / 1st / 1st	
Jun, 29	Rosewell Irish National	130 yards / 300	2nd / 1st	

	Foresters' Games, Dalkeith	yards / Half-mile	/ 1st	
Jul, 4	Penrith Friendly Society Sports, England	300 yards hurdles	2nd	
Jul, 6	Musselburgh Gardeners' Games	300 yards / Wheelbarrow race	2nd / 2nd	15s
Jul, 13	Jedburgh Border Games	Hurdles / 300 yards hurdles	2nd / 2nd	
Jul, 16	Airth Annual Games	120 yards	2nd	
Jul, 17	Racing and Highland Gathering, Dunfermline	300 yards	4th	
Jul, 19	Thornton Highland Games, Lochty Bridge	120 yards / 300 yards / 300 yards consolation	DNP / DNP / 1st	
Jul, 20	Kelso Games	440 yards / Half-mile / Hurdles / Hop, step and leap	3rd / 1st / 2nd / 2nd	
Jul, 22	Kinross Games	300 yards	2nd	
Jul, 27	Langholm Common Riding	100 yards / 100 yards shoe race / 120 yards / Half-mile / 100 yards hurdles	1st / 1st / 2nd / DNP / 1st	
Aug, 3	Strathallan Games, Bridge of Allan	110 yards / 440 yards hurdles	1st / 3rd	
Aug, 10	Lauder Games	130 yards / 200 yards / 440 yards	3rd / DNP / 2nd	
Aug, 15	Alva Gymnastic Games	200 yards / 300 yards / 1,200 yards	4th / 3rd / 1st	
Aug, 17	St Ronan's Border Games, Innerleithen	120 yards / 150 yards / 300 yards / Obstacle race	DNP / 2nd / 3rd / 2nd	
Aug, 24	Workington Summer Sports and Band	120 yards	3rd	

		Contest, England			
Aug, 31		Ullswater Sports, Pooley Bridge, England	440 yards / Half-mile	1st / 1st	
Sep, 14		Powderhall, Edinburgh	130 yards	DNP	
Sep, 28		Powderhall Handicap, Edinburgh	300 yards	1st	£8

Running as Jimmy Curran, professional

Date	Games	Event/s	Place	Prize
Nov or Dec	Third Regiment Armory, Philadelphia, Pa.	1,000 yards v Nellie Brookmeyer	1st	

1908

Date	Games	Event/s	Place	Prize
Jan, 16	Park Square Coliseum, Boston, Ma.	Five man, ten mile relay v Alfie Shrubb	2nd	
Jan, 23	Third Regiment Armory, Philadelphia, Pa.	Four man, six mile relay v Alfie Shrubb	2nd	
Feb, 5	Third Regiment Armory, Philadelphia, Pa.	1,000 yards v Al Nash	1st	
Feb, 22	Third Regiment Athletic Sports, Philadelphia, Pa.	One mile	Unk.	
Apr, 3	Tamaqua, Pa.	One mile v Tall Feather	1st	
Apr, 4	Mahanoy City, Pa.	Unk.	Unk.	
May, 30	Athletic, Motor Cycle and Dancing Carnival, Philadelphia, Pa.	Half-mile / One mile	2nd / 1st	
Jun, 13	Northeastern Burns Club Scottish Games,	Half-mile / One mile	2nd / 1st	

293

	Philadelphia, Pa.			
Jun, 27	Laceworkers of America Games, Philadelphia, Pa.	Half-mile / One mile	1st / 1st	
Jul, 4	Royal Oak Lodge, Sons of St George Games, Trenton, N.J.	Unk.	Unk.	
Jul, 11	Ancient Order of Hibernians' Irish National Games, Philadelphia, Pa.	One mile / Four miles	2nd / 2nd	$20+
Aug, 1	49th Annual Scottish Games, Philadelphia, Pa.	Half-mile / One mile	1st / 1st	
Aug, 15	Foresters Annual Jubilee, Philadelphia, Pa.	Half-mile / One mile / Two man, two mile relay	1st / 3rd / 1st	
Aug, 29	25th Annual Outing and Games of the Journeymen's Bricklayers' Protective Union, Philadelphia, Pa.	880 yards / One mile	1st / 2nd	$13
Sep, 7	Central Labor Union 8th Annual Picnic, Trenton, N.J.	120 yards / One mile	DNP / 1st	$50
Sep, 7	White City, Trenton, N.J.	Two miles	1st	$15
Sep, 12	Order of St George, Philadelphia, Pa.	One mile	3rd	
Nov, 26	Thanksgiving Sports, Trenton, N.J.	Two miles v Bobby Hallen	Unk.	
Nov, 26	Central Park, Trenton, N.J.	Four man, eight mile relay v Alfie Shrubb	2nd	

1909

Date	Games	Event/s	Place	Prize
Feb, 11	Third Regiment Armory, Philadelphia, Pa.	1,000 yards v Al Nash	1st	
Feb, 25	Third Regiment Armory, Philadelphia, Pa.	1,000 yards v Al Nash	1st	
Mar, 5	69th Regiment Armory, New York	Five miles	1st	$50
Mar, 8	Madison Square Garden, New York	Six-day-go-as-you-please	DNF	
Mar, 9	Essex Troop Armory, Newark	Five miles	3rd	
Mar, 10	Madison Square Garden, New York	Two man, six mile relay v Bobby Hallen	2nd	
Mar, 13	Madison Square Garden, New York	Two miles	1st	
Jun, 12	8th Northeastern Burns Club Scottish Games, Philadelphia, Pa.	One mile	1st	
Jul, 5	2nd Annual Irish Games, Philadelphia, Pa.	Half-mile / One mile	1st / 1st	
Jul, 17	White City, Erdenheim, Pa.	1,000 yards / Two mile relay	1st / 1st	
Jul, 25	United Brewers' Assoc. Games, New York	440 yards / One mile	3rd / 1st	
Jul, 31	Loom Fixers' Assoc., Philadelphia, Pa.	Half-mile / 1,000 yards / One mile	1st / 1st / 1st	
Aug, 14	Foresters' Annual Jubilee, Philadelphia, Pa.	One mile / Potato race	1st / 3rd	
Sep, 6	53rd New York Caledonian Club Games, New York	One mile	1st	

1910

Date	Games	Event/s	Place	Prize
Feb, 19	Fairhill Park, Philadelphia, Pa.	Marathon Relay	Unk.	
Jul, 2	Connaught Men's BB Patriotic Society of Philadelphia, Pa.	440 yards / One mile / Long jump / Hop, skip and jump	1st / 1st / 2nd / 3rd	$24
Aug, 1	Wilkes-Barre Caledonian Club, Pa.	Half-mile / One mile / Three miles / High jump	1st / 1st / 3rd / 3rd	
Aug, 6	51st Annual Scottish Games, Philadelphia, Pa.	100 yards / 220 yards / Half-mile / One mile / Pole vault	1st / 3rd / 2nd / 2nd / 3rd	
Sep, 5	New York Caledonian Club	440 yards / One mile	2nd / 1st	

1911

Date	Games	Event/s	Place	Prize
Jul, 22	Foresters' Annual Jubilee, Philadelphia, Pa.	One mile	1st	$8

1912

Date	Games	Event/s	Place	Prize
Jun, 29	Clan-Na-Gael Sports, Philadelphia, Pa.	220 yards hurdles / 440 yards hurdles / High jump / Pole vault	2nd / 1st / 3rd / 3rd	
Aug, 3	53rd Annual Scottish Games, Philadelphia, Pa.	Half-mile / 220 yards hurdles /	2nd / 3rd / 1st	

		Hop, step and jump		
Sep, 1	33rd Sons of St George Games, Gloucester City, N.J.	Half-mile / Potato race	3rd / DNP	
Sep, 2	New York Caledonian Club, Long Island	Pole vault	2nd	

1913

Date	Games	Event/s	Place	Prize
Jul, 12	Jedburgh Border Games	800 yards / One mile	1st / 3rd	
Jul, 19	Kelso Games	Half-mile / Half-mile handicap	1st / 1st	£2
Jul, 26	Clyde Football Club Sports, Glasgow	One mile handicap	3rd	
Jul, 28	Forfar Athletic Football Club Games	Half-mile / Half-mile consolation	DNP / 1st	
Jul, 29	Blairgowrie and Rattray Highland Games	One mile / 750 yards	2nd / 1st	
Aug, 2	Morpeth Olympic Games, England	Half-mile	1st	£8 10s
Aug	Powderhall, Edinburgh	Unk.	Unk.	
Aug, 16	St Ronan's Border Games, Innerleithen	Half-mile handicap / Race Around Town	1st / 1st	
Aug, 21	Carnwath Red Hose Games, England	Half-mile / Three miles (Red Hose)	1st / 2nd	
Aug, 23	Whittingham Games, near Alnwick, England	One mile	1st	
Nov	Mercersburg Academy, Pa.	50 yards v Albert Robinson	2nd	

1914

Date	Games	Event/s	Place	Prize
Aug, 1	55th Annual Scottish Games, Philadelphia, Pa.	Half-mile / 220 yards hurdles / Pole vault	1st / 1st / 2nd	

1915

Date	Games	Event/s	Place	Prize
Feb, 22	Mercersburg Academy, Pa.	800 yards v Ted Meredith	1st	
Aug, 7	56th Annual Scottish Games, Philadelphia, Pa.	Half-mile	1st	
Dec, 26	Mercersburg Academy, Pa.	Cross country v Donald Hellfrich and Harry Smock	1st	

1916

Date	Games	Event/s	Place	Prize
Aug, 5	57th Annual Scottish Games, Philadelphia, Pa.	Half-mile / One mile	1st / 1st	

1917

Date	Games	Event/s	Place	Prize
Aug, 4	58th Annual Scottish Games, Philadelphia, Pa.	Half-mile / One mile	1st / 1st	

1920

Date	Games	Event/s	Place	Prize
Aug, 7	61st Annual Scottish Games, Philadelphia, Pa.	One mile relay	1st	
Dec, 25	Powderhall Christmas Half-Mile, Edinburgh	Half-mile	DNP	

1921

Date	Games	Event/s	Place	Prize
Jul, 9	Jedburgh Border Games	800 yards / One mile	1st / 2nd	60s
Jul, 23	British Legion Sports, Dumfries	Half-mile / One mile / Hop, step and jump	1st / 2nd / 1st	
Jul, 30	Langholm Common Riding	220 yards / Half-mile	3rd / 3rd	
Aug, 13	Greenlaw Games	Half-mile / One mile / Hop, step and jump	1st / 2nd / 2nd	
August, 20	St Ronan's Border Games, Innerleithen	Half-mile / Race Around Town	3rd / 1st	

1922

Date	Games	Event/s	Place	Prize
Mar, 20	Franklin Field, Philadelphia, Pa.	v high school and college coaches	Unk.	

Jimmy's eastbound Atlantic journeys[*]

Depart date	Depart	Ship	Destination	Arrival date
3 Dec 1911	NYC	SS *Finland*	Dover	13 Dec 1911
14 Jun 1913	NYC	RMS *Caledonia*	Glasgow	23 Jun 1913
11 Dec 1920	NYC	SS *Finland*	Southampton	Dec 1920
11 Jun 1921	NYC	RMS *Cedric*	Liverpool	20 Jun 1921
1922	NYC			
28 Jun 1924	NYC	RMS *Majestic*	Cherbourg	4 Jul 1924
18 Jun 1932	NYC	RMS *Transylvania*	Glasgow	26 Jun 1932
19 Jun 1935	NYC	RMS *Berengaria*	Southampton via Cherbourg	25 Jun 1935
19 Jul 1947	NYC			Jul 1947
21 May 1948	NYC	RMS *Queen Mary*	Southampton via Cherbourg	27 May 1948
Jun 1950				Jun 1950
2 Jun 1953		Aircraft	Prestwick nr Glasgow	2 Jun 1953
1954		Aircraft		1954
May 1957	NYC	SS *United States*	Southampton via Le Havre	6 Jun 1957
May 1960	NYC	Aircraft	Prestwick nr Glasgow	May 1960

[*] It is believed Jimmy made 18 journeys to Europe, of which information exists about 15. Of these 15, 10 were made aboard a ship, and three by aeroplane. The remainder are unknown.

Jimmy's westbound Atlantic journeys

Depart date	Depart	Ship	Destination	Arrival date
5 Oct 1907	Liverpool	RMS *Lusitania*	NYC	12 Oct 1907
Jan 1912			NYC	Jan 1912
4 Sep 1913	Liverpool	RMS *Celtic*	NYC	13 Sep 1913
22 Jan 1921	Southampton	RMS *Aquitania*	NYC	30 Jan 1921
3 Sep 1921	Southampton	RMS *Aquitania*	NYC	9 Sep 1921
15 Aug 1922	Liverpool	SS *Pittsburgh*	Philadelphia	Aug 1922
30 Aug 1924*	Liverpool	RMS *Baltic*	NYC	8 Sep 1924
26 Aug 1932	Glasgow	SS *Tuscania*	NYC	4 Sep 1932
11 Sep 1935	Southampton	RMS *Berengaria*	NYC via Cherbourg	17 Sep 1935
1947				1947
8 Sep. 1948	Southampton	RMS *Queen Mary*	NYC	13 Sep 1948
1950				1950
13 Sep 1953	Prestwick nr Glasgow	Aircraft	NYC	14 Sep 1953
Mar 1954		Aircraft	NYC	22 Mar 1954
10 Jul 1957	Southampton	SS *America*	NYC	Jul 1957
Sep 1960	Rome	Aircraft	NYC	9 Sep 1960

---

* Jimmy was originally scheduled to return on 16th August on the RMS *Adriatic* but cancelled his trip for an unknown reason, possibly to watch Eric Liddell's final race in Scotland

Mercersburg Academy Penn Relays victories

Year	440 yards	Mile	Two Miles	Medley
1912		3.27 ⅕		
1915		3.28 ⅘		
1923		3.31 ⅕		
1924		3.29 ⅗		
1925	43 ⅘	3.28		
1926	43 ⅗			
1927	42 ⅘			
1929	43 ⅗			
1930	44	3.28 $^3/_{10}$		7.50 $^8/_{10}$
1931		3.34 $^9/_{10}$		
1932	43	3.28		
1933	42.5			
1934	44.6			
1935	43.2			
1936			8.08.6	
1938	43.2			
1939	42.2			
1942	43.1			
1943	44.2			
1945	45.2			
1947	44.1			
1948	43.7			
1950	42.9	3.27.4		
1951	44.1	3.28.8		
1953	44.6			
1955		3.30.3		
1961	44.6			
Victories	20	11	1	1

Endnotes and Sources

Notes

xviii   'Timings': N. Linthorne, Design and Material in Athletics, in Aleksandar Subic [ed.], *Materials in Sports Equipment*, Woodhead Publishing, 2019, p423

Prologue • 290

1-4   The stories of Jimmy's golfing and walking feats were published in a multitude of sources. These include, but are not limited to: Believe It Or Not – By Ripley, *Hartford Courant*, 17 November 1938; Curran, Mercersburg Coach, Visits Syracuse Friends, *Syracuse Herald*, 22 March 1939; Prep School Sports: Mr. Curran of Mercersburg Is A Braw Scot Who Backs Up His Words With Deeds, *New York Times*, 23 February 1953; Prep School Sports: Mercersburg Track Coach, 74, Takes a 28-Mile Walk to Prove a Point, *New York Times*, 11 Jan 1954; Spotlight On Sports, *Hagerstown Daily Mail*, 8 Feb 1963; They'll Miss Wee Scot at the Relays, *Philadelphia Inquirer*, 11 Feb 1963; Mercersburg's Olympic Tradition, in *Mercersburg Magazine*, Volume XI, No.5, Summer 1984; Track coach aced golf endurance test, *Palm Beach Daily News*, 18 May 2004; Michael Strauss, *Digging Out Stories*, unpublished and undated typescript

1   'prep school': prep, or preparatory, schools are, often, elite, private, fee-paying institutions which ready students for university. Although fees are generally high, many students are accepted on academic or sporting scholarships.

1   'tammy': an abbreviation of Tam o' Shanter, a hat named after the eponymous hero of the poem by Scotland's national bard, Robert Burns

1   'On any given day … a kilt': Telephone interview with Henry Thresher, 9 April 2015

1   'He carried with him … three balls': one newspaper reported that he carried cold tea and sweet chocolate with him

JIMMY CURRAN

1   'But on this ... sped away from him': Telephone interview with Henry Thresher, 9 April 2015

1   'He was a diminutive man ... average jockey': *Philadelphia Evening Bulletin*, February 1963

1   'As the years ... Barry Fitzgerald': Whilst Jimmy and Barry Fitzgerald do bear a passing resemblance, this humorous correlation was likely due to Fitzgerald's portrayal of Father Fitzgibbon in the 1944 film *Going My Way* where he wore round spectacles much like those worn by Jimmy

3   'He would ... could do': Interview with Mike Lewis, 21 May 2015

3   'His granddaughter ... be exhausted': Email from Laurie Danaher, 23 April 2020

3-4   'By noon ... bee sting': Curran Sets Record for Marathon Golf on Academy Course, *unknown newspaper*, 1938

4   '8.12pm': The exact start and end times vary from one report to the next. The precision of the times reported in the *Reading Times*, 15 November 1928 – a 5.05am start and an 8.12pm finish – mark this article out as having obtained this information from a knowledgeable source.

4   'As he passed ... grown into five': Prep School Sports: Mr. Curran of Mercersburg Is A Braw Scot Who Backs Up His Words With Deeds, *New York Times*, 23 February 1953; Spotlight on Sports, *Hagerstown Daily Mail*, 8 February 1963

Chapter 1 • The Queen's Shilling

6   'And then there were ... acres of grazing': Rev. Robert Douglas, *General View of the Agriculture of the Counties of Roxburgh and Selkirk; with Observations on the Means of their Improvement*, Richard Phillips, London, 1798, p309

7   'The weight of wool ... great manufactories': David Bremner, *The Industries of Scotland their Rise, Progress, and Present Condition*, Adam and Charles Black, Edinburgh, 1869, pp189-191; Robert Hall, *The History of Galashiels*, Alexander Walker & Son, 1898, pp301-307; Karen McKechnie, *A Border Woollen Town in the Industrial Revolution*, Longmans, Green and Co. Ltd, London and Harlow, 1968, pp38-40 and p77; Margaret C. Lawson, *Guid Auld Galashiels*, Galashiels, 1998,

ENDNOTES AND SOURCES

p3; Kevin Binfield [ed.], *Writings of the Luddites*, Johns Hopkins University Press, Baltimore, 2004, pp110-112; Martin Rorke, Dennis Gallagher, Charles McKean, E. Patricia Dennison, Gordon Ewart, *Historic Galashiels: Archaeology and Development*, Council for British Archaeology, 2011, pp31-36

7   Lade: a man-made waterway diverted from a natural water source for use in textile processes

7   'In 1833 ... great perfection': Hall, op. cit., pp116-117

7   'The number of mills ... the skyline': www.galashielshistory .com [Accessed 24 January 2017]

7   'That year Galashiels ... hanging space': The Great Exhibition, *Dumfries and Galloway Standard*, 2 April 1851

8   'Thus the ... further afield': www.galashielshistory.com [Accessed 24 January 2017]

8   'Dorothy Wordsworth ... thatched cottage': Dorothy Wordsworth, *Recollections of a Tour Made in Scotland*, Yale University Press, New Haven & London, 1997, p206

8   'Toilets were ... wash-houses': Lawson, op. cit., pp43-47

8   Haar: a sea fog common to the east coast of Scotland and northern England

8   'And a growing ... music teachers': Lawson, op. cit., p43; McKechnie, op. cit., pp12-13

8-9   'By mid-century around 120 ... especially badly': W.W. Knox, *A History of the Scottish People: Health in Scotland 1840-1940* – www.scran. ac.uk/scotland/pdf/SP2_3Health.pdf [Accessed 4 November 2017]

9   'From 1849 ... domestic use': Hall, op. cit., pp127-137

9   'In October 1875 ... tainted milk': Public Health, *Southern Reporter*, 9 September 1875

9   'Without the benefit ... Overhaugh Street': Death Certificate of John Curran – 775/00 0098 [Sourced from www .scotlandspeople.gov.uk, 31 March 2015]

9   'As was common ... named John': Birth Certificate of John Curran – 775/00 0009 [Sourced from www.scotlandspeople .gov.uk, 31 March 2015]

9   'Three years later ... into mourning': Death Certificate of Jane-Ann Curran – 775/00 0001 [Sourced from www.scotlandspeople .gov.uk, 31 March 2015]

10   'And just over a year ... his grandfather': Birth Certificate of James

JIMMY CURRAN

Curran – 775/00 0031 [Sourced from www.scotlandspeople.gov.uk, 21 March 2015]

10 'As a Roman … name, Michael': Confirmation of James Curran, Our Lady and St Andrew RC Church, Galashiels, Confirmation Register – MP7811166 [Sourced from www.scotlandspeople.gov.uk, 31 March 2015]

10 'He arrived … in the world': Hall, op. cit., p471

10-11 'In June 1887 … Meigle Hill': ibid., pp152-153; Galashiels, *Southern Reporter*, 23 June 1887

11 'A year before … Auld Lang Syne': Hall, ibid., p159; Galashiels Burns Demonstration, *Edinburgh Evening News*, 20 July 1896

11 'Jimmy's love of Burns … *Gala Water*': Philadelphia Scottish Border Club, *Southern Reporter*, 24 February 1910; Borderers in America, *Hawick News and Border Chronicle*, 2 September 1910

11 'Burns' *Braw Lads O' Gala Water*': Jimmy is also known to have sung *Bonnie Dundee*

11 'The following year … smaller fires': Queen Victoria's Diamond Jubilee, *Southern Reporter*, 24 June 1897

11 'In 1904 … to 1906': Tom F. Cunningham, *Your Fathers the Ghosts: Buffalo Bill's Wild West In Scotland*, Black and White Publishing, 2007

12 'In 1883 Michael … the lieges': Police Court Cases, *Southern Reporter*, 19 July 1883; Police Court Cases, *Southern Reporter*, 21 February 1884

12 'Three years later … of the peace': Police Court Cases, *Southern Reporter*, 24 March 1887; Police Court Cases, *Southern Reporter*, 7 April 1898

12 'But it was … was dropped': Police Court Cases, *Southern Reporter*, 17 April 1879

12-13 'The scale of the … Europe and Yorkshire': Clifford Gulvin, *The Tweedmakers: A History of the Scottish Fancy Woollen Industry 1600-1914*, David & Charles, Newton Abbot, 1973, pp140-147; Sir A. Conan Doyle at Galashiels, *Edinburgh Evening News*, 31 March 1905

13 'With less … viable option': www.galashielshistory.com/page2.html [Accessed 24 January 2017]

13 The Queen's Shilling: known as the King's Shilling when the monarch was male, it was a nominal payment made to army recruits upon joining the British Army. Although the practice was ended in 1879, the use of the phrase was still active by the end of the 19th century and it still occasionally used over 100 years later.

ENDNOTES AND SOURCES

14   Merse: a flat area of land bordering a water course

14   'On 19th July … valuable assistance': Rev. R.W. Weir, *The History of the 3rd Battalion King's Own Scottish Borderers 1798-1907 with many interesting illustrations*, Dumfries, [1908], pp101

14   'On the south-eastern … quarter-mile distance': Ordnance Survey, 2nd edition, 25" to the mile, 1897/1899 – maps.nls.uk /view /82905222 [Accessed 16 August 2017]

14   Sexton: a church officer whose role it is to look after the maintenance of the buildings and connected graveyard

14-15   'They had cinder … in the morning': Seizure Proves Fatal to Jimmy Curran at 83, *Harrisburg Patriot-News*, 8 February 1963

15-16   'A competition area … Regimental Theatre': Scottish Borderers' Centenary, *Dumfries and Galloway Standard & Advertiser*, 24 August 1898; A Military Church Services, *Dumfries and Galloway Standard & Advertiser*, 24 August 1898; The Militia Training, *Dumfries and Galloway Standard & Advertiser*, 24 August 1898

16   'After a night of disturbances … headed south': A Militia Disturbance in Dumfries, *Scotsman*, 26 August 1898

16-17   The trains carrying … a single line': The Salisbury Plain Manoeuvres – how the troops were removed. Interview with Mr S. Fay, *North Wilts Herald*, 16 September 1898

17-18   'After more marching … a ceasefire': *The Autumn Maneuvers of 1898: Austria-Hungary, France, Germany, Great Britain, Russia and Switzerland*, Government Printing Office, Washington, 1900, pp67-117

18   'On 8th September … men were dismissed': The Army Manoeuvres, *Scotsman*, 29 August 1898; The Army Manoeuvres, *Scotsman*, 30 August 1898; The Army Manoeuvres, *Scotsman*, 3 September 1898; The Army Manoeuvres, *Scotsman*, 5 September 1898; The Army Manoeuvres, *Scotsman*, 6 September 1898; Army Manoeuvres, *Scotsman*, 8 September 1898; The Army Manoeuvres, *Scotsman*, 9 September 1898; The Military Manoeuvres: The Review on Boscombe Down, *The Times*, 9 September 1898; The Army Manoeuvres, *Scotsman*, 10 September 1898; Rev. R.W. Weir, *King's Own Scottish Borderers*, op. cit., pp107-110

18   'It appears that … regular army': National Archives, GBM WO97 4626 030

18   But, perhaps cognisant … clean-shaven': Brigadier-General H.R. Kelham, *The 1st Battalion Highland Light Infantry 1899-1901*,

unpublished, [1923], p134

18   Trews: trousers. Unlike most Scottish regiments, whose soldiers wore the kilt, the HLI wore trews, although just days after arriving in South Africa these were discarded in favour of more apposite khaki trousers.

19   'The success of the previous ... smaller scale': A Fight That Failed, *Shipley Times and Express*, 8 July 1899

19   'And these failings ... berated the cadets': Major A.F. Mockler-Ferryman, *Annals of Sandhurst: A Chronicle of the Royal Military College from its Foundation to the Present Day with a Sketch of the History of the College Staff*, London, 1900, pp59-61

19-20 'The military response ... national importance': Tony Mason, Eliza Riedi, *Sport and the Military: The British Armed Forces 1880-1960*, Cambridge University Press, 2010, p17

20   'In the 1890s ... hockey, etc': Sir Charles Harington, *Tim Harington Looks Back*, John Murray, London, 1940, p12

20   'In August 1899 ... cricket ball': Sports at Hamilton Garrison, *Glasgow Herald*, 11 August 1899

20   'A month later ... hop, skip and jump': A H.L.I. Athlete, *Highland Light Infantry Chronicle*, Volume IV, No.4, October 1904, p107; Meredith's work due to Curran's coaching, *Detroit Free Press*, 18 August 1912

Chapter 2 • Kelham's Warriors

This chapter relied heavily on two sources. Brigadier-General Henry Kelham's *The 1ˢᵗ Battalion Highland Light Infantry 1899-1901*, his day-by-day account of his experiences in the Boer War. It was written in 1923, but has gone unpublished. The Highland Light Infantry's *Chronicle* magazine also contained a vast amount of detailed information, with a strong focus on battles undertaken, as well as regimental events such as football, cricket and athletics.

22   'For many centuries ... colony's courts': A.P. Newton and E.A. Benians [eds], *The Cambridge History of the British Empire, Volume VIII, South Africa, Rhodesia and the Protectorates*, Cambridge University Press, Cambridge, 1936, p321

ENDNOTES AND SOURCES

23   'The *Daily Telegraph* ... must have': *Daily Telegraph & Courier*, 11 October 1899

23   'On 11th October ... from Britain': Robert Ross, *A Concise History of South Africa*, Cambridge University Press, 2008, pp23-90

23-24   'During October ... the latter group': *Highland Light Infantry Chronicle*, Volume II, No.13, January 1900, p454

24   'The main body ... was going badly': *Highland Light Infantry Chronicle*, Volume IV, No.2, April 1904, p49

24   'If this anxiety ... get into it': Coach Considers Enlisting, *Buffalo Evening News*, 22 June 1942

24   'Almost three weeks ... the Modder River': *Regimental Records of the 1st Battalion Highland Light Infantry Formerly the 71st Highland Light Infantry, 1777 to 1906*, Dinapore, 1907, pp196-197

24   'In the early ... Magersfontein Ridge': *A Handbook to the Boer War with General Map of South Africa and 18 Sketches and Plans*, Gale and Polden Limited, London and Aldershot, 1910, p60

25   'One soldier ... neck and died': A Soldier's Terrible Fall, *Glasgow Herald*, 13 December 1899

25   *Kildonan Castle*: in 1909, Mohandas Karamchand Gandhi, soon to be known as Mahatma, would write the book *Hind Swaraj*, or *Indian Home Rule*, onboard the *Kildonan Castle*

25   'As the ship was on ... maiden voyage': Felicity Potter [ed.], *To the Sea in Ships: Captain J.C. Robinson of the Union-Castle Line – and his brother Damnation Joe (Captain J.T. Robinson)*, Royd House, 2013, pp76-83

25   'As it pulled out ... *Auld Lang Syne*': The Scene at Southampton, *Western Gazette*, 5 January 1900; Departure of the Kildonan Castle, *London Standard*, 4 January 1900; To-day's Embarkations, *Morning Post*, 3 January 1900; The Transvaal War, *Hampshire Advertiser*, 6 January 1900; *Highland Light Infantry Chronicle*, Volume II, No.13, January 1900, pp454-455

26   'Almost immediately ... flow of vomit': *Hampshire Advertiser*, 17 January 1900

26   'And for those ... a regular pestilence': E.J. McWeeney, On Immunity Against Infectious Disease, with special reference to Anti-Typhoid Inoculation in *Journal of the Statistical and Social Inquiry Society of Ireland*, Volume XIII, 1915, pp231-254

26   'Anti-typhoid fever ... high fever': *Highland Light Infantry Chronicle*, Volume II, No.13, January 1900, p439; Winston Spencer Churchill,

London to Ladysmith via Pretoria, Longmans, Green, and Co., London, New York and Bombay, 1900, p10

26   'As a result ... killed in battle': E.J. McWeeney, On Immunity, ibid., pp238-241; Vincent J. Cirillo, Arthur Conan Doyle (1859-1930): Physician during the typhoid epidemic in the Anglo-Boer War (1899-1902) in *Journal of Medical Biography*, Volume 22, Issue 1, 2013, pp2-8; Julian Ralph, *War's Brighter Side*, C. Arthur Pearson, London, 1901

26-27   'But any thoughts ... in South Africa': A Plucky Youth: Determined to Fight, *London Daily News*, 23 January 1900

27   'But a dampener ... four days later': Shipping Intelligence, *Glasgow Herald*, 9 January 1900; Deaths at Sea, *Glasgow Herald*, 24 January 1900; *Hampshire Advertiser*, 17 January 1900

27   'A man had also fallen ... *Aurania's* trip': *Highland Light Infantry Chronicle*, Volume IV, No.2, April 1904, pp49-50

27   'Before them lay ... rousing speech': The Transports, *Birmingham Daily Post*, 23 January 1900; The Transports, *Liverpool Mercury*, 23 January 1900

28   'The word veldt ... cracked earth': *The Union-Castle Atlas of South Africa: A series of 21 plates, printed in colour, containing 36 maps and diagrams. With an account of the geographical features, the climate, the mineral and other resources, and the history of South Africa. And an index of over 6,000 names*, The Union-Castle Mail Steamship Co., Ltd., London, 1903, p8

28   'But as graced ... a soldier': *Highland Light Infantry Chronicle*, Volume II, No.16, October 1900, p548; Kelham, op. cit.., pp272-293

28   Mauser: the Mauser was a rifle originally produced in Germany and licensed to countries throughout the world. The version used by the Boers, the M1895, was produced in Sweden.

28   'On 5th February ... 65 wounded': *Highland Light Infantry Chronicle*, Volume II, No.14, April 1900, pp468-469

28   'The men then ... of Jacobsdaal': *Highland Light Infantry Chronicle*, Volume II, No.14, April 1900, p470; Kelham, op.cit., p79

28-29   'Two days later ... numbers killed': Kelham, ibid., pp82-84 and p166

29   Mufti: civilian clothes

29   'That evening ... Cross overhead': *Highland Light Infantry Chronicle*, Volume II, No.14, April 1900, p470; Kelham, op. cit., pp87-88

29   'On 5th March ... accoutrements': Kelham, ibid., pp89-91

29   'After a nine-day stay ... Highland Brigade': *Highland Light Infantry Chronicle*, Volume II, No.14, April 1900, p472; ibid., pp97-98

29   Basutoland is now modern-day Lesotho. Poor relations with the Orange Free State had seen it become a Crown dependency in 1868, and by the time of the Second Boer War relations with the Orange Free State were still poor. This saw them give free access to the British Army.

29   'Over a 15-day spell … ending up in Winburg': *Highland Light Infantry Chronicle*, Volume II, No.14, April 1900, pp473-474; Kelham, op. cit., pp107-114

29   'After a short stay … cock feathers': *Highland Light Infantry Chronicle*, Volume II, No.15, July 1900, p502

29-30   'On 22nd May … two miles marched': *Highland Light Infantry Chronicle*, Volume II, No.15, July 1900, pp503-505; *Highland Light Infantry Chronicle*, Volume IV, No.1, January 1902, pp690-691; Kelham, op. cit., pp117-133 and pp259-266;

30   'Around 60 years later … and no fun': Email from Jef Evans, 6 January 2020; Jimmy was using poetic licence to make a point. He never actually made it to Pretoria, the closest he came being Heilbron, 126 miles to the south.

30   'And so just … your bellies': Kelham, op. cit., pp134-136

30-31   'The Boers had … becoming demoralised': ibid., pp137-140

31   'When the soldiers … all starving': *Highland Light Infantry Chronicle*, Volume II, No.15, July 1900, pp503-505; ibid., 134-149

31   'But the Boers were aware … crossed it': Kelham, op. cit., pp150-167

31   'Henry Kelham … and game': Highland Light Infantry Chronicle, Volume IV, No.1, January 1902

31   'Another book … indescribable charm': *The Union-Castle Atlas* op. cit., p22

31-32   'Each of Kelham's … his memoirs': *Highland Light Infantry Chronicle*, Volume IV, No.1, January 1902, pp718-725; Kelham, op. cit., pp158-163

32   'For part of the war … Douglas Haig': Facebook post by Tom Danaher, 27 March 2015

32-33   'On the morning … special praise': Kelham, op. cit., pp179-190

33   'The operation proved … to the north': ibid., p201

33   Landrost: magistrate

33   'In early August … fun of the occasion': *Chronicle*, Volume IV, No.1, January 1902, p719; Kelham, op. cit., pp202-203

33-34   'And still the … three-day march': Kelham, ibid., pp204-221

34   Picquets: advance groups of soldiers sent out to provide an outer line of defence against any enemy incursion

34   'Jimmy spent his first … didn't compete': *Highland Light Infantry Chronicle*, Volume III, No.1 & 2, January/April 1901, pp593-597; Kelham, op. cit., pp245-260

34   'But despite … from Smithfield': Kelham, ibid.' pp261-279

34   'By early 1901 … and Rouxville': ibid., p283

34   'On Jimmy's birthday … next month': *Highland Light Infantry Chronicle*, Volume III, No.1 & 2, January/April 1901, p580

34   'And while Hughes-Hallett … through Basutoland': *Highland Light Infantry Chronicle*, Volume IV, No.1, January 1902, p721; Kelham, op. cit., pp279-293 and 348-349

35   'Regardless, they … goals to 2': Kelham, ibid., pp314-315

35   'With the threat … bid you farewell': ibid., pp322-323; Trevor Royle, *Fighting Mac: The Downfall of Major-General Sir Hector Macdonald*, Mainstream Publishing, 2003; MacDonald's successes in South Africa were no protection from the events that were to follow in his life. Rumours of a sexual liaison with a Boer prisoner had circulated in South Africa, but rumours became accusations in the closer confines of Ceylon. And his alienation of the wrong people saw his supposed indiscretions wind their way through the inhibited mores of Edwardian society, finally reaching the ears of King Edward VII. Feeling hounded from all quarters, and with a court martial imminent, he committed suicide in a hotel room in Paris. Within three months a Government Commission had exonerated him, noting that it had found not 'the slightest particle of truth' in the rumours.

35   'Then, in late May … around Queenstown': *Highland Light Infantry Chronicle*, Volume III, No.1 & 2, January/April 1901, p602; Kelham, ibid., pp327a-332

35-36 'Three weeks … absolutely Arctic': *Highland Light Infantry Chronicle*, Volume III, No.1 & 2, January/April 1901, pp602-603; *Highland Light Infantry Chronicle*, Volume IV, No.1, January 1902, p725

36   'Jimmy was dispatched … the next year': *Highland Light Infantry Chronicle*, Volume III, No.7, July-October 1902, p773

36   'And while Jimmy … to Herschel': *Highland Light Infantry Chronicle*, Volume III, No.3 & 4, July/October 1901, p644, *Highland Light Infantry Chronicle*, Volume IV, No.1, January 1902, p725

36   'In early May … Venter's Drift': *Highland Light Infantry Chronicle*,

Volume III, No.7, July-October 1902, p773

36   'A blockhouse ... corrugated havens': *Highland Light Infantry Chronicle*, Volume III, No.6, April 1902, pp747-748; Kelham, op. cit., pp337-347

36   'The relentless threat ... our last moon': Kelham, ibid., p205

36-37   'And if the threat ... fresh water': *Highland Light Infantry Chronicle*, Volume III, No.3 & 4, July/October 1901, p652; *Highland Light Infantry Chronicle*, Volume IV, No.1, January 1902, p701, p708 and p715

37   'A local farmer's ... their accuracy': Kelham, op. cit., pp338-339

37   'At the close ... World Wars': Greencastle, *Chambersburg Public Opinion*, 14 March 1951

37-38   'G Company was ... seven hours': *Highland Light Infantry Chronicle*, Volume III, No.7, July-October 1902, p778; A photograph showing the train approaching the Koffiebus and Teebus mountains is held within an album in the Royal Highland Fusiliers Regimental Museum in Glasgow.

38   'Port Elizabeth ... or speed': *Highland Light Infantry Chronicle*, Volume III, No.7, July-October 1902, p778 and pp783-787; *Highland Light Infantry Chronicle*, Volume III, No.8, January 1903

38-39   'Jimmy had cemented ... under fire': Halswelle Retires With Great Record, *Washington Times*, 5 July 1909

39-40   'In the last days ... returning to camp': *Highland Light Infantry Chronicle*, Volume III, No.8, January 1903, pp804-810

40   'But sport was ... 60 years': *Highland Light Infantry Chronicle*, Volume III, No.8, January 1903, pp812-813; Halswelle Retires With Great Record, *Washington Times*, 5 July 1909; Halswelle was given handicaps of five yards in the 100 yards, and 12½ yards in the 220 yards, but refused them and ran off scratch

Chapter 3 • The Long Journey Home

42   'On 12ᵗʰ January ... order of the day': *Highland Light Infantry Chronicle*, Volume III, No.9, April 1903, pp838-839 and p842

42   Tilting the bucket: a game that would see one man pushing another in a wheelbarrow. The man in the barrow would attempt to thread a 'lance' through a small hole in a board. Failure to do so would tip a

bucket of water over both men.

42　　Placing the pig's eye: a game that would see a pig drawn on the ship's deck, and a blindfolded man would attempt to place an 'eye' in the correct place on the body – similar to pinning the tail on the donkey.

43　　'The stay in the port ... undrinkable water': Rev. C.W. Isenberg's account of a visit to Mount Sinai, in *Church Missionary Paper for the Use of Weekly and Monthly Contributors*, No.LXXVI, Christmas, 1834, Church Missionary Society; John Hood, *Australia and the East; Being a Journal Narrative of a Voyage to New South Wales with a Residence of some Months in Sydney and the Bush and the Route Home by Way of India and Egypt*, London, 1843, p431

43　　'With no war ... half-mile championships': *Highland Light Infantry Chronicle*, Volume III, No.10, July 1903; Meredith Brought Out by J. Curran, *Boston Herald*, 30 August 1912

43-44　'On 10th March ... Pyramid of Saqqara': *Highland Light Infantry Chronicle*, Volume III, No.10, July 1903, pp868-869

44　　'Given this transfer ... December 1903': Attestation of James Curran [Sourced from Find My Past, 26 January 2015]; Jimmy also won the King's South Africa Medal, with clasps for 1901 and 1902, but it is unknown when he received it. His former comrades in the HLI received theirs in a ceremony in India on 24th December 1903.

44-45　'The final phase ... he had left': Captain Godfrey Trevelyan Williams, *The Historical Records of the Eleventh Hussars Prince Albert's Own*, London, 1908, p291

45　　'But in June ... finally succumbed': Attestation of James Curran [Sourced from Find My Past, 26 January 2015]; Death Certificate of Edward Curran – 775/00 0136 [Sourced from www.scotlandspeople .gov.uk, 31 December 2015]; Proposed Consumptive Sanatorium for the Borders, *Southern Reporter*, 22 May 1902

45　　'In July ... by the King': Williams, op. cit., pp291-292

45-46　'On the 8th ... heather on fire': Demonstration at Galashiels: Sports and Fireworks, *Border Telegraph*, 11 August 1903; Athletics, *Southern Reporter*, 13 August 1903; Most newspapers only listed those who placed in an event. In theory an athlete could take part in every race at a sports day and, if they failed to place in any of them, we would likely never know he had competed.

46　　'On 24th August ... the half-mile': Military Sports at the Curragh, *Kildare Observer and Eastern Counties Advertiser*, 29 August 1903

46 'But first he … scouting movement': Williams, op. cit., p292

Chapter 4 • Gala Hailes Villa and the Mighty Glasgow Rangers

48 'One derby game … between the players': Gala Renton v. Hailes Villa, *Border Telegraph*, 26 January 1904

48 'But lack of league form … Walkerburn 4-2': Football, *Southern Reporter*, 7 April 1904

48 'A month later … hearty reception': Football, *Southern Reporter*, 19 May 1904

48-49 'In order to raise … Glasgow Celtic': a 'friendly' is a non-competitive game, usually used as a warm-up for early season league and cup games; Celtic and Heart of Midlothian finished first and second in the Scottish League, Rangers fourth. The Scottish Cup was won by Heart of Midlothian.

49 'Jimmy was deemed … for tea': Trial Football Match at Galashiels, *Border Telegraph*, 10 April 1906

49 'And so it was … at a discount': Rangers v. Border XI, *Border Telegraph*, 1 May 1906

50 'But before Jimmy … content': Gala Hailes Villa v. Selkirk – Border League Championship, *Border Telegraph*, 1 May 1906

Chapter 5 • The Best Half-Miler in Scotland

52-53 'But determining … in their favour': Montague Shearman, *Athletics and Football*, Longmans, Green, and Co., London, 1887, pp200-204, pp208-211

53-54 'A Scottish runner … ten times over': David Mason and Ian Stewart, *Mr Struth: The Boss*, Headline Publishing Group, London, 2013, pp30-32; A.R Downer, in his *Running Recollections*, notes that stealing yards in this way was a common occurrence

54 'In the 1880s … the bookmakers': Dash Across Ocean Longest on Record, *Washington Post*, 31 May 1915

54 'Another highlights … follow suit': The Edinburgh New Year

Handicaps, *Bell's Life in London and Sporting Chronicle*, 6 January 1883

55 'To remedy this ... an amateur': Important Amateur Conference: New Amateur Definition, *Leicester Chronicle and the Leicestershire Mercury*, 23 November 1895

55-56 'The following year ... in Scotland': National Records of Scotland, GD370 1/1/1; National Records of Scotland, GD370 1/1/2

56 'Seeing the Scottish ... Berwick-upon-Tweed': Border Amateur Athletic Club, *Edinburgh Evening News*, 7 October 1895; Border Amateur Athletic Association, *Edinburgh Evening News*, 9 March 1896

57 'Wyndham Halswelle's views ... chance of victory': Halswelle Retires With Great Record, *Washington Times*, 5 July 1909

57 'Alfie Shrubb ... he collected': A photograph depicting Shrubb standing amongst his winnings is shown in Rob Hadgraft, *The Little Wonder: The Untold Story of Alfie Shrubb World Champion Runner*, Desert Island eBooks, 2012

57 'This was also ... to friends': Duncan Hamilton, *For the Glory: The Life of Eric Liddell*, Doubleday, 2016

57 'They believed ... amateur sport': Amateur & Professional Athletics, *Isle of Wight Observer*, 14 June 1884

57-58 'In 1933 ... amateur code': J.K. Ballantyne, Amateur Athletics in the Borders, in *Fifty Years of Athletics: An Historical Record of the Scottish Amateur Athletic Association 1883-1933*, Scottish Amateur Athletic Association, Edinburgh, 1933, p44

58 'Individuals and teams ... form or another': Cases of amateur suspensions are commonplace. One of the most interesting and moving, recounting the career of John Tarrant, is told in Bill Jones' *The Ghost Runner*. In Scotland the bloody-mindedness of the amateur authorities is clearly visible in the story of Scotland's greatest ever sprinter, George McNeill. McNeill's story is told in his autobiography – *The Unique Double*. If a story most aptly sums up the mindset of the amateur authorities it is that of Andy Williamson, a 10-year old who was banned from athletic competition due to having received a prize of a 10p packet of sweets. Further information on Williamson's story can be found in the *Glasgow Herald*, 10 August 1985.

58 'Alfie Shrubb ... amateur circuit': Hadgraft, op. cit.

58-59 'So, in 1882 ... jail sentence': Jeremy Crump, Athletics, in Tony Mason, *Sport in Britain: a social history*, Cambridge University Press, 1989, p51; The following reports are a sample of the prosecutions that took place in the late 19ᵗʰ and early 20ᵗʰ centuries – A Professional Runner Sent to Jail, *Edinburgh Evening News*, 18 October 1884; A Mean Fraud by Running Men, *Dundee Evening Telegraph*, 7 October 1889; The Charge Against an Essex Athlete, *Essex Newsman*, 2 December 1893; Alleged Impersonation at Lincoln Bicycle Sports, *Lincolnshire Chronicle*, 5 June 1900; Amateur Athlete Sent to Gaol, *Gloucester Citizen*, 21 October 1902

59   'Two years after ... hard labour': Athletes Charged with Conspiracy, *Cheshire Observer*, 18 October 1884

59   'In the late ... a professional': Dilwyn Porter and Stephen Wagg [eds], *Amateurism in British Sport: It Matters Not Who Won Or Lost*, Routledge, London and New York, 2008, p3

59   'And Alfred Downer ... for manslaughter': A.R. Downer, *Running Recollections and How to Run: Being an Autobiography of A.R. Downer, Champion Sprinter of the World*, Gale & Polden Ltd,. London, 1899, p38

60   'In 1903 a letter ... Scot free': National Records of Scotland, GD370 1/1/3

60   'In 1906 a correspondent ... prizes on offer': Border Games Decaying, *Edinburgh Evening News*, 21 August 1906

61   'Backers of the best ... both parties': Downer, op. cit.; David F. Town, *Hot Foot: Walter Knox's Remarkable Life as a Professional in an Amateur World*, Kindle Edition, 2014

61   'Alfie Shrubb was able ... finance for him': Hadgraft, op. cit.

61-62   'His childhood friend ... lose a race': "Doctored" Runners, *Dundee Courier*, 15 April 1908; Lauder, *Berwickshire News and General Advertiser*, 15 August 1922

62   'As such there were ... legal means': Sporting Comments, *Morning Post*, 29 October 1894; English Athletic Notes, *Edinburgh Evening News*, 7 June 1906

62   'The committee ... previous year': Norman Dovey, *One Hundred and Fifty Years of the Alva Gymnastic Games*, N. Dovey, 2006, pp14-15

62   'In 1906 ... the morn': *Border Telegraph*, 30 April 1907; Sporting Jottings, *Border Telegraph*, 11 June 1907; A Selkirk Minister and the Common-Riding, *Southern Reporter*, 13 June 1907

62   'Weel Johnny ... the morn': The translation is 'Well, Johnny, if there's to be no betting we may go and seek a job tomorrow'

62-63   'Over the next ... time of 4.28': Athletics: Edinburgh Pharmacy Club Sports, *Edinburgh Evening News*, 9 June 1904; Edinburgh Pharmacy

Sports, *Edinburgh Evening News*, 10 June 1904; Eastern Athletic Notes, *Scottish Referee*, 10 June 1904; Success of a Gala "Ped", *Border Telegraph*, 14 June 1904

63 'Powderhall track in Edinburgh': Powderhall, until 1970, hosted the world famous Powderhall Sprint, now known as the New Year Sprint. Luminaries such as Jack Donaldson, Barney Ewell, and George McNeill competed in it.

63 'John McGough': The Irish born and Scottish bred McGough at one time held all Scottish records from 1,000 yards to four miles and, in 1906, set a new Scottish record for the mile. In 1906 and 1908 he represented Great Britain at the Athens and London Olympics. In 1906 he won a silver medal in the 1,500 metres, but in 1908 came third in his 1,500 metres heat and failed to progress.

63 'In the next ... Arthur Duffey': Scottish Cycling Meet Races, *Scotsman*, 20 June 1904; Athletics: Leith Shamrock Cycling Club Sports, *Edinburgh Evening News*, 21 July 1904; *Border Telegraph*, 26 July 1904

63 'A further ... exciting finish': The St Bernard's Sports, *Edinburgh Evening News*, 11 July 1904; Eastern Athletic Notes, *Scottish Referee*, 15 July 1904

63 'The Championship ... the SBAAA': The Strang Steel Challenge Cup, *Edinburgh Evening News*, 8 July 1899

63-64 'This was given ... five year history': Athletics, *Border Telegraph*, 2 August 1904; Sports and Pastimes, *Berwickshire News*, 16 August 1904

64 'Some years later ... amateurs in Scotland': Sporting Jottings, *Border Telegraph*, 22 July 1913

64 'In early August ... William Torrie': Primrose League Sports, *Southern Reporter*, 11 August 1904

64 'Jimmy was ... Hyman of Dublin': Celtic F.C. Sports, *Dundee Evening Post*, 13 August 1904; Celtic Sports at Parkhead, *Scotsman*, 15 August 1904; Athletics: Celtic F.C. Sports, *Glasgow Herald*, 16 August 1904

64-65 'Jimmy had ... splendid runner': Wearin' the Green, *Scottish Referee*, 15 August 1904; Sprints, *Scottish Referee*, 15 August 1904; The Curran family still own the trophy won by Jimmy at this event.

65 'A week later ... the afternoon': Eastern Athletic Notes, *Scottish Referee*, 26 August 1904; Leith Sports Society, *Field*, 27 August 1904

65 'In September ... club captain': Gala Harriers Club, *Border Telegraph*, 13 September 1904

65 'He spent ... 20 seconds': Field and Fen, *Scottish Referee*, 10 October

1904; Harriers, *Southern Reporter*, 3 November 1904; Field and Fen, *Scottish Referee*, 4 November 1904; Harriers, *Southern Reporter*, 17 November 1904; *Border Telegraph*, 26 November 1904; Harriers, *Border Telegraph*, 6 December 1904; Harriers' Sports, *Jedburgh Gazette*, 7 January 1905; *Border Telegraph*, 28 March 1905

65   'Often he would ... far behind': The Old Gala Club, *Galashiels*, The History Press, 2011, p85

65   'These local runs ... top 12': The Harriers, *Edinburgh Evening News*, 10 February 1905; Harriers, *Dundee Courier*, 13 February 1905; Harrires [sic.], *Falkirk Herald*, 15 February 1905

65   'Jimmy's first race ... two miles': Rugby, *Scottish Referee*, 10 April 1905; Club Sports at Melrose, *Southern Reporter*, 13 April 1905; Eastern Athletic Notes, *Scottish Referee*, 28 April 1905; Edinburgh Harriers' Sports, *Southern Reporter*, 2 June 1905; Edinburgh Harriers Sports, *Sporting Life*, 6 June 1905

66   'Strangely his move ... G. Gordon': Amateur Runners Become Professionals, *Southern Reporter*, 15 June 1905

66   'Summer games and gatherings': The most well known of these gatherings were the Highland Games, but in the Borders they tended to be known as Common Ridings

66   'In June ... basket and stone': Hawick Common-Riding, *Southern Reporter*, 15 June 1905; Selkirk Common-Riding, 1905, *Southern Reporter*, 22 June 1905; Jedburgh Border Games, *Scotsman*, 10 July 1905; St Ronan's Border Games, *Southern Reporter*, 24 August 1905

66-67   'Compare this ... a miner': Arthur L. Bowley, *Wages in the United Kingdom in the Nineteenth Century: Notes for the Use of Students of Social and Economic Questions*, University Press, Cambridge, 1900; 20/- equals £1

67   'It is likely ... three places': Handicaps at Powderhall, *Scotsman*, 16 October 1905

67   'The world famous ... soon after': Edinburgh New Year Handicap, *Edinburgh Evening News*, 3 January 1906

67   'A week later ... 40-45 yards': Pedestrianism, *Scotsman*, 7 May 1906

67-68   'Jimmy's first known ... the hurdles': Selkirk Common-Riding, *Southern Reporter*, 21 June 1906

68   'In the following ... behind Duffus': West of Scotland Highland Games, *Scotsman*, 9 July 1906; Armadale Highland Games, *Scotsman*, 14 July 1906; Kelso Games, *Southern Reporter*, 26 July 1906; Greenlaw Games, *Berwickshire News and General Advertiser*, 31 July 1906; Alva

Gymnastic Games, *Scotsman*, 11 August 1906

68   'He strode … half-mile': Jedburgh Border Games, *Scotsman*, 16 July 1906; Jedburgh Games, *Southern Reporter*, 19 July 1906; Lochgelly Highland Games, *Dundee Courier*, 19 July 1906; Cleikum Ceremony at Innerleithen, *Southern Reporter*, 23 August 1906; Bute Highland Gathering, *Scotsman*, 25 August 1906; Cowal Highland Games, *Scottish Referee*, 27 August 1906

68   'In 1940 … running means': Scotch Games Said Colorful, *Waynesboro Record Herald*, 2 April 1940; Jimmy was still giving this talk 11 years later, this time at Greencastle Rotary Club, as detailed in 'Scotch Games' are Described at Rotary Meet, *Waynesboro Record Herald*, 13 March 1951; Mercersburg's Olympic Tradition, in *Mercersburg Magazine*, Volume XI, No.5, Summer 1984, p5

68   'September and October … nearest opponent': Half-mile Handicap at Powderhall Edinburgh, *Scotsman*, 17 September 1906; Half-Mile Handicap Winners at Powderhall, *Dundee Courier*, 8 October 1906

68-69   'In December … with ease': Newcastle £100 125 Yards Handicap, *Sporting Life*, 24 December 1906; Newcastle £100 Handicap: Victory of Eastman, *Sporting Life*, 26 December 1906

69   'As 1906 turned … in the process': The Powderhall Handicap, *Scotsman*, 3 January 1907; Pedestrianism: Conclusion of Powderhall Handicaps, *Aberdeen Press and Journal*, 4 January 1907; Powderhall Handicap, *Scottish Referee*, 4 January 1907

69   'Two days … £8 prize': The Edinburgh Gymnasium Handicap, *Scotsman*, 5 January 1907; The Gymnasium Handicap Winners, *Dundee Courier*, 5 January 1907; Pedestrianism: The Edinburgh Handicaps, *The Sportsman*, 5 January 1907; Scottish New Year Gala, *Sporting Life*, 5 January 1907

69   'The most glowing … in Britain': Sporting Jottings, *Border Telegraph*, 8 January 1907

69-70   'In the quiet … were married': Marriage Certificate of James Curran and Janet Mabon – 775/00 0013 [Sourced from www.scotlandspeople.gov.uk, 21 March 2015]; Marriage record of James Curran and Janet Mabon, in the parish of Our Lady & St Andrew, Galashiels – MP/78/1/1/1 [Sourced from www.findmypast.co.uk, 7 December 2019]; www.catholic.org /encyclopedia/view.php?id= 8048 [Accessed 13 March 2016]

70   'In many ways … feigning offence': Email from Laurie Danaher and

ENDNOTES AND SOURCES

Alanna Berger, 29 January 2017; Email from Alanna Berger, 23 April 2020

71 'His parents ... east of the town': Fall Down Stairs, *Southern Reporter*, 18 January 1906

71 'The Welshman ... be heading over': Athlete's Notebook, *Aberdeen People's Journal*, 21 September 1907

71 'So Jimmy paid ... RMS *Lusitania*': Drew Keeling, The Voyage Abstracts of the Cunard Line as a Source of Transatlantic Passenger Fares, 1883-1914 in *Business Archives Sources and History*, 96, 2008, pp.17-20 and p34

72 'The period of ... finished unplaced': Pedestrianism, *The Sportsman*, 26 March 1907

72 'In early April ... the handicap': Handicaps at Powderhall Grounds, Edinburgh, *Scotsman*, 8 April 1907

72 'Later in the month ... failed to win': Pedestrianism, *The Sportsman*, 20 May 1907

72 'The season began ... the mile': Highland Games, *Scottish Referee*, 3 May 1907

72 'A month later ... toed the mark': Sporting Jottings, *Border Telegraph*, 4 June 1907

72-73 'Days later ... at Dalkeith': Sporting Jottings, *Border Telegraph*, 11 June 1907; Selkirk Common Riding Sports, *Scotsman*, 17 June 1907; Swinton Games, *Berwickshire News & General Advertiser*, 25 June 1907; Rosewell Irish National Foresters, *Scottish Referee*, 1 July 1907

73 'His schedule ... and Jedburgh': Musselburgh Gardeners Games, *Scottish Referee*, 8 July 1907; Jedburgh Border Games, *Scotsman*, 15 July 1907; Births, Marriages, and Deaths, *Border Telegraph*, 23 July 1907; Birth Certificate of Mary Davidson Curran – 775/148 [Sourced from www.scotlandspeople.gov.uk, 21 March 2015]; Davidson was the maiden name of Janet's mother

73 'A small ... consolation race': Airth Annual Games, *Falkirk Herald*, 17 July 1907; Highland Gathering at Dunfermline, *Dundee Courier*, 18 July 1907; Thornton Highland Games, *Dundee Evening Telegraph*, 19 July 1907; Thornton Highland Games, *Fife Free Press & Kirkcaldy Guardian*, 20 July 1907

73 'The following day ... annual games': Athletics: Kelso Games, *Southern Reporter*, 25 July 1907

73 'Two days later ... Kinross Games': Kinross Highland Games,

Fifeshire Advertiser, 27 July 1907; Kinross July Fair and Games, *Kinross-shire Advertiser*, 27 July 1907

73-74 'On 27th July ... second place': Langholm Sports, *Scotsman*, 29 July 1907

74 'A week later ... 110 yards handicap': Strathallan Games, *Dundee Courier*, 5 August 1907

74 'He continued ... year's defeat': Lauder, *Southern Reporter*, 15 August 1907; Alva Gymnastic Games, *Alloa Advertiser*, 17 August 1907; The Games, *Southern Reporter*, 22 August 1907; Norman Dovey, *One Hundred and Fifty Years of the Alva Gymnastic Games*, N. Dovey, 2006

74 'At one of his ... take seconds': Sporting Jottings, *Border Telegraph*, 20 August 1907

74 'With the Scottish ... 120 yards handicap': Workington, *Sporting Life*, 26 August 1907

74 'A week later ... half-mile': Ullswater Sports, *Lancashire Evening Post*, 2 September 1907; Sporting Jottings, *Border Telegraph*, 3 September 1907

74 'A sprained ankle ... in Edinburgh': Sporting Jottings, *Border Telegraph*, 10 September 1907

74 'A 130 yards ... in the process': Handicaps at Powderhall Grounds, Edinburgh, *Scotsman*, 16 September 1907; Pedestrianism, *The Sportsman*, 30 September 1907

75 'In the four ... has ever produced': Sporting Jottings, *Border Telegraph*, 18 June 1907; Sporting Jottings, *Border Telegraph*, 25 June 1907; Athlete's Notebook, *Aberdeen People's Journal*, 21 September 1907

75 'In late September ... Atlantic Ocean': A Noted Gala Athlete, *Border Telegraph*, 8 October 1907

Chapter 6 · Ameriky Bound

77 'At the beginning ... 18 hours': E.J. Hobsbawm, *Industry and Empire: From 1750 to the Present Day*, Penguin Books, 1985, p93; Richard Brown, *Society and Economy in Britain 1700-1850*, Routledge, 1991, p84; David Powell, *Nationhood and Identity: The British State Since 1800*, I.B. Tauris Publishers, London and New York, 2002, p38

77 'And in their shadows ... carpet bag': Mercersburg Academy's Track Coach Has Earned Title of King of Realm, *Philadelphia Record*, 3 June 1928

ENDNOTES AND SOURCES

78 'Jammed up hard ... the river': www.old-merseytimes.co.uk/ lplpageant 1907.html [Accessed 22 May 2015]

78 'The city ... warehouses galore': Ordnance Survey 25" to the mile, CVI.6, Revised: 1906, Published: 1908; Ordnance Survey 25" to the mile, CVI.10, Revised: 1906, Published: 1908

78 'Three Graces': The Dock Office, later known as the Port of Liverpool Building, was opened in 1907 and was joined by the Royal Liver Building (1911) and the Cunard Building (1916). The close proximity of the three saw them identified locally as the Three Graces, so named after Antonio Canova's marble sculpture depicting the three daughters of Zeus.

78 Newspaper vendors ... Goodison Park': The Lusitania's Second Trip, *Liverpool Echo*, 4 October 1907; Football in Prospect, *Liverpool Echo*, 4 October 1907

78-79 'Horse-drawn carts ... through daily': Christian Fredericksen and Rick Fredericksen [ed.], *Lusitania Diary*, 2015

79 'Arriving in the city ... Line passengers': Sean Dennis Cashman, *America in the Age of Innocence: The Progressive Era and World War I*, New York University, 1988, p156; Kevin Brown, *Passage to the World: The Emigrant Experience 1807-1940*, Seaforth Publishing, 2013, p41

79-80 'The complex was ... Line physician': United States Immigration Commission, *Reports of the Immigration Commission*, Washington, 1907-1910, Volume 4, pp85-87; Fredericksen [ed.], op.cit.

80 'Living conditions ... the better': H. Phelps Whitmarsh, The Steerage of To-day: A Personal Experience in Century, in *The Century Illustrated Monthly Magazine*, Volume 55, New Series Volume 33, November 1897 to April 1898, pp528-543; Edward A. Steiner, *On the Trail of the Immigrant*, Fleming H. Revell Company, New York, Chicago, Toronto, London and Edinburgh, 1906, pp37-38 and p77

80 'Only a month ... Lincoln Cathedral': Liverpool Museum, Letter by C.R. Minnitt to Mrs E.M. Poole, 9 July 1907, DX/2284

80-81 'And the physical ... François Boucher': Greg King and Penny Wilson, *Lusitania: Triumph, Tragedy, and the End of the Edwardian Age*, St Martin's Press, New York, 2015; www.rmslusitania.info [Accessed 14 July 2016]

81 'Its 25 Scotch ... prove successful': Lusitania Arrives; Broke All Records, *New York Times*, 11 October 1907

81 'On leaving the dock ... tranquil oceans': Lusitania's Second Trip,

Dundee Courier, 7 October 1907; Lusitania, *North Devon Gazette*, 15 October 1907

81-82   'The journey itself … ship's piano': Broughton Brandenburg, *Imported Americans: the story of the experiences of a disguised American and his wife studying the immigration question*, Frederick A. Stokes Company, New York, 1904, p195; Fredericksen [ed.], op. cit.

82   'Not quite five … human beings': "Lusitania": Regains Blue Ribbon of Atlantic, *Western Times*, 12 October 1907

82-83   'Celebrations in steerage … ship's stokers': Sure Lusitania Can Go Even Faster, *New York Times*, 12 October 1907; Bransby Williams, *An Actor's Story*, Chapman & Hall, London, 1909, pp144-146; Brandenburg, op. cit., pp199-200; J. Kent Layton, *Lusitania: An Illustrated Biography*, Amberley Publishing, 2015

83   'That same purser … Lucy Tania': Lusitania's Trip, *Danville Republican*, 24 October 1907

83   'The liner remained … breaking ship': "Lusitania's" Triumphs, *Manchester Courier and Lancashire General Advertiser*, 12 October 1907; Williams, op. cit., p146

84   'And so Jimmy … weak and helpless': Steiner, op. cit., p72

84-85   'From the baggage … bald patch: Steiner, ibid., pp64-67; Barbara Benton, Ellis Island: A Pictorial History, Facts on File Publications, New York and Oxford, 1987, pp48-74; Peter Morton Coan, *Ellis Island Interviews: In Their Own Words*, Facts On File, New York, 1997, pp164-165

85-86   'So as Bransby … Jersey Terminal': Mark Hambourg Arrives, *New York Times*, 12 October 1907; Bransby Williams, *Bransby Williams, by Himself*, Hutchinson, London, 1954

86   'In the early … Harrisburg, Pennsylvania': Jedburgh Man's Death in America, *Jedburgh Gazette*, 12 September 1924

86   'That job was … head to toe': James J. David, *The Iron Puddler: My Life in the Rolling Mill and What Came of it*, Grosset & Dunlap, New York, c1922, pp90-92; *Wages and hours of labor in the iron and steel industry:1907-1924*, US Government Printing Office, Washington, 1925, p66; *Reading Times*, 15 November 1938; David S. Landes, *The Unbound Prometheus: Technological change and industrial development in Western Europe from 1750 to the present*, Cambridge University Press, Cambridge, 2003, p218

86   'corner the stock': Cornering the market on a commodity or stock is

324

a means by which to fix the price

86-87   'But Jimmy … almost doubled': Carola Frydman, Eric Hilt, and Lily Y. Zhou, *The Panic of 1907: JP Morgan, Trust Companies, and the Impact of the Financial Crisis*, p2; Elmus Wicker, *Banking Panics in the Gilded Age*, Cambridge University Press, Cambridge, 2000, p110; Federal Reserve Bank of Boston, *Panic of 1907* – www.bostonfed.org/about/pubs /panicof1.pdf [Accessed 12 May 2015]

87   'Jimmy had barely … to 3,809': Will Resume January 6, *The Morning News*, 23 December 1907

87-88   'At one of these … drooping moustache': Hit By 16-Pound Hammer, *Tyrone Daily Herald*, 16 April 1908; "Scotty" Seriously Injured, *The Pennsylvanian*, 14 April 1908; Mercersburg Academy's Track Coach Has Earned Title of King of Realm, *Philadelphia Record*, 3 June 1928

88   'If Mike Murphy … the job': Payne, Stewart and Foran: Curran Watched Stars Star on Cinders First, *St Petersburg Independent*, 24 April 1960

88-89   'Born in Westboro … we considered': Greatest of All Athletic Trainers, *Cincinnati Enquirer*, 9 June 1913

89-90   'But Murphy … one mile': Mike Murphy Occupies Unique Position in Athletic World, *Washington Post*, 13 December 1908

90-91   'A coach without … his charge': *Boston Daily Globe*, 11 November 1894; The Baseball Trainer, *Logansport Pharos*, 21 April 1910; Trainer Mike Dee To Stay With Phillies, *Pittsburgh Press*, 3 January 1911, p20; First Aid To Charley-Horse, *The Day Book*, Volume 1, Number 154, 25 March 1912, pp13-15

91   'The rubber … random jobs': The Baseball Trainer, *Logansport Pharos*, 21 April 1910

91   'Jimmy's fellow … physical adviser': Mike Dee Dies at 86, *Philadelphia Inquirer*, 21 December 1954

91   'In 1913 … athletics field': Harry Andrews, *Training for Athletics and General Health*, C. Arthur Pearson, London, 1911, pp21-22; Consistent Training is Secret of Kolehmainen's Great Feats, *Washington Post*, 23 February 1913

91   'So Jimmy … race winnings': Training Big Teams, *Washington Post*, 3 December 1905

Chapter 7 • A Race Like No Other

94 'Halswelle's star … blue blood': Halswelle Retires With Great Record, *Washington Times*, 5 July 1909

94 'With possibilities … the workshop': Edinburgh Harriers' Meeting at Powderhall, *Scotsman*, 7 June 1909

95 'Halswelle was … James Lightbody': The 400 Metres Foot Race, *Sheffield Evening Telegraph*, 30 April 1906; Upsets in Olympics, *Washington Post*, 25 December 1911; Bill Mallon, *The 1906 Olympic Games: Results for All Competitors in All Events, with Commentary*, McFarland & Co. Inc, Jefferson, North Carolina and London, 1999, pp37-42

95 'An injury … 400 metres': Hero From a Forsaken Generation, *The Herald*, 21 July 2008; Both records were eventually beaten by men who were to find a degree of fame in their own right, outside athletics. His 300 yards record fell, in 1961, to Menzies Campbell, who served as a Member of Parliament from 1987-2015. His 440 yards record was beaten, in 1934, by Godfrey Rampling, whose daughter Charlotte would go on to become an actress of note. The 440 yards time was not beaten by another Scot until John McIsaac bettered it in 1958.

95 'But before … Edward VII': Dr Bill Mallon M.D. and Ian Buchanan, To No Earthly King: The United States Flag-Bearing Incident at the 1908 Olympic Games Opening Ceremony, in *Journal of Olympic History*, September 1999 – http://isoh.org/wp-content/uploads/2015/04/99.pdf [Accessed 9 May 2020]

95 'White City Stadium': The term White City was first coined to describe the temporary amusement park at Chicago's World Columbian Exposition in 1893. Thereafter it was commonly used for many amusement parks and stadia across America and the rest of the world. Jimmy is known to have raced at at least two – in Trenton and Philadelphia – while both Wyndham Halswelle and Jimmy's son competed at London's White City Stadium.

95-96 'What followed … the Americans'; Queen Honors Victors, *New York Tribune*, 26 July 1908; Bill Mallon and Ian Buchanan, *The 1908 Olympic Games: Results for All Competitors in All Events, with Commentary*, McFarland & Company, Inc., Jefferson, North Carolina, 2000, pp328-331

96 'And even the crowd … to desist'; A Bitter Wrangle Over Olympic

ENDNOTES AND SOURCES

Race, *New York Times*, 24 July 1908

96-97   'Lining up … in the final': Sensation at the Stadium, *Scotsman*, 24 July 1908; Robbed of Victory, *Washington Post*, 24 July 1908; A Bitter Wrangle Over Olympic Race, *New York Times*, 24 July 1908; *Fifty Years of Athletics: An Historical Record of the Scottish Amateur Athletic Association 1883-1933*, Scottish Amateur Athletic Association, Edinburgh, 1933, p56; Mallon and Buchanan, *1908 Olympic* Games; op. cit., pp52-55, p333 and p364; Edward S. Sears, *Running Through the Ages*, 2nd edition, McFarland & Co. Inc., Jefferson, 2005, pp188-190; A summary of events is given at www.sports-reference.com/olympics/summer/1908/ATH/mens-400-metres.html [Accessed 14 February 2016] and it provides details of the dispute over the US rules and also accounts by both Halswelle and Carpenter; The version of events given by newspapers varies, with British publications almost wholly echoing Halswelle's view that he was driven to the edge of the track. US newspapers were less supportive, with the *Washington Post* denying any elbowing took place, and that Carpenter had Halswelle well beaten as they entered the final straight. The *New York Times* was more circumspect, noting that the athletes had gone wide on the final bend, but that it could see no foul. The opinions of officials were also split, again generally on national lines. Bill Mallon and Ian Buchanan note that photographic evidence points towards the fact that Carpenter did indeed drive Halswelle to the periphery of the track.

97   'Just when Halswelle … ever seen run': Halswelle Retires With Great Record, *Washington Times*, 5 July 1909

Chapter 8 • A Roller Skater, Two Indians, a Welshman and the Great Alfie Shrubb

For a solid overview of amateurism and professionalism in American sport, see Ted Vincent, *The Rise and Fall of American Sport: Mudville's Revenge*, University of Nebraska Press, Lincoln and London, 1994

99-100   'One evening … Park Track': Mercersburg Academy's Track Coach Has Earned Title of King of Realm, *Philadelphia Record*, 3 June 1928; The Old Sport's Musings, *Philadelphia Inquirer*, 15 January 1936; One article notes that the day after his race against Nellie Brookmeyer he was actually taken to Washington Park.

100 'A typical … around 2,000': Curran Outran Indian, *Topeka State Journal*, 5 February 1908; http://carlisleindian.dickinson .edu/sites/ all/files/docs-ephemera/NARA_1327_b154 _f6077.pdf

100 'Within weeks … highly of Jimmy': Bob Dunbar's Sporting Chat, *Boston Herald*, 3 December 1907

100-101 'Organised athletic … years later': Howard J. Savage, Harold W. Bentley, John T. McGovern and Dean F. Smiley, *American College Athletics*, Bulletin Number Twenty-Three, Carnegie Foundation for the Advancement of Teaching, New York, 1929, p17; Emily Ann Donaldson, *The Scottish Highland Games in America*, Pelican Publishing Company, Gretna, 1986 pp23-50; Ronald A. Smith, *Sports and Freedom: The Rise of Big-Time College Athletics*, Oxford University Press, Oxford and New York, 1988, pp99-111

101 'The growth … hill runs': Savage, ibid., p15

101 'But it was … coast colleges': Sears, ibid., pp66-67

101-102 'And many colleges … against Yale': Smith, ibid., pp147-164

102 'A year after … we compete': William T. Reid Jr., Football and Coaching in *Harvard Graduates' Magazine XV*, March 1907, p400

102 'When Jimmy … 100 yards': For an in-depth report of this record-breaking race see Alexander Kidd, The Fastest Sprint: How Arthur F. Duffey Made a New World's Record, in *Outing: An Illustrated Magazine of Sport Travel Adventure and Country Life*, Volume XL, April-September 1902, Outing Publishing Company, New York, pp433-439

102-103 'Duffey wanted … far enough': Many Organizations Represented at Protective Basketball Dinner, *Brooklyn Standard Union*, May 1907

103 'On hearing … keep out': Fate of Y.M.C.A. Will Be Decided at A.A.U. Meeting, *Washington Times*, 14 November 1907

103-104 Duffey's admission … on Duffey': To Prosecute Duffey Legally, If Possible, *New York Times*, 29 October 1905; President Maccabe Arraigns Former Georgetown Sprinter, A.F. Duffey, *New York Times*, 21 November 1905; Sears, ibid., pp167-168

104 'He was not … in America': Quaker Athletes Fight the A.A.U., *Brooklyn Daily Eagle*, 24 January 1908; Bob Dunbar's Sporting Chat, *Boston Journal*, 28 January 1908

105 'In January 1908 … actually happened': Kanaly Accepts Challenge from James Curren [sic.], *Daily Kennebec Journal*, 21 January 1908

ENDNOTES AND SOURCES

105   'Later in the year ... and $500': Curran's Broad Challenge, *Boston Herald*, 14 August 1908

105   'promoter for Jimmy': Within two years of arriving in America Jimmy had had a number of managers or, more accurately, promoters. Four are known – Arthur Duffey, Jack Roden, Al Nash, and Jack Cavanagh. Jimmy also acted as a manager/promoter, this position being noted on a letterhead produced for Al Nash and available to view at http://carlisleindian.dickinson.edu/sites/all/files/docs-ephemera/NARA_1327_b154_f6077.pdf [Accessed 19th January 2019]

105   'Jimmy's first known ... Shrubb's lead': Indians to Race Shrubb, *Boston Herald*, 13 January 1908; *Shrubb Outruns Five Men*, The Evening World, 17 January 1908; Shrubb Wins 10-Mile Race, *Boston Daily Globe*, 17 January 1908; Invincible Shrubb Again Victorious, *Boston Post*, 17 January 1908

106   'A week later ... tennis shoes': Al Shrubb Wins the Relay Race, *Philadelphia Inquirer*, 24 January 1908; Shrubb Outruns Four Men in Six-Mile Race, *Indianapolis News*, 24 January 1908; Shrubb a Winner, *Victoria Daily Colonist*, 13 February 1908

106   'Conversely it meant ... 25 yards': Curran and Tallfeather, *Philadelphia Inquirer*, 22 February 1908; Trenton Runners in Phila. Event, *Trenton Evening Times*, 22 February 1908

106   'Races were limited ... 1,000 yards race': Roden's Band Touring State, *Philadelphia Inquirer*, 5 April 1908

106-107 'Next he headed ... the other': *Hammond Lake County Times*, 2 April 1908; Burns Club Holds Games, *Philadelphia Inquirer*, 14 June 1908; Seaman Won Half: Second in Mile Run, *Trenton Evening Times*, 14 June 1908

107   'Over the next ... $20 richer': "Jack" Cody Will Referee the Walk, *Trenton Evening Times*, 14 June 1908; Geo. Seaman Finished Second in Two Races, *Trenton Sunday Times*, 28 June 1908; Seaman Won Twice, *Trenton Evening Times*, 29 June 1908; Royal Oak Lodge Ready for Games, *Trenton Evening Times*, 2 July 1908; Seaman Won $20, *Trenton Evening Times*, 13 July 1908; Caledonian Club Holds Its Sports, *Philadelphia Inquirer*, 2 August 1908

107   'On 29th August ... prize money': Banner Outing for Bricklayers, *Philadelphia Inquirer*, 30 August 1908; Billy Paul Won Great Mile Race, *Trenton Evening Times*, 31 August 1908

JIMMY CURRAN

107   'On 7th September ... purse of $50': Alcock Won in Handicap Match, *Trenton Evening Times*, 8 September 1908

107   'Billy Paull': Paull was one of Jimmy's athletes at the University of Pennsylvania, having earlier attended Mercersburg Academy

107   'After the race ... profitable day': Labor Day Race at White City, *Trenton Evening Times*, 3 September 1908; Two Mile Race at White City Park, *Trenton Evening Times*, 7 September 1908; Curran Won at White City, *Trenton Evening Times*, 8 September 1908; Curran Defeats Paul, *Philadelphia Inquirer*, 8 September 1908

107-108 'Five days later ... world record': Shrubb's 5-Mile Race, *New York Times*, 13 September 1908; Shrubb Makes World's Record, *Philadelphia Inquirer*, 13 September 1908

108   'Jimmy's exhausting ... Franklin Field': Manifest of SS *Furnessia*, Glasgow to New York City, 19 September 1908

108   'The first was ... Percy Smallwood': Best Distance Men in the World Entered, *Trenton Evening Times*, 22 November 1908; Thanksgiving Day Races, *Trenton Evening Times*, 23 November 1908

108   'The result ... won out': English Champion Wins Against Four, *Washington Times*, 27 November 1908; Shrubb Easily Defeats Relay of Four in 8 Miles, *Buffalo Courier*, 28 November 1908

109   'Jimmy's first ... the winner': Dorando Matched With Smallwood, *Washington Times*, 3 February 1909; Welsh Runner is Beaten, *Rock Island Argus*, 12 February 1909; Smallwood Quit in Indoor Race, *Philadelphia Inquirer*, 12 February 1909; *Sporting Life*, 1 March 1909

109   'On 5th March ... the process': White Quits Race With Matt Maloney, *New York Times*, 6 March 1909; Maloney Wins Marathon, *The Sun*, 6 March 1909

109   'Three days ... tenth hour': Six Day Race is Begun at Awful Pace, *Glen Falls Daily Times*, 8 March 1909; Long Run in New York, *Duluth Evening Herald*, 8 March 1909; Pedestrians Start in Six-Day Race, *New York Times*, 8 March 1909; Pedestrians in Seven-Day Race, *Anaconda Standard*, 8 March 1909

109-110 'Two days later ... finished third': Dorando in Newark Tonight, *New York Press*, 9 March 1909; Dorando Will Run at Newark Tonight, *Washington Times*, 9 March 1909; Pride of Pittsburg: Great Welsh Fleet Foot, *Evening Express and Evening Mail*, 29 April 1909

110   'Interspersed throughout ... two laps': Swedish Runner Wins 10-Mile Race, *New York Times*, 11 March 1909

110   'Next was ... first place': Weary Walkers' Grind Near Its End, *New York Times*, 13 March 1909

110   'But so many ... three months': Three Famous Runners Prominent in the Public Eye, *Idaho Statesman*, 29 August 1909

110   'Curious as to ... most races': *Scottish Referee*, 3 May 1909; Powderhall Grounds, Edinburgh, *Sporting Life*, 11 May 1909; Murray Wins Half-Mile Handicap, *Sporting Life*, 27 December 1909; David A. Jamieson, *Powderhall and Pedestrianism: The History of a Famous Sports Enclosure*, 1870-1943, W. & A.K. Johnston, Edinburgh, 1943

110   'But if ... mile race': Burns Club Sports, *Philadelphia Inquirer*, 13 June 1909

110   'In early July ... half-mile races': Curran Stars in Irish Track Meet, *Philadelphia Inquirer*, 6 July 1909

110   'A fortnight later ... his partner': Curran Wins 1000-Yard Run, *Philadelphia Inquirer*, 17 July 1909

110-111 'The following weekend ... professional run': Two New Pros Do Well, *The Sun*, 26 July 1909

111   'A week later ... the races': Curran Stars in River Sports, *Philadelphia Inquirer*, 1 August 1909

111   'On 14th August ... potato race': Foresters Race at Central Park, *Philadelphia Inquirer*, 15 August 1909

111   'By 6th September ... easy victory': Muller's Five-Mile Run, *New York Times*, 7 September 1909

Chapter 9 • Mercersburg

Much of the background material in this chapter was derived from Matt J. Webber's immensely detailed *Dropping the Bucket and Sponge: A History of Athletic Training 1887-1941*, published in 2013.

113   'Alfie Shrubb ... eventually sacked': Hadgraft, op. cit.

113   'Alvin Kraenzlein ... patchy at best': *The Karux*, The Boys of the Mercersburg Academy, 1918, pp115-116

113   'Only time ... his stride': Sport Brief, *Waynesboro Record Herald*, 3 March 1941; Mercersburg Coach Marked 70th Birthday With Aggressive Game of Handball, *Sunday Bulletin*, 15 January 1950; *Philadelphia Evening Bulletin*, January 1950; Email from Jef Evans, 27

JIMMY CURRAN

November 2018

113-114 'It came … over to Jimmy': Cross Country, *The Pennsylvanian*, Volume XXV, No.21, 18 October 1909

114 'Before Boston … Mike Murphy': 1913 Defeats Mercersburg, *The Pennsylvanian*, Volume XXV, No.37, 3 November 1909

114 'Less than … were good': Cross Country Team Wins, *The Pennsylvanian*, Volume XXV, No.41, 8 November 1909

114 'The team travelled … poor performance': Cornell Wins Again, *The Pennsylvanian*, Volume XXV, No.53, 22 November 1909; *Lincoln Daily News*, 4 September 1912

114 'By autumn … the University': Mike Murphy's Influence, *Washington Post*, 25 June 1905; Princeton's New Trainer, *New York Times*, 10 February 1910; From a discussion with Doug Smith, Mercersburg Academy archivist, 3 September 2018

114 'But in order … baseball team': *Philadelphia Inquirer*, 30 December 1909; Local Jottings, *Sporting Life*, 8 January 1910; Tex Ramsdell to Run Abroad, *Indianapolis Star*, 18 June 1911

115 'He would … to possess': The Good Trust Guarding Thirty Thousand Collegians, *San Francisco Call*, 29 October 1911

115 'Approached by … Jimmy Curran': Mercersburg Group Send Coach Overseas, *Harrisburg Telegraph*, 7 June 1924

115 'And so … plus a house': Borderers in America, *Hawick News and Border Chronicle*, 2 September 1910

115 'Jimmy didn't … his life': Curran, New Track Coach, *Mercersburg Academy Alumni Quarterly*, November 1910, Volume 5, No.2, p9; Spotlight on Sports, *Hagerstown Daily Mail*, 8 February 1963

115-116 'In 17 years … Oxford of America': Girard's Talk of the Day, *Philadelphia Inquirer*, 10 January 1929

116 'The school placed … his predecessors': *The Karux*, Mercersburg Academy, 1950, p113

116 'By early century … University of Michigan': *The Karux*, The Boys of the Mercersburg Academy, 1918, pp115-116

117 'It was an opportune … years later': *The Karux*, The Boys of the Mercersburg Academy, 1918, pp5-6

117 'In 1813 … modern athlete': Walter Thom, *Pedestrianism; or, an account of the performances of celebrated pedestrians during the last and present century; with a full narrative of Captain Barclay's public and private matches; and an essay on training*, Aberdeen, 1813, pp221-248

ENDNOTES AND SOURCES

117   'In the following ... from it': For example see C.J. Michôd, *Good Condition: A Guide to Athletic Training for Amateurs or Professionals*, Robert Hardwicke, London, 1874; R.V. Somers-Smith, G.P. Beckley and A.W. Pollard, *Athletic Training. Prize Essays*, Simpkin, Marshall & Co., London, 1882

117   'But by the ... maximum potential': Randolph Faries, *Practical Training for Athletics, Health and Pleasure*, Outing Publishing Company, New York and London, 1897

118   'In 1913 ... the sport': Michael C. Murphy, *Athletic Training*, Charles Scribner's Sons, New York, 1914

118   'By the late ... premature death': James C. Whorton, 'Athlete's Heart': The Medical Debate Over Athleticism, 1870-1920, in *Journal of Sport History*, Volume 9, No.1, Spring 1982, p37

118   'In 1899 ... life-threatening occurrence': Aaron L. Baggish and Malissa J. Wood, Athlete's Heart and Cardiovascular Care of the Athlete: Scientific and Clinical Update, in *Circulation*, 2011, 123 (23), pp2723-2735

118-119   'Although scepticism ... Mike Murphy': Felix Deutsch and Emil Kauf, *Heart and athletics: clinical researches upon the influence of athletics upon the heart*, The C.V. Mosby Company, St Louis 1927, p172

119   'The dangers ... strengthened it': Murphy, ibid., pp150-153

119   'It is said ... other sprinters': Crouch Start in Athletics, *Meridien Morning Record*, 12 December 1912; Jimmy Ryan Said to have Invented Crouch Start, *Pittsburgh Press*, 10 February 1913; Murphy Invents Crouch, *The Spokesman-Review*, 22 March 1913; Who Originated the 'Crouch Start'?, *Brooklyn Daily Eagle*, 30 June 1936; Edward S. Sears, *Running Through the Ages*, 2nd edition, McFarland & Co. Inc., Jefferson, 2005, pp96-98. Those claiming the invention of the crouching start include an Aboriginal sprinter called Bobby McDonald, US champion Tommy Lee, multiple world record holder Lon Myers, and Irishman Jimmy Ryan.

119-120   'To shave them ... his weaknesses': Murphy's View on Training, *Pittsburgh Press*, 6 November 1904

120   'And where ... a season': Murphy, ibid., pp173-174

120   'And when ... elastic bandages': Mike Murphy Occupies Unique Position in Athletic World, *Washington Post*, 13 December 1908; Sickness of Mike Murphy, Trainer, Handicap to Olympic Athletes, *Anaconda Standard*, 28 January 1912; Matt J. Webber, *Dropping the*

JIMMY CURRAN

Bucket and Sponge: A History of Athletic Training 1887-1941, 2013

120   'Randolph Faries ... mental harmony': Faries, ibid., p97

120   'George W. Orton ... would be fatal': R.V. Somers-Smith, G.P. Beckley and A.W. Pollard, *Athletic Training. Prize Essays*, Simpkin, Marshall & Co., London, 1882; George W. Orton, *Athletic Training for School Boys*, The British Sports Publishing Co., Ltd, Spalding's Athletic Library, No.16, London, 1907

120   'Even the great ... wrapping paper': Murphy, ibid., pp71-72

120-121   'And Jimmy ... weakening effect': Mercersburg Star Track Trainer Follows His Own Set of Rules, *Harrisburg Courier*, 23 April 1916

121   'He also ... long stride': *Mercersburg Magazine*, Volume XI, No.5, Summer 1984, p5; Jeremy Schaap, Triumph: The Untold Story of Jesse Owens and Hitler's Olympics, Houghton Mifflin Harcourt, 2008; Email from David Emory Jr, 9 December 2016

121   There have been three incarnations of the Williams Cup. It was first presented to the school in 1905, and then in 1923 and 1949, all by members of the Williams family.

121   'In 1915 ... standout athlete': Penn. Gets Bang-up Schoolboy Athletes, *Johnson City-Endicott Record*, 16 October 1915

121-122   'Larry Lattomus ... of course': Email from Larry Lattomus, 7 July 2015

122   'Lester Cagle ... high hurdler': Telephone interview with Seth Cagle, 6 July 2019

122   'A decade later ... Eric Liddell': Conway Enters Olympic Field, *New York Telegram and Evening Mail*, 5 May 1924

122   'In the 1950s ... breathing techniques': Letter from Henry Thresher, 8 May 2015

122   'And a long ... for height': Telephone interview with Andy Anderson, 12 February 2019

122-123   'According to Paul ... exchange zone': Paul F. White, *How Sir James Michael Curran Influenced My Life*, unpublished, 2016

123   'This relentless ... sloppiness': Email from Larry Lattomus, 7 July 2015

123   'Indeed, in his ... the baton': Email from Gus Ormrod, 25 July 2016

123   'Charles Hill ... help today': Prep School Sports, *New York Times*, 12 November 1956

123   'And Bob Batdorf ... trained themselves': Email from Bob Batdorf, 12 March 2018

123   'So respected ... his knowledge': J.E. ('Ted') Meredith [ed.], Middle Distance and Relay Racing, American Sports Publishing Company, Spalding Track and Field Series of Athletic Textbooks No.502B, New York, 1925; Although no evidence was found that Jimmy authored, part-authored, or offered advice about this book, his name is listed in the acknowledgements. It is not listed in the acknowledgements of any previous books, which suggests he was involved to some extent in the publication of this edition.

123   'This standing ... the track': Turners' Relay Team to Use New Baton-Passing System, *Philadelphia Inquirer*, 28 March 1946

123-124 'And his intimate ... his wounds': Jimmy Curran's Quartet Wins 31st Relay Crown, *Waynesboro Record Herald*, 1 May 1961

124   'In 1942 ... be broken': How to Run a Four-Minute Mile, *Pittsburgh Sun-Telegraph*, 21 April 1942

124   'When the Scottish ... he turned': *Boston Globe*, 31 December 1912

124   'And Jack Green ... Easter break': Jack Green Places Fourth in Rodman Wanamaker "660" Race, *Shippensburg News-Chronicle*, 23 February 1932

124   'Jimmy's over-riding ... under pressure': Mercersburg Track Trainer Follows His Own Set of Rules, *Harrisburg Courier*, 23 April 1916

124-125 'Food, he told ... upset stomach': Mercersburg Track Trainer Follows His Own Set of Rules, *Harrisburg Courier*, 23 April 1916; J.E. Ted Meredith, *Dear Mums, Poverty and War – A Working Boy's Story, 1936-1947*, 2001; Letter from Henry Thresher, 8 May 2015

125   'On a trip ... such fancies': Arthur F. Duffey, *How To Sprint*, The British Sports Publishing Co., Ltd, Spalding's Athletic Library No.8, London, [1906], p45

125   'In 1913 ... with him': Consistent Training is Secret of Kolehmainen's Great Feats, *Washington Post*, 23 February 1911

125   'A boy ... aspire to': Mr Curran Addresses Y.M.C.A., *Mercersburg Academy Alumni Quarterly*, November 1918, Volume 14, No.1, pp17-18

125   'Jimmy had ... runs himself': Curran Develops Noted Harriers, *Evening Public Ledger*, 6 December 1917

125-126 'He had learned ... record height': Murphy is Crowned the Wizard Trainer of the Civilized World, *Butte Miner*, 9 August 1908

126   'Gus Ormrod ... a chance': Email from Gus Ormrod, 27 July 2016

126   'And this belief ... his career': Halswelle Retires With Great Record,

Washington Times, 5 July 1909

126   'Sprinter Paul White … stressful meets': White, op. cit.

126-127 'In 2015 … go wrong': Rebecca Adlington and Mark Foster, Discussion at Swimming World Championships, BBC1, 6 August 2015

127   'In 1898 … sporting performance': Norman Triplett, The Dynamogenic Factors in Pacemaking and Competition, in *The American Journal of Psychology*, Volume 9, No.4, July 1898, pp507-533

127   'In 1920 … sports psychology': https://andydriska.wordpress.com/2011/06/26/a-brief-history-of-sport-psychology [Accessed 9 September 2016]

127   'Mike Murphy … an evangelist': Charles Halsted Mapes, *The Man Who One Day a Year Would Go Eelin, and Some Other Little College Things - Mostly Athletic*, G.P. Putnam & Sons, London and New York, 1913, p16

127   'Mike Dee … frame of mind': Mike Dee Dies at 86, *Philadelphia Inquirer*, 21 December 1954

127-128 'Jimmy's opening … any good': Mercersburg Track Trainer Follows His Own Set of Rules, *Harrisburg Courier*, 23 April 1916

128   'Charles Moore … faith in me': Moore, Jr with Herzog, *One Hurdle at a Time: An Olympian's Guide to Clearing Life's Obstacles*, Edgemoor Ink, 2017, p56

128   'Andy Anderson … the height': Telephone interview with Andy Anderson, 12 February 2019

128   'On one occasion … the race': Letter from Don D. Hill to Albert L. Watson Jr, 20 December 1984, in Mercersburg Academy Archive

128   'Jimmy would … good efforts': White, op. cit.

128   'Jef Evans … his hand': Email from Jef Evans, 26 November 2018

128-129 'In 1957 … jump of 23' 5½': Telephone interview with Andy Anderson, 12 February 2019; As of February 2019, Anderson's jump of 23' 5½" still stands as the school record

129   'Ted Meredith … 440 yards': Claim That Robinson Can Beat Ted Meredith, *Sunday Union*, 19 January 1913

129   'After winning … in myself': Moore, *One Hurdle*, op. cit., p57

129   'Jef Evans … had before': Email from Jef Evans, 13 January 2020

129   'By the late … coming meet': Email from Gus Ormrod, 27 July 2016

129   'And if a private … r-r-r-r-race': J.E. Ted Meredith, *Dear Mums, Poverty and War – A Working Boy's Story, 1936-1947*, 2001

ENDNOTES AND SOURCES

129-130 'But he was ... offer support': Email from Gus Ormrod, 25 July 2016

130 'Jef Evans ... had none': Email from Jef Evans, 26 November 2018

130-131 'And very occasionally ... mentioned again': Telephone interview with Andy Anderson, 12 February 2019

131 'On at least ... the team': Jimmy Curran Speaks at Dinner Honoring Championship Teams, *Waynesboro Record Herald*, 29 March 1946

131 'Whilst perfect ... needed advice': Telephone interview with Henry Thresher, 9 April 2015

131-132 'Gus Ormrod ... do it again': Email from Gus Ormrod, 25 July 2016

132 'In the 1950s ... the school': Prep School Sports, *New York Times*, 8 October 1956; Reader Extolls the Sport of Tubing, *New York Times*, 3 May 1959; Emails from Christopher Montgomery, 27 December 2015 and 12 January 2016

132 'It was said ... for Mike': Mapes, op. cit., p16

133 'In 1930 ... his tyres': *The Karux*, The Students of the Mercersburg Academy, 1930, p230

133 'Five years later ... developing film': Sporting Gossip, *International Herald Tribune*, 14 August 1935

133 'And in 1957 ... cost money': *Penn to Name Track Coach*, New York Times, 6 May 1957

133 'On his retirement ... after lunch': Robertson Retires at Penn; Famous Olympic Coach, *Philadelphia Inquirer*, 8 July 1947

133-134 'And Ed Pollock ... to spend': *Philadelphia Evening Bulletin*, February 1963

134 'Spurred on ... free of charge': *The Karux*, The Students of the Mercersburg Academy, 1922, p188; Letter from Henry Thresher, 8 May 2015

134 'Scot's [sic.] Thistle': A Philadelphia benevolent society founded in 1796 to aid Scottish immigrants

134 'But he was ... which war': Email from Laurie Danaher, 11 August 2019

134 'In 1957 ... coming out': Email from Hank Spire, 22 December 2015

134-135 'And just ... the track': Email from Harry Pickle III, 25 December 2015

135 'And even ... start line': Email from Harper Girvin, 11 January 2016

136 'In the years ... pair of heels': Curran Develops Noted Harriers, *Evening Public Ledger*, 6 December 1917

136 'Whilst Jimmy ... did impart': Telephone interview with Henry

Thresher, 9 April 2015

136   'In 1923 … his daughter': *Mercersburg Academy Alumni Quarterly*, October 1923, Volume 19, No.1, p38

136   'And in 1927 … best man': Yale Man Closes College Career With Marriage, *New York Herald Tribune*, 7 October 1927; Letter from Don D. Hill to Albert L Watson Jr, 20 December 1984

136-137   'For Jef Evans … got on well': Email from Jef Evans, 8 December 2018

137   'Jimmy was offered … leave Mercersburg': New Track Coach Considered, *Daily Pennsylvanian*, Volume XXXI, No.151, 13 April 1916; Arthur Duffey's Comment on Sports, *Boston Post*, 15 April 1916; Penn to Name Track Coach, *New York Times*, 19 April 1916; Robertson May Land Job as Penn Coach, *New Castle News*, 20 April 1916; Many Colleges After Mercersburg Coach, *Evening Public Ledger*, 15 May 1918; Live Tips and Tricks, *Boston Daily Globe*, 15 September 1922; Notes of School Sports, *Boston Globe*, 24 March 1924; Mercersburg Group Send Coach Overseas, *Harrisburg Telegraph*, 7 June 1924; A search was made in the Phillips Exeter Academy archives for information on Jimmy's interview for the head coaching role, but none was found.

137   'In 1906 … around $7,500': Murphy to Quit Yale, *Boston Evening Transcript*, 29 May 1905; Makes a Hit at Princeton, *Washington Post*, 26 November 1911; On 13 December 1908 the Washington Post printed an article stating that Mike Murphy was earning $10,000 a year, but Matt J. Webber, in *Dropping the Bucket and Sponge*, notes that this figure is erroneous. United States Bureau of the Census, *The Statistical History of the United States: From Colonial Times to the Present*, Basic Books Inc., Publishers, New York, 1976, p164; Brudnick, Ida A., *Salaries of Members of Congress: Recent Actions and Historical Tables*, Congregational Research Service, Washington, D.C., 2014, p11

137   'A fellow … college presidents': Archibald Rutledge, *When Boys Go Off to School*, Fleming H. Revell Company, New York, London and Edinburgh, 1935, p19

137-138   'Examples can … golf irons': Mercersburg Group Send Coach Overseas, *Harrisburg Telegraph*, 7 June 1924; Grads Fete Coach of Mercersburg, *Philadelphia Inquirer*, 28 April 1950; Coach Honored … Curran Is Given Trip to Europe, *Hagerstown Morning Herald*, 23 January 1960

138 'Jimmy, his … wry smile': *Philadelphia Evening Bulletin*, January 1950

139 'Jimmy's team … Princeton Freshmen': The Weekly Bulletin, *Daily Princetonian*, Volume 35, No.103, 24 November 1910

139 'The result … individual honours': Barringer School Wins Run, *Baltimore Sun*, 6 November 1910; Barringer High Winner, *Daily Princetonian*, Volume 35, No.115, 7 November 1910

139 'A week later … again victorious': Mercersburg Loses Cross Country, *Pittsburgh Gazette Times*, 13 November 1910

139 'The track season … Penn Relays': Hopkins Wins Meet, *Baltimore Sun*, 12 February 1911; Cornell and Pennsy Win Relay Titles, *New York Times*, 30 April 1911

139 'Victories at … Princeton meet': F. & M. Scholastic Meet, *Philadelphia Inquirer*, 7 May 1911; Hill School's Tiger Meet, *New York Times*, 14 May 1911; Mercersburg Wins Meet From Penn Freshies, *Pittsburgh Gazette Times*, 30 May 1911

Chapter 10 • The Greatest Year

Much of the information relating to Ted Meredith was sourced prior to reading John Jack Lemon's wonderful biography of Meredith, *Immortal of the Cinder Path*. However, upon receiving a copy from the author I was able to double-check my facts and add additional information based on this work.

141 'In 1908 … in London': "Ted" Meredith's Great Race, *Boston Evening Transcript*, 15 August 1912; How It Feels To Be Winner, *Helena Independent Record*, 18 August 1912

141 'His family … a bricklayer': Harold Wilson Jr, Schoolboy Ted Meredith's Amazing Stockholm Games, in *Journal of Olympics History*, 16, July 2008, No.2, p15 – http://isoh.org/wp-content/uploads /2015/03/181.pdf [Accessed 9 May 2020]

141-142 'His own introduction … certain death': Analysis of the Style of James E. Meredith, National Quarter-Mile Champion, *New York Times*, 26 March 1916

142 'At this time … the mile': James C. Curran [sic.], Training the World's Half-Miler: How "Ted" Meredith, The Wonderful School-boy Athlete and Olympic Champion, Was Developed, in *The Illustrated*

Outdoor World and Recreation, Volume 48, The Outdoor World Publishing Company, New York, 1912, p36

142   'Jimmy was effusive … his tuition': John Jack Lemon, *Immortal of the Cinder Path: The Saga of James "Ted" Meredith*, Choice Publishing, 2015, p35 and p44

142-143   'Jimmy headed … to attend': American Runner a Near Muhlenberg [sic.], *Allentown Morning Call*, 9 July 1912; The only other example I could find of a school interested in Meredith was Phillips Academy Andover

143   'During his time … sports events': Wilson Jr, op. cit., pp15-16

143   'The school's drive … to either': Mercersburg Academy, *New York Herald Tribune*, 16 October 1957; David Emory, *One Hundred Years of Life: Mercersburg, 1893-1993*, Mercersburg Academy, 1993, p78

144   'Towards the end … son Thorne': Article by Meredith Gives Interesting Data About Robinson Ex. '15, *Mercersburg News*, 16 April 1921

144   'Murphy was … real speed': Mike Murphy Found Schoolboy Runner, *Washington Times*, 11 May 1913; The Latest "Phenom", *Syracuse Daily Herald*, 12 May 1913

144-145   'The track … one mile relay': Barringer Boys Outclass Rivals, *New York Times*, 4 February 1912; J.E. Ted Meredith, *Dear Mums, Poverty and War – A Working Boy's Story, 1936-1947*, 2001

145   'Two weeks later … one mile relay': Georgetown Runners Lead, *New York Times*, 18 February 1912

145   'Competing in … college race': Stars of Track and Field Shine in Rain, *New York Tribune*, 28 April 1912; Pennsylvania Wins Its Relay Honors, *New York Times*, 28 April 1912; Mercersburg Star May Go To Olympiad, *Pittsburgh Press*, 18 May 1912

145   'Indeed, so … Wall of Fame': https://pennrelays.wordpress.com /the-stars-of-the-relays/relays-wall-of-fame [Accessed 9 May 2020]

146   'But if Sullivan … 1.55 respectively': Five Records Lowered, *Washington Post*, 5 May 1912; Meredith Makes Fast Time for Quarter and Half at Princeton Interscholastic Games, *New York Times*, 5 May 1912

146   'Over the course … first places': Schoolboy Equals Quarter-Mile Mark, *New York Times*, 19 May 1912; Meredith the Star, *New York Times*, 26 May 1912

146   'Meredith was … every one': Curran, *Outdoor*, op. cit., p36; Wilson Jr,

op. cit.

146 'His faith … Meredith's entry': Arthur Duffey's Column, *Boston Post*, 1 June 1912

147 'Days before … in 1.53 ⅘': Arthur Duffey's Column, *Boston Post*, 7 June 1912; Curran, *Outdoor World*, op. cit., p36

147 'Arthur Duffey's *Boston Post* office': In his post-athletics career, Duffey became a sports journalist for the *Boston Post*

147 'In the final … different approach': World's Marks Go at Olympic Trials, *New York Times*, 9 June 1912; Curran, *Outdoor World*, op. cit., p55

147 'Two days later … for Stockholm': American Athletes Are Given Fine Send-Off, *Pittsburgh Gazette Times*, 15 June 1912

148 'The ship … team's mascot': Boy Hides on Finland to see Olympic Games, *New York Evening World*, 14 June 1912

148 'Every attempt … on deck': James E. Sullivan [ed.], *The Olympic Games Stockholm 1912*, American Sports Publishing Company, New York, 1912, p37; America's Athletic Team, *New York Times*, 11 June 1912; American Athletes Sail for Stockholm, *New York Times*, 15 June 1912; U.S. Athletes Sail, *Washington Post*, 15 June 1912; U.S. Athletes Train on Ship, *Washington Post*, 16 June 1912; Train Faithfully on Ship, *Washington Post*, 17 June 1912

148 'After a short … to Stockholm': American Athletes Arrive in Antwerp, *New York Times*, 25 June 1912; Sullivan, op. cit., p239

148-149 'The 19-year-old … the final': Meredith's Rise Due to Coach Curran, *Chester Times*, 13 August 1912; Analysis of the Style of James E. Meredith, National Quarter-Mile Champion, *New York Times*, 26 March 1916; Mercersburg's Olympic Tradition, in *Mercersburg Magazine*, Volume XI, No.5, Summer 1984, p5

149-150 'On the day … a schoolboy': Plan Reception for Olympic Champion, *Chester Times*, 9 July 1912; Meredith a Boy Wonder, *Norwich Bulletin*, 12 July 1912; Analysis of the Style of James E. Meredith, National Quarter-Mile Champion, *New York Times*, 26 March 1916; Mel Sheppard, Great Old Distance Runner, Credits Ted Meredith with having given him his Greatest Thrill in Olympic Competition, *Pittsburgh Press*, 10 July 1932; When Meredith and Sheppard Were Olympic Rivals, *New York Times*, 31 December 1943; Mercersburg's Olympic Tradition, in *Mercersburg Magazine*, Volume XI, No.5, Summer 1984, p5

150   'On receiving ... coaching career': "Ted" Meredith's Great Race, *Boston Evening Transcript*, 15 August 1912; Mercersburg's Olympic Tradition, in *Mercersburg Magazine*, Volume XI, No.5, Summer 1984, p10

150   'His fellow ... ever witnessed': Robertson Retires at Penn; Famous Olympic Coach, *Philadelphia Inquirer*, 8 July 1947

150   'And Meredith ... the finish': Americans' Lead in Olympics Grows, *New York Times*, 14 July 1912; "Ted" Meredith's Great Race, *Boston Evening Transcript*, 15 August 1912

150   'The day after ... of 3.16.6': U.S. One-Milers Win by Good Margin, *Philadelphia Inquirer*, 16 July 1912

150-151   'As the Games ... silvers and bronzes': Sweden won a grand total of 65, but leadership of the medal table is based on the gold medal tally

151   'In a letter ... a second': Sports Miscellany, *Glasgow Herald*, 10 June 1912

151   'In the lead ... Alvah Meyer': A photograph of Meredith and Meyer in their car appeared the following day in the *New York Tribune*

151   'William Gaynor': Gaynor was shot in the neck during an assassination attempt in 1910. The bullet remained lodged in his neck, and may have been a factor in his death three years later.

151-152   'And those celebrations ... Jim Thorpe': Thousands Cheer Olympic Victor, *New York Tribune*, 25 August 1912; Gotham Lauds U.S. Athletes, *Washington Post*, 25 August 1912; Olympic Champions Cheered and Dined, *New York Times*, 25 August 1912

152   'Two days later ... of Media': Reception for Olympic Team, *Washington Post*, 26 August 1912; Wilson Jr, op. cit., p18

152   'Jimmy travelled ... Gustaf V': Media Burns Red Fire in Honor of Meredith, *Chester Times*, 28 August 1912; Meredith Gets Big Send Off at Media, *Philadelphia Inquirer*, 28 August 1912; Lemon, op.cit., p118

152-153   'Soon after ... a model': Mercersburg College Gets Fine Painting, *Washington Herald*, 26 March 1914; Valerie G. Therrien, Under the Eye: The Victor, in *Mercersburg Magazine*, Winter 2003, p33

153   'Jimmy significantly ... pole vault': Connaught Men in Track Event, *Philadelphia Inquirer*, 3 July 1910; Jimmy Lee Starred in Scottish Games, *Philadelphia Inquirer*, 7 August 1910

153   'A month later ... five mile race': Hans Holmer in Front, *New York Times*, 6 September 1910

153   'The following year ... prize of $8': Foresters Hold Annual Jubilee,

Philadelphia Inquirer, 23 July 1911

153   'Foresters' courts': The Foresters was a fraternal organisation, with members drawn from across society

153-154   'At the Scottish ... step and jump': Jimmy Lee Starts in Scottish Meet, *Philadelphia Inquirer*, 4 August 1912

154   'The following ... pole vault': Caledonian Club Sports, *New York Times*, 3 September 1912

154   'The following year ... the rest': Email from Jef Evans, 26 November 2018

154   'Only two athletes': Carlisle did in fact turn up with a team of seven, but were almost wholly reliant on Thorpe and Tewanima

154   And so ... Thomas Fields': Robinson, Maxfield and Fields Star in Big Meet, *New York Press*, 8 June 1913; Title Meet Easy for Mercersburg, *New York Times*, 8 June 1913

154   'Such was ... on campus': Drop Basketball at Mercersburg, *Syracuse Daily Herald*, June 1913

154-155   'The season ... particularly impressive': Mercersburg Boys Win, *New York Times*, 11 May 1913; Hill School Adds Athletic Honors, *New York Times*, 25 May 1913

155   'Jimmy had expected ... Dan Kelley': Faster Than Meredith, *Baltimore Sun*, 17 January 1913; Claim That Robinson Can Beat Ted Meredith, *Sunday Union*, 19 January 1913

155-156   'And in the ... Penn State': Robinson a Marvel in Athletic World, *Washington Times*, 4 May 1913; *Spalding's Official Athletic Almanac, 1914*, American Sports Publishing Co., 1914, p124 contains a photograph of Robinson crossing the line in the 220 yards race, with the opposition in the far distance; *Mercersburg Academy Alumni Quarterly*, April 1921, Volume 16, No.3, p17; Article by Ted Meredith Gives Interesting Data About Robinson's 220, *Mercersburg News*, 16 April 1921; Speed Beyond Belief, *Detroit News*, 20 October 1947

156   'By May 1913 ... professional meets': Timely Bits of Sport, *New York Tribune*, 28 May 1913; Accused of "Pot Hunting", *Boston Evening Transcript*, 5 June 1913; Robinson to Europe, *Indianapolis Star*, 8 June 1913; Arthur Duffey's Column, *Boston Sunday Post*, 8 June 1913; Sentiment Spoils a Trip, *Athletic News*, 16 June 1913

156   'In later years ... the Olympics': Telephone interview with Henry Thresher, 9 April 2015

156   'He had never ... position of chairman': The Philadelphia Scottish

Borderers, *Jedburgh Gazette*, 17 December 1909; Philadelphia Scottish Border Club, *Southern Reporter*, 24 February 1910; Borderers in America, *Hawick News and Border Chronicle*, 2 September 1910

156   'In 1910 ... topped trophy': Athletics, *Southern Reporter*, 15 September 1910; Gala Harriers Club, *Southern Reporter*, 30 March 1911; Gala Harriers Club Sports Meeting, *Southern Reporter*, 6 August 1925

156-157   'But before ... crowd of mourners': "Mike" Murphy, Dean of U.S. Trainers, Dead, *New York Tribune*, 5 June 1913; Mike Murphy's Body Solemnly Sent Away, *Philadelphia Inquirer*, 10 June 1913

157   'After the funeral ... local newspaper': Sporting Jottings, *Border Telegraph*, 10 June 1913

157   'Travelling second ... acute bronchitis': A Century of Census, National Records of Scotland, December 2012 – www.scotlandscensus.gov.uk/documents/censusresults/release1a/rel1ap opchartall.pdf [Accessed 3 December 2018]; Annual Report of the Registrar General of Births, Deaths and Marriages for Scotland 2013 159th Edition, Chapter 11, 14 August 2014 – www.nrscotland.gov.uk /files//statistics/annual-review-2013/html/rgar-2013-first-world-war.html [Accessed 3 December 2018]; Death Certificate of John Curran – 775/00 0049 [Sourced from www.scotlandspeople .gov.uk, 21 March 2015]; Death Certificate of John Curran – 775/00 0097 [Sourced from www.scotlandspeople.gov.uk, 21 March 2015]

157   'Trip he would make at least 17 times': Jimmy is believed to have made one trip across the Atlantic that did not involve visiting Scotland – in 1935 when he worked at Donald MacJannet's summer camps in the French Alps.

157   'Two trips ... the culprit': Lawson, op. cit., p40

157   'Many years later ... seen inebriated': Email from Jef Evans, 12 January 2020

158   'Just a month ... Temperance Hotel': The Old Gala Club, *Galashiels*, The History Press, Stroud, 2011; Alex F. Young, *Old Galashiels*, Stenlake Publishing, 2006

158   'Indeed, in his ... tourists arrived: Live Tips and Tricks, *Boston Daily Globe*, 26 July 1913

158   'His first race ... his prize': Jedburgh Border Games, *Southern Reporter*, 17 July 1913

158   'A week later ... the latter': Kelso Games, *Southern Reporter*, 24 July 1913

ENDNOTES AND SOURCES

158   'He then travelled ... yards advantage': Clyde Football Club Sports, *Scotsman*, 28 July 1913; Season's Record is Made at Forfar by W.R. Knox, *Dundee Courier*, 29 July 1913; Blairgowrie and Rattray Highland Games, *Blairgowrie Advertiser*, 2 August 1913

158-159 'His intent ... in Morpeth': This is supposition on my part, but it is unlikely, indeed nigh on impossible, that Jimmy journeyed the 160 miles to or from Morpeth, where he definitely ran, to attend both events.

159   'In 1873 ... £8 10s': Morpeth Olympic Games, *Morpeth Herald*, 8 August 1913

159   'On his return ... younger days': St Ronan's Border Games, *Southern Reporter*, 21 August 1913; Carnwath Red Hose Games, *Scotsman*, 22 August 1913; Seizure Proves Fatal to Jimmy Curran at 83, *Harrisburg Patriot-News*, 8 February 1963

159-160 'Two days ... ahead of him': Whittingham Games, *Yorkshire Post and Leeds Intelligencer*, 25 August 1913

160   'An injury ... returned home': Live Tips and Tricks, *Boston Daily Globe*, 27 September 1913

160   'In later years ... Military Tattoo': Facebook posts from Tom Danaher, Jean Cornelius and Laurie Danaher, 15 March 2015 and 23 April 2015; Email from Laurie Danaher and Alanna Berger, 29 January 2017

160   'Military Tattoo': The Royal Edinburgh Military Tattoo first took place in 1950, as part of the Edinburgh International Festival. It features performances by military bands on the esplanade of Edinburgh Castle. It is highly likely that Jimmy attended at least one of these events.

160   'Meredith had moved ... held in America': Decathlon Prize Goes to Goelitz, *Chicago Daily Tribune*, 4 July 1913

161   'At the annual ... both names': Twenty-First Annual Field Day Observed, *Mercersburg News*, 21 November 1913

161   'Soon after ... Robinson's armoury': Dual Meet Held, *Mercersburg News*, 21 November 1913

161   'William 'Sparrow' Robertson': Robertson's two claims to fame were a writing style that was 'devoid of *syntax* and even more of elementary *grammar*', and for having invented the Old Pal cocktail

161   'The aim ... the profession': "Pro" Trainers to Meet, *New York Times*, 30 December 1913; Professional Trainers Are After Protection,

Washington Times, 30 December 1913; Trainers Frown on Pro-Amateur Races, *The Sun*, 31 December 1913; *Evening World*, 3 June 1918; Form New Body to Help Sports, *The Capital Times*, 3 June 1918; Coaches and Trainers Form an Association, *Boston Sunday Globe*, 2 June 1918; College Track Coaches Form an Organization, *Boston Globe*, 4 June 1918

161-162 'The following ... the school': Robinson is Excused from Further Study, *Harrisburg Telegraph*, 31 December 1913; School Dismisses Champion Athlete, *Allentown Democrat*, 31 December 1913; Harry Goelitz to Join Illini, *Chicago Daily Tribune*, 3 January 1914

161   'Hogmanay': The Scots word for the last day of the year

162   'Barry Cantwell': Cantwell, like Goelitz, hailed from Oak Park. When Cantwell died of a heart attack, in 1937, Goelitz acted as a pallbearer.

162   'But were ... as misdemeanours': The argument that it is unlikely that these transgressions were the sole reason for expulsion, was put forward by Mercersburg Academy's archivist, Doug Smith

162   'In later years ... athletics altogether': Curran's Biography More Exciting Than Fiction, *Philadelphia Inquirer*, 30 April 1939

162   'For a short ... team trophy': Capital Athletes Fail, *Washington Post*, 10 May 1914; Two-Man Team Wins Scholastic Meet, *Ithaca Daily News*, 11 May 1914; As the News Breaks in World of Sport, *Houston Daily Post*, 17 May 1914; *The Karux*, The Boys of the Mercersburg Academy, 1915, p107; 50th Year – And Still Molding Stars, *Philadelphia Inquirer*, 25 April 1957

162   'Keewatin Academy': Keewatin Academy was based in Wisconsin during the summer months, and Florida during the winter

162   'The defeat ... major ones': Athletic Stars Crop Out in Baltimore Track Meet, *Washington Post*, 16 February 1914; Summaries of Events, *Washington Post*, 26 April 1914; Mercersburg Boys First, *New York Times*, 3 May 1914

162   'Soon after ... his powers': Track Team Favorite Barred in Athletics, *Sandusky Star-Journal*, 16 February 1916; Pick-Ups From Fields of Sport, *Houston Post*, 21 August 1916; Speed Beyond Belief, *Detroit News*, 20 October 1947; Email from Art Whiting, 3 February 2019

163   'Furthermore ... taught them': Soccer May Become a School Sport, *Mercersburg News*, 27 January 1911; *The Karux*, The Students of the Mercersburg Academy, 1919, p120; *The Karux*, The Students of the Mercersburg Academy, 1934, p152; *The Karux*, The Students of the

Mercersburg Academy, 1935, p172

163   'Academy's soccer team': In 1930 Jimmy was featured in *Ripley's Believe It Or Not* for having dropkicked a football 50 yards in bare feet

163   'The school's YMCA ... of a Coach': Hard Work at Mercersburg, *Philadelphia Inquirer*, 1 October 1910; 1914 Ties Mercersburg, *Daily Princetonian*, Volume 35, No.103, 24 October 1910; Mercersburg Nosed out by the Penn Freshmen, *Pittsburgh Gazette Times*, 30 October 1910; Mercersburg School Closes Its Season, *Philadelphia Inquirer*, 13 November 1910; Curran Gives Talk on "Training Experiences", *Mercersburg Academy Alumni Quarterly*, February 1914, Volume 9, No.1; Y.M.C.A, Reception, *Mercersburg Academy Alumni Quarterly*, October 1917, Volume 13, No.1, p3; School Notes, *Mercersburg Academy Alumni Quarterly*, January 1923, Volume 18, No.2, p22

163   'For the rest ... British Housewife': Woman's Club, *Waynesboro Record Herald*, 8 November 1948

163   Jimmy continued ... in 1950': News of Washington County and Vicinity, *Hagerstown Morning Herald*, 2 May 1950

163   'And he even ... for him': Faculty Dinner, *Mercersburg News*, 29 January 1915

Chapter 11 • The Master Mechanic

165   'Within months ... master mechanic': *Sporting Chronicle*, 1912; Of Interest to All, *Mercersburg News*, 18 October 1912; Arthur Duffey's Column, *Boston Post*, 30 April 1913; Untitled article on Lawson Robertson and Arthur Chapple, 1913

165-166   'The role ... be paid': English Bid for Curran, *New York Tribune*, 18 March 1914; Daily Sport Review by Hal Sheridan, *Trenton Evening Times*, 18 March 1914; Jimmy Curran, Developer of Robinson and Meredith, Sought as Trainer of English Athletes for Olympic Games, *Oregon Daily Journal*, 29 March 1914; Town, op. cit.

166   'Within months ... his employment': Council Minutes of the British Olympic Association, 15 January 1914 and 7 October 1914

166   'And so ... Philadelphia': Relay and Track, *Mercersburg Academy Alumni Quarterly*, May 1914, Volume 19, No.2, p12; *Miami Herald*, 9 May 1914; *Milwaukee Journal*, 31 May 1914; *Oregon Daily Journal*, 14 June 1914

166-168   'The Meadowbrook ... a schoolboy': *Meadowbrook Club Year Book*,

1916; *Meadowbrook Club Year Book*, 1918

169   'Zimmerman Telegram': The Zimmerman Telegram was an attempt, made by Germany and intercepted and decoded by British intelligence, to draw Mexico into a war with the United States

169   'In August … regulation changed': Posters Here Calls British to Colors, *Philadelphia Inquirer*, 19 July 1917; Coast Artillery Again Recruiting, *Philadelphia Inquirer*, 4 August 1917; Plea For Recruits at Scottish Games, *Philadelphia Inquirer*, 5 August 1917

169   'British Recruiting Mission': These missions emerged throughout America after its entry into the war on 6th April 1917. Prior to that they were deemed illegal, in an attempt to maintain American neutrality.

169-170   'In April … non-committal': The War Department, *Commission on Training Camp Activities*, Washington, DC, War Department, 1917; *New York Sun*, 27 April 1918

170   'Jimmy fell … US Army': World War I Registration Card – 2171/42351 [Sourced from www.ancestry.com, 4 October 2017]

170   'After the US … and 64': World War II Registration Card – U695 [Sourced from www.ancestry.com, 4 October 2017]; www.newberry.org/old-mans-draft [Accessed 4 December 2018]

170-171   'In 1916 … one occasion': Scottish Clans in Field Games, *Philadelphia Inquirer*, 2 August 1914; Scottish Games of Caledonian Club at Central Park, *Philadelphia Evening Ledger*, 5 August 1916; Meinin Victor in 5-Mile Race at Scotch Carnival, *Philadelphia Inquirer*, 6 August 1916

171   'coatee': Now known as a Bonnie Prince Charlie jacket

171   'For the next … into consideration': Meinin Victor in 5-Mile Race at Scotch Carnival, *Philadelphia Inquirer*, 6 August 1916; Curran Victor in Half-Mile Run, *Evening Public Ledger*, 4 August 1917

171-172   'On 14th November … mid-race': Evander Childs Boy Wins Cross country, *The Sun*, 15 November 1914; Interscholastic Cross Country Champions, *Philadelphia Inquirer*, 20 December 1914; Memorial Parade Marshal Recalls Soap Plant Guide Job, *Tonawanda News*, 9 May 1964

172   'If the boys … single point': Smith Leads in Mercersburg Meet, *Philadelphia Inquirer*, 22 November 1914; Boughton of Newark, Noses Out McHale, of Central High, For First Place. Mercersburg Wins, *Evening Ledger – Philadelphia*, 26 November 1914; Interscholastic Cross Country Champions, *Philadelphia Inquirer*, 20 December 1914; Cross

ENDNOTES AND SOURCES

Country, *Mercersburg Academy Alumni Quarterly*, February 1915, Volume 10, No.2, p13

172   'An author … next meets': Athletics: Track Review, *Mercersburg Academy Alumni Quarterly*, February 1915, Volume 10, No.2, p35

173   'In February 1915 … lap to go': *The Karux*, The Boys of the Mercersburg Academy, 1915, p173; "Ted" Meredith Runs Coach Curran Exhibition, *Mercersburg News*, 26 February 1915

173   'In February the … Peddie Institute': Taylor Cleans Up at Erasmus Meet, *Brooklyn Daily Eagle*, 7 February 1915; Mercersburg Squad Captures Trophy, *Brooklyn Daily Eagle*, 18 April 1915

173   'A week later … in 49 ⅗': Penn's Relay Team Breaks Mile Record, *The Sun*, 25 April 1915

173   'But the schedule … middle distances': Mercersburg Gets Third Leg on Cup, *Ithaca Daily News*, 3 May 1915

173-174 'A week later … mile record': Mercersburg Victors, *Philadelphia Record*, 9 May 1915

174   'The penultimate … the meet': Hill School Athletes Star in Senior Meet, *Philadelphia Record*, 16 May 1915

174   'A week later … Head Coach': Mercersburg Wins Scholastic Meet, *New York Herald*, 23 May 1915

174-175 'At the Columbia … one man': Mercersburg Boys Win Columbia Run, *The Sun*, 14 November 1915

175   'Two weeks later … respectively': New Cross Country Mark, *The Sun*, 26 November 1915

175   'In an effort … over it': Triple Entente has Race War, *Mercersburg News*, 3 December 1915

175   'The track team … Interscholastics': Mercersburg Lads Best in New York University Meet, *The Sun*, 16 April 1916

175-176 'On 29th April … five yards': St. Alban's Winner of Titles in Relay, *Washington Post*, 30 April 1916

176   'But if … Princeton meets': Lafayette Ties for Second, Hutch Fourth at Ithaca, *Buffalo Courier*, 7 May 1916; Mercersburg Lads Win Princeton Meet, *The Sun*, 14 May 1916

176   'And then … the mile': Tech Loses Meet at Mercersburg, *Harrisburg Telegraph*, 8 May 1916; Live Tips and Tricks, *Boston Daily Globe*, 13 May 1916

176   'So, on 20th May … previous record': Schoolboy Record for Mile Broken, *Brooklyn Daily Eagle*, 21 May 1916

176   'The final ... good distance': Mercersburg Wins Big Track Meet, *Philadelphia Inquirer*, 21 May 1916

176-177 'For the 1916/17 ... coming seasons': Many Stars Enter High School Games, *Brooklyn Daily Eagle*, 25 February 1918

177   'Allen Woodring ... athletic feats': *Evening Public Ledger*, 15 May 1918; *Harrisburg Evening News*, 21 August 1920; Onondogan Yearbook (Syracuse University), 1922, p198

177   'Swede impressed ... Championship': Flushing High Boy is Victor in Long Race, *New York Tribune*, 12 November 1916

177   'In the New Year ... Penn Relays': Tech and Brewer Win in Penn Relay Games, *Washington Post*, 29 April 1917; Mercersburg Now Owns N.Y.U. Cup, *Brooklyn Daily Eagle*, 22 May 1917

177   'In May ... Hill School': Another Trophy for Mercersburg, *Philadelphia Inquirer*, 12 May 1917

177-178 'A week later ... mile race': Hill School Wins Middle States Meet, *Philadelphia Inquirer*, 19 May 1917

178   'After two ... scholastic circles': Swede Wins Park X-Country Title, *Philadelphia Evening Public Ledger*, 29 November 1917

178   'For once ... schoolboy coaches': Curran Develops Noted Harriers, *Philadelphia Evening Public Ledger*, 6 December 1917

178   'The track ... Mercersburg victorious': Devanney Wins the "1,000", *New York Herald*, 3 March 1918

178   'The following ... Penn Relays': Ray Sets New Record at Wanamaker Meet, *Daily Standard Union*, 21 March 1918; Pittsburgh Wins Penn. Relay Meet, *Joplin News Herald*, 28 April 1918

178-179 'But victories ... secure victory': Easy for Mercersburg, *Philadelphia Inquirer*, 1 May 1918; Mercersburg Runs Away With Title, *Philadelphia Inquirer*, 4 May 1918; Mercersburg Wins Meet, *New York Times*, 12 May 1918

179   'So successful ... single team': Many Stars Enter High School Games, *Brooklyn Daily Eagle*, 25 February 1918; All America Athletic Teams for the Year 1918, *The Sun*, 29 December 1918; Crawford is Only Local Lad on National Scholastic Team, *Brooklyn Daily Eagle*, 30 December 1918

179   'As the new ... Reading Railroad': Tragic Death for Athlete, *Harrisburg Telegraph*, 9 August 1918

179   'And Jimmy ... Camp Lee, Va.': *Harrisburg Telegraph*, 19 August 1918; Star Schoolboy Sprinter Enrolls at University [sic.], *Syracuse Journal*,

September 1919

179 'Jimmy's 1918/19 … fifth place': George Douglas Wins Cross Country Run, *Norwich Bulletin*, 29 November 1918

179 'With the race … Pennsylvania': *Philadelphia Evening Public Ledger*, 30 November 1918

179-180 'The season … the latter': Mercersburg Wins Meet From Harrisburg Tech, *Philadelphia Inquirer*, 21 April 1919; Close Victory for Hill School Lads, *Philadelphia Inquirer*, 18 May 1919

180 'There were few … Penn Relays': Penn Relay Meet Summaries, *New York Tribune*, 2 May 1920

180 'Harry Bigelow … State Championships': Thomson Captures High Hurdle Race, *New York Times*, 15 February 1920; Joie Ray Unable to Lower Record, *New York Times*, 31 March 1920; Friends Near the Top, *Baltimore Sun*, 9 May 1920; Mercersburg Victor in Big Track Meet, *Evening Public Ledger – Philadelphia*, 22 May 1920

180-181 'With the conflict … in Antwerp': Captain Joseph Mills Hanson [ed.], *The inter-allied games, Paris, 22nd June to 6th July, 1919*, 1919; Colonel Wait C. Johnson and Elwood S. Brown [eds.], *Official Athletic Almanac of the American Expeditionary Forces, 1919: A.E.F. Championships: Inter-Allied Games*, American Sports Publishing Co., New York, 1919

181 'Upon the announcement … final resurrection': Wilson Jr, op. cit.; Lemon, op. cit., p117

181 'He began … 52 seconds': Fast Spurt Wins Mile for Curtis, *New York Times*, 13 June 1920; O'Brien Retains Title in Quarter, *New York Times*, 20 June 1920

181 'The Olympic trials … Oxford University': Ted Meredith "Comes Back" For Olympiad, *New York Tribune*, 19 July 1920

181-182 'At the first … 880 yards': New York Stars Shine on Track, *New York Times*, 27 June 1920

182 'From Philadelphia … his race': Five Marks Fall on Harvard Field, *New York Times*, 18 July 1920; Lever Falls During Race; Fails to Make Olympic Team, *Utica Daily Press*, 20 July 1920; Lever had been a serious Olympic prospect. So much so that he had applied for a passport before his race.

182 'Another who … Point graduates': Shields, of Penn., Candidate for the Modern Pentathlon, *Washington Post*, 22 March 1920; Train for Pentathlon, *New York Times*, 23 June 1920

182 'The numbers … the decathlon': New York Stars Shine on Track,

New York Times, 27 June 1920; Le Gendre Stars in Olympic Trials, *Washington Post*, 10 July 1920; Le Gendre is Third as Records Fall, *Washington Post*, 11 July 1920; Star Performance Mark Trial Heats, *Washington Post*, 17 July 1920; Team of 132 Stars to Represent U.S., *New York Times*, 19 July 1920; Ted Meredith "Comes Back" For Olympiad, *New York Tribune*, 19 July 1920

182-183 'And so ... its destination': Olympic Athletes Sail for Antwerp, *New York Times*, 27 July 1920; Work On Way To Antwerp, *New York Times*, 29 July 1920; Officials Blamed by U.S. Athletes, *New York Times*, 8 August 1920; John E. Findling and Kimberly D. Pelle (eds.), *Encyclopedia of the Modern Olympic Movement*, Greenwood Press, Westport, Ct., 2004, p73; Lemon, op. cit., pp117; Footage of the on-board training, as well as some of the events in Antwerp was, until recently, available to view on You Tube, but has been removed.

183 'A delay ... Olympisch Stadion': Olympic Stars Delayed at Sea, *Akron Beacon Journal*, 2 August 1920; Rush Work on Lodgings, *Chicago Tribune*, 7 August 1920; American Olympic Athletes Hold First Workout in Antwerp Stadium, *Washington Post*, 8 August 1920

183 'The first ... took silver': Landon Sets New Olympic Record in High Jumping, *New York Times*, 18 August 1920; Olympic Games. Canada's Great Hurdle Racer, *Manchester Guardian*, 19 August 1920

183 'Two years later ... at Mercersburg': *Evening Public Ledger – Philadelphia*, 22 September 1922

183-184 'Larry Shields ... closing yards': Hill Again Victor; Meredith in Final, *Philadelphia Inquirer*, 20 August 1920; Sport Chat, *Pittsburgh Post-Gazette*, 25 August 1920

184 '3,000m team race': Each team in the 3,000m team race starts with five or six runners. The runner finishing in first place receives one point, the runner in second received two, and so on. Only the first three runners from a team are counted towards the final score. Of the teams who medal, only their top three finishers receive a medal. So, in 1920, the US team won event, but Larry Shields, who was the fourth placed American, did not receive a medal. Four years later, the rules had changed, with all team members receiving a medal.

184 'Philip Baker': A year after the Games, Baker would add his wife's surname to his, becoming Philip Noel-Baker. He would serve as an MP and, upon retirement, as a peer. In 1959 he won the Nobel Peace Prize.

184 'Two days later ... a medal': Finn Wins Marathon; More Records Broken, *Washington Evening Star*, 23 August 1920

184 'Harry Goelitz ... Gore Vidal': Hamilton Sets Decathlon Mark, *New York Times*, 11 July 1920

184 'At the event ... the former': Bill Mallon and Anthony Th. Bijkerk, *The 1912 Olympic Games: Results for All Competitors in All Events, with Commentary*, McFarland & Company, Inc., Jefferson, North Carolina, 2003

184-185 'For Meredith ... breaking team': U.S. Athletes Sew Up Olympic Title, *Philadelphia Inquirer*, 21 August 1920; American Athletes Win Championship, *Philadelphia Inquirer*, 24 August 1920

185 'But as a ... fellow athlete': Sport of the Times, *New York Times*, 6 March 1936

185 'Woodring had ... own merits': Charles William Paddock, *The Fastest Human: Autobiography of Charles William Paddock*, Thomas Nelson & Sons, New York, 1932; *New York Times*, 21 August 1920

185-186 'If Woodring ... star runner': On the Sport Firing Line, *Syracuse Daily Journal*, August 1920

186 'A week after ... relay team': America Triumphs in Colombes Games, *Philadelphia Inquirer*, 30 August 1920

186 'As he had ... the Olympics': Mr Curran Academy Representative at Olympic Dinner, *Mercersburg News*, 9 October 1920; Notes, *Mercersburg Academy Alumni Quarterly*, Volume 16, No.2, January 1921, pp11-12

Chapter 12 · Ru-u-un Laddie

188 'The children ... childhood memory': Email from Stephen Curran, 1 July 2018

188 'In July 1920 ... the final': Christmas Half-Mile Handicap at Powderhall, *Scotsman*, 27 December 1920; Information from Alanna Berger via email from Laurie Danaher, 26 April 2020

188-189 'Middle-distance ... as Chuck': Erasmus to Lose Star, *New York Times*, 28 January 1920; Marvin Rick Stars, *Brooklyn Daily Eagle*, 26 April 1920

189 'Rick appears ... half-mile races': Marvin Rick Stars, *Brooklyn Daily Eagle*, 26 April 1920

189 'They were ... for Liverpool': 'Chuck' Taylor Stars in Meet, *Brookville*

American, 28 April 1921; Mercersburg is Winner, *New York Times*, 8 May 1921; Hill School First in Princeton Meet, *New York Times*, 15 May 1921; 'Chuck' Taylor on Way to Europe to Compete in Sports, *Brookville American*, 16 June 1921; Ray Breaks Mile and a Half Mark; Murphy Shatters Jump, *Baltimore Sun*, 2 February 1922; *Philadelphia Inquirer*, 23 April 1922; Two Local Quartets Score in Penn Meet, *Washington Post*, 30 April 1922; Mercersburg Academy Again Wins High and Prep School Meet Held at Swarthmore, *Philadelphia Inquirer*, 7 May 1922; Mercersburg Academy Easily Wins the Tome School Meet, *Baltimore Sun*, 21 May 1922; Facebook message from David Taylor, 15 June 2019

189   'Before he began ... of 22' 1'": The Championships, *Exeter and Plymouth Gazette*, 4 July 1921; Sporting Jottings, *Border Telegraph*, 6 July 1921; Two Jolly Rogers, *Pittsburgh Gazette Times*, 20 August 1922

190   'The first ... first place': Jedburgh Border Games, *Southern Reporter*, 14 July 1921

190   'A week ... and jump': Sports at Dumfries, *Sunday Post*, 24 July 1921

190   'Over the next ... first places': Langholm Open Events, *Yorkshire Post and Leeds Intelligencer*, 1 August 1921; Greenlaw Games, *Berwickshire News and General Advertiser*, 16 August 1921; St Ronan's Games, *Scotsman*, 22 August 1921; St. Ronan's Border Games, *Southern Reporter*, 25 August 1921

190   Jimmy returned ... two years': Athletics: Inter-School Sports, *Southern Reporter*, 29 June 1922; Amateur Sports of Galashiels, *Southern Reporter*, 13 July 1922; Email from Laurie Danaher, 26 April 2020

190-191 'Cox's first ... the lurch': Mercersburg is Victor, *New York Times*, 5 November 1922; Mercersburg Wins Prep School Run, *New York Times*, 12 November 1922; Distance Run to Mercersburg, *Washington Post*, 1 December 1922; Frank Hussey Defeats La Vin in Sprint Race at Erasmus Games, *New York Tribune*, 10 February 1923; Watch Fails to Run as Hussey Runs Fast, So Record is Lost, *New York Tribune*, 22 February 1923; World Record Set in Beating Oxford, *New York Times*, 29 April 1923; Mercersburg Wins Tech Track Meeting, *Pittsburgh Gazette Times*, 6 May 1923; Mercersburg Lands School Track Title, *Philadelphia Inquirer*, 20 May 1923

191   'In November ... third place': Yale Run is Won by Mercersburg, *New York Times*, 11 November 1923; Cox Leads Large Field in Schoolboy Cross Country for Kirby Cup at Van Cortlandt Park, *New York*

Tribune, 18 November 1923; Cox Wins Columbia Cross-Country Run, *New York Times*, 18 November 1923; Champ Bill Cox Leads Pack Home, *Boston Daily Globe*, 30 November 1923

191   'And on the …4.24 mile': Millrose Results, *Philadelphia Inquirer*, 31 January 1924; Huntington in Second Place, *Boston Daily Globe*, 16 March 1924; Mercersburg Blazes Trail at Princeton, *Boston Daily Globe*, 11 May 1924; Frank Hussey Does Century in 9 4-5S, *Boston Daily Globe*, 18 May 1924

191   'At the Millrose … notable victories': Mercersburg Runs to a New World's Record, *Boston Daily Globe*, 30 January 1924; Murchison Flashes to Victory in Meet, *Philadelphia Inquirer*, 9 March 1924

191   'And as … notable victories': National Mark Set in Schoolboy Jump, *New York Times*, 16 March 1924; Mercersburg Wins School Track Meet, *New York Times*, 11 May 1924; New Utrecht Looms Up Strong at Franklin Field, *Brooklyn Daily Eagle*, 18 May 1924; Frank Hussey Stars As Jimmy Curran's Boys Capture Title, *Philadelphia Inquirer*, 18 May 1924; Hussey Lowers Penn Mark to 9 4-5 Seconds, *New York Tribune*, 18 May 1924

191   'In late April … 100 yards': World's Record Set by Boston College, *New York Times*, 27 April 1924; British Champion Liddell Hero in Defeat; Many Penn Carnival Marks Equalled and Broken, *Brooklyn Standard Union*, 27 April 1924; Penn Relay Summaries, *New York Herald Tribune*, 27 April 1924

191-192   'The season … high jump': High School Stars Advance Rapidly, *Canton Daily News*, 25 May 1924

192   'For all Jimmy's … schoolboy tour': Indoor Track, *Mercersburg Academy Alumni Quarterly*, October 1923, Volume 19, No.1, p19

192   'The school … fully deserved': H.M.J. Klein, *A Century of Education at Mercersburg, 1836-1936*, Mercersburg Academy, 1936, p558

192   'Irvine would … for $450': Mr. Curran Speaker on Olympic Games, *Mercersburg News*, 26 September 1924

192   'Frank Conway … losing out': Conway Enter Olympic Field, *New York Telegram and Evening Mail*, 5 May 1924; Dowding, Ascher and Norton Win in Eastern Tests, *Washington Post*, 8 June 1924; Scholz Sets 100-Meter Record, *Atlanta Constitution*, 8 June 1924; Eight Schoolboys Qualify for Final Olympic Team Try-Outs, *New York Tribune*, 8 June 1924

192   'Holding up … past performances': Dowding, Ascher and Norton

JIMMY CURRAN

Win in Eastern Tests, *Washington Post*, 8 June 1924; 3,000 Meter Run Won by Devaney, *New York Times*, 9 June 1924; The Olympic Games: America's Wonderful Team Fine Record of Athletic Superiority, *Observer*, 22 June 1924; Stepping High for Dad, *Philadelphia Inquirer Magazine*, 20 July 1952

192-193 'In mid-June … Fairbanks Jr': Paris Wildly Cheers U.S. Team on Arrival, *New York Times*, 26 June 1924

193 'Training continued … the victims': American Athletes Race to the Rescue When Twenty Fires Sweep French Village, *New York Times*, 27 June 1924

193 'In July … the Games': Mercersburg Group Send Coach Overseas, *Harrisburg Telegraph*, 7 June 1924; Jimmy Curran Orders Meal While in Paris, *Mercersburg News*, 30 October 1924; It is possible that Jimmy travelled alone and met up with the others once in France

193 'Jimmy's early … a salad': "Jimmy" Curran Tells of Olympics, *Mercersburg Academy Alumni Quarterly*, October 1924, Volume 20, No.1, pp27-28; Jimmy Curran Orders Meal While in Paris, *Mercersburg News*, 3 October 1924

193 'On 5th July … his death': *Gloucestershire Echo*, 5 July 1924; U.S. President Bereaved: Death of Calvin Coolidge Jr, *Edinburgh Evening News*, 8 July 1924

194 'Almost a year … human soul': School Friends Honor Memory of Coolidge Jr., *Amsterdam Evening Record*, 2 June 1925

194 'Jimmy's greatest … was successful': Stepping High for Dad, *Philadelphia Inquirer Magazine*, 20 July 1952; Email from Dave Johnson, 14 January 2019

194 'Moore could … relay race': Empire Athletes Beaten, *Manchester Guardian*, 21 July 1924

195 'Marvin Rick … worthy fourth': Yankee Stars Go Into Lead in Olympics, *Chicago Daily Tribune*, 8 July 1924; American Sprint Kings Bring Added Laurels to Old Glory, *Philadelphia Inquirer*, 10 July 1924

195 'But the real … Harvard stadiums': Records Fall as Eastern Athletes Try for Places in Finals for Olympic Team, *Philadelphia Inquirer*, 8 June 1924; Olympic Finals Produce More Records, *Buffalo Courier*, 15 June 1924; Olympic Track and Field Results, *Philadelphia Inquirer*, 15 June 1924

195 'Considered the … the final': World Mark Broken Twice in 400 Meters, *New York Times*, 12 July 1924

195   'But Cox's ... the Olympics': William Cox Refuses to Run Sunday Race, *Mercersburg News*, 6 December 1924

195-196   'Any minor ... bronze medal': Finland Captures Marathon, Closing Race of Olympics, *Washington Post*, 14 July 1924; "Jimmy" Curran Tells of Olympics, *Mercersburg Academy Alumni Quarterly*, October 1924, Volume 20, No.1, p28

196   'The reason ... Harriers' Sports': E.H. Liddell at Gala, *Edinburgh Evening News*, 15 August 1924; Sports of All Sorts, *Edinburgh Evening News*, 18 August 1924; Gala Harriers' Sports, *Southern Reporter*, 21 August 1924; Mr Curran Speaks on Olympic Games, *Mercersburg News*, 26 September 1924

196   'It is likely ... 350 yards': *Border Telegraph*, 4 August 1925

196   'The Mercersburg ... individual victor': Wm. Cox, of Rochester Tech., for 3d Consecutive Time Captures Columbia X-Country Run, *New York Tribune*, 16 November 1924

196   'The following ... individual stars': Paavo Nurmi Shatters Two World Records in Mile and a Half Race at the Millrose Games, *New York Herald Tribune*, 29 January 1925; New Utrecht-Hill Tie in Title Meet, *New York Times*, 15 March 1925; Mercersburg and New Utrecht Athletes Win in Princeton Meet, *New York Herald Tribune*, 10 May 1925; New York Boys Star in Penn School Games, *New York Herald Tribune*, 17 May 1925; New York Schoolboys Break Two National Track Records, *New York Tribune*, 14 March 1926; Mercersburg Academy Triumphs in Princeton Schoolboy Track Meet for Third Straight Year, *New York Tribune*, 9 May 1926

196   'The team ... yards relay': Two Records are Broken, One Tied in Penn Relays, *Gazette Times*, 25 April 1925; Palmyra High Victorious in 3 Races at Penn Relays, *Philadelphia Inquirer*, 26 April 1925; Penn Relays Summary, *Pittsburgh Gazette Times*, 24 April 1926; Many Athletes Will Compete, *Chester Times*, 7 May 1926

196-197   'But the stand-out ... track team': Berlinger, Penn Freshman, is Promising Decathlon Prospect, *New York Herald Tribune*, 4 March 1928; Quaker Freshman New Decathlon Hope of U.S., *Hartford Courant*, 11 March 1928

197   'Despite a slow ... Penn Relays': Stuyvesant High Wins Interscholastic Meet, *Boston Daily Globe*, 10 February 1927; Wide Shatters Two of Nurmi's World's Marks in Philadelphia, *New York Tribune*, 20 March 1927; Mercersburg First in Princeton Meet, *New*

York Times, 8 May 1927; Mercersburg Wins Penn Track Meet, *New York Times*, 22 May 1927; *The Karux*, The Students of the Mercersburg Academy, 1928, pp154-155; Curran Watched Stars Star on Cinders First, *St Petersburg Independent*, 24 April 1960

197   'In the quarter ... mile team': Many Athletes Will Compete, *Chester Times*, 7 May 1926; Lord Burghley Bows to Yank in Penn Meet, *San Francisco Chronicle*, 30 April 1927; Two World Records and U.S. International Wins Feature Opening of Meet, *Schenectady Gazette*, 30 April 1927; *The Karux*, The Students of the Mercersburg Academy, 1928, pp150-151

197   'Berlinger was ... performance': *The Karux*, The Students of the Mercersburg Academy, 1928, p151

197-198   'Arriving at ... 12 seconds': Mercersburg Lad Wins Columbia X-Country Jaunt, *Brooklyn Daily Eagle*, 13 November 1927; Cobb, of Mercersburg Academy, Wins Interscholastic Distance Run, *New York Herald Tribune*, 11 November 1928

198   'Cobb's success ... Interscholastics': Ira Singer Wins Interscholastic Sprint Titles at Newark Games, *New York Herald Tribune*, 8 February 1928; Mercersburg Lads Win Track Honors, *Philadelphia Inquirer*, 22 April 1928; Penn Relay Summaries, *New York Herald Tribune*, 28 April 1928; Mercersburg Defeats Quaker Freshmen, *Philadelphia Inquirer*, 6 May 1928; Mercersburg Wins Fifth Title, Taking Princeton Track Meet, *New York Herald Tribune*, 13 May 1928; Mercersburg Wins Scholastic Track Title for 5th Year, *New York Herald Tribune*, 20 May 1928

198   'The 1928 ... badly beaten': Scenes at First Annual Devitt Prep Scholastic Meet, *Washington Post*, 22 April 1928; Hahn Smashes U.S. 800-Meter Record, *Daily Boston Globe*, 17 June 1928; Gibson Betters World Record for 400-Meter Hurdles at Stadium, *New York Herald Tribune*, 17 June 1928

198   'At the final ... to Amsterdam': Doherty is Winner of Decathlon Title, *New York Times*, 6 July 1928

198   'And so ... in Philadelphia': U.S. Coaches Order Rest for Athletes, *New York Times*, 12 July 1928

198-199   'The decathlon ... point barrier': Finnish Athletes Win 2 More Titles in Olympic Games, *New York Times*, 5 August 1928

199   'Three years later ... in Amsterdam': Barney Berlinger Wins Decathlon in Penn Relays, *Daily Capital News*, 25 April 1931

ENDNOTES AND SOURCES

199 'In 1931 ... five display': Berlinger Wins Sullivan Medal, *The Telegraph*, 31 December 1931; Berlinger May Not Compete in Olympics, *Reading Eagle*, 15 June 1932

199 'In the conspicuous ... year previously': Katherine Mearls Retains Title, Finishing Fast, *Boston Globe*, 9 September 1928; Track, *Mercersburg Academy Alumni Quarterly*, January 1929, Volume 24, No.2, p85

199-200 'At the first ... of 4.25.4': Williams Winner in 45-Yard Dash, *New York Times*, 13 February 1929; Two Relay Titles Retained by N.Y.U., *New York Times*, 27 April 1929; Lermond Runs Great Mile at Penn Meet, *Daily Boston Globe*, 28 April 1929; Mercersburg Retains Title in Princeton School Track Meet, *New York Herald Tribune*, 12 May 1929; Mercersburg Wins Penn School Meet, *New York Times*, 19 May 1929

200 'A victory ... Penn Interscholastics': Mercersburg Leads Plebes in Track Meet, *Baltimore Sun*, 4 May 1930; Hill Takes Title, Scoring Five First in Princeton Meet, *New York Herald Tribune*, 11 May 1930; Crowley Breaks Mile Record at Schoolboy Meet, *New York Herald Tribune*, 18 May 1930

200 'But the team's ... such as this': No Bay State Victors in Penn Relay Carnival, *Daily Boston Globe*, 26 April 1930; Summaries of Events in Penn Relay Carnival, *New York Times*, 26 April 1930; St. James and Manual Show in Picture, *Brooklyn Daily Eagle*, 26 April 1930

200 'To put this ... June 1934': M'Williams Picked to Lead Trackmen, *Daily Princetonian*, 2 June 1934

200-201 'This preceded ... in college': U.S. Track Stars Leave for Europe, *New York Times*, 18 June 1934; Rangers Sports, *Scotsman*, 6 August 1934; Time Out, *Daily Princetonian*, Volume 60, Number 58, 25 April 1935

201 'Later that year ... and effort': Hogan Elected to Captain 1936 Squad of Cindermen, *Daily Princetonian Special Bulletin*, 30 May 1935

201 'Jimmy's time ... silverware': Fulton Trophy Room Completed in the Gym, *Mercersburg News*, 10 October 1931

201 'Ironically, victories ... in 1932': Stella Walsh Ties World Sprint Mark, *Philadelphia Inquirer*, 13 February 1931; Lowell High Relay Team Breaks the Track Record, *Daily Boston Globe*, 15 March 1931; Summaries of Penn Relay Carnival, *New York Times*, 25 April 1931; Mercersburg Runners Win Tri-Track Meet, *Baltimore Sun*, 3 May 1931; Hill School Wins Princeton Scholastics, *Allentown Morning Call*, 10 May 1931; Hill School Athletes Win Princeton Meet, *New York Herald*

Tribune, 10 May 1931; Penn Track Meet to Mercersburg, *New York Times*, 17 May 1931; Mercersburg Captures Track Meet at Penn, *New York Herald Tribune*, 17 May 1931; Three Records Broken as Mercersburg Wins Penn Schoolboy Meet, *Brooklyn Daily Eagle*, 17 May 1931; Renwick, Michigan Star, Wins Sprint in Annual W.V.A. Games, *Charleston Daily Mail*, 14 February 1932; Navy Plebes Lose Meet, *New York Times*, 24 April 1932; Navy Track Teams Win and Lose, *Washington Post*, 24 April 1932; 3 Penn Relay Marks Fall, *Washington Post*, 30 April 1932; 25,000 Watch Penn Win One-Mile Relay, *New York Times*, 1 May 1932; Gains 3D Victory to Capture Trophy, *New York Times*, 15 May 1932

201 'It isn't known … quite likely': After Twenty-Two Years, *Mercersburg News*, 5 December 1931

201-202 'After the 1931/32 … in America': Penn's Relay Team Races to World Record, *Chicago Daily Tribune*, 8 March 1931; For the Game's Sake, *New York Sun*, 9 May 1933; Through---But Never to Be Forgotten, *Troy Times*, 26 May 1933; Bill Carr, Victor in 1932 Olympics: Winner of 400-Meter Race Dies in Tokyo at 56, *New York Times*, 15 January 1966

202 'Carr's assault … record time': Sexton of N.Y.A.C. Tops Shot-Put Mark, *New York Times*, 16 July 1932; Carr, Penn, Victor in 400-Meter Run, *New York Times*, 17 July 1932

202 'He cruised … the Games': Texas Girl Wins Hurdles for U.S., *Washington Post*, 5 August 1932; Carr of U.S. Wins Title at Olympics, *New York Times*, 6 August 1932; William A. ("Bill") Carr, '29, Adds to Mercersburg's Athletic Record, *Mercersburg Academy Alumni Quarterly*, 1932

202 'In the last … 1952 Olympics': Relay Teams Clip Marks at 400 and 1,600 Meters Before Crowd of 75,000, *Washington Post*, 8 August 1932

203 'With the Olympics … 500 others': Civic Reception to Overseas Visitors, *Border Telegraph*, 5 July 1932

203 'It was the … March 1929': *Waynesboro Record Herald*, 26 March 1929; Certificate of Naturalization, 1384894 [Sourced from Franklin County Archives] Jimmy's naturalisation document details his journey west on the *Lusitania*. By signing it, he declared that he will renounce all 'allegiance and fidelity' to all foreign powers, and most notably King George V.

203 'The trip was … Gala Water': Laird of Abbotsford: Centenary Gifts

to Braw Lad and Lass, *Southern Reporter*, 7 July 1932; A montage of footage of the main events from the 1932 Braw Lads' Gathering is available to view: www.youtube.com/watch?v=PFymoCWpS0M [Accessed 7 August 2015]

203 'Mercat Cross': From the 12th century, Scottish towns given rights to hold a weekly fair or market were allowed to build a mercat, or market, cross. It was usually placed centrally in a town or city and in later years often served as a gathering place during communal events.

203 'Jimmy was … a judge': An article in the Edinburgh Evening News on 4 July 1932 suggests that the elder Curran did take part in the event as an athlete, but there is no overwhelming evidence that this was actually the case. It is likely that Jimmy Jr's name on the race card was mistaken for his.

203-204 'Jimmy Jr … his heat': Braw Lads' Gathering: The Sports Council, *Border Telegraph*, 5 July 1932; Braw Lad from U.S.A., *Southern Reporter*, 7 July 1932; Sports and Races, *Southern Reporter*, 7 July 1932

204 'It would not … his degree': James M. Curran Jr., *A Geological Pilgrimage to the Scottish Highlands Including Further Comments on the Durness-Beekmantown Problem*, unpublished thesis, 1935

204 'A year … Arts degree': 447 Members of Graduating Class Will be Awarded Degrees at 188th Commencement Ceremonies in Front of Nassau Hall, *Daily Princetonian*, Volume 30, Number 93, 18 June 1935

Chapter 13 · Highs and Lows

206 'By early … his career': Carr Will Retire After 1933 Season, *New York Times*, 26 January 1933

206 'But only two … was over': Carr's Running Days At College Are Over, *New York Times*, 19 March 1933

206 'Refreshed after … of 1927': Wykoff Annexes 50-Yard Sprint, *New York Times*, 19 February 1933; Summaries of Yesterday's Events in the Penn Relays, *New York Times*, 29 April 1933; Gorton High Squad Wins Heat in Penn Relays, But Fails to Qualify, *Herald Statesman*, 29 April 1933; Penn Relay Meet Summaries, *New York Herald Tribune*, 29 April 1933; Hill School Again Captures Title in Princeton Games, *Times-Union*, 7 May 1933; Richmond Schoolboy Wins "C" Meet as 4 Marks Fall, *Washington Post*, 21 May 1933; Track, *Mercersburg Academy*

JIMMY CURRAN

Alumni Quarterly, Winter 1933, Volume XXXIII, No.2, p54

206   'The team's ... Square Garden': Queens Boys Star at Scholastic Track and Field Meet, *Long Island Daily Press*, 24 February 1934; *The Karux*, The Students of the Mercersburg Academy, 1934, p163

206   'The team ... 44.4 seconds': West Philly Wins Public High Mile Relay; West Catholic Triumphs, *Philadelphia Inquirer*, 28 April 1934

206-207   'With just the ... shot put': School Meet Won by Mercersburg, *New York Times*, 13 May 1934

207   'In the fall ... 15 of these': Schoolboy Cross Country Phenom Gives Credit to Strict Training, *Hagerstown Daily Mail*, 3 January 1934
'The school's first ... away victorious': Plebe Harriers Beat Mercersburg, 21-34, *Washington Post*, 11 November 1934

207   'From the race ... by a yard': School Cross Country Title Won by Leonard Dauenhauer of Syracuse, *New York Times*, 30 November 1934

207   'The track season ... 440 yards': St. Benedict's Prep Takes Track Title, *New York Times*, 24 February 1935

207   'The remainder ... Bill Bradway': Georgetown Frosh Swamped in Track, *Washington Post*, 21 April 1935

207   'A further victory ... 43.2 seconds': Torrance Shows Way With World Record as Nine Marks Fall in Penn Carnival, *New York Times*, 27 April 1935

207   'But just ... Hill School': Team Honors Go to Hill School and Union High in Track Meet at Princeton, *New York Times*, 5 May 1935

208   'In the summer – Spanish sculptor': Ted Meredith's Coach to Teach in France, *International Herald Tribune*, 1 June 1935; Sporting Gossip, *International Herald Tribune*, 27 June 1935; Sporting Gossip, *International Herald Tribune*, 28 June 1935; Sporting Gossip, *International Herald Tribune*, 12 August 1935; Sporting Gossip, *International Herald Tribune*, 18 August 1935; Coach Curran Returns, *Washington Post*, 21 September 1935; Robert Gildea, *Fighters in the Shadows: A New History of the French Resistance*, Faber & Faber, 2015

208   'For a fee ... mutual respect': Email from Helen Stec, Tufts University Archives, 19 October 2018, with information derived from MS024.002.204.00002; https://www.macjannet.org/our-founders.html [Accessed 27 December 2018]

208   'But there was ... the Atlantic': Email from Alanna Berger, 20 November 2018. The bust now has pride of place in the home of one

ENDNOTES AND SOURCES

of Jimmy's granddaughters.

208   'The commemoration ... the school': Coach Curran Honored, *Chambersburg Public Opinion*, 25 April 1935

208-209 'That same evening ... coaching career': Track Coach to be Honor Guest, *Hagerstown Morning Herald*, 25 April 1935; Fete Jim Curran, Famous Coach, *Philadelphia Inquirer*, 26 April 1935

209   'This triumvirate ... sound body': *The Karux*, The Students of the Mercersburg Academy, 1935, p2

209-210 'If Jimmy's stock ... was charged': Email from Jef Evans, 6 November 2018

210   'Plaudits were ... Ed Powers': Navy Plebe Harriers Defeat Mercersburg, *Washington Post*, 3 November 1935

210   'The early track ... Princeton Games': Summaries in the Millrose Meet, *New York Times*, 2 February 1936; Mercersburg Record-breaking Two Mile Team Standout as School Quartets, *Philadelphia Inquirer*, 26 April 1936; Features and Flashes from Franklin Field, *Daily Pennsylvanian*, Volume LII, No.129, 27 April 1936; Mercersburg, Bel Air Win High School Meet, *Washington Post*, 3 May 1936; Class A Honors in Princeton Meet Are Captured by Mercersburg Track Team, *New York Times*, 17 May 1936

210   'Since 1908 ... Czech team': Ted Meredith Grooms Czech Olympic Team, *Ogden Standard-Examiner*, 19 May 1936

210-211 'By the 1930s ... financial position': Mrs. Coolidge Sees Chapel Dedicated, *New York Times*, 14 October 1926; Emory, op. cit., pp24-27; History Behind Stained Glass in the Chapel, *Mercersburg News*, 8 October 2015

211   'With no project ... its halls': *The Flowering of Mercersburg: Seventy-five Great Years 1893-1968*, p17

211-212 'Indeed, so serious ... each day': Discussion with Doug Smith, Mercersburg Academy archivist, 3-4 September 2018

212   'sprints': the sprint events, in this context, are considered to be the 100m, 200m and 400m

212   'But while ... school's headmaster': Academy Founder is Given Honors, *Altoona Mirror*, 12 October 1936; David F. Chapman, *A Challenge to Youth: Biography of Robert Henry Michelet*, Grit Publishing Company, Williamsburg, 1943, p55; A Tale of Two Statues, in *Mercersburg Magazine*, Volume 36, No.1, Spring 2009, p3

212-213 'The Carr bronze ... of Pennsylvania': Academy Founder is Given

363

Honors, *Altoona Mirror*, 12 October 1936; Irvine Memorial Seat Dedicated, *Chambersburg Public Opinion*, 12 October 1936; *The Karux*, The Students of Mercersburg Academy, 1937, pp120-123; Jean McGill, *The Joy of Effort: A Biography of R. Tait McKenzie*, Clay Publishing Company, Ontario, 1980, pp223-224; A Tale of Two Statues, in *Mercersburg Magazine*, Volume 36, No.1, Spring 2009, p3

213   'The Navy Plebes ... many decades': Mercersburg Beats Navy Plebe Harriers, *Washington Post*, 8 November 1936

213   'He laid down ... at Princeton': *The Karux*, The Students of Mercersburg Academy, 1937, p152; 8 Meet Marks Set in School Games, *New York Times*, 28 February 1937; Syracuse's Stick Team Routed, 14-3, *Washington Post*, 2 May 1937; Maryland Stars Win, *Cumberland Times*, 2 May 1937; Track Honors to Mercersburg, *New York Times*, 9 May 1937

213-214 'The track team ... same venue': *The Karux*, The Students of Mercersburg Academy, 1937, p152; Olympic Ace Gets Double in Features, *Washington Post*, 7 March 1937

214   'Jimmy's attempts ... Princeton Games': School Track Aces Smash 8 Records, *New York Times*, 27 February 1938; Summaries of Penn Relay Carnival, *New York Times*, 30 April 1938; Mercersburg Wins Crown in Prep School Track, *New York Herald Tribune*, 8 May 1938

214   'The season ... of 1.57.5': Interscholastic Summary, *Daily Boston Globe*, 22 May 1938

214   'Since returning ... hand-offs': Curran's Biography More Exciting Than Fiction, *Philadelphia Inquirer*, 29 April 1939

214   'Their first chance ... the Games': Summaries of the Millrose Games, *New York Times*, 6 February 1938; Spec Town Cracks Mark in Two Heats, *Washington Post*, 6 February 1938

214-215 'They soon ... Ed Beetem': Mercersburg Academy Trackmen Defeat Penn Freshmen Runners, *Philadelphia Inquirer*, 12 February 1939

215   'It was ... long jump': Evander and Seton Hall Capture National A.A.U. Championships, *Brooklyn Eagle*, 26 February 1939; 5 Records Broken in Schoolboy Tests, *New York Times*, 26 February 1939

215   'Strong results ... of 1.25.2': Johnny Munski Smashes Flat-Track Mile Record in Maryland-Fifth Meet, *Baltimore Sun*, 12 March 1939; Armory Track Summaries, *Baltimore Sun*, 12 March 1939

215   'If Jimmy's ... the record': Curran's Biography More Exciting Than Fiction, *Philadelphia Inquirer*, 29 April 1939; Penn Relay Summaries,

ENDNOTES AND SOURCES

New York Times, 29 April 1939

215   'medley relay': A combination of four distances – one mile, 880, 440, and 220 yards

215   'The final meet … Olympic team': Honors on Track to Mercersburg, *New York Times*, 14 May 1939

216   'First up … J.P Morgan': Elite Throng Embassy Garden to Greet British Royalty, *Salt Lake Tribune*, 9 June 1939; And Everybody Came to King and Queen's Party, *Ogden Standard-Examiner*, 11 June 1939; Attends Embassy Review, *Waynesboro Record Herald*, 12 June 1939

216-217   'Just a week … for publication': News From America, *Edinburgh Evening News*, 1 July 1939; Mile Fiasco: As Seen By Scot At Princeton, *Edinburgh Evening News*, 1 July 1939; A video of the race is available to view on You Tube – www.youtube.com/watch?v=0iFAa3KD5Yc [Accessed 3 December 2018]

217   'His students … Mercersburg track': 47th Field Day, *Mercersburg Academy Alumni Quarterly*, Winter 1940, Volume XXXV, No.2, p36; Bill Cox and Eddie Shields had both run faster mile times on the Mercersburg track, but Milne's mile was completed in poor weather conditions. Jimmy believed that if the weather has been more conducive to athletics his time would have eclipsed those recorded by Cox and Shields.

217   'Milne followed … annual defeat': Navy Plebes Win in Cross Country, *Washington Post*, 12 November 1939

217   'The school's … meet record': World Hurdle Mark Tied Twice in Meet, *Washington Post*, 11 February 1940; Loughlin Annexes U.S. Track Title, *New York Times*, 25 February 1940

217   'In April … Atlantic Championships': Morgan Sets Mile Record, *New York Times*, 7 April 1940

217-218   'The remainder … against Yale': Cornell Wins Track Meet Handily; Frosh Defeat Mercersburg, *Ithaca Journal*, 18 March 1940; Seton Hall Prep Captures 2 School Titles in Relay, *Philadelphia Inquirer*, 27 April 1940; State Track Frosh Bow to Mercersburg, *Pittsburgh Press*, 5 May 1940; Mercersburg Trims Penn Fresh on Track, *Philadelphia Inquirer*, 12 May 1940; Navy Plebe Trackmen Beat Mercersburg, *Baltimore Sun*, 19 May 1940; One-Man Team, *Brooklyn Citizen*, 14 June 1940

218   'Unlike 1914 … to help': *Hagerstown Daily Mail*, 26 October 1940; Nearly Everyone in School Buys a Ticket for Jimmy's 'Galashiels Comfort Fund', *Mercersburg News*, 26 October 1940; Donations to

Comforts Fund, *Border Telegraph*, 18 March 1941; http://mhs.mercersburg.org/blog/38 [Accessed 3 December 2018]

218 'The torpedoed ship ... a baton': Curran's Biography More Exciting Than Fiction, *Philadelphia Inquirer*, 30 April 1939; Navy Plebe Trackmen Win Over Mercersburg, *Baltimore Sun*, 11 May 1941; *The Karux*, The Senior Class of Mercersburg Academy, 1941, p149

218-219 'Fate did ... the gun': Overbrook Trackmen Take Two Titles in Carnival, *Philadelphia Inquirer*, 26 April 1941

219 'The season ... Penn Relays': Seton Hall Wins School Track Title, *Philadelphia Inquirer*, 23 February 1941; 2 Titles Won by Overbrook, *Philadelphia Inquirer*, 26 April 1941

219 'And so ... and Robinson': Future Book, *Sarasota Herald Tribune*, 22 December 1941; Kirk Recalls Lessons His Father Taught Him, *Philadelphia Inquirer*, 22 April 1943; Quaker Star Heads Field in Penn Relays, *Washington Post*, 23 April 1943

219 'Despite the ... six events': Mercersburg Cup Won by Paul Cowie, *Brooklyn Eagle*, 25 November 1941; Field Day, *Mercersburg Academy Alumni Quarterly*, Winter 1942, Volume XXXVII, No.2, p67

219 'But things ... the season': *The Karux*, The Senior Class of Mercersburg Academy, 1942, p141

219 'And the school's ... Seton Hall': Summaries of U.S. School Meet, *New York Times*, 1 March 1942; *The Karux*, The Senior Class of Mercersburg Academy, 1942, p141

219-220 'At the Penn ... relay team': Summaries of Penn Relay Carnival, *New York Times*, 25 April 1942; Baltimore Poly Upsets Mercersburg in 'C' Club Track Meet, *Washington Post*, 17 May 1942

220 'As America ... winning run': Mercersburg Ace Has Measles, *Philadelphia Inquirer*, 25 April 1943; Sports Roundup, *Hanover Evening Sun*, 21 May 1943

220 'But Jimmy's ... the Boers': Monday Matinee, *Asbury Park Press*, 22 June 1942

220 'One of those ... the Bulge': Dick M'Fadden Dies in Action, *Waynesboro Record Herald*, 19 December 1944; Ann Hull, *Cumberland Valley: From Tuscarora to Chambersburg to Blue Ridge*, Arcadia Publishing, Charleston, 2011, p125

220 'The next two ... Williams Cup': Wins Track Award, *Altoona Mirror*, 1 November 1943

220-221 'In 1944 ... to disqualification': Loughlin, Mercersburg Capture U.S.

ENDNOTES AND SOURCES

Interscholastic Track Titles, *New York Times*, 27 February 1944

221 'And the following ... 880 yards': N.Y.U, Dartmouth, Michigan Capture Titles at Penn Relays, *New York Herald Tribune*, 29 April 1944; Mercersburg Captures Track Meet in Capital, *Baltimore Sun*, 21 May 1944; St Michael's Upsets, Takes Prep School Title, *Philadelphia Inquirer*, 28 January 1945; Loughlin and Hill Capture Crowns in National Interscholastic Track, *New York Times*, 25 February 1945; Mercersburg Win on Track, *Philadelphia Inquirer*, 22 April 1945; The Summaries, *New York Times*, 28 April 1945; Plebe Trackmen Win, *Washington Post*, 6 May 1945

221 'The 1945/46 season ... he was': Stepping High for Dad, *Philadelphia Inquirer Magazine*, 20 July 1952

221 'But when Moore ... help you': Moore, Jr with Herzog, op. cit., p59

221 'Mercersburg's season ... Navy Plebes': *The Karux*, The Senior Class of Mercersburg Academy, 1946 p183; Summaries of Track Meet, *New York Times*, 26 January 1946; Mercersburg, Loughlin Win U.S. School Track Titles, *Philadelphia Inquirer*, 24 February 1946; Mercersburg Wins in Tennis, Track, *Philadelphia Inquirer*, 21 April 1946; Summaries of Penn Relays, *New York Times*, 27 April 1946 ; Plebes Beat Mercersburg, *Philadelphia Inquirer*, 12 May 1946

221-222 'While Moore's ... the dais': *The Karux*, The Senior Class of Mercersburg Academy, 1947, pp193-194

222 'At the Inquirer ... Penn Relays': Philadelphia Track Summaries, *New York Times*, 25 January 1947; Slade Meet's Star with Four Firsts, *New York Times*, 23 February 1947; Illini Narrowly Misses 4 Titles, *Chambersburg Public Opinion*, 28 April 1947

222 'In the summer ...the proceedings': Borderers' Gay Welcome to Royal Family, *Scotsman*, 19 July 1947; Jimmy outlived all three of his known childhood friends, William and John Torrie, and A.D. Lawson. He was in Galashiels, in 1954, when John died.

222 The 1947/48 season ... Penn Relays': Bayonne Sets Relay Mark; Mercersburg Quartet Wins, *Philadelphia Inquirer*, 24 January 1948; U.S. Track Crown Won By Boys High, *New York Times*, 22 February 1948; Ormrod, Shelly Win in Spiked Shoe Meet, *Philadelphia Inquirer*, 14 March 1948; Brooklyn High Sets Relay Mark, *Philadelphia Inquirer*, 24 April 1948

222-223 'Gus Ormrod ... a scholarship': Moorestown Youth Wins Section B Run, *Philadelphia Inquirer*, 16 November 1947; Ormrod, Shelly Win in

Spiked Shoe Meet, *Philadelphia Inquirer*, 14 March 1948; Brooklyn High Sets Relay Mark, *Philadelphia Inquirer*, 24 April 1948; Email from Gus Ormrod, 25 July 2016

223 'By the summer ... Wembley Stadium': Mercersburg Academy Proud of Work of Alumni in Olympic Games, *Harrisburg Evening News*, 13 August 1948

223 'All did not ... the Games': Cochran Acts Quickly, Ties New Record, *Philadelphia Inquirer*, 31 July 1948; Kirk Won't Run in '400' Hurdles, *Philadelphia Inquirer*, April 28, 1949; Jeff Kirk, Former Penn Track Star, *Philadelphia Inquirer*, February 26, 1976

223 'Jimmy's thoughts ... gold medals': Email from David Emory Jr, 9 December 2016; Email from Laurie Danaher, 8 January 2019; Email from Laurie Danaher, 26 April 2020

223 'After the Games ... writer's descendants': Curran Describes Scotland Trip, *Waynesboro Record Herald*, 20 October 1953

224 'The start of ... Freshmen team': *The Karux*, Grit Publishing Company, Williamsport, Pa., 1950, p178

224 'In January ... team spirit': Inquirer Track Summaries, *Philadelphia Inquirer*, 22 January 1949; Ormrod, St. Thomas Team Win Spiked Shoe Trophies, *Philadelphia Inquirer*, 13 March 1949

224 'The strength ... two points': Kiski Nips Mercersburg in Track, *Pittsburgh Post-Gazette*, 22 May 1949

224-225 'He now ... 220 yards': Trojans Win County Track Championship, *Nassau Daily Review-Star*, 6 June 1949; Long Island Trackmen Win West Point Meet, *Nassau Daily Review-Star*, 13 June 1949

225 'By the time ... Jesse Owens': Capital Mile Taken Easily by Gehrmann, *Rochester Democrat and Chronicle*, 15 January 1950; Thresher's Record for Meet in Washington Legitimate, *Nassau Daily Review-Star*, 17 January 1950

225 'A loss ... Millrose Games': Wilt Takes Mile Tying Meet Mark, *New York Times*, 9 February 1950; Summaries of the Meet, *New York Times*, 19 February 1950

225 'Days later ... the final': Badgers Quiet Down, *Brooklyn Daily Eagle*, 13 February 1950

225 'Just weeks later ... 6.4 seconds': Thresher Only Tenth of Second Off 60 Yard Mark, *Nassau Daily Review Star*, 20 February 1950

225 'And he continued ... before them': Thresher's 0:06.2 in '60' Betters World Record, *Philadelphia Inquirer*, 19 March 1950

225 'The following ... emerged victorious': Mercersburg 1st; Thresher Does 9.6, *Philadelphia Inquirer*, 23 April 1950; Mercersburg Wins in Track, *Washington Post*, 23 April 1950

226 'A week later ... the honours': Mercersburg and Cardozo Score Outstanding Victories, *Philadelphia Inquirer*, 29 April 1950; Summaries of the Penn Relays, *Philadelphia Inquirer*, 30 April 1950

226 'The following ... the world': Thresher Sets '100' Record, *Philadelphia Inquirer*, 7 May 1950; Youth in a Hurry, *Farmington Daily Times*, 12 May 1950

226 'Thresher's summer ... Hook Stadium': Pioneer Club Annexes the Metropolitan A.A.U. Junior Track Team Title, *New York Times*, 5 June 1950

226 'A week ... the 220': Fuchs and Appel Set Meet Marks as N.Y.A.C. Retains Track Title, *New York Times*, 11 June 1950

226 'Things didn't ... MacDonald Bailey': Gehrmann Wins in Stretch, *Wisconsin State Journal*, 14 January 1951; Morgan's Bragg Outstanding in Evening Star Track Meet, *Pittsburgh Courier*, 20 January 1951

226 'The elation ... been stolen': Not Fastest Man, *Doylestown Daily Intelligencer*, 22 January 1951; Thresher is Timed in 5.3 For 50 Yards, *Syracuse Herald Journal*, 26 January 1951

226 'It may ... Millrose Games': Richards Vaults 15-1 in Millrose Games, *Long Beach Press Telegram*, 28 January 1951

226 'But a runner ... 6.4 seconds': Mercersburg and Boston Trade Win School A.A.U. Team Track Titles; 2 Marks Set, *New York Herald Tribune*, 18 February 1951

226 'And he went ... Woodberry Forest': Felton Betters MAAAU Record, *Philadelphia Inquirer*, 4 March 1951; Thresher Run 9.6 '100', *Philadelphia Inquirer*, 22 April 1951

226-227 'Further wins ... sodden track': Navy Plebes Triumph in Track Meet, 65-52, *Baltimore Sun*, 13 May 1951; Morgan State Retains Relay Title in Meet, *Baltimore Sun*, 11 June 1951; NYAC Holds AAU Title; Dreyer, McKenley Set Marks, *Philadelphia Inquirer*, 17 June 1951

227 'A blip ... in Berkeley': Los Angeles A.C. Gains Track Title, *New York Times*, 24 June 1951

227 But Thresher's ... February 1950': Dean of Track Keeps in Trim Playing Handball, *New Castle News*, 8 February 1950

227 'But then ... to recuperate': Thresher, Track Star, Stricken with Polio, *Niagara Falls Gazette*, 24 August 1951; Athlete Gets Visit from Sister

Kenny, *New York Times*, 29 August 1951

227   'But in … Olympic trials': Thresher Launches Olympic Bid in NYAC Games, *Nassau Review-Star*, 3 June 1952

227   'The feeling … was ended': Olympic Berth for Thresher?, *Nassau Review-Star*, 12 June 1952; Letter from Henry Thresher, 8 May 2015

227   'Jimmy had … meter hurdles': Veteran Mentor Rates Moose Top Quarter-Miler [sic.], *Syracuse Post Standard*, 9 July 1950

227   'If evidence … his technique': Telephone interview with Seth Cagle, 6 July 2019

227-227   'He was also … down to 13': Winning Every Race, in *Mercersburg Magazine*, Summer 2008, Volume 35, No.2, p28

228   'Moore fulfilled … win places': U.S. Olympic Track Trials End Today, *San Rafael Daily Independent Journal*, 28 June 1952; Here's 1952 U.S. Olympic Track Squad, *Arizona Republic*, 29 June 1952

228   'And so, 28 … the quarters': Stepping High for Dad, *Philadelphia Inquirer Magazine*, 20 July 1952

228-229   'In the final … Olympic Games': American Hoopsters Top Russians in 86-58 Game, *Nevada State Journal*, 29 July 1952; Moore, Jr with Herzog, op. cit.

229   'Jimmy's desire … against Miller': Faculty Defeats Boys' Group in Hand Ball, *Mercersburg News*, c1940; 64-Year-Old Coach Keeps in Condition, *Albany Times-Union*, 22 June 1945; Mercersburg Coach Marked 70th Birthday With Aggressive Game of Handball, *Sunday Bulletin*, 15 January 1950

229   'In 1949 … physical condition': Mercersburg Halls Inspire Human Faith, *Philadelphia Inquirer*, 12 November 1949

229   'Jimmy was … Christmas present': Prep School Sports, *New York Times*, 21 December 1953

229   'six-league boots': Strauss appears to have made an error in using the term 'six-league boots.' Seven-league boots are a common feature in European folklore such as *Jack the Giant Killer* and *The Bee and the Orange Tree*. More recently they have appeared in the works of authors as diverse as C.S. Lewis, Terry Pratchett, Mark Twain and Zane Grey.

229   'Since his youth … the Appalachians': Email from Laurie Danaher and Alanna Berger, 29 January 2017

229   'In 1951 … been effective': Jimmy Curran Home, *Waynesboro Record Herald*, 20 December 1951

229-230   'And where better … 11 miles': Mercersburg Track Coach, 74, Takes a 28-Mile Walk to Prove a Point, *New York Times*, 11 January 1954

230 'The early … ever recorded': St. Augustine's of Brooklyn, Cardozo of Washington Triumph in Penn …, *New York Times*, 26 April 1953; Boys High Takes Mile and St. John's Prep Two Mile Event at Penn Relays, *New York Times*, 1 May 1955

230 'Some good … pole vault': 3 Records Set, 2 Tied in Spiked Shoe Track, *Philadelphia Inquirer*, 20 March 1955; Penn Relay Summaries, *Philadelphia Inquirer*, 1 May 1955

230 'But by … the way': Knapp Sets Two Records, Ties 3d in Track Meet, *Philadelphia Inquirer*, 21 March 1954; Penn Relay Summaries, *Philadelphia Inquirer*, 25 April 1954; St. James Trackmen Second in Meet, *Hagerstown Daily Mail*, 24 May 1954; 3 Records Set, 2 Tied in Spiked Shoe Meet, *Philadelphia Inquirer*, 20 March 1955; Mercersburg Wins Track Meet, 64-52, *Philadelphia Inquirer Public Ledger*, 17 April 1955; Mercersburg Ace Sets Three Marks, *Philadelphia Inquirer*, 8 May 1955; Mercersburg Victor Over SMA in Track, *Philadelphia Inquirer Public Ledger*, 15 May 1955; Millrose Summaries, *New York Times*, 5 February 1956; Two Records Fall, Four Equaled As 629 Vie in Spiked Shoe Track, *Philadelphia Inquirer*, 11 March 1956; Brooklyn Schoolboys Sweep Penn Relay Championships, *New York Herald Tribune*, 29 April 1956; Relay Summaries, *Philadelphia Inquirer*, 29 April 1956; Inquirer Summaries, *Philadelphia Inquirer*, 26 January 1957; Lower Merion Close 2d For National Track Title, *Philadelphia Inquirer*, 24 February 1957; Mass. Stars Finish Second in 2 Events, *Daily Boston Globe*, 24 February 1957; Hearn, Batdorf Repeat as 9 Marks Crash in Spiked Shoe Track Meet, *Philadelphia Inquirer*, 24 March 1957; Mercersburg Victor, *Philadelphia Inquirer*, 14 April 1957; Hill Sch. Trackmen Beat Mercersburg For 1st Win, *Philadelphia Inquirer*, 21 April 1957; Penn Relay Summaries, *Philadelphia Inquirer*, 28 April 1957; St. Francis Prep, Jackson Set Records in Penn Relays, *New York Herald Tribune*, 28 April 1957; 6 Track Marks Fall Mercersb'g Wins, *Philadelphia Inquirer*, 5 May 1957; Batdorf Wins AAU Shot Put Title, *Lebanon Daily News*, 22 February 1958; Track Honors to Mercersburg, *Philadelphia Inquirer*, 4 May 1958; *The Karux*, 1959, p131

230-231 'But if the … this is America': $500 Stopwatch Bill Worries Scotsman, *New York Times*, 21 May 1956

231 'And the Olympics … track career': Letter from Henry Thresher, 8 May 2015

231   'Despite the … fine boy': Mercersburg Ace to Pole Vault in Inquirer Meet Friday, *Philadelphia Inquirer*, 19 January 1958

231   'Jimmy was represented in Australia': Jimmy almost had two students at the Games. James A Morefield was a hammer thrower and was selected as an alternate. No throwers withdrew so Morefield was never called upon.

231-232 'Had he been … no good': Cruz Can Vault, But He Doesn't Brag, *Philadelphia Inquirer*, 27 September 1960

232   'But those … gets him': Mercersburg Ace to Pole Vault in Inquirer Meet Friday, *Philadelphia Inquirer*, 19 January 1958

232   'Jimmy did see … the trade': Coach, 79, Rewarded, *New York Times*, 2 February 1959

232   'In April 1957 … Penn Relays': Jimmy Curran Feted by Former Track Aces, *Philadelphia Inquirer*, 26 April 1957; More About Curran of Mercersburg, *New York Times*, 6 May 1957; Prep School Sports, *New York Times*, 6 May 1957

232   'A ringing endorsement … anyone anywhere': 50th Year – And Still Molding Stars, *Philadelphia Inquirer*, 25 April 1957

232   'In the stadium … these days': Coach, 79, Rewarded, *New York Times*, 2 February 1959

233   'Years later … anybody's way': Track Coach Aced Golf Endurance Test, *Palm Beach Daily News*, 9 May 2004

233   'In May … athlete was': Email from Jef Evans via Doug Smith, 14 January 2019

233   'Just six months … may obtain': Ted Meredith, All-Time Track Great, Dies at 64, *Towanda Daily Review*, 6 November 1957; Former Coach, Ex-Stars Attend Meredith Rites, *Philadelphia Inquirer*, 8 November 1957; Lemon, op. cit., p160

233-234 'While the 1957/58 … 13 ¼ feet': Track Honors to Mercersburg, *Philadelphia Inquirer*, 4 May 1958

234   'Days later at … all the others': Puerto Rican Wins in Track at Mercersburg, *Lebanon Daily News*, 22 May 1958; *The Karux*, 1959, p132

234   'Jimmy wanted … New Orleans': Scot Takes High Road, *New York Times*, 19 May 1958; Coach, 79, Rewarded, *New York Times*, 2 February 1959; Email from Jeannie Cornelius, 4 December 2018

234-235 'On another trip … his transformation': Email from Stephen Curran, 1 July 2018

235   'The trip … two others': Houston Track Summaries, *Waco Tribune-*

Herald, 8 June 1958

235   'The 1958/59 … Williams Cup': Soldier Bragg Flies High, *Philadelphia Inquirer*, 2 February 1959; Coach, 79, Rewarded, *New York Times*, 2 February 1959; Ace Vaulter Tops 14' 6" in New York Garden Meet, *Mercersburg News*, 7 February 1959; Inquirer Track Games Summaries, *Philadelphia Inquirer*, 14 February 1959; 2 Marks Fall, 3d Equalled in Spiked Shoe Track Meet, *Philadelphia Inquirer*, 22 March 1959; *The Karux*, 1959, p131; *The Karux*, 1960, p34

235   'The following year … bright spots': Morgan First in Mile Run, *Baltimore Sun*, 24 January 1960; Frosh Bow to Mercersburg, *Gettysburg Times*, 9 May 1960

235   'On 7th January … in Rome': Curran is Given Trip to Europe, *Hagerstown Morning Herald*, 23 January 1960; *The Karux*, 1960, p34

235   'As was his way … relay race': Mr James M. Curran, *unknown newspaper*, February 1963; Telephone interview with Janette Adams, 26 March 2018

235-236 'Cruz returned … beat Bragg: Cruz Can Vault, But He Doesn't Brag, *Philadelphia Inquirer*, 27 September 1960; The Olympic pole vault scoring was changed soon after – when two or more athletes finished on the same height, the one had failed the least number of heights overall would finish above the one with the greater number of fails. Had this scoring system been in place during 1960 Cruz would have won bronze.

236   'After Rome … his daughters': Mercersburg, *Hagerstown Morning Herald*, 15 September 1960

236   'Entering his final … them all': Undefeated Cross Country Team, *Chambersburg Public Opinion*, 3 December 1960

236   'Before the track … Sonny Liston': Writers to Fete Van Brocklin, Ditka at Dinner, *Philadelphia Inquirer*, 23 January 1961

Chapter 14 • He run a good race

238   'Jimmy had … unknown reasons': Mercersburg Preppers Win One for Curran, *Harrisburg Patriot-News*, April/May 1960; Jimmy Curran's Quartet Wins 31st Relay Crown, *Waynesboro Record Herald*, 1 May 1961

238   'During the summer … man's nap': White, op. cit.

238   'White would … away present': Jimmy Curran's Quartet Wins 31st

Relay Crown, *Waynesboro Record Herald*, 1 May 1961; Williams Cup Winner Annexes Symbol of All-Around Track Ability, *Mercersburg News*, 27 May 1961; White, ibid.

238   'Penn Relays gold watches': The watches are unique. The 12 numbers are replaced by the word PENNSYLVANIA.

239   'As late ... started yesterday': Mercersburg Ace to Pole Vault in Inquirer Meet Friday, *Philadelphia Inquirer*, 19 January 1958

239   'His body ... his retiral': Death Certificate of James Curran – 015412-63; Email from Laurie Danaher, 11 August 2019

239   'In May 1961 ... with ease': Trackmen Take 10 of 12 First to Annihilate Gettysburg 80-28, *Mercersburg News*, 20 May 1961

239   'A month later ... relay team': Eight Records Broken in County Track, Field Meet, *Chambersburg Public Opinion*, 14 June 1961

239   'And so, one ... silver tray': Honoring 4 Retiring Members of Faculty, *Mercersburg News*, 1961; Mercersburg Academy Graduate, *Waynesboro Record Herald*, 6 June 1961; Four Faculty Members of Mercersburg Retire, *Hagerstown Morning Herald*, 20 June 1961

239   'Outwardly he was ... this one': Jimmy Curran's Quartet Wins 31st Relay Crown, *Waynesboro Record Herald*, 1 May 1961

240   'Before his retirement ... the javelin': Seizure Proves Fatal to Jimmy Curran at 83, *Harrisburg Patriot-News*, 8 February 1963

240   'But for all ... the athletes': V. Tracksters Outrun Hill 20-37, *Mercersburg News*, 28 October 1961; Here and There in Sports, *Waynesboro Record Herald*, 20 April 1962; Email from Jef Evans, 8 December 2018

240   'On 3rd February ... the process': 16-foot Vault, Kidd Mile Top Philly Games, *Nevada State Journal*, 3 February 1963; A Cruz Sails to 16 – And a Kidd Cruises, *Binghamton Sunday Press*, 3 February 1963

240   'The following day ... each other': Email from David Emory Jr, 9 December 2016

240   'Later that day ... final kiss': Here and There in Sports, *Waynesboro Record Herald*, 8 February 1963; Email from Laurie Danaher, 29 January 2017

241   'he returned to Galashiels regularly': Jimmy and Janet's Scottish family also returned the favour, regularly visiting the Currans in Mercersburg. In 1947, for example, Janet's brother and sister, James and Nan, visited for three months.

241   'thick Scots brogue': Jimmy's Scots brogue was regularly the butt of

good-natured jokes at the hands of his students, as detailed throughout this book. In addition, visitors to the school occasionally struggled to understand him. In 1918, after hearing Jimmy speak at an assembly, a female visitor to the school remarked, 'Why, that man that made the announcements about the track meet this morning could hardly speak English at all.'

241-242   'In his time … in history': Ex-Devil Swimmer Takes Silver, *Chambersburg Public Opinion*, 1 August 1984

241   'he had trained 16 Olympians': This number includes Wyndham Halswelle in Scotland, and two athletes – Harold Barron and Larry Shields – at the Meadowbrook Club. It is possible a number of others passed through his hands at Meadowbrook as well as at the University of Pennsylvania.

242   'In the days … every way': *"He r-r-r-run a go-o-o-o-d r-r-r-race."*, [1963], p4

242   'The *Harrisburg* … sports figures': Seizure Proves Fatal to Jimmy Curran at 83, *Harrisburg Patriot-News*, 8 February 1963

242   'Ed Pollock … world of sport': *Philadelphia Evening Bulletin*, February 1963

242-243   'Ron Smith … of forgetting': They'll Miss Wee Scot at the Relays, *Philadelphia Inquirer*, 11 February 1963

243   'And his impact … well-being': Board Hears of Two Dists, Merger Plan, *Chambersburg Public Opinion*, 12 February 1963

243   'Some of the … Coach': Curran's Biography More Exciting Than Fiction, *Philadelphia Inquirer*, 30 April 1939

243   'Jimmy Stewart': Stewart was not the only one of the Jimmy's athletes who went on to some degree of fame on the silver screen. John Payne made almost 60 movies, most notably *Miracle on 34th Street*, whilst Dick Foran made over 80 movies, being best known for western musicals. Gail Robinson was a body double for John Wayne and had bit parts, most uncredited, in a number of films.

244   'The next morning … Alumni Association': Curran Rites, unknown source, February 1963

244   'He was buried … outlived him': www.findagrave.com /memorial/ 175512572/james-michael-curran

244   'Paul White … to greatness': White, op. cit.

244   'Henry Thresher … outstanding person': Telephone interview with Henry Thresher, 9 April 2015

244   'Christopher Montgomery ... not enemies': Email from Christopher Montgomery, 5 January 2016

244-245 'In 2008 ... Mentor, Legend': Winning Every Race, in *Mercersburg Magazine*, Volume 35, No.2, Summer 2008, p27; Charles H. Moore, Jr with James Cockerille, *Running on Purpose: Winning Olympic Gold, Advancing Corporate Leadership, and Creating Sustainable Value*, Edgemoor Ink, 2017, pp65-66 and p69

245   'And, for this ... an honor': Email from Jef Evans, 21 January 2020

245   'In all of them ... mighty task': www.mercersburg.edu/about/meaning-mercersburg

246   'Through the years ... of Galashiels': Step Songs Attract Crowd, *Mercersburg News*, 1918; Commencement Exercises, *Mercersburg Academy Alumni Quarterly*, Volume 14, No.1, November 1918, p17; Klein, op. cit., p558; Grads Fete Coach of Mercersburg, Philadelphia Inquirer, 28 April 1950; Curran is Given Trip to Europe, *Hagerstown Morning Herald*, 23 January 1960; *The Karux*, 1960, p34

246   'In the wake ... at trackside': *"He r-r-r-run a go-o-o-o-d r-r-r-race."*, [1963]; Jimmy Curran Honored Today, *Waynesboro Record Herald*, 20 May 1972; Track Dedicated to Jimmy Curran, *Chambersburg Public Opinion*, 23 May 1972

247   'Things did not ... mile run': It's Simply a Matter of Inches at M-Burg All-Weather Track, *Chambersburg Public Opinion*, 28 June 1972; Email from Jef Evans, 2 January 2019

247   'It is unclear ... the campaign': From a postcard sent to former athletes, 10 May 1994

247   'In the basement ... Rican alumni': Coach Curran at 80 Has 50 Years Here, *Mercersburg News*, 1960

247   'In 1999 ... Hall of Fame': www.ptfca.org/hall-of-fame [Accessed 14 January 2019]; Email from Dave Johnson, 14 January 2019

247   'But in 2007 ... his inclusion': Emails from Neil Renton to Jay Quinn, 26 June 2007 and 30 October 2008

Biographies

250   'Mike Murphy': Murphy, op. cit.

250   'Mike Dee': Mike Dee, Phillies' Trainer, Is All There With the Strong Arm Stuff, Philadelphia Inquirer, 12 January 1911; Mike Dee Dies at

ENDNOTES AND SOURCES

86; Trained Sports Greats, *Philadelphia Inquirer*, 21 December 1954

251   'James Lee': Galashiels Sportsman's Death, *Edinburgh Evening News*, 20 July 1939

251   'Bill Struth': Mason and Stewart, op. cit.

251   'Johnny McHugh': John McHugh Dies, U.S. Track Starter in '24 Olympics, *Philadelphia Inquirer*, 2 November 1924; John McHugh Dead, *New York Herald Tribune*, 2 November 1951; Benevolent Gunman, *New York Times*, 7 November 1951

251-252   'Walter Knox': Town, op. cit.

252   'Arthur Duffey': Duffey, First to Run 100 in 9 3-5 Secs., Dies at 75, *Boston Daily Globe*, 25 January 1955; http://duffeydash .blogspot.com [Accessed 15 December 2019]

252-253   'Al Nash': http://carlisleindian.dickinson.edu/sites/all/files/docs-ephemera/NARA_1327_b154_f6077.pdf [Accessed 19th January 2019]; Famous Indian Runner Dies Following an Operation; Started at Carlisle School, *Harrisburg Telegraph*, 23 January 1918; Indian Athlete Had York Chum, *York Daily*, 25 January 1918

253   'Alfie Shrubb': Hadgraft, op. cit.

253   'Jack Roden': John Roden Dies; Former Athlete, *Philadelphia Inquirer*, 11 October 1943

253   'Wyndham Halswelle': How Captain Halswelle Died, *Highland Light Infantry Chronicle*, Volume XV, No.1, January 1915, pp68-69

254   'Tall Feather': One of Greatest Distance Runners, Tallfeather Once Ran from Milwaukee to Chicago at 42, *Green Bay Press-Gazette*, 15 June 1949

254   'Percy Smallwood': Smallwood Resigns, *Louisville Courier Journal*, 2 June 1922; New Photo Unites Kin, *New York Daily News*, 31 January 1950; Smallwood Was a Runner of His Day, *Atlanta Constitution*, 10 July 1952; Meilyr Emrys, *Percy Smallwood: The Forgotten "Welsh Wonder"* [Paper presented at the North American Society for Sport History's 40th annual conference, Berkeley, Ca.], 2012

254   'Jim Thorpe': Joseph Bruchac, *Jim Thorpe: Original All-American*, Penguin Group, 2006

255-256   'Ted Meredith': Wilson Jr, op. cit.; Lemon, op. cit.

256   'Wallace 'Pete' Maxfield': Pete Maxfield in Medical Corps, *The Lafayette Weekly*, 31 October 1917; "Pete" Maxfield in Training, *The Lafayette Weekly*, 26 March 1919; Hanson [ed.], op. cit.; The Maxfield Boys, *Bloomfield Independent Press*, 28 July 1939

256 'Eugene 'E.P.' Hammitt: Eugene P. Hammitt Dies of Heart Attack, *The Oil City Derrick*, 9 October 1972; www.fold3.com /page/ 641435356-eugene-p-hammitt [Accessed 14 January 2019]

256-257 'Theodore Dale': Theo Dale is Dead in France, *Scranton Republican*, 12 November 1918; www.findagrave.com/memorial/56339477 [Accessed 27 February 2019]

257 'Albert Robinson': *United States Federal Census*, 1940; Speed Beyond Belief, *Detroit News*, 20 October 1947; Email from Art Whiting, 3 February 2019

257 'Harry Goelitz': Goelitz Called Second Thorpe by E.C. Brown, *Chicago Examiner*, 29 June 1913, Goelitz Breaks A.A.U. Record, *Oak Leaves*, 11 July 1914; Thorpe's Successor Being Searched For, *Janesville Daily Gazette*, 16 July 1914; Chicago Hurdler Sets New World's Record, *Chicago Examiner*, 26 July 1914; Goelitz to Antwerp, *Oak Leaves*, 7 August 1920; American Olympic Star Badly Hurt, *Washington Post*, 15 November 1921; A Carload of Horses, *Oak Leaves*, 12 May 1923; At the Horse Show, *Oak Leaves*, 19 July 1924; Wins a Horse Show, *Oak Leaves*, 29 January 1927; Oak Park Pioneer Son Harry Goelitz Dies, *Oak Leaves*, 19 May 1971

258 'Harold Barron': *The Blueprint*, Volume XIX, 1926; Coaches Design New Track Hurdle to Prevent Falls, *Alton Evening Telegraph*, 8 July 1930; Barron Resigns as Coach, *Yonkers Statesman*, 2 August 1930; *United States Federal Census*, 1940

258 'Harold 'Boots' Lever': Harold B. Lever Dies in Florida, *Bridgeport Post*, 19 April 1963; Bridgeport Executive Dies on Golf Course, *Hartford Courant*, 20 April 1963

258-259 'Larry Shields': Hanson [ed.], op. cit.; *Pot Pourri*, 1960, p8; M. Lawrence Shields, 81, *Boston Globe*, 25 February 1976

259 'Eddie Shields': Rutgers Loses Greatest School Boy Runner by his Decision Not to Take up College Career, *New Brunswick Home News*, 22 July 1916; Shields, of Penn., Candidate for the Modern Pentathlon, *Washington Post*, 22 March 1920; Edward Shields, *Tampa Tribune*, 19 September 1970

259 'Harvey 'Beck' Reed': Reed-Campbell Engagement, *New York Times*, 11 June 1921; Dist. 4 School Board Candidates, *Orlando Evening Star*, 1 May 1968; Deane Smith Successful in Comeback, *Orlando Sentinel*, 8 May 1968; Deaths, *Orlando Evening Star*, 5 November 1968; His Pingry Journey: Ed Cissel '39 Shares Memories of Being a Student, Teacher

and Coach, *The Pingry Review*, May 2015, p46; Email from Christine Ameduri, 7 March 2019

259-260 'Allen Swede': Allen Swede, Tiger Crack, Quits Team, *Bridgeport Telegram*, 10 November 1921; Memorials, *Princeton Alumni Weekly*, Volume 78, 1977, p20

260 'Allen Woodring': Allen Woodring, Gold Medal Winner in 1920 Olympics, *Tampa Bay Times*, 17 November 1982

260 'Elmer Smith': Waltham to Line Up Today, *Boston Post*, 23 September 1914; Penn, Gets Bang-Up Schoolboy Athletes, *Johnson City-Endicott Record*, 16 October 1915; Elmer Smith Star of Millrose Meet, *Philadelphia Evening Public Ledger*, 24 January 1918; Penn Suffers Loss of Smith, Her Star Track Athlete, *Buffalo Courier*, 17 April 1920; He'll See the Sights at Age 91, *Fort Lauderdale News*, 18 November 1967; Tours Are Provided for Shut-ins, *Fort Lauderdale News*, 11 December 1967

260 'Frank Ward Conway': Frank Ward Conway, *Pittston Gazette*, 20 August 1957

260-261 'Henry Charles 'Chuck' Taylor': Email from David Taylor, 1 November 2019

261 'Marvin Rick': Facebook message from Carol Rick Gibbons, 1 January 2019

261-262 'Charles 'Crip' Moore': Hurdler Moore Loses Fingers, *Pottsville Republican*, 4 August 1925; Deaths and Funerals, *Fort Myers News-Press*, 6 May 1983; Moore, Jr with Cockerille, op. cit, pp49-51 and pp59-62

262 'George 'Buck' Hester': Ex-Olympic Star George Hester Dies, *Indianapolis News*, 8 December 1951; Hester, Oldtime Prep Sprint Champion, Dies, *Detroit Free Press*, 11 December 1951; Wolverines to Induct 10-Man Class into Hall of Fame, *US Fed News Service*, 31 July 2009

262 'Bill Cox': Olympic Hero Cox Has Lost Ultimate Race, *Rochester Democrat and Chronicle*, 5 June 1996

262 'Gail Robinson': www.imdb.com/name/nm2167966; Email from Doug Smith, 9 February 2019

263 'Barney Berlinger': Email from Barney Berlinger Jr, 9 January 2020

263 'Terrell 'Tex' Cobb': Dr. Terrell Cobb Dies; Osteopath and Sailor, *Providence Journal*, 3 September 1970

263 'Bill Carr': Carr, a Day Late for Princeton, Speeds to World Mark for Penn, *New York Herald Tribune*, 19 July 1932; Bill Carr Buried at Pine

Bluff, *Camden News*, 28 January 1966

263-264 'Bill Estes': www.legacy.com/obituaries/news-press/obituary .aspx? n=william-edwin-estes&pid=18665157 [Accessed 27 February 2019]

264 'Bill Bradway Jr': *Military Reserve Posture Hearing [No.66]: Hearing Before Subcommittee No.3 of the Committee on Armed Services, House of Representatives, Eighty-Seventh Congress, Second Session*, U.S. Government Printing Office, Washington, 1962, pp5475-5476; Capt. Bradway in vacant seat, *Coronado Journal*, 16 May 1968

264 'Charles Mutchler': Mutchler-Varney, *Sherbrooke Telegram*, 4 March 1943; Obituaries, *Orlando Sentinel*, 13 December 1986

264-265 'Steve Szumachowski': Adirondack Dist. AAU Championship Meet Scheduled Today, *Schenectady Gazette*, 15 June 1946; Email from Jerry A. Madden, 1st March 2019; http://schenectady.ss12.sharpschool .com/common/pages/DisplayFile.aspx?itemId=2603154 [Accessed 2 January 2020]; www.findagrave.com/memorial /155495278/ stephen-a.-szumachowski [Accessed 13 May 2018]

265-266 'Jack White': Central Hall Headliners, *Lebanon Daily News*, 4 November 1969; Jack Howard White '38, *Princeton Alumni Weekly*, 21 September 1983; Jack Harlan [sic.] White, 1916-1983, *The Columbus Academy Magazine*, Fall 1983, pp24-25

266 'Ed Beetem': Beetem Also Too Big, *Philadelphia Evening Bulletin*, 18 June 1942; Email from Joseph-James Ahern, 27 November 2019

266 'Austin Kellam': Heat in Arabia Very Humid, Not Dry as Many Believe, *Binghamton Sunday Press*, 22 August 1954; A. Kellam, Insurance Agent, Dies, *Binghampton Press and Sun-Bulletin*, 6 December 1984; Austin M. Kellam '44, *Princeton Alumni Weekly*, Volume 86, 9 October 1985, p48

266-267 'Paxson 'Pax' Gifford': Email from Benjamin G. Gifford, 31 January 2019

267 'Jack Milne': Jack H. Milne Sr., 69; honoured for lengthy service to athletics, *Philadelphia Inquirer*, 29 September 1988; https://running indians.wordpress.com/2011/10/11/jack-h-milne-a-legendary-toms -river-high-school-runner [Accessed 14 January 2019]; www.trschools.com/trhof/inductee.asp?ID =30 [Accessed 14 January 2019]

267-268 'Ed Burrowes': Edward Burrowes, Milton, Veteran of World War II, *Sunbury Daily Item*, 14 April 1959; www.findagrave .com/memorial /168233772/edward-burrowes [Accessed 13 May 2018]

ENDNOTES AND SOURCES

268   'Ed Morgan': Death Notices, *Camden Courier-Post*, 2 June 1978; E.J. Morgan Sr, *Philadelphia Inquirer*, 3 June 1978; Email from Doug Smith, 9 February 2019

268   'Jack Watt': http://new.npaaa.org/wp-content/uploads /NPAAA - Program-2006.pdf [Accessed 13 May 2018]

268   'Ted Meredith Jr': Three NAA Members Will Submit Papers at Paris Conference, *NAA Bulletin – Management Accounting*, June 1965, p10; J.E. Ted Meredith, *Lt. Ted Meredith, USNR, PT Boat Officer, Stories from 50 Years Ago*, iUniverse.com, Inc., 2000; James E. "Ted" Meredith in *Strategic Finance*, Volume 88, Issue 7, January 2007, pp22-23

269   'Bob Ufer': Ailing Bob Ufer Says He'll be Ready for U-M Season, *Detroit Free Press*, 21 August 1981; Voice of Wolverines, Bob Ufer, Falls Silent, *Detroit Free Press*, 27 October 1981

269   'Dick McFadden': Missing in Action, *Hagerstown Morning Herald*, 15 December 1944; Dick M'Fadden Dies in Action, *Waynesboro Record Herald*, 19 December 1944; Six Inducted into South Central Pennsylvania Sports Hall, *Gettysburg Times*, 23 October 1990; Ann Hull, *Cumberland Valley: From Tuscarora to Chambersburg to Blue Ridge*, Arcadia Publishing, Charleston, 2011, p125

269   'Jeff Kirk': Jeff Kirk, Former Penn Track Star, *Philadelphia Inquirer*, 26 February 1976

269   'Paul Cowie': Newark, Rutgers Defeat Princeton Nine, *Princeton Alumni Weekly*, 26 April 1946; Time Out, *Daily Princetonian*, 8 May 1947; Tigers Beaten, 13-7, in Close Struggle as Cowie is Star, *Daily Princetonian*, 13 October 1947; Sport Slants, *Camden News*, 3 November 1947; Mark F. Bernstein, *Princeton Football*, Arcadia Publishing, 2009, p73; Paul F. Cowie, 54, publishing executive, *Boston Globe*, 6 February 1978; Obituaries, *Westport Fairpress*, 9 February 1978

270   'Gus Ormrod': Email from Gus Ormrod via A.C. Ormrod, 21 May 2020

270-271   'Charles Moore Jr': Moore, Jr with Cockerille, op. cit.; Moore, Jr with Herzog, op. cit.

271   'Dewey Lee Yoder': Steven Olderr, *The Pan American Games: A Statistical History, 1951-1999*, McFarland & Co., Inc., Jefferson, North Carolina and London, 2003, p110; https://library.uafs.edu/sites/ librarydev.uafs.edu/files/Departments/fshsj/34-02 _complete_issue .pdf [Accessed 26 January 2019]

271   'Bob Black': www.mohnfuneralhomeandcremationservices.com/

obituary/1987615 [Accessed 7 February 2019]; Email from Holly Roper, 7 February 2019

271-272 'Lester Cagle': www.legacy.com/obituaries/name/lester-cagle-obituary?pid=188022391 [Accessed 7 July 2019]; Email from Seth Cagle, 11 July 2019

272 Henry Thresher': https://justaroundhere.com/index.php/all-sections/names-faces/it-s-nice-to-know-you/239-meet-hank-thresher; Telephone interview with Henry Thresher, 9 April 2015; Letter from Henry Thresher, 8 May 2015

272-273 'Larry Lattomus': Sigma Phi Remembers our friend and brother Larry Lattomus, C'52 with this excerpt from *A Place in the Sun* – https://issuu.com/sigmaphi-cornell/docs /lattomusexcerpt_sm_1_ [Accessed 15 January 2019]; Telephone interview with Diane Carey, 17 May 2020

273-274 'Jef Evans': Email from Jef Evans, 6 January 2020

274 'Malcolm 'Andy' Anderson': Telephone interview with Andy Anderson, 12 February 2019

274 'Rolando Cruz': *Consumer's Resource Handbook*, The White House Office of the Special Assistant for Consumer Affairs, 1979, p73

275 'Bob Batdorf': www.eldridgeco.com/team/robert-a-batdorf [Accessed 2 March 2019]

275 'Paul White': Email from Paul White, 23 February 2019

275-276 'Tom Danaher': Email from Laurie Danaher with additional text supplied by Maria Danaher, 19 February 2020

Major International Games Competed in by Jimmy's Athletes

277 'Intercalated Games, Athens, 1906': Mallon, *1906 Olympic Games*, op. cit.

277 'Olympic Games, London, 1908': Mallon and Buchanan, *1908 Olympic Games*, op. cit.

278 'Olympic Games, Stockholm, 1912': Bill Mallon and Ture Widland, *The 1912 Olympic Games: Results for All Competitors in All Events, with Commentary*, McFarland & Company, Inc., Jefferson, North Carolina, 2001

ENDNOTES AND SOURCES

278-279 'AEF Championships, Stade Pershing, Paris, 1919': Colonel Wait C. Johnson and Elwood S. Brown [eds.], *Official Athletic Almanac of the American Expeditionary Forces, 1919: A.E.F. Championships: Inter-Allied Games*, American Sports Publishing Co., New York, 1919

279 'Inter-Allied Games, Stade Pershing, Paris, 1919': Captain Joseph Mills Hanson [ed.], *The inter-allied games, Paris, 22nd June to 6th July, 1919*, 1919; Colonel Wait C. Johnson and Elwood S. Brown [eds.], *Official Athletic Almanac of the American Expeditionary Forces, 1919: A.E.F. Championships: Inter-Allied Games*, American Sports Publishing Co., New York, 1919

280-281 'Olympic Games, Antwerp, 1920': Bill Mallon and Anthony Th. Bijkerk, *The 1920 Olympic Games: Results for All Competitors in All Events, with Commentary*, McFarland & Company, Inc., Jefferson, North Carolina, 2003

281 'Colombes Games, Paris, 1920': America Triumphs in Colombes Games, *Philadelphia Inquirer*, 30 August 1920

Races featuring Jimmy Curran / G. Gordon

296 '19 February 1910': This race was originally scheduled for 12 February. It was cancelled and rescheduled for 19 February, but it is unclear whether the race eventually took place.

Index

Only major race meets are noted.

All ships are indexed by their prefix, either HMS, HMT, RMS or SS.

AAU = Amateur Athletic Union
AAA = Amateur Athletic Association
AEF = American Expeditionary Forces
IS   = Interscholastics

INDEX

INDEX

INDEX

INDEX

INDEX

INDEX

INDEX

The Author

CRAIG STATHAM has worked in Scotland's heritage sector for 20 years. In 2013 he published an acclaimed biography of Bruce Springsteen, the first author to cover only the years prior to the release of *Born to Run*.

Looking for a new subject to write about, he undertook extensive research, before finding Jimmy lurking in the stories of more famous athletes. The result of five years' work is presented here.

He lives with his family in Newbattle, just outside Edinburgh, and can often be seen running through the grounds of the nearby 12th century Cistercian Abbey. If he listens closely enough, he swears he can occasionally hear whispers in the trees that sound decidedly like Jimmy purring 'He r-r-run a go-o-o-od r-r-r-r-race'.